FRANCIS PARKMAN

FRANCIS PARKMAN

by

Howard Doughty

Harvard University Press

Cambridge, Massachusetts

London, England

1983

This Harvard University Press paperback
is published by arrangement with the
Macmillan Company.

Printed in the United States of America
10 9 8 7 6 5 4 3 2 1

Library of Congress Cataloging in Publication Data

Doughty, Howard, 1904–
    Francis Parkman.

    Reprint. Originally published: New York: Macmillan,
1962.
    Bibliography: p.
    Includes index.
    1. Parkman, Francis, 1823–1893. 2. Historians—
United States—Biography. I. Title.
[E175.5.P28D68 1983]   973'.072024 [B]   82–21394
ISBN 0–674–31775–0 (pbk.)

FOR

NEWTON ARVIN

—✠ FOREWORD ✠—

A critical study of Francis Parkman by a person who is not himself an historian, either professional or amateur—and even as a layman no more than a casual reader of history—would appear a somewhat quixotic undertaking. At least, I have felt it to be so. Still, in the end, historical writing, whatever its special province and special techniques, fulfills itself only on grounds accessible to the layman; and a layman's examination of an historical work on these grounds may have the value that can attach to an outsider's view. At any rate, having read and reread Parkman from an early age, and having found in what has been written about him relatively little that helped to explain my impulsion to do so, I have made the experiment of attempting the task myself.

My main concern in this book is Parkman's histories. The man, however, is so much of a piece with his work, and so much of his life is in his work, that I have found the biographical form best suited to my purpose.

For assistance that made possible the beginnings of this study I am indebted to the Library of Congress Grants-in-Aid for Studies in the History of American Civilization; and to Mrs. Elizabeth Ames and the Corporation of Yaddo. It would never have been finished without the capacity for endurance and fortitude of my wife, Frances Wilde Doughty.

H. N. D.

—◄ ACKNOWLEDGMENTS ►—

I am indebted to the Massachusetts Historical Society for permission to quote from the MS. "Sept. 1841" account of Parkman's first Magalloway trip and from other unprinted items among the Parkman Papers; to Mrs. Langdon P. Marvin and the *Harvard Library Bulletin* for extracts and quotations from Parkman's letters to Mrs. Marvin's grandmother, Mary Dwight Parkman, and from other letters among the Marvin MSS.; and to Harper and Brothers and Mason Wade for quotations from *The Journals of Francis Parkman* (New York, 1947), edited by Mason Wade.

──⊰ CONTENTS ⊱──

CHAPTER I

BOSTON AND THE FELLS

❧ ❧ ❧

Francis Parkman was born in Boston, on Beacon Hill, September 16, 1823—and born to the full quantum of "advantages" in the way of wealth, social position, and social background that these natal circumstances suggest.

On the paternal side he was the son of the Reverend Francis Parkman, pastor of the New North Church, and a pillar of orthodox Unitarianism; and a grandson of Samuel Parkman, the twelfth child of a country minister, who had come to the city as a boy and, as Josiah Quincy put it, had risen "through assiduity and talent . . . to eminence and opulence among the merchants of Boston." So we find Samuel in 1800 part owner of the *Herald* of Salem, trading to India, or earlier, venturing "6 gross gimblets" and "12 gross buttons" in the famous voyage of the *Columbia,* under Captain Gray, that opened up the Northwest fur trade with China; thus, in sum, laying the foundations of the kind of fortune, and one of the largest of its kind, from which most respectable nineteenth century Boston wealth derived. Merchant prince and Federalist grandee, he looks at us from his portrait with mild, bland gaze, and was remembered as a man of courtly presence and manners, faultlessly dressed in a brass-buttoned blue coat, a diamond on his ruffled shirt front. He died the year after his grandson was born, but the boy's family were later to occupy the impressive town house he had built at 5 Bowdoin Square—a three-story pilastered brick mansion in the Federalist style, adorned at the entrance with a semicircular Doric-columned porch and shaded by tall horse chestnut trees. The sloping ground behind was laid out in terraces, which Samuel devoted to the cul-

1

ture of fruit, a certain variety of bergamot pear in which he specialized becoming famous among connoisseurs.

The most salient figure in the further reaches of the Parkman
line is the philoprogenitive clergyman, Samuel's father, the Reverend
Ebenezer Parkman, elected minister of Westborough in 1724, when
he was twenty-one, and holding the post until his death at the age of
eighty: a masterful spirit whose instinct of command his great
grandson was to share. A theocrat of mark in a still theocratic age,
he was the voice of authority for his part of the state in all matters
of religion and politics. "He magnified his calling," says Edward
Wheelright, "and was careful not to lower its dignity, wielding almost despotic power with firmness guided by discretion and tempered with kindness." As witness of his influence he was styled on
his tombstone "the first Bishop of the Church in Westborough." A
divine of the old militant stamp, he had been an Indian fighter in
his day, and three of his sons saw military service, one at Ticonderoga, the other two in the Revolution; William, the boy who
shouldered a musket at Ticonderoga, leaving a diary of the campaign
which his great-nephew put to effective use in *Montcalm and Wolfe*.
The Reverend Ebenezer also assiduously kept a diary, where, among
much else of interest, we read that he bought from his father a
Negro slave named Maro, whose death a year later he thus quaintly
records: "Dark as it has been with us, it became much darker about
the sun-setting, [when] the sun of Maro's life Sat."

On the maternal side, through the Halls and the Brookses of
Medford, the boy's ancestry also ran to clerics, comprising the three
Cottons—John, the second John, and Rowland—eminent for learning and divinity in the early days of the colony, and descending in
the eighteenth century through the Reverend Edward Brooks of
Medford, another fighting parson, who, according to his son, rode
to the skirmish at Lexington "with his gun on his shoulder, and in
his full-bottomed wig," though his chief feat of the day seems to
have been saving the life of a wounded British officer. Later, as the
chaplain of a continental frigate, he was taken prisoner and confined
at Halifax. His daughter, Joanna Cotton Brooks, married Nathaniel

Hall of Medford, a distiller, like his father before him, of the town's most famous product, at one time a representative in the state legislature, but early broken by ill health. Nathaniel's daughter Caroline, in turn, became the second wife of the Reverend Francis Parkman, of which union young Francis was the first child. Caroline's forebear, the above-mentioned Edward Brooks, figures, one may note, as the crossing-point in the lineage of perhaps the two greatest of American historians, for his son Peter Chardon Brooks, Joanna Hall's brother, was the grandfather of Henry Adams; Adams and Parkman being thus second cousins through their mothers, though Adams was by fifteen years the younger of the two. Peter Chardon Brooks, like Samuel Parkman, laid a solid material foundation for the intellectual pursuits of his descendants; indeed, his fortune, based on marine insurance, was accounted the largest of his time in New England. But the order of Samuel's own endeavors is perhaps indicated by the fact that his Bowdoin Square mansion is recorded in 1822 as taxed on a real-estate valuation "the same as . . . P. C. Brooks."

Yet, except for a certain romantic pride in the Huguenot strain that came to him through the Chardon connection of the Brookses, Parkman was never particularly concerned with his ancestry. Nor had he need to be as an authentic scion of the social order its elements had coalesced to create: that tight-knit Federalist patriciate, which, with its roots in the Puritan and Revolutionary past, had consolidated itself after the Revolution by a splendid commerce, had reshaped its ancestral Puitanism to more amenable accord with its condition, and, on the national scene, had presided over the birth and early days of the Republic. Furthermore, whatever its subsequent fortunes, it was to show a remarkable genius for conserving and renewing its material base and perpetuating itself as a social entity. But if the boy could take his social origins for granted, and if he was to be stamped through life with their patrician imprint, nevertheless there was much in his nature and temperament to set him at odds with this Federalist-Unitarian world as it had come to be in his father's generation, and as his father exemplified it; and much, likewise, to heighten for him the tension of the pressures from without that assailed it in the time of his own growing up. And, as it happened, an experience of his boyhood, cutting across the grain of his Boston life, at once fostered the elements of this incipient conflict of temperament and environment, and gave it an original and creative direction.

But to this we shall return. Meanwhile, we have to do with the boy's father and his world—the world of Federalism in its mild Indian summer of decline between the Jeffersonian and Jacksonian revolutions, whose ethical expression and quasi-official religion was the mild, decorous, rational, and respectable Unitarianism, hitting the mean between the spirituality of Channing and the earnestness of Theodore Parker, of which the Reverend Francis Parkman was a leading light. A pupil of Channing's, Dr. Parkman had continued his theological studies at Edinburgh, and in 1813 was installed as pastor of the New North Church, where he remained until a few years before his death in 1852. He published many papers on moral and theological subjects; and—besides completing the donation begun by his father Samuel to endow at the Harvard Divinity School the Parkman Professorship of Pulpit Eloquence and the Pastoral Care—he was efficiently active in furthering the work of a host of worthy philanthropic organizations: The Congregational Charitable Society, the Society for the Relief of Aged and Indigent Clergymen, the Orphan Asylum, the Medical Dispensary, the Massachusetts Bible Society, and the like. In person a small man, with pleasant voice and expressive face, kindly, courteous, and affable by nature, his most distinctive trait was a strain of ready verbal felicity, which, turned to effects of wit and humor, was the marvel of his eulogists. "In the commonest conversation . . . ," says one of them (E. P. Whipple),

without the slightest hesitation, sentence after sentence would glide from his tongue, indicating the most consummate command of the resources of language, and every word moistened with the richest humor, and edged with the most refined wit. His voice, in its sweet, mild, unctuous smoothness, aided the effect of his expression. His style in conversation, unlike his style in his writings, evinced a creative mind. It was individual, original, teeming with felicities of verbal combination, and flexible to the most delicate variations of his thought.

In some respects, indeed, this gift of verbal prestidigitation gave him almost the character of an eccentric. "He still survives," Lowell writes of him at the end of the century, "in traditions of an abundant and exquisite humor, provoked to wilder hazards, and set in stronger relief (as in Sterne) by the decorum of his cloth." These "wilder hazards" may have been, in part, the result of a manic-depressive tendency, for it is also recorded that Dr. Parkman's geniality was sometimes overshadowed by fits of melancholy; and in 1845 he had to take a trip abroad to recover from a nervous breakdown.

But, however individual the traits that won for him the soubriquet of "the clerical humorist," they were, as may be surmised, of a sort less likely to be appreciated in the home circle than at large; and, furthermore, they were offset by other traits that give the impression of a chilling enough correctness and conventionality. "Even in his less restrained hours . . . ," Bishop Huntington notes, "it was his custom . . . to insist with considerable scrupulousness on those clerical proprieties and formalities that formerly, more than now, distinguished the ministerial vocation." So whatever his originality of speech, the manner of his letters is ministerially thin and flat to a degree, and indicative of the limitations that made his son's bents and proclivities, however tolerantly he indulged them, blankly incomprehensible to him. Almost compulsively social, affable, kind, dignified, correct, unimaginative, not "deeply interior," or in the slightest degree "volcanic, or sulphureous, or explosive with wrath however 'holy' "—to quote from O. B. Frothingham's characterization of the Unitarian type—Dr. Parkman had the misfortune to sire an offspring in whom such qualities, and others beyond the purview of the Unitarian ethos, ran strong. For his high-mettled son, in turn, the ministerial calling, the "decorum of the cloth," and much else his father personified were to be lifelong irritants and the subjects of a variety of incisive sallies. Thus, one of the earliest anecdotes of his childhood is an example of the sort—the execution of a spirited sketch of three devils carrying off on their pitchforks three ministers in a flutter of Geneva bands and gowns, while he sat quietly drawing at a window during an interview with his father of a notably sentimental female parishioner, who asked to be shown what such a well behaved child was doing. In later life, according to his first biographer, his favorite appellation for the clerical tribe was "vermin"—if not without exception of individuals—and he wrote on the occasion of a boy's being named after him: "I hope the youngster will do honor to the name. He should be brought up to some respectable calling and not allowed to become a minister." But one could trace almost indefinitely the ramifications of reaction against the clerical milieu of his rearing: his aversion, for instance, to the saintly Channing, his father's revered teacher, and the preacher of his ordination sermon; or his refusal to concern himself in any way with the chair his father and grandfather had founded at the Divinity School; or, when he had settled with his wife in a cottage in Dorchester, his dry enumeration, among the burdens of a householder, of "an impending visit from the tax-gatherer" and "petitions for the furtherance of charitable enterprises which, as I am informed, the son of my father will not fail to promote." How different a father-image the boy had constructed for himself is evident from the recurring sketches in his early journals of sturdy ancients, Revolutionary veterans, and the like, even to picturesque old rips, but all as far removed as conceivable from the paternal aura of clerical proprieties, worthy charities, and "sweet, mild, unctuous smoothness." Few boys could have been less fitted by nature to sustain the traditionally difficult rôle of clergyman's son.

But if his father was a disappointment, the boy's bonds with his mother, on the contrary, were close and strong. "Whatever characteristics Frank inherited from his parents came from her," his sister Lizzie wrote. "He was like her in many ways, and the expression of his face grew more and more like hers. She had, I think, a peculiar tenderness toward him, her eldest child." A devoted wife and mother, and the favorite of an intimate circle of friends and relations, but "too retiring and self-distrustful to share her husband's marked social traits," her chief characteristic was a strain of "deep feeling" guarded by a "great though never cold reserve." Her son was to share to a preeminent degree this vein of inwardness, this capacity for deep emotion, at odds with a constitutional diffidence. For the rest, according to another memorialist, Mrs. Parkman possessed strongly developed ethical principles, coupled with "gentleness in practice" and a "perfect charity" toward individuals; a strong vein of common sense and practical wisdom, great penetration into character, and a fund of quiet humor. Here too we note much that, in its own context, was to mark the development of the son; the feeling for character, the ethical and pragmatic bent, the combination of strong principles of judgment with justice to individuals. The bond between these two "deeply interior" natures is evident enough from the mother's easy, intimate, and highly readable letters, edged with her dry humor. "We are all now in the midst of ministers," she writes her son, "perhaps you have forgotten that this is Anniversary Week. You would be forcibly reminded of it, if you could look in upon us. . . . Tomorrow, I expect eighteen to dinner. Father is enjoying it much. I can't say so much for the rest of us."

Besides Frank, born, as I have said, in 1823, four other children (together with Dr. Parkman's daughter by his first wife, Sarah Cabot) completed the family circle: three girls, Caroline, Mary, and Eliza, born between 1825 and 1832; and another son, John Eliot, born in 1834. Young Frank was to grow up much idolized by his sisters, the youngest of whom, Eliza or Lizzie, in the end devoted herself wholly to his welfare. His brother Eliot, recorded to have been of a sunny and vivacious disposition, made the very unministerial and un-Unitarian choice of the Navy for a career, and after boyhood figured infrequently at home. Taken prisoner during the Civil War (the circumstances of his imprisonment were related by his brother at the time, in a letter to the *Boston Advertiser*) he survived other risks and chances of his profession to lose his life in a trivial accident at the age of thirty-eight.

But among the older generation of the boy's kin there remain other figures on whom we must cast a glance. These comprise particularly his father's brothers, Samuel and George Parkman, if only for the intrinsic interest of their cases. Each of them, as it happened, became the focus of a notoriety highly out of accord with Brahmin and clerical proprieties. Samuel, to be sure, is merely the familiar figure of the black sheep, which any well placed Boston family might be expected to produce as inevitably as it produced Unitarian ministers. Still, the scandal he caused during his nephew's boyhood, involving a divorce from his wife and permanent exile to Europe, seems to have been a thorough performance of its kind. The nickname of "naughty Sam" which still lingers in family tradition, and the intimate knowledge of Parisian night life with which we find him solacing his ostracism, suggest one explanation as to the nature of his misfeasances. They also appear, however, to have taken a graver form. At least, an anonymous chronicler, who published in 1846 under the title of *Our First Men*, a fascinatingly annotated calendar of "those persons taxed in the city of Boston, credibly reported to be worth one hundred thousand dollars," makes the following entry under the name of Samuel's wife, Mary Mason:

A daughter of the late Jonathan Mason, the divorced wife of Samuel Parkman . . . who left the country years ago, charged with certain forgeries, and now resides in Italy.

Whatever the circumstances, the transgressions of her errant spouse were still an issue with the redoubtable Mary Mason when young Frank had grown up. Indeed she flatly forbade her son, a third Samuel, to visit his father—an edict which the young man spiritedly defied—and one surmises from a letter of Mrs. Parkman's that she had had to defend as spiritedly a similar visit by Frank on his European trip of 1844. However that may be, the nephew found his uncle—then resident in Paris, not in Italy—quite unperturbed by Bostonian tabus and altogether at ease in Zion, to whose mysteries—the Bal Mabille, and the like—he proved a highly knowledgeable guide. "I like to see a thing done thoroughly," is the young man's comment.

But naughty Sam's long-forgotten case was of an ordinary enough variety. George Parkman, on the contrary, achieved, if involuntarily, a unique, resounding, and lurid kind of publicity which time has far from obliterated. It was he, of course, who was the victim of Professor Webster of Harvard in that celebrated murder that set Boston by the ears—a murder provoked, in one view, by the victim's vindictive pursuit of a financially harried man, consequent to the discovery that a cabinet of minerals pledged to him by Webster as security on a loan was later pledged for the same purpose to George Parkman's brother-in-law, Robert Gould Shaw. But whether or not George Parkman's later conduct can be described as vindictive, his original impulse in his dealings with Professor Webster was evidently enough one of generosity; and his nephew, at any rate, who was himself to manifest a strong dislike of being cheated, had no patience with pleas in mitigation. "Prof. Webster of Cambridge, whom perhaps you know," he wrote E. G. Squier at the time, "was sentenced to death yesterday for murdering my uncle . . . in order to prevent the exposure of numerous frauds and swindling transactions of which he, Webster, had been guilty. All the town has been in commotion, and the feeling of satisfaction at the result of the trial is, I believe, universal." Indeed, in view of the influences brought to bear on Professor Webster's behalf, the case was widely regarded as a test of Massachusetts justice, evoking from Chief Justice Lemuel Shaw, who presided at the trial, a classic charge to the jury on the probative nature of circumstantial evidence (in this instance chiefly, it will be recalled, a set of false teeth which survived the attempt to destroy the victim's body and were identified by his dentist).

But apart from his posthumous celebrity, George Parkman was a person of mark in his own right, and decidedly an original. As a young man he had studied medicine in Paris, and brought home ideas on the treatment of the insane greatly in advance of his time, ideas which he did much to help realize. Though he gave up practice as a physician at the death of his father, the merchant Samuel, he retained a lively interest in his early profession, donating the site for the new building of the Harvard Medical College, which later became the scene of his murder. At the same time, as a businessman, he very energetically augmented his share of his father's fortune—and cut a figure in this capacity that made him a curiosity of the Boston streets. Credited with five hundred thousand dollars in *Our First Men*, "Parkman, George," we there read, was

bred a physician but practices as a speculator in real estate. He owns a vast many cheap built tenements, let at high rents; and as he is his own rent collector, and keeps no horse, he may be seen at almost any hour moving rapidly through the city. To judge from the expression of his face—so deceptive is physiognomy—he might be mistaken for a man without a sixpence; yet many a poor family has partaken of his unostentatious beneficence, which, perhaps, he will not thank us for proclaiming. He has lately given a site for a new medical college.

But medicine and real estate by no means exhausted the range of this humane, crusty-kind, eccentric, public-spirited collector of his rents, who once, during a cholera epidemic, offered his own house to the city for a hospital. Very much a man of parts and intellect, he drew to himself a variety of original spirits. Thus we find him assembling at his table such diverse figures as Emerson, John Quincy Adams, or Fanny Kemble. Or, again, we find him fostering the career of a promising unknown like Alexander Jackson Davis, that fantastic genius of American architecture, whose stay in Boston in 1827–1828 proved particularly formative, largely through George Parkman's encouragement. Both he and his equally versatile friend, Dr. Jacob Bigelow—later young Francis's father-in-law—were ardent amateurs of Davis's subject and had made collections of architectural models to which they enthusiastically gave the young student access, besides befriending him personally, and making it possible for him to browse on the extensive library of books in his field at the Boston Athenaeum.[1] Similarly, another original spirit,

[1] Like George Parkman, Jacob Bigelow came to a melancholy if not so drastic an end, losing his mind and then his eyesight—though not before translating *Mother Goose* into Latin. An accomplished classicist himself,

James Audubon, recounting his visit to Boston in 1834, pays his respects to his "most worthy and generous friend, George Parkman, Esq., M.D." With the aid of the doctor, Audubon spent two days trying to suffocate with fumes of charcoal and sulfur a live golden-headed eagle which he had acquired to make a drawing of and was forced in the end to stab. The strain of this experiment in euthanasia and of sketching his subject before *rigor mortis* set in so upset him that he had to put himself for a time under his friend's hospitable care. One fundamental trait of George Parkman, indicated by the rapidity of his walk noted in *Our First Men*, deserves our attention. This was his "never flagging energy," to quote Oliver Wendell Holmes—an overruling compulsion to "strenuous personal activity which extended to every movement and expression." Even to the quickness of gait, his nephew was to exhibit in a marked degree the same turn of constitution.

Thus, then, the paternal generation could hardly be said to be lacking in offsets to the established patterns of Federalist-Unitarian respectability, and certainly not in variety and saliency of character. No doubt, likewise, other figures of defectors or originals presented themselves for the boy's comtemplation among the vast Brooks cousinage on his mother's side, or the solid clans of Blake, Tuckerman, and Shaw, into which his father's sisters had married. There was much, furthermore, in the particular New England-Boston quality of these very solidities and respectabilities that would engage his loyalties and command his adherence. Nevertheless, cir-

---

he had earlier written a polemic on *The Limits of Education* of the most pronounced anticlassical, scientific-utilitarian cast. Besides his solid achievements as a physician—his *Discourse on Self-Limited Diseases*, emphasizing natural recuperative powers, was largely responsible for stopping the practice of indiscriminate dosing and bleeding—he also did botanical work of some importance. One, perhaps dubious, fruit of his architectural interests was Mt. Auburn Cemetery, the idea of which he conceived, and for which he designed the curious Sphinx monument to the Civil War dead. His son Henry Jacob Bigelow was likewise a well known physician; and his grandson, William Sturges Bigelow, was the orientalist and convert to Buddhism who figures in Henry Adams's circle of friends.

cumstances had combined to create a more than usually sharp cleavage of generations between this world of late Federalist Boston and its more gifted or imaginative sons. Now forced out of politics, it was dominated by business, in the prosaic and parochial forms of manufacturing or real estate to which it was profitably converting the older profits of a great world commerce. Its only acceptable alternatives to business as a career were comprised in a narrow choice of law, medicine, or the ministry. For all the solid virtues of this world, its range of thought and ideas was equally limited. And, finally, about its whole edifice, the winds of change, which are always blowing, happened at the juncture of the boy's growing up, to be blowing with peculiarly disturbing force. With what force and how close to home they were blowing *Our First Men* makes evident in its entry for the boy's uncle-in-law, Robert Gould Shaw, with whose family he was to be on a particularly intimate footing. Senior partner of "one of the wealthiest and largest commercial houses in the city," and rated at a million dollars, the elder Shaw, we are informed, had "obtained his capital to begin upon, by marriage with a daughter of old Sam. Parkman," and had signally increased it by "heavy and very successful investments in real estate." His children, however, our guide tartly continues,

do not all of them conform exactly to his notions of aristocratic propriety, nor seem to be entirely persuaded that the great art and duty of life is to make money and to keep it. One of them is an "associationist," a great friend and supporter of the Brook Farm Phalanx; another has recently adopted the Catholic religion, and has gone to Rome to prepare himself for a missionary priest; a third, an accomplished and much admired lady, has recently married a son of Nat. Greene, the postmaster of Boston, a Unitarian minister, recently settled in Brookfield, and, to the horror and admiration of all her Boston acquaintants, lives without servants and does her own work!

Here, indeed, was mutiny in the citadel; and a breaking of the way that led from Robert Gould Shaw to his abolitionist grandson of the same name.

Young Frank, to be sure, was hardly susceptible to the particular ferments of change at work in the Shaw household—or, at least, only so far as he came for a little within the orbit of his slightly older and much admired cousin Joseph's conversion to Catholicism. For the rest, indeed, no son of his forefathers could have been more stanchly proof against the enticements of "associationism" or any cognate manifestation of the Transcendental-Reformist afflatus that so largely inspired this conflict of generations. Nevertheless he had his own reckonings to make with the world of the fathers, his own directions to find, his own path to break—and one, though it led in the end so far afield from Brook Farm as the tepees of the Sioux, no less rich in discoveries. But, meanwhile, we must return to the episode of his boyhood that saw the beginning of these developments and shaped their nature.

This experience was, of course, his rustic sojourn in Medford, during the impressionable period from his eighth to his thirteenth year, at the edge of the wild tract of land known as the Five Mile Woods, or, later, the Middlesex Fells. He says of himself that his early childhood was "neither healthful nor buoyant" and that as a child he was "sensitive and restless, rarely ill, but never robust." Whatever more specific this may indicate, something was wrong enough for his parents to take the rather drastic, but, as it proved, salutary step of sending him away to live at his Grandfather Hall's farm, bordering on the Fells, in West Medford. Here Nathaniel Hall, having met reverses, had retired in broken health, with his wife, and his son Peter Chardon Hall, who took over the running of the fifty-acre farm. In this household of grandparents and bachelor uncle, the youngster, it is evident, was left pretty freely to the pursuit of his own devices. For his schooling he went a mile or so away to Medford, to a Mr. Angier's, averred to have been a well conducted establishment, but where he says he "learned little," and from which, others recall, he often played truant. At any rate, in his own recollections, the Halls and school hardly figure beside the attractions of the place itself—the wonderland of the Fells, a few rods from the Hall farm—and the activities of which it was the scene.

The Middlesex Fells are today a municipal park, laid out in bridle paths and seamed with automobile highways. Even so they keep a touch of wildness; and merely glanced at in passing, the landscape is strange and distinctive: a rough, boulder-strewn, densely wooded, glacial terrain, with gleams of water from the ponds in its hollows, and a broken skyline of abrupt, rock-ledged little hills. Some attempt was apparently made in the early days of the colony to cultivate this waste, but it proved intractable even for New England farmers. In the boy's time it lay uninhabited and unimproved, a little enclave of sufficiently primeval wilderness within eight miles of the heart of Boston. Here for four years he roamed untrammeled and at large; exploring its alluring recesses; collecting eggs, insects, and minerals; trapping squirrels and woodchucks; stalking birds with a bow and arrow; and, with all the passionate intensity of his nature, falling completely in love with the place and its life. When he came back to the city, the experience had impressed itself indelibly on his imagination; and, enhanced by contrast, nurtured in memory, or working subconsciously, was to set up a tension of opposites that henceforth ruled his life, shaping it, if at cost and pain, to centrally creative ends.

The experience, in itself, was by no means an extraordinary one. But, in the first generation to be exposed in youth to a new kind of urban life, such experiences could have decisive results. The boy's growing up coincided precisely with the transformation of the sharply individuated, half rural little Boston of thirty or forty thousand souls at the time of his birth into the generic megalopolis of the nineteenth century, the *fourmillante cité* of the Industrial Revolution, his uncles' "real estate," and a novel separation of man from his natural environment. In face of these new conditions of an urban rearing, society had as yet—before the days of school athletics or the institutionalizing of the "out-of-doors"—made little provision for its young, and least of all for a type of boy as motor-oriented, as "somatatonic" in constitution, as craving of activity and free range, as Dr. Parkman's son happened to be. For such a boy, then, if he also happened to be imaginatively sensitive, it is little wonder, under such conditions, that the image of the Fells, counterpoised to the image of the city, should implant itself so deeply. Henry Adams, exposed a little later to the same environment, was to write that the contrast of town and country, of Boston and Quincy, was "the most decisive force he ever knew." To be sure, similar conditions on the European scene had begotten similar responses; and these, as Romantic literature had already voiced them, were to have their share in what Parkman was to make of the image of the Fells. Nevertheless, few other responses of the sort were nourished from such an imperative pressure of innate needs or bear the stamp of more authentically personal origins.

And, within this larger context, other appositions of Boston and the Fells deepened sufficiently the aftereffects of the experience. Nor, indeed, did certain recalcitrances of the Old Adam fail to manifest themselves at the time. Thus, the Saturday afternoon appearance of his father in a gig, to take him home for a Boston Sunday, are recorded to have kindled a lively resentment, expressed on the drive back, by a show of gaping and staring at the familiar sights of the city as if he were a green country boy. So, again, bringing up the rear of the family procession home from church, headed by his father, in the dignity of his gown, with Mrs. Parkman on his arm, the youngster is once recalled to have enlivened the occasion by displaying, to the amusement of passersby, a dead rat he had picked up, held out at arm's length by the tail.

But the life of the Fells had its term; and at thirteen the boy came back to Boston for good—and now, or shortly after, in 1836 or 1837, to the mansion his grandfather had built in Bowdoin Square, vacant apparently as a result of his Uncle Samuel's enforced exile. (Before this his family had lived first in Allston Street, where he was born, and later in Green Street, both nearby on Beacon Hill.) Likewise, the age of overt savagery and boyish mischief now past, the youngster settled down conformably enough, on the surface at least, to his new pattern of life, attending creditably, in preparation for Harvard, Mr. Gideon Thayer's academy for young gentlemen in Chauncey Place, where, with strange misapprehension, his be-

havior was even characterized by one of his teachers as "docile."
For the time being, the passions and volitions stirred to life by the
Fells ran underground.

Nevertheless, he had his extracurricular pursuits. The Fells, as
well as awakening his imaginative capacities, had also awakened as
strongly his faculties of observation and stimulated the beginning
of scientific interests. The first direction of this bent was of course
toward "natural history," for the pursuit of which place and circumstances were so opportune. At Mr. Angier's school his pockets
are recalled to have bulged with specimens collected on his walk
from the Halls—comprising on one occasion a live snake—and these
interests survived the phase of boyish "collecting" to develop into
the effective working knowledge of geology, topography, flora
and fauna, unobtrusively evident in his histories. On his return from
the Fells, however, his scientific pursuits took the form, for the
time being, of a passionate absorption in chemistry, or at least in
the concocting of chemical experiments. Parkman later deprecated
this unguided enthusiasm as giving him little of the real rudiments
of the science and involving "a lonely, confined, unwholesome sort
of life, baneful to mind and body." But this seems an overcolored
view; and these activities are known to have had their lighter side,
such as administering shocks to a row of girls by means of a homemade electric machine. Furthermore, they were also a feature of a
far from lonely or unsocial enterprise, which, at this time, though
he fails to mention it in his own recollections, equally enlisted his
energies.

This was the organizing and keeping afoot of an amateur acting
company, the "Star Theater," which, for two seasons, gave regular
performances on Saturday afternoons in Dr. Parkman's unused
coachhouse—and by no means to wholly juvenile audiences. The
members, recruited from boys of the neighborhood, including
Parkman's cousins, the younger George Parkman, and Joseph and
Quincy Shaw, wrote or adapted the plays they put on, painted the
scenery, made the costumes, and printed their own playbills. Young
Frank seems to have been very much a leading spirit of the enter-

prise, functioning as manager, actor, stagehand, scene designer, and lighting expert, besides contributing the chemical displays which were an added attraction of the performances. On-stage, because of his high-pitched voice and delicate complexion, he most often took feminine parts, such as that of Katharina in *The Taming of the Shrew*, or of Distaffina in *Bombastes Furioso*, a ribald little burlesque, in which he scored a particular hit. He also distinguished himself as the title character of *The Dumb Boy of Genoa*, a part played wholly in pantomime—his talents for which, indeed, we have already seen him deploying off-stage on his drives back from the Fells.

And, in fact, most of the Star's repertory, running, as it naturally did, to farce and burlesque, to parody, caricature, and the grotesque, struck a vein which was to prove lastingly congenial and was to manifest itself in various connections. So we find Parkman on his trip to Italy held spellbound by the Pulcinella (Punchinello) shows he discovered at Naples, and the stylized antics of which he records minutely and at length in his journal.[2] Likewise, in later life, his own comic invention, for the entertainment of his children or grandchildren, ran in kindred channels of burlesque fantasy: highly apocryphal biographies of Old Testament prophets, for instance; or parodies, composed during his hours of insomnia, such as one on Longfellow's "Psalm of Life," of which cats were the heroes. And

---

[2] I went tonight to the Teatro Sebeto. . . . The piece was a deep tragedy, full of love, jealousy, and murder; dungeons, trap-doors, etc. Pulcinella here assumed the character of a pilgrim. . . . His entree . . . was in the midst of the most tragic part. The father of the distressed lady was busy bemoaning his afflictions on his knees, with clasped hands. Pulcinella kneeled down behind him and caricatured all his motions most ludicrously. . . . Pulcinella then has a scene to himself with two girls, each of whom falls in love with him, and treat[s] him with sugar-plums. Some of his evolutions are very particularly indecent. Pulcinella is a most original character. . . . In a terrific scene of incantation and sorcery which I saw today, [he] pretended at first to be very much frightened, but seized an opportunity to knock over Death himself, who was rising out of a fiery pit to seize him. He kicked a sultan in the face. He is always present in every tragic or pathetic scene, turning the whole to ridicule by his ludicrous caricatures or his affected sympathy.

finally, in his history itself, the baroque phantasmagoria he created out of the materials on which *The Jesuits in North America* is based owes much, in its elements of savage farce and illusionistic *grotesquerie*, to the tastes which found their account on the boards of the Star, or in the "little boxes" of the *commedia de l'arte*, along the quay at Naples. For the rest, this venture of the Star obviously involved the fruitful exercise of a nascent instinct for leadership, and as obviously bears the marks of the thoroughness of application and the exacting standards of competence its leading spirit was to bring to all his undertakings. It is perhaps characteristic that he passed it over in his accounts of his youth to dwell disparagingly on his chemical pursuits—the only one of his ardors and enthusiasms which did not contribute, in one way or another, to the working out of his master purposes.

But with the onset of adolescence both the Star and chemistry were swept aside by a ferment of new interests. The dormant image of the Fells, revived by a trip with his family to New Hampshire, now reasserted itself with overmastering force; the backwoods and the wilderness became a passion; and the manipulation of retorts and crucibles gave way to an inordinate craving for physical activity and an inordinate concern with physical prowess. At the same time, the boy discovered the world of books, into which he plunged with the same overmastering passion. Likewise, his own creative instincts were touched to life; and, half despising a literary career, he began to conceive literary projects and nurture literary ambitions. Declaring itself at fifteen or sixteen, this ferment of oddly assorted predilections was remarkably soon—by the time of his sophomore year in college—to reach its peak and crystallize into the purpose of a life's work.

Meanwhile, nourishing his enthusiams in secret, the boy, as I have said, went conformably enough on his Boston-Brahmin way. However little the Chauncey Place School could satisfy his insistent drive to bodily activity, the *diable-au-corps* that now possessed him, it appears to have performed its intellectual functions amenably to his needs and to have ministered fruitfully to his nascent literary impulses. A fair enough scholar in Greek and Latin, he is said to have excelled particularly in the "rhetorical department"; and, in later life, recalled with appreciation the work of his English teacher, William Russell, who encouraged his pupils to write translations in prose and verse, from Homer and Virgil, "insisting on idiomatic English, and criticizing in his gentle way anything flowery or bombastic." This kind of practice accorded well enough with spontaneous promptings to composition, inspired by his own reading and his boyish fancies of a "life of action and a death in battle"— the versifying of incidents of heroic achievement from Scott's novels, and the like, such as a version of the tournament scene in *Ivanhoe*, which served for a time at Mr. Thayer's as a school declamation piece.

This has been lost, however; and the one surviving example of his schoolboy compositions runs along other lines, and represents the feeling for fact that ballasted his imaginative impressionability. His discovery of literature had by no means atrophied the scientific interests engendered by the Fells. Thus while he was versifying *Ivanhoe*, we also find him writing an essay on "Studies of Nature," where, along with a defense of the utility of such studies, he emphasizes their enhancement of imaginative pleasure:

We are all born with an instinctive fondness for the beauties of nature. We all take pleasure in viewing a lofty mountain, a fertile valley, or a clear stream. . . . But suppose a man who has made nature his study . . . to be placed where we were, and to be looking upon the same objects. The black and precipitous rocks which lie piled in confusion above him, remind him of the period when that mountain emerged from the plain impelled by some irresistible subterranean power. He notices the deposits which through successive ages have accumulated at its base, and compares the present appearance of that valley, enlivened by grazing herds, with its aspect in former ages, when it perhaps formed the bed of a stagnant lake, the abode of monsters, now happily extinct.

Already, these solemn schoolboy reflections indicate an instinctive recognition of fact and actuality as the proper grist for the workings of their author's particular kind of imagination; and already, their emphasis on the historic sense—which geology was then so excitingly quickening—brings us close to the field of history itself as common ground for the faculties that were diversely seeking their account in poetry and in science.

And, of course, we have always to reckon in Parkman with the bent indicated by this essay: this instinct for fact, this concern with the actual and with what, in the light of reason, could be demonstrated to have produced it—the rational-scientific elements of his nature that were indispensable to his making as an historian. But complementary elements were equally indispensable; and for the time being, in the quick unfoldings of adolescence, the world of literature disputed sway over his imagination only with the haunting vision of the wilderness. For the substance of his reading, Scott and Cooper figure large; likewise, Byron, Coleridge, and, to a less degree, the other Romantics; but its core was an impassioned and catholic ranging through the whole field of English poetry, and the discovery, above all, of Milton and Shakespeare. He gave himself to the exploration of this new world with the ardor and intensity he brought to all his pursuits; and much of what he thus ingested and assimilated remained *verbatim* in his memory throughout his life. Indeed, few adolescent awakenings of the sort could show a more magistral taking possession of the realms which literature opens to the spirit. And few, likewise, could show a more direct and intuitive finding of the way to what, on various levels, was particularly to nourish his own spirit. "He had a great enthusiasm as a youth for Milton," says his classmate, O. B. Frothingham; "Shakespeare he had always by him." One can conceive the depth of response to the ring and clangor of the verse—"sonorous metal blowing martial sounds"—as he made his way through the opening books of *Paradise Lost;* and the shock of recognition with which he came across the figure of the Miltonic Satan, so much an archetype of his own heroic-tragic La Salle. But the beginnings of his traffic with Shakespeare are richest of all in their suggestion of deepening recognitions and affinities. The work of no other historical writer is more Shakespearian in its kinship of dramatic creativeness that so absolutely imposes the world of its own making on our imagination; or in its kinship of feeling for this human show of things, as it has being of and for itself, in the tragic interest of its splendor and frailty *sub specie temporis.*

This may seem to bring us at one bound from the boy to the mature man. Nevertheless, as I have said, Parkman's development was in fact rapid enough. As early as his sophomore year at college, his instinct for fact and his instinct for imaginative creation had found their common center in the discovery of his historical vocation; and his passion for the wilderness had led to the discovery of a subject which enlisted that passion equally in the service of his calling. By the time he was nineteen the ferments of adolescence had clarified in self-knowledge; the decisions that determined his life's course had been taken; and all his diverse interests had come to focus on the grand design of the "forest drama" of the Franco-English contest for North America.

Or so at least it seemed at the time, and so at long last it triumphantly proved to have been. The calling of historian has seldom declared itself more unequivocally, or evoked a more unequivocal response. But, meanwhile, the strange discordances of the young man's nature were not after all to be so easily reconciled in the service of his chosen task; and there were dangers in his path which he had not foreseen. Above all there was danger in the very quality of his nature that could be counted his greatest asset—the *vivida vis animi,* the passionate, whole-souled, unremitting energy of spirit with which he gave himself to whatever purpose engaged him. To the degree that the all-absorbing, many-faceted purpose of a life's work began to engage him, so this "pernicious intensity" of application, working on both body and mind, raised itself to a pitch that a nature at once so inwardly excitable and so rigidly self-contained could not long endure. Signs of overstrain and nervous exhaustion soon began to manifest themselves, to which the young man characteristically responded by spurring himself on the more strenuously the more ominous such manifestations became. This cycle of heightening tensions had its inevitable effect; and already, by the beginning of his senior year in college, he had suffered the first of an increasingly grave series of breakdowns.

Moreover, it was precisely the most pleasing aspect of his task, as he first conceived it, which presented the strongest incentives to overdrive himself. He realized well enough that, for his purposes, one "prime condition of success" was an "unwearied delving in dusty books and papers": those labors of research which—though somewhat to our skepticism—he professed to dislike, he was later to perform with an exhaustiveness and thoroughness that made his work, in no relative sense, a landmark of historical scholarship. But, for the moment, he also reached "the agreeable yet correct conclusion" that "the time for this drudgery was not come"; and that his "present business" was to range the wilderness, impregnate himself with his theme, fill his mind with "impressions from real life," and "bring himself as near as might be to the times with which he was to deal." In sum, duty confirmed predilection, and, for the first item on his agenda, he could give himself unreservedly to the pursuit of that image of the Fells under the sign of which his work itself was conceived. And, as to ultimate results, the decision was indeed a correct one. Nothing contributed more to the distinctive character of his histories than the series of wilderness forays that began with his college vacation trips and reached their culmination on the Oregon Trail.

But it was here also, as I have said, that the tendency to drive himself beyond his limits particularly worked havoc. He had come to the Fells as a somewhat puny child, somehow impaired in health, and had been made whole—or so it seemed—by the life of free physical activity he had led there. But this always transient wholeness of boyhood could not be maintained, nor the specter of impairment entirely exorcised. Thus when in adolescence the psyche fixed again upon the image of the Fells, its elements had come to comprise an exaggerated concern with physical prowess and hardihood, sprung in turn from an exaggerated dread of physical deficiency, which gave an almost obsessive quality to the interaction of drives that combined to overstimulate his energies. On these physical grounds, above all, the spur of sheer will power was to be applied at any sign of flagging or faltering—the remedy of "persistent violence which I thought energy"—and here above all the inner struggle that gave rise to these tensions was to be fought to a finish, until, in the wreck of his health which his pursuit of the image of the Fells at last entailed, he confronted face to face the specter that had hagridden him.

But all this was still hidden from the freshman, just turning seventeen, who entered Harvard in the fall of 1840, as yet only on the verge of the momentous commitment he was to make the following year. And whatever indications of trouble began to appear amid the excitements of that commitment, he kept them strictly to himself, as he kept to himself his plans and purposes and the enthusiasms that engendered them. Even among his intimates, inklings of his pursuits passed merely for signs of an amusing eccentricity—"Injuns on the brain," as one of them put it. For the rest, he figured on the Harvard scene as a favorable specimen of his social class and type: active in college affairs; outwardly self-possessed and reserved, even by New England standards; but with a frankness and candor of manner that dispelled constraint; and abounding in force and fire when aroused.

During his freshman year he roomed in Holworthy Hall with B. A. Gould, son of the headmaster of the Boston Latin School, and in later life a well known astronomer. The two boys had never met before, this arrangement having been their fathers' idea; and, as Parkman put it years afterward at a banquet in Gould's honor, the beginnings of their "chumship" were a "little breezy, I might say squally." But, with the aid of some advice from Dr. Gould on the virtues of mutual forbearance, these initial dissensions were smoothed over, and the pair became and remained good friends. For the rest of his college course, however, Parkman roomed alone, first at the corner of Garden Street and Appian Way, and then in Massachusetts Hall, taking his meals at Mrs. Schutte's, a popular, moderate-priced boarding place, with a mixed and lively clientele. Here, on the principle of opposites, he was absurdly nicknamed "The Loquacious," from his marked capacity for sustaining in conversation the rôle of listener and observer. "Catholic in his likings," according to Edward Wheelright, and "rather fond of calling on his class-mates, with whom he was always popular," he seldom, it seems, asked them to his own room in return. His inclinations were not those of a solitary, however; nor did the preoccupations for the sake of which he thus guarded his privacy keep him from playing his part in the little world of the college, or making what was to be made of what it had to offer.

What it had to offer was limited in some respects, and in some respects very much to the young man's purpose. Socially speaking, to be sure, the Harvard of his time could not, in the nature of things, have been for a born Bostonian a vastly broadening experi-ence. Except for a small if colorful Southern contingent, the stu-dents were still almost entirely New Englanders—some, like Park-man, children of privilege; the greater part from families of moderate or small means; but all, in the general American perspective, cut from pretty much the same piece of cloth. On the other hand, what the college lacked in range, it made up for in social cohesiveness. Minuscule by modern standards—the whole tale of the student body, the Schools of Divinity, Law, and Medicine included, came in Parkman's time to well under five hundred—this very smallness of numbers, reinforced by the prescribed curriculum which every collegian followed, made membership in a class more or less equiv-alent to membership in a club, of itself conferring a certain equality of status. If the world of the college was a small one, it was one that could be intimately and thoroughly known, and free of the abysmal cleavages that began to mark its social composition after the Civil War.

Likewise college life itself proliferated with clubs and societies, of which Parkman's time was the golden age. "It is difficult to see," says Professor Morison, touching this period of Harvard's history, "how any student, unless invincibly unsocial in temperament and tastes, could have been wholly unclubbed. Lack of money or of social background was no bar." Parkman, possessing both, together with an unusual range of interests, was correspondingly to the fore in a diversity of such organizations—or rather very sketchily organized and informal groupings as they still were. Thus, among other clubs, we find him a member of the Institute of 1770, then a literary and debating society; Secretary of the Natural History Society, as well as its "Curator of Mineralogy"; President of Hasty Pudding; and a founder and leading spirit of a more purely convivial group known by its initials as the C.C. (Chit-Chat) Club, recruited from his closer friends. The Harvard world was hardly without its social differentiations. Parkman's more intimate companions were boys of his own general background, especially the livelier spirits among this élite, such as George Cary, wit and bonvivant; or the future painter, William Morris Hunt, whose exuberance finally led to a permanent severance of his connections with the college. Nor did the young man at all stint his own share of the gentlemenly diversions that means and social standing put at his command—a sufficient consumption of ale, porter, and flip; dinners at Murdoch's Tavern; wine parties in Massachusetts Hall; expeditions to the theater and to balls in Boston; and the like. Still, the general frame of the college microcosm made for cohesion rather than divisiveness, or at least facilitated a diversity of intercourse, of which the young Brahmin seems to have rather gone out of his way to take advantage.

One also notes, incidentally, the forensic nature of much of the activity of clubs and societies—the prevalent taste for the reading of papers, speechmaking, and debating as forms of sociality. Parkman appears to have found such activities particularly congenial, and spoke often and forcefully in debates. Once, assigned to defend the highly distasteful affirmative of the question, "Does attendance on theatrical exhibitions have a bad effect on the mind and morals?" he is recalled to have startled his audience by changing sides in the middle. He is also recalled to have spoken on the question, "Whether the Republic of the United States is likely to continue?" though on which side is not known. For the college "exhibition" of his sophomore year he declaimed an English version of the "Speech of an

Insurgent Plebeian" from Machiavelli's *History of Florence;* and the following year gave two original dissertations—which one wishes were extant—one on the subject, "Is a man in advance of his age fitted for his age?" and the other on "Romance in America." But his most notable forensic effort was an iconoclastic assault on the Puritans—from whom he and most of his audience were descended —delivered at the Institute of 1770, and demonstrating "in a very original and humorous style the front, flank, and rear of their offending." The topic was one to which he was to return.

One aspect of Parkman's student life, however, was very much off the usual range of his day. His manner in debate, always forcible and trenchant, is said also to have been sometimes downright belligerent—as if, perhaps, he were bringing to these verbal clashes the same spirit of combat that would later have found its outlet in competitive sports. This lack, at any rate, as conspicuous then as its opposite has become since, he did his best to supply on his own by a rigorous program of physical activities, of which his vacation wilderness expeditions were the most notable. Here, as will be seen from the discomforts of his companions on these forays, he had developed a taste that had by no means yet been generally inculcated among the young of his social class; and he pursued in an equally disconcerting spirit the usual forms of desultory student exercise—rowing on Fresh Pond, or pedestrian or hunting excursions into the still unsuburbanized Cambridge countryside, conducted at a pace that made them a trial of endurance to classmates who shared them. Likewise he threw himself with the same overstrained energy into developing special skills—perfecting his marksmanship by constant rifle practice; taking boxing lessons from a retired pugilist; and later, in law school, bringing his horsemanship to a professional level under the direction of a quondam circus rider. As we shall see, at the beginning of his senior year, the immoderate use to which he put the facilities of the newly built college gymnasium was the immediate cause of the breakdown that sent him to Europe.

Meanwhile, the young man was also making what he could of the college for more formal educational purposes. Here the Harvard of the forties presented a decidedly mixed prospect. In part it was the nucleus of an embryonic university, with a stir of innovations, new departures, and intellectual vitality. Nevertheless, in larger part, it was still, for the average collegian, little more than a boys' boarding school, dispensing by rote in daily graded recitations a prescribed regimen of Greek and Latin classics; and governing its charges by a complicated system of petty disciplinary regulations, calculated to keep them in a permanent state of tutelage. Coming to it with a genuinely original bent of mind and a rare maturity of self-knowledge as to his needs, Parkman attempted to cut his cloth accordingly; slighted, as he says, "all college studies which did not promote" his purposes; and "pursued with avidity such as had a bearing upon it, however indirect." This course of action led in his freshman year to a flat failure in mathematics, the time he should have spent preparing for which he chose to spend fowling on the Cambridge marshes. This experience seems to have sobered him, however, and thereafter a passable accommodation was achieved between his own interests and the requirements of the college—which last, perhaps, also proved less unpalatable than they at first appeared. Thus, during his sophomore year he was permitted an "elective" in history—a matter of fairly recent innovation—and in Edward Tyrell Channing he encountered, and responded to, a teacher of composition, who, during his long tenure of the Boylston chair of rhetoric, left the impress of his work on a whole galaxy of New England literati. At any rate, Parkman's academic career was not so erratic that he failed to win a due modicum of official honors, election to Phi Beta Kappa, and "high distinction" in history at graduation.

Furthermore, whatever quantum of mere rote and routine—of "effete and futile scholasticism," to use his own later phrase—could be charged against the college's academic regimen, it had at least the merit of making no very exacting demands on the time or attention of spirits inclined to scholarly pursuits beyond its official purview. Indeed, as it happened, the Harvard of the forties disposed of resources for the furtherance of such pursuits as the young man's —at least as they were undertaken in a private and voluntary capacity—that he could hardly have come on elsewhere. For one thing, its library was the best in the country, and, through such acquisitions as that of the Ebeling collection and the Obadiah Rich collection, unexcelled in the world at the time for its Americana. Likewise, in the person of Jared Sparks, appointed in 1839 to the newly created McLean professorship of history, it possessed both the first occupant of any such post at an American seat of learning, and, by virtue of Sparks's interests, the first also to concern himself with his own country's past. As Sparks's biographer, H. B. Adams, puts it, this appointment, with its recognition of history, and of American history, as worthy of admission to the circle of accepted academic subjects, "marked the dawn of a new era in American scholarship." [3] Not dimmest among the evidences of such a dawn is a little note—in substance simply a request for bibliographical

[3] Born to poverty and a self-made man ("From the Carpenter's Bench to the Presidency of Harvard College" is the subtitle of James Parton's sketch of him), Sparks worked his way through Exeter and Harvard, entered the ministry, and established a flourishing outpost of Unitarianism at Baltimore. Later, as owner-editor of the *North American Review*, he had made the magazine both financially profitable and the equal in quality of its English analogues. With the publication (1834–1837) of his monumental *Washington*, he was at the height of an equally successful career in letters and scholarship, and very much of two minds as to accepting the post his alma mater pressed on him. (He had earlier declined the Alford chair of philosophy, economics, and politics.) He voices his misgivings in a letter of October 3, 1838, to Edward Everett:

"The corporation of the college, as you know, made me a proposal upon which I have not yet decided. In some respects it promises well, but there are various bearings to it which are not altogether satisfactory. You are acquainted with the state of public feeling in regard to the college. There is a general conviction that it is on the decline, and that there are radical faults somewhere. No one seems to know what these faults are; and no one that I have heard of has suggested a remedy. Can a man join an institution in such a condition, with much hope of usefulness or efficiency?"

Later, both Everett and Sparks were to feel the force of these misgivings in their own brief and unhappy terms as successive presidents of the college. Sparks, in this capacity, earned the name of academic "reactionary" for his opposition to the innovations he had earlier helped to establish. The "elective system," he felt, had been sufficiently tried and had been found wanting as a remedy for the college's ills.

The sense of "radical faults" in the condition of the college which Sparks's 1838 letter indicates was to be shared over the years by an increasing number of alumni, including Parkman himself, until the election

information—of which Sparks was the recipient in the spring of 1842. Dated April 29, and superscribed "From Francis Parkman, Jr., Soph. Class," it reads:

Dear Sir:

I am desirous of studying the history of the Seven Years' War, and find it difficult to discover authorities sufficiently minute to satisfy me. I wish particularly to know the details of military operations around Lake George—the characters of the officers—the relations of the Indian tribes— the history, the more minute, the better, of partisan exploits—in short, all relating to the incidents of the war in that neighborhood. Could you furnish me through the Post Office with the names of such authorities you can immediately call to mind, you would do me a great kindness.

                                        Yours with great respect

Sparks, on his part, promptly dispatched the requested list, and went on to invite intercourse of a less formal kind:

                                                    Apl. 30, 1842

Mr. F. Parkman,

I send you a list of books relating to the Old French War. If you wish further information, I shall be happy to see you, and afford you any facilities in my power.

                         Yours

This little transaction, of a sort as rare then in the way of traffic between student and teacher as it was later to become routine, was the beginning for Parkman of the first and perhaps the most important of the long series of scholarly friendships, which, in their personal as well as their professional amenities, form such a pleasing aspect of his career. As he was to discover—if he did not already know—the "facilities" Sparks proffered him were of a kind almost unique at the time. Sparks himself, properly speaking, was hardly a writer of history at all; and a stricter conception of editorial method than his has rendered obsolete the stately, multivolumed compila-

---

of Eliot as president in 1869—with which, as we shall see, Parkman, had much to do—began a new epoch in American higher education.

tions of texts on which his contemporary fame rested—*The Life and Writings of George Washington, The Diplomatic Correspondence of the American Revolution,* the Gouverneur Morris papers, the writings of Franklin, and the rest. Nevertheless, these works were the fruit of investigations, both in America and in Europe, which were the first systematic exploration of the primary sources of early American history, and a conclusive demonstration for future writers of it of the indispensability of mastering such sources. In particular, by gaining admission to the English and French archives—a matter in itself of a some difficulty at the time—Sparks had broken the way to wholly virgin territory, among the riches of which, indeed, he had noted some of the basic materials for just such a project as, fifteen years later, his young correspondent proposed.[4]

The sophomore-historian, on his part, at the critical juncture of his own investigations which his letter indicates, could have found no one better qualified than Sparks to indicate what he would ultimately have to do to come by "authorities sufficiently minute to satisfy me," or better able to help clarify the decisions he was arriving at as to his immediate course of action. For a spirit so eminently capable of making its way on its own, the relationship, even at the start, was perhaps hardly that of pupil and master. Still, for what pertains to the scholarly side of Parkman's work, if any single individual is to be credited with a formative rôle in his development, it is Sparks.

For the rest, Sparks was in many ways the epitome in letters and learning of the respectable Boston Unitarianism of Parkman's father's generation. Thus, in the interest of its sense of decorum, he had groomed Washington and his other subjects for their place on the shelves of a gentleman's library by emending their spelling, punctuation, grammar, and phrasing as freely as if he were editing con-

---

[4] *Journal,* Paris, December 25, 1828: "In the Dépôt de la Guerre are also papers relating to the Canadian wars, embracing Montcalm's correspondence in full, and the correspondence of Dieskau and other French officers engaged in those wars. It will be useful in a history of the 'Old French War.' "

tributions to the *North American Review*. Likewise, he was the voice of Unitarian rationalism and didacticism in his views of historical writing. Much as he admired the scholarship of his quondam student's *Pontiac* (which Parkman dedicated to him) he was uneasy at its lack of the kind of overt moralizing he considered the hallmark of historical profundity. In particular, he felt, Parkman had failed to improve the opportunity offered by the affair of the "Paxton Boys" to enforce "one of the great lessons of history, showing what passion is capable of doing when it defies reason." Obviously, for probing the meaning of history, the elements of the younger man's genius that could dispense with moralistic "lessons" of this sort opened into a world beyond his distinguished senior's ken.

Nevertheless, Sparks himself had entertained one passion that came dangerously close to defying reason—and one that made for a very special bond of interest with his junior. The most ardent wish of his life had been to be a traveler or explorer; and perhaps the main reason for his entering the ministry was the hope that it might be the means of taking him to Africa as a missionary. His regret at having had to abandon this project inspires one of the few passages in his journals of deeply personal emotion—quickly tempered, as it is, to a note of rational resignation. The passage occurs in the entry of his 1828 journal following the one cited above:

December 26th.—The last morning of my residence in Paris. It has been passed with M. Caillé in my own apartments. Caillé is the fortunate man who has just returned from his tour of Timbuctoo and through the interior of Africa. . . . I am rejoiced to have seen, so soon after his return, the first man who has accomplished an undertaking so arduous in itself, which for ten years has tempted me at times in a manner almost too powerful to resist. It is true, indeed, that a combination of very small circumstances prevented my resolving to make the attempt, and turned the tenor of my life in another direction; and I confess that I look back at this moment with some regret on the failure of this more than half-formed purpose. But I can only say that I have submitted to a fatality, a series of events which I was not able to control, and I doubt not the wisdom of Providence in the result.

Likewise, as a surrogate for these thwarted inclinations, Sparks's first historical work had been his memoir of the traveler John Ledyard; and later, with his lives of Marquette and La Salle for the Library of American Biography, of which he was editor, he entered territory where he was the direct precursor of his young correspondent—who was to nourish his own kindred interests by giving rein with such un-Unitarian vehemence to the passion which Sparks had forgone. Thus there were double grounds for Parkman's dedication of *Pontiac* to Sparks "as a testimonial of high personal regard, and a tribute of respect for his distinguished services to American history." At Sparks's death in 1866, his widow, knowing her husband's wishes, made over to Parkman his collection of material relating to La Salle.

But as to the Harvard setting that saw the beginning of this relationship, the academic connection seems almost fortuitous. In the conditions of the time and even considering the fact that Parkman's father was an Overseer of the college and Sparks an old family friend, the little exchange of letters that opened the relationship is not least remarkable for having taken place at all between any Harvard student, "soph" or otherwise, and any member of the faculty. And if, even on the scholarly side, the "lucubrations" of the tyro-historian take us this far beyond the usual academic range of things, so much the more, the inner drama of creative conception of which they were one result, and the matrix of which was the young student's passion for the wilderness. This had its main practical effect in the vacation expeditions of his freshman and sophomore years, which framed the inception of his grand design, and constituted, the first unwittingly, the second consciously, the most original element of his preparations for realizing it. But with these *Ausflüge* we reach altogether the other pole of the dualities that had ruled his life since the ascendancy of the Fells. Obviously they demand a chapter of their own—the more so since he himself has left a detailed record of them.

CHAPTER II

THE MAGALLOWAY
AND LAKE GEORGE

⚜ ⚜ ⚜

Parkman's freshman vacation trip began as an ordinary collegian's walking and climbing excursion along the much-traveled tourist routes of the White Mountains. Nor at the start did he have definite plans for anything more ambitious. But it is obvious from his journal that he was on fire to be off the beaten track; and he soon contrived to turn his vacation outing into a miniature exploring expedition through a section of northern New England until then hardly penetrated, except by Indians and a few white hunters and boundary surveyors. His companion was a classmate, Dan Slade, a rangy six-footer and good walker, whose length of stride had made him a not too reluctant partner of Parkman's Cambridge excursions. But the deeper backwoods were more than he had bargained for; he had no taste for gratuitous hardships; and the trip was punctuated by a good many quarrels between its initiatory spirit and his balky second.

The pair started from Alton Bay, on the south shore of Lake Winnipesaukee, where they had arrived from Boston on July 19, 1841, in a Tartarean hot spell. Making their way on foot up the west shore of the lake to Red Hill—which they stopped to climb, over Slade's objections—they took the stage across to Conway, and then up Crawford Notch to Tom Crawford's pioneer inn in the heart of the range. Here they broke their journey for a few days to make the ascent of Washington which was the climax of this familiar itinerary of early White Mountain travel. But here too, for Parkman, the trip began to take on a character satisfactorily out of the ordinary.

For one thing, under the promptings of the wilderness scene, he involved himself in an adventure which nearly cost him his neck; at the same time he was experiencing the first intoxications of falling in love; and from the father of the young lady who thus took his fancy he received the information which sent him into the untraveled wilderness to the north.

The near fatality occurred on an excursion he made by himself, the first day of his stay at the Notch House, up the ravine of the famous avalanche that in 1824 had overwhelmed the Willey family. Scaling the ledges that blocked the floor of the ravine, he found himself in a position where he could neither advance nor retreat, and was forced to attempt a flanking movement up the rotten rock of the side wall. Here, halfway up, with "certain destruction" below if he lost his grip, two stones gave under his weight and left him grasping the treacherous rock face by only his fingertips. But he kept his wits, and remembered the jackknife he had brought with him. Freeing a hand by gingerly kicking a place for his feet, he got the knife out of his pocket, and managed to open it with his teeth. Then, by alternately scooping hollows for his feet and thrusting the blade into the crumbling rock for a handhold, he finally reached a projecting tree root and could haul himself to safety. The propulsion of a hundred-pound boulder over the edge of the gulf from which he had just escaped duly celebrated this feat of untaught Alpinism. He writes of the incident in his journal as "the most serious adventure it was ever my lot to encounter," as, at the age of seventeen, it was, though it was to be followed by others of equal or greater gravity. But, however creditable to his coolness and nerve, it has a quality of unconsidered rashness which it shares with none of these subsequent encounters. Indeed he had engaged himself in the venture on just such a sudden impulse, occasioned by an article of Professor Silliman's, describing the author's own attempt to climb the avalanche ravine, in which he had been stopped by the transverse ledges. Coming to these same ledges, Parkman recalled the article, determined that the " 'inaccessible precipices' " which had cooled the professor's scientific ardor should prove no barrier to me," and forthwith set himself to scale them in this mood of bravado. Having once courted danger out of foolhardiness and proved his mettle, he was not again to find himself in as dire or direr straits without having weighed the risks.

But at seventeen such considerations would have been intolerably priggish. Furthermore, as I have said, other influences besides those of the wilderness and Professor Silliman were contributing to heighten the legitimate exhilarations of almost breaking one's neck. These emanated from one of a party of girls whose agreeable acquaintance Parkman and Slade had made on the coach ride from Conway—the vivacious and spirited Miss Pamela Prentiss of Keene, New Hampshire, stopping at the Notch House with her father. The acquaintance thus begun could not help but be improved by the young man's recital of his adventure, however much he made light of it; and, as is evident from his journal, matters progressed rapidly in the heady air of the horseback climb of Washington, which took place the following day. "Two of the party fell from their horses," he writes,

three of the ladies were faint-hearted, and all of them tired with one exception—Miss Prentiss of Keene, whose strength and spirit and good humor would have invigorated at least a dozen feeble damsels.

Nor did the attraction prove a passing one. In fact, with subsequent visits to Keene, it ripened, as we shall see, into the major *affaire du cœur* of Parkman's early life; an affair, which, with its White Mountain opening, he later memorialized in his novel *Vassall Morton*, whose heroine, Edith Leslie, is partly modeled on Pamela Prentiss.

But, for the moment, the main effect of these stirrings was to sharpen the boy's urge to be off the beaten track, which, for the rest, was now given a definite aim by what he learned from Mr. Prentiss of Dixville Notch to the north, which the State Geological Survey had just brought to general notice, and of the Umbagog-Magalloway region beyond, where a sparse frontier of settlement thinned out to all but virgin wild, still abounding in moose and other game. Fired by Mr. Prentiss's report, he resolved at once to get himself if possible to these alluring fastnesses. Nor were such promptings lessened by an exuberant bushwhacking scramble he made up "The Rock of the Notch" (Mt. Willard) the last day of his stay at Crawford's—"there was a path," he notes, "but I did not avail myself of it"—nor by the tedium of the inn when he got back at noon to find the Keene party gone, the weather turned to rain, and for company, only a certain Mr. and Mrs. Plummer—"a couple of the most consummate fools I ever saw." He was not put in any more charitable frame of mind the next morning by the spectacle of the Plummers' departure for Washington, the lady uttering "the most piercing shrieks her limited power of lungs could compass the moment she was seated in the saddle."

Nevertheless, partly on the chance of catching up with the Prentisses, he finished out the regular tourist round of the White Mountains, north and west from Crawford's to the Ammonoosuc, then down Franconia Notch to the Old Man of the Mountain—Hawthorne's "Great Stone Face"—and the Flume and Pool at Lincoln. Though he had visited Franconia with his family three years before, the twenty-two-mile hike from Crawford's put him in a less irritable mood; and at Lincoln another bushwhacking expedition, conducted on the principles of his scramble up Mt. Willard, wholly restored his buoyancy. This was to the aforementioned Flume and Pool, two showpieces of White Mountain scenery, now sufficiently tamed, but in Parkman's day still in a state of primitive wildness and requiring the services of a guide to reach; the Pool, indeed, does not ordinarily seem to have been visited. Parkman insisted on doing without a guide, and led off in the wrong direction, having failed to note that the Flume was on a branch of the Pemigewasset, not on the main stream. Thus, to a volley of expostulations from Slade ("Hang your dirty Flume . . . I wish we had never come"), the pair had to struggle through the depths of the virgin forest, "dense and dark, and the ground strewn with fallen trunks in various states of decay," until they reached the clifflike banks of the stream and could follow it back to the Pool and the road. (The Flume, which he had missed altogether, he explored later in the day with a guide from the tavern at Lincoln.) This was Parkman's first real experience of aboriginal deep forest, in its foison of growth and decay, and his eagerly recorded impressions of it and of the stream itself, were later to form the basis of a remarkable forest piece in *The Old Régime*. But however imaginatively fruitful, this experience, like his more serious climbing adventure at Crawford's, also left its imprint in another way. As he notes, he had after all made a "grievous mistake" for lack of preliminary inquiries as to the exact lay of the land; and, if later he was to engage himself with equal ardor in more perilous adventures, their perils were not owing to a repetition of this kind of heedlessness.

But meanwhile, with the scenic "lions" of the White Mountain region duly viewed, and the Prentisses apparently beyond reach, he was free to set about what had become for him the main business in hand. As a first step, he hurried Slade north through Franconia Notch again to Lancaster, where Mr. Prentiss had told him an Indian guide, named Anantz, might be procured. Anantz proved to be absent, but he had the good luck to fall in with the Geological Survey party, from whom he obtained the practical information he needed for the realization of his plan. Thus, its head, Dr. Jackson (Emerson's brother-in-law, later famous for his experiments in anesthesia) gave him a detailed briefing on the equipment and management of backwoods excursions; and M. B. Williams, who had been up the Magalloway the year before, loaned him a sketch map to copy, told him where temporary guides could be engaged, and told him how much he ought to pay them (a "most valuable piece of information," Uncle George's nephew notes, "for otherwise I could not guard myself from imposition"). These practical details fixed in mind, there still remained the problem of dealing with Slade, who, appalled by Dr. Jackson's catalogue of requisites—some of the most important of which, such as blankets, the couple lacked —was again on the verge of mutiny. He sullenly gave in, however, to the "full battery of arguments" which the more masterful spirit of the two opened on him; and the pair proceeded by wagon up the Connecticut to Colebrook. Here, after a dreary Sunday, they took off at last for the backwoods, Parkman, if not Slade, at the keenest pitch of anticipation. "We left Colebrook and civilization this morning, Our journey lieth not, henceforward, through pleasant villages and cultivated fields, but through the wild forest and among lakes and streams which have borne no bark but the canoe of the Indian or the hunter. This is probably the last night we shall spend under a roof."

The country to which he was going was still in the frontier state —a stagnant, backward-turning eddy of the main current to the West. In the eighteen-twenties a few settlers had pushed east through Dixville Notch or north from Umbagog as stragglers in a final attack on the New England wilderness which, if it had not lost its momentum, might have transformed northern Maine to farmland clear to the valley of the St. Lawrence. But the superior attraction of the fabulous midland soil had brought it to a halt, and already abandoned cabins or bare foundation walls could be seen in the sparse clearings. A rough forest track led through Dixville Notch to Captain Bragg's little lumbering settlement (now Errol, New Hampshire) on the Androscoggin, a few miles west of where the Magalloway entered it. An even rougher track followed the Magalloway north past more clearings to the jumping-off place above the rapids at what is now Wilson's Mills. From here all beyond to Canada was an unbroken wilderness, with the little river reaching up to the heart of it.[1]

On his way to the edge of settlement on the Magalloway, Parkman was seeing a pioneer region for the first time and his social prejudices did not prevent him from avidly noting the details: the herd of half-wild cattle in an abandoned meadow beyond Dixville Notch (the scenery of which he found disappointing); the skin of a fresh-killed bear nailed up on Captain Bragg's barn to dry; the dugout canoe that took him across the Magalloway; the scanty

[1] An artificial lake, Lake Aziscoos, formed by the construction of a dam at Wilson's Mills in 1911, now covers the route of Parkman's expedition. The head of the present lake, at the junction of the Magalloway and the Little Magalloway, is the point where he turned back.

clearings choked with the trunks and stumps of the original burning off; the dwellings of the settlers, "mere hovels built of logs and
roofed with bark"; the single-room interior with its great rough-
stone fireplace filling a whole wall; the appearance and speech of
the uncouth but admirably sturdy inhabitants—Bennet, "strong and
hardy and handsome," weather-tanned darker than an Indian; or
Lombard, who was to be his guide, dull-featured but powerfully
framed. Parkman watched with curiosity the Bennet family cutting
for hay the rank grass that grew between the stumps of their clearing and piling it on sleds, "wheels being seldom to be had in this
region." He noted the advance of civilization in the shape of handsome, well built barns, the product of a newly introduced sawmill,
appended to the still primitive dwelling cabins. At Lombard's he was
introduced to backwoods cooking and backwoods appetite, the
doughnuts and pancakes at supper oozing with grease that daubed
the faces of the boys as they wolfed them down, "five or six young
ogres who [ate] as I never saw man eat before."

The settler's "hovel"—in other words, the celebrated log cabin
of the American frontier—was hardly a sentimental symbol for the
unreconstructed young Federalist, to whom the victory of the
Whigs a year before, when, in an orgy of conservative demagog-
uery, the log cabin had taken its place as an American folk myth,
was scarcely less distasteful than the earlier triumphs of Jacksonism. He pointedly sets down his preference for fresh milk to greasy
doughnuts, and a night in the woods to the possibility of dirty sheets;
and he would have been glad to exchange Lombard for "an Indian
or a dare-devil hunter and run the risk of the latter's more questionable fidelity." Like travelers before and after him, he found the
pioneer indifferent to the scenery. " 'I wish them mountains was
furder off. You're welcome to take them down to Portland or
wherever you belong if you're mind to and we'd pay you for the
job too,' " was Lombard's response to his praise of Aziscoos and
Half Moon which shut the sunlight from the settler's good bottom
land. "These fellows," in fact, had no notions except utilitarian
ones and wrought the most deplorable havoc to the forest by their

burnings, creating patch after patch of ghastly ruin "at some leisure day when they conceived that no harm could possibly arise from destroying a few acres of woods to make a clearing which in the course of some few years would be fit to raise a few potatoes"— well conducted persons, one supposes, sending out for their potatoes to Faneuil Hall Market. Obviously, in these precincts of the Jacksonian *demos*, the young scion of the patriciate it had rejected had his spleen to vent, his social and political grudges to air. But just as obviously, and most to the point, he also brought to these uncouth regions a gift of observation that transcended notions, sympathetic or unsympathetic; and set the impress of actuality on what he saw and recorded, independently of opinions. And here—impatient as he was to get himself to the more congenial realms of the Indian and the hunter—the compulsion to see and record was to stand him in particularly good stead. Indeed, except as he revisited the region the next year, he was to see nowhere else, with such fresh eyes, and at such close range, a type of settlement nearer in appearance and modes of life than this little backwater to the American forest frontier of his histories.

But meanwhile the wilderness was his present goal. Under the shadow of Mt. Aziscoos, just over the Maine line, a settler named Lombard (or "Lumber" as the name was pronounced) farmed the next to last clearing up the Magalloway. Here a day's march brought Parkman and Slade after a night at Captain Bragg's. Lombard proved willing to leave his haying for a few days; and Parkman made arrangements with him for the use of his boat and his services as guide. The expedition was to start the next morning. That night, "as an initiation into the mode of life which we are about to enter upon," he and Slade camped in the forest nearby. This was, it appears, Parkman's first night in the open, and his first experience of the night world of the woods whose daylight spell was already so strong upon him. His record of it is a prototype of the unforgettable bivouacs of his histories—the bed of balsam and spruce, and the magic chiaroscuro of the campfire, "illuminating with its glare the tall trees around, whose trunks stood strangely out in the light, relieved against the black darkness beyond."

To make the evening entirely memorable, the boy for the first time also came face to face with a real Indian (though not in the wild state). After he and Slade had shaken themselves down "as well as could be expected for novices," Lombard came out to their fire with a stranger. The visitor was silent for a while, but "when the strange man spoke, his accents showed him to be an Indian, which in the flickering and shadowy light I had not before discovered." He was Jerome, a nephew of Anantz, the hunter-guide whom Parkman failed to find at Lancaster. Jerome was planning a hunting trip on the Magalloway and, unlike Lombard, had no haying to get back for. The boy saw an opportunity to realize the plan of pushing through to Canada that had been in the back of his mind since he had talked with the Survey party in Lancaster, and made an agreement with Jerome for a rendezvous at a point thirty miles up the stream. Then, if circumstances were right, Jerome could take over from Lombard and guide Parkman and Slade to the Canadian settlements, a five days' journey above the rendezvous. Otherwise the boys could come back with Lombard. The plan was a dubious one, given the state of Slade's morale and the little party's lack of supplies and equipment, and it was not destined to be realized. Nevertheless the idea of it quickened the excitement of this night of initiation.

In the morning Lombard's boat was fetched by sledge and oxen up the three-mile carry around the rapids, so overgrown that a way had to be cleared by ax: "Considerable of an enterprise, sir," as the backwoodsman put it. At the end of the portage in a little opening of the woods on the river bank was a broken-down cabin, "the last vestige of man's hand we should meet," in which Lombard had wintered many years before, when he first came to the country. Here they made some repairs to the skiff (the craft was the *bateau* of the northern woods, built of wood rather than canvas or bark, but on canoe lines and paddle-propelled—Parkman describes Lombard's as about twelve feet long, three feet wide in the middle; and "so light that a man could carry it with the greatest ease"). Then with Lombard shouting, "Now for Canada," the expedition pushed from the shore. Parkman was embarked for the first time on a wilderness stream, and in fact seems hardly to have been in a canoe before. "My experience with the paddle was very limited," he writes, "and my companion's none at all." But, eager to get on, he quickly picked up the knack of it, and in an hour or two "had attained in my own conceit at least, a wondrous facility."

The Magalloway was a typical forest river of the north. From the head of the rapids where Parkman put off, it reached through miles of dense woods to a marshy tract called the Meadows, where trees gave way to rank grass and bushes, and the current twisted in endless meanders. Here among the bushes were little ponds, "a grand resort of the moose," who came there in the heat of the day to cool themselves in the water and keep off the flies. Beyond the Meadows the river became more difficult, breaking into white water over a rocky bed, shallow enough in places so that one had to get out and wade to lighten the boat, and here and there blocked by a barricade of drift timber over which the craft had to be lifted by main force. Finally a quiet stretch brought one to the deep, forest-darkened basin which marked the confluence with the Little Magalloway and was the meeting place agreed on with Jerome. Both streams offered a route northward to Canada, the main branch by way of Parmachenee Lake, Lake Megantic, and the Chaudière; the western branch by way of the Salmon River and the St. Francis. As has been said, Parkman was not to follow either of these routes, but on his 1842 trip he was to see more of the Little Magalloway, one of whose upper tributaries he reached across the gloomy, densely forested range of mountains that border the Magalloway valley on the west.

The chief incident of the first day's paddle was an excursion up a side stream to catch fish—chub and trout. Here Parkman and Slade first encountered the full fury of the insects that infest the northern woods in early summer—mosquitoes "which swarmed in unprecedented numbers," clouds of black flies, "as if a blast of red-hot sand was beating against our faces," and "another accursed race, denominated from its microscopic dimensions 'no-see-'ems,' [whose] bite is like the prick of a needle, but not half so endurable" and who "insinuate themselves through pantaloons, stockings, and everything else." But Parkman, whose delicate skin made him particularly vulnerable to their attacks, stuck by his fishing until he had a good catch, and bore the marks of his persistence for days afterwards in the shape of swollen bites that made him look as if he had had the smallpox. Even in the boat the flies were so thick that the voyagers had to keep a smudge going in a frying pan at the bow.

That evening, after an eighteen-mile paddle, they made a belated camp on a high bank of the river, keeping up an enormous fire to ward off the chill, as Parkman and Slade were without blankets. Again Parkman dwells in fascinated detail on the night world of the woods: the bed of spruce boughs, the broad glare of the campfire on the water. "Soon the moon came up and glistened on the still river and half lighted the black forest. An owl, disturbed by the glare of our fire, sent forth a long wild cry from the depths of the woods and was answered by another louder and closer to us . . . then all was still as death again but the roar and crackling of our fire."

The next day brought them to the bends and twists of the Meadows, with its rank grass and marshy pools, where Parkman excitedly hoped to find moose. Images of game had haunted him from the time he had talked with Williams; and the chance for hunting was one of his main incentives for coming to the Magalloway. All along the river broods of wild duck plashed among the alders; an eagle or two had appeared overhead; and "every instant huge bitterns would rise and sail slowly away"; but of bear and moose he had so far seen only the tracks. He had no better luck in the Meadows, though he followed a fresh trail to one of the ponds, whose muddy banks were "as full of the tracks as I have seen a road after a herd of cattle has passed." But his expectations were not in the end to go unrewarded, and the next day he was to have the satisfaction of bringing down his first big game.

In the afternoon they had passed the Meadows and reentered the forest between high banks from which old moss-hung pines reached out over the water. After poling and dragging their way up the "rips," they came to the place where the Little Magalloway joined the main stream and Jerome had agreed to meet them. The water of the tree-shadowed basin ran deep and clear, and they could see shoals of trout moving along the bottom. On the tongue of land between the two streams, near the mouth of the smaller, they found the cleared space and the ashes and charred logs of a hunter's camp site, which they took over for their own bivouac. They had got in early enough this evening to make a proper camp. Up the Little Magalloway Parkman and Lombard caught a mess of magnificent trout, "none of them being less than a foot long," and Lombard built a lean-to of boughs, in front of which they broiled their fish for supper. Again the campfire streamed up "throwing its fierce glare on water and forest for many a rod around." The no-see-'ems were outrageous, but the boy dozed off to a troubled sleep. In the middle of the night he woke, chilled to the bone by the river mist. There was no sound in the pitch darkness but the monotonous tumble of the river, and the fire had burned down to a heap of dull red embers. Waking up Slade, he got him to help collect more wood by the light of strips of birch bark, then lay watching the replenished flame send its sparks streaming like fireflies through the boughs of the trees. He dozed again, dreaming of his disastrous mathematics examination in Cambridge, "when a sudden sound between a shout and a scream dissipated the horrid vision." A shadowy form emerged across the darkness of the water, there was the light grating sound of a canoe beaching, and in an instant Jerome the Indian, who had hailed them from the river, stood by the fire, punctual to the rendezvous, which had been appointed for sunrise. He had paddled since nine o'clock the day before to keep it, and fell asleep as soon as he had wrapped himself in his blanket.

So the wilderness night wore on. It was sunrise when the boy woke again. The others, white and red, still slept like logs around the remains of the fire. A little way off Jerome's dog sat quietly on its haunches, and his long-barreled gun projected from the end of the birch-bark canoe drawn up by the boat on the shore. From the sleeping camp Parkman watched the light break above the dense wall of trees across the misty river, tingeing the tops of giant pines and hemlocks that reached above the level of the rest—a scene that "apart from the excitement and interest of its solitude, was worth much toil to look upon" and a scene that twenty-four years later was to figure to remarkable effect in the climactic episode of *Pioneers*.

Before breakfast a council of war took place as to the party's next move. Parkman reluctantly came to the conclusion that, as things were, pushing on to Canada was out of the question. The boys' equipment and supplies for such a trip were of the scantiest. They were without tent, fly-dope, or most important of all, blankets. All Lombard had been able to spare them in the way of provisions was six pounds of bread, some salt, and some butter. Except for one or two good catches even the fishing had been a disappointment, and with bigger game they had had no luck at all. Even so, Parkman might have chanced it, if it hadn't been for his companion, but Slade's morale by now had completely collapsed, and he refused point-blank to consider going on. "The poor devil was sick of the woods, and, as he has told me since, had passed the preceding day in absolute misery; indeed, I divined as much, for he looked the picture of despair as he sat with his long legs coiled up in the bottom of the boat which he nearly overset every five minutes in convulsive efforts to gain a comfortable position." His night had not made him any more cheerful, and the decision was taken to turn back. After breakfast the little fleet of boat and canoe put off downstream. Jerome on the way up had wounded a moose and went on ahead to track it if he could.

Parkman did not take easily the defection of his second that caused the abandonment of the Canadian enterprise he had conceived. Striking a rarely subjective note, he wrote of it in a narrative of the trip he fashioned from his journal entries shortly after:

It was in vain to attempt to rouse him by holding before his romantic vision pictures of adventures to be achieved and glory to be won in the wilderness. . . . I would have given worlds for a companion hardy, resolute, and enthusiastic; as it was, I was to all intents and purposes alone.[2]

[2] Untitled manuscript, endorsed "Sept. 1841," Parkman papers, Massachusetts Historical Society. I have drawn on this manuscript elsewhere for factual or descriptive details that do not appear in the journal itself.

This was by no means the only light in which he came to view the episode. He was to have difficulties of the same sort with H. O. White, the companion of his sophomore wilderness expedition; and both experiences induced some long second thoughts on the qualities of successful leadership, the gifts that inspire a "willing, not a constrained obedience," and his own failures as leader on these early expeditions to establish this kind of rapport. But, already, in what he makes of this little Magalloway drama of Slade's disaffection, we discern the germ of what he was afterward to make of the tragedy of La Salle and his mutinous followers.

But whatever chagrin he may have felt at the moment was soon dissipated. After the boat had gone a few miles, with Jerome out of sight in advance, suddenly a moose—the one Jerome had shot at the night before, as it proved—sprang from the woods, "splashed through the river, shook the water from its sides, gazed at us an instant, and was gone." Parkman was about to follow its tracks into the woods when around a bend they heard the snap of a gun missing fire. Even Slade seized a paddle and they "swept around the curve like lightning." There, on one bank of the stream, was the moose lumbering into the bushes, and Jerome on the other, picking the lock of his gun with anything but Indian impassivity. A contest of marksmanship followed in which Parkman had the satisfaction of outshooting the Indian, even though his gun was only a light fowling piece charged with bullets, which, however, it luckily carried "with tolerable accuracy." "I raised my gun and fired. The moose tumbled head over heels from the bank into the river, my ball having struck the center of the hump between the shoulders, cut directly through the back-bone, and having been stopped only by the skin of the neck. The unhappy beast lay some time in the shallow water; then staggering convulsively to her feet, she stood with drooping head, unable to move a yard. The Indian fired; the ball whistled by her ears, yet she did not stir. I reloaded, and, aiming at the eye, hit her just beneath the roots of the ear, the bullet grazing the skull and passing out the other side. A stagger was the only result. Jerome now advanced into the water, took a long and careful aim, and drove his ball through the skull midway between the eyes. The moose sank into the water, blood spouted an instant from her nostrils, and she lay dead." Being a female, the animal had of course no antlers, "but her body was larger than a horse's." The dog, who had tracked her, bounded through the shallows to worry the carcass, until Parkman and Jerome dragged it up the bank. Lombard kindled a smudge, and he and Jerome skinned the moose and cut her up.

Coming back to the forks of the Magalloway the next year, the young man dryly cut this adventure down to size: "The old place . . . was the spot which had listened to Slade's lugubrious lamentations; the extreme point of my last year's pilgrimage; the place where Jerome had joined our party; and to crown all, it was scarce five miles distant from the scene of that astounding exploit of knocking over the wounded moose." This was a tame prelude to the risks and challenges of buffalo hunting on the Oregon Trail. Still, the experience had the peculiar satisfactions of all "firsts"; and, next to exploration itself, it was the experience he had most hoped for on this little expedition.

Meanwhile, a noontime gorge of venison by the still smoldering fire of their first night's encampment brought the material reward of his and Jerome's performance; and the rest of the trip was a long but easy downstream paddle to the portage, which the party reached at sunset. After a night in Lombard's barn, and a ten-mile paddle below the rapids to Captain Bragg's, Parkman and Slade walked the rest of the way to Colebrook by a forced march of thirty miles, which Parkman characteristically began by a plunge into the icy waters of Clear Stream to counteract the soporific effects of an enormous breakfast at Bragg's of pie, cake, and bread. Proceeding variously by foot, wagon, and stage, the pair reached the railhead at Nashua on the 13th of August and took the afternoon train to Boston. "Thus ended my expedition up the Magalloway; something of an undertaking in itself, but, I trust, only the 'beginning of greater things.' "

The expedition was indeed the "beginning of greater things," both of the same kind, and as the precipitant of Parkman's historical undertaking. But it also had more specific literary effects, immediate and remote, at which we must glance. The impulse to literary expression that from the start had mingled with his vision of the wilderness is evident of course from the current journal he kept of the trip—the first of his remarkable travel journals, to be followed, particularly, by that of his Lake George trip and return to the Magalloway the next year, the European journal of his senior year, and the Oregon Trail journal two years later. The interest of these journals and the qualities of writing they evince hardly need be enlarged on.

The journal form and manner have their limitations, however, and shortly after his return from the expedition, Parkman felt impelled to recast his field notes of the Magalloway part of the expedition as a more connected and continuous narrative. The result, embodied in the little unprinted "Sept. 1841" manuscript, already referred to, is his first and very tentative effort to convert the raw material of direct observation to something that, without impairing the actuality of the experience, would give a fuller and deeper sense of its imaginative meaning. In intention, at least, his instinct was not at fault. Much expanded with fresh detail, his last wilderness night, for instance, and the moose hunt the next day, now stand out, as they do not in the more cursory journal entries, with the climatic force he actually felt the events to have had. Likewise, for "atmosphere," a passage in his retelling of the first day of the voyage is an evocation of the wilderness in its swarming plenitude of floral and faunal life, which already hints at the symbolic intimations that were to gather to cumulative effect around similar visions of the wilderness that recur through Parkman's work. On the other hand, for one or two such descriptive successes, we have to note a good many failures—perhaps the most egregious of which is precisely the first version, developed from a bare hint in the journal, of that Magalloway sunrise scene, later metamorphosed as we shall see, into one of the most effective passages of *Pioneers*. For narrative structure and movement, the "Sept. 1841" ms. achieves what it set out to achieve; but for color and atmosphere, the writing is too often overlabored and "literary" as compared with the direct, incisive prose of the journal; and execution fails intent in this effort at a more highly wrought, more imaginatively evocative kind of prose, which would bring the experience nearer to Parkman's deeper sense of it. As we shall find, when we come to his *Knickerbocker* stories and *The Oregon Trail*, this stylistic problem was to beset other attempts to give more coherent and expressive form to the data of his journals. Nor was it always to be entirely solved in his histories.

Yet, on the whole, history proved emphatically to be the medium most congenial to eliciting the inward pattern of meaning of these early experiences, as Parkman felt them; and nowhere more triumphantly so in what he was finally to make of this first Magalloway voyage. As we shall have occasion to note in detail, his memories of it, as the journal and particularly the "Sept. 1841" ms. revived them, provided the evocative core of his account in *Pioneers* of Champlain's famous Ottawa voyage—the culminating episode of the book, and an apotheosis of the figure of the explorer, and the central, Western drives the explorer exemplifies, hardly matched elsewhere in Western literature. No subsequent wilderness experience was to make quite such an imaginative impression on Parkman as his own miniature exploration of the Magalloway, or was to be converted more effectively to the uses of history. However fumbling and tentative, the "Sept. 1841" ms. was a first step in the process.

But meanwhile, of course, it was the discovery of history itself as the field for the deployment of his gifts and powers that was the main result of this first wilderness expedition and the literary efforts it inspired. Between September and April of Parkman's sophomore term there occurred the momentous crystallizing of aims of which I have spoken, the conception in its essentials of what was to be a life's task and the beginnings of his preparation for it in a turmoil of aspirations, misgivings, pragmatic calculations, and imaginative excitement, of which he has left his own record in his autobiographical letters.

My favorite backwoods were always in my thoughts. At first I tried to woo this . . . mistress in verse; then I came down to fiction, and at last reached the sage though not flattering conclusion that if I wanted to build in her honor any monument that would stand, I must found on solid fact. Before the end of the sophomore year my various schemes had crystallized into a plan of writing the story of what was then known as the "Old French War" . . . [a plan] later enlarged to include the whole course of the American conflict between France and England; or, in other words, the history of the American forest; for this was the light in which I regarded it. My theme fascinated me, and I was haunted by wilderness images day and night. . . . While not exaggerating the importance of my subject, I felt that it had a peculiar life of its own, to me irresistibly attractive. I felt far from sure that I was equal to the task of rekindling it, calling out of the dust the soul and body of it and making it a breathing reality. I was like some smitten youth plagued with harrowing doubts as to whether he can win the mistress of his fancy. I tried to gauge my own faculties, and was displeased with the result. Nevertheless, I resolved that if my steed was not a thoroughbred, I would at least get his best paces out of him, and I set myself a strenuous course of training for the end in view . . . spending my summer vacations in the woods . . . [and] reading such books, as I thought suited, in a general way, to help me towards my object. I pursued these lucubrations with a pernicious intensity, keeping my plans and purposes to myself, while passing among my companions as an outspoken fellow.

So Parkman to Martin Brimmer forty-five years later. As we have seen, the young man, even at the time, did not keep his purposes altogether secret, or evolve his plans in quite such an atmosphere of isolation as one would suppose from his own reminiscences. Still, it is clear from his April, 1842, letter to Sparks how fast and how far he had come on his own in the few months since he had conceived his subject. And whatever light Sparks could throw on his further prosecution of it, it is also clear that he had already determined his immediate program of "filling my mind with impressions from real life," and "bringing myself as near as might be to the times with which I was to deal." For these purposes, still confined to a history of the "Old French War," a visit to Lake George was obviously the most present item, and was the first objective of his sophomore vacation plans. But he was by no means finished with the deeper wilderness, and completed the expedition with a traverse from the north of the rough country that divides the Connecticut Lakes from the valley of the Magalloway—a route that finally brought him out at his starting place of the year before. This part of the expedition, as with his idea of pushing through to Canada on his first Magalloway trip, was the abridgement of a more ambitious scheme. He originally planned to trek from the Connecticut Lakes through the heart of the Maine wilderness to Mt. Katahdin (the existence of which had become generally known only a few years earlier, through the explorations of Dr. Jackson), but he had likewise to give up this idea because of his companion's recalcitrance. He had chosen to go with him on this second expedition Henry Orne White of the class of '43, whose prowess as an angler would have seemed, like Slade's pedestrian abilities, to make him a promising candidate for the backwoods. But White found the hardships of wilderness living as little to his taste as Slade had, and proved as impervious to the enthusiasms which urged on his friend.

Meanwhile, these enthusiasms were intensified for Parkman by the specific historical purposes he now had in view. At Lake George, furthermore, he was not only seeing for the first time an important scene of the action of the work he had begun to envisage—but the scene, likewise, of the book which was the literary influence responsible for his discovery of this subject. Thus it is a double ferment of excitement that we feel rising in his journal as the sites whose names his boyhood reading of *The Last of the Mohicans* had already made portents came into view on the hot July stage ride from Saratoga that brought him and White to the village of Lake George (or Caldwell, as it was then known).

Here the pair put up at the inn for a couple of days, while Parkman inspected the tree-grown ruins of Fort William Henry and other historical remains. The weather was overcast and muggy; and he exhausted himself in his enthusiasm by bushwhacking three miles in the suffocating heat up Mt. Prospect to get a panorama of the lake. As usual, he drove himself the harder, the more out of sorts he felt. (Indeed the condition of irritability, overstimulation, and nervous fatigue in which he had come from Boston already strikes an ominous if passing note in the general exuberance of the 1842 journal.) The

next day, to his relief, he and White put off in a hired rowboat for
Diamond Island where they began their exploration of the lake by
camping for the night. Caldwell was already a tourist resort: Parkman had found the inn full of fashionable New Yorkers ("all of a
piece") who stared at him and White in their rough clothes. The
lake itself, however, was still a demiwilderness. Except for scattered
clearings and a hamlet or two, the primeval forest clothed its shores
much as when Rogers's and Marin's bands had ranged them, and
they had looked down on the flotillas of Montcalm or Lord Howe.

Parkman's tensions began to relax the next morning as a stiff
south wind tempered the heat and sent the boat at a fast clip down the
east shore to the island-studded Narrows. Here was the most spectacular part of the lake, and the scene, as Parkman notes, of the
canoe chase in *The Last of the Mohicans*. The boys landed at the
point of Tongue Mountain, where White went off shooting, while
Parkman swam across the smother of whitecaps in the strait to one
of the islands, from which in spite of the haze the "view down the
lake was the finest water-scene I ever saw." When the wind fell a
little toward sunset they took the boat over to another island where
they made their second camp.

The wind held the next day, driving the mists before it, and Parkman's enthusiasm grew as he and White kept on through the Narrows, and the mountain-framed vistas revealed themselves in a dramatic counterchange of light and shadow: "The water was a dark
glistening blue, with lines of foam on the crests of the waves; huge
shadows of clouds coursed along the mountains. The little islands
would be lighted at one instant by a stream of sunshine falling on
them and almost making their black pines transparent, and the next
moment they would be suddenly darkened and all around be glittering with a sudden burst of light from the opening clouds."

The pair spent most of the day exploring among the islands in the
Narrows, White trailing a line for bass. In the afternoon they landed
at Sabbath Day Point where they found they could get supper and
a bed at the "rickety, dingy, shingle palace" of an old man who oc-

cupied part of it and let the rest. His tenants were a couple with a progeny of "youthful giants and ogresses" who "calculated" on removing to Illinois in the fall. The old man himself was a revolutionary pensioner, "Captain Patchin by name, and stout-hearted, hale, and clever by nature"—a sturdy ancient of eighty-six, still handsome and muscular, who three years before had danced with great applause at a country party. Parkman was fascinated by his stories of the Indian campaigns around Fort Stanwix, or of Quebec, where he had been sent as a prisoner of war. With this appeal to his special interests and his usual responsiveness to any genuine saliency of character, his social prejudices at once dissolved, and he enthusiastically excepted the captain and his household from the general anathemas on the inhabitants of the region with which his journal bristles—"a race of boors about as uncouth, mean, and stupid as the hogs they seem chiefly to delight in." The next day, too, he spent agreeably enough in the company of one of these boors, young Myrtle Bailey, of the Brobdignagian brood lodging at the captain's, "a simple, good-natured, strong-handed, grinning son of the plough," who took him on a rattlesnake hunt up the mountain in back of the point. From a precipice overhanging the lake, the panorama of which from these heights was the "noblest view" he had yet had of it, he scared the crows by firing off his new rifle into the gulf below. Frontier-fashion he had christened the weapon with a personal name, "Satan," in honor, no doubt, of the hero of his favorite *Paradise Lost*.

After this break in the boat journey, Parkman explored the lower part of the lake as thoroughly as he had the upper, with a stop at Garfield's (now Hague) to replace a broken oar; a night's encampment under the cliffs of the Nose across from Rogers's Slide at the beginning of the outlet; and the next day a twelve-mile row in the teeth of the wind back to Captain Patchin's to pick up some laundry. At Garfield's, while the carpenter was making a new oar, Parkman bushwhacked up a valley in back of the settlement and came across a chasm resembling, as he notes, the Flume at Franconia. The place drew him with the same curious spell and again he records his impressions in fascinated detail—the fallen logs of the wood, the sheer rock walls, the strange plunging noise of the water, "apparently from underground."

A spell too, for Parkman at least, hung over the spot where they camped for the night under precipices that had witnessed "the passage of twenty vast armies," where there was "not an echo but had answered to the crack of rifles and the screams of dying men." White, however, was allergic to the *frisson historique* of their romantic situation. Parkman had chosen for a camp site a little roofless log hut they had found in a deep hollow, which, sheltered from the wind as it was, turned out to be an inferno of no-see-'ems. White had begun to have enough and said so, volubly and emphatically. With the next day's twelve-mile grind up the lake against a head wind he broke into open revolt. " 'Are you going to back out?' said I. 'Back out, yes; when I get into a scrape, I back out of it as quick as I can.' . . . Lake George he called a 'scrubby looking place'—said there was no fishing in it—he hated camping and would have no more of it—he wouldn't live so for another week to save his life, etc., etc." A familiar scene was repeating itself, but Parkman was now an old hand at dealing with mutiny, and was as much worried over White's lack of cash, which would make it necessary to abandon the Katahdin trip, as over his threats of desertion. After dining at Patchin's who welcomed the pair "as cordially as if we were his own children," they rowed down to Garfield's again. Here Parkman put his still contumacious follower ashore at the inn, retired to an island, washed his one pair of pantaloons, camped out by himself for the night, and, the point of honor satisfied, rejoined White at Garfield's the next morning. A couple of days' loafing at the inn restored for the time being the harmony of the expedition, which on the 26th proceeded down the outlet to Ticonderoga without incident. The chief event of Parkman's stay at Garfield's was the arrival at the inn of William Caldwell, the principal landowner of the region, whose father, like the grandfather of the Jameses, was an Irish emigrant who had built himself a fortune by trading at Albany. The progress of the great man through his domains was marked by exactions of deference, firings of salutes, and so forth—a very un-Bostonian pomp of place, which the young patrician, one generation further removed from commerce, did not fail to score. His reflections on the follies of the newly rich were not sweetened by having to share his room with two of the nabob's retinue.

At Ticonderoga Parkman of course explored the old fortress—then unrestored and vandalized by the townspeople, who used it as a stone quarry—and the scenes around it of Abercrombie's repulse and Amherst's siege, which he was often to examine again. He had not been prepared for the extent and size of the masonry walls of the fort, reaching in the oldest part sheer down to the level of the lake. After making arrangements to send the rowboat back to Caldwell, he and White embarked for Burlington, on one of the luxurious lake boats which, among little else in America, won unstinted praise from Dickens who traveled up Lake Champlain in the same year.

Parkman's traverse of northern Vermont took him through the Mt. Mansfield region to Lake Memphramagog, shrouded in rain clouds when he saw it, and then across the border to the flourishing town of Stanstead in southern Quebec. Here the last flicker of a boundary dispute, to be settled that summer by the Webster-Ashburton treaty, signalized itself in the presence of a small detail of British infantry. The atmosphere was hardly warlike, however, as natives, soldiers, and the visitors from across the line fraternized on Sunday morning in a session of psalm singing in the inn kitchen, which ended in a rendition of "America" with "God Save the Queen" added at the close of each stanza. From the fertile levels of Stanstead Plain Parkman and White followed a rough forest track back through the Vermont hills, past occasional clearings and log cabins, to Canaan on the Connecticut, his route being in part that of Rogers's Rangers on their retreat from St. Francis in 1759. From Canaan they went on up the river to the edge of habitation on the First Connecticut Lake, where Parkman engaged a settler named Abbot to come with them on what was to be his most ambitious and, as it proved, his last venture in forest living. He had suffered a serious check on the way in to the lake through an accident to his rifle which had split the stock and broken off the breech pin—"worse than anything that could have happened, short of the loss of our cash"—but he determined to go on. He had worked up White to something resembling enthusiasm by inflaming his mind with visions of the Magalloway trout, and the opportunity was too good to miss, in spite of the fact that the weapon he counted on for game was now practically useless. Abbot did not know the country in the direction in which Parkman planned to go, but "this was nothing to the purpose—a compass was guide enough," and he hired the burly farmer's services for a dollar a day.

The preparations for the expedition took a day or two, and Parkman again had a chance to observe backwoods life at close range and again sets down what he saw in sharp detail: "We went in to supper, which was served in rough style, but had the virtue of cleanliness as did the whole place—children excepted. . . . . Abbot was a rough-hewn piece of timber enough, but his wife was a perfect barbarian, as far as entire absence of all manners can make one, but both were equally open and hospitable. Henry tried the polite, but I judged it best to do at Rome as the Romans do, and I believe got along best. We spent that evening about their enormous cavern of a fireplace, whence a blazing fire gleamed on rows of suspended stockings, the spinning wheel, the churn, the bed, and walls covered with an array of piled up cheeses, plates, milkpails, and clothes; all clean and all in order; while the older children were dodging about the furniture of the crowded room and the younger ones venting precocious snorings from a box under the bed." Abbot, unlike the majority of his neighbors, turned out to be a Whig in politics—he had named one of his children Henry Harrison—and astonished his guests by erudite references to democratic levelers and the bed of Procrustes, "all this while he was squatting on his homemade chair, one leg cocked into the air, shirt-sleeves rolled up to his elbows, bushy hair straggling over his eyes, and eating meanwhile as if his life depended on his efforts." He was a great reader of history and much else (except fiction, which he detested) and once, acting as his own counsel, had successfully defended himself in court against a clever lawyer.

Abbot's cabin and one other were the last outposts of settlement in the region. From them an overgrown bridle path ran to the Second Connecticut Lake beyond which lay the same unbroken wilderness Parkman had penetrated from the south the year before. To the southeast of the lake the land rose in a dreary sweep of forest to the semicircle of shapeless, huddled, wooded ridges that separate the Connecticut watershed from the valley of the Magalloway—Prospect, Stub Hill (the highest of the range at 3,607 feet) Diamond Ridge, Magalloway Mountain to the south, more peaked than the others, Bosebuck out of sight to the east. A through road now leads past the Connecticut lakes across the Canadian border, and lumberers have of course been busy with the virgin forest of Parkman's time, but the region is still a forbidding one; easy to get lost in, even for those familiar with it, from its densely wooded character and lack of distinctive topographical features; and, virtually unmapped and wholly trailless as it was when Parkman came to it, altogether as exacting a terrain for bushwhacking by compass as the northern wilderness could offer. If he had had to forgo his Katahdin plan, he had chosen a sufficiently arduous substitute.

He, White, and Abbot began their traverse on the fourth of August. They expected to cross the Second Connecticut Lake on a raft which Abbot kept there, but found it had disappeared over the rapids at the outlet and had to build a new one. This improvised craft brought them to the eastern shore, where they landed in an alder swamp, White managing to tumble overboard in the process. Setting their course SE by compass, they plunged into the almost impassible tangle of rocks, gullies, undergrowth, and blowdowns that lay before them. "It was a constant straining of muscle and sinew. Boughs slapped us in the face, swarms of flies stung us; we trod on spots apparently solid and sank to the thighs in masses of rotten timber. . . . Now and then there was a 'windfall'—a disgusting feature of forest scenery, owing its origin to the passage of a whirlwind, sweeping down the trees and piling them in masses. One of them, in a hollow place, where a gorge opened from the mountain, presented an aspect singularly unpleasing. It was of old date, for the forest had grown up, around, and over it. . . . Some [of the fallen trees] were a mass of pulp, delicately coated with a sleek green moss, which, pressed with the finger, oozed water like a sponge. Others, less perishable, or lifted higher from the earth, still showed fight against the elements, and scores of red cedars in particular bristled out of every part of the pile in an execrable chevaux-de-frise." [3]

White, who had hurt his foot the day before, made matters worse by lagging behind so that the other two had to stop every few minutes and endure the black flies while they waited for him to catch up. This did not improve the already strained relations between him and Abbot. Parkman kept his impatience in check, cannily aiming to gentle White along until that unfortunate would find it more formidable to try to turn back than to keep going.

Afternoon brought them over the first ridge to a little valley where a brook half hidden in brushwood and fallen trees made its way through the thick growth of fir, spruce, and birch. Parkman and Abbot were for going on up the second and higher ridge, but White had had enough, so they camped by the brook, making a supper from the scanty provisions they had brought with them—bread, rice, butter, tea, and salt. Again the campfire cast its magic light into the depths of the wood, as the early darkness of an overcast day settled in and

[3] The first part of this passage is from Parkman's journal; the last part from an article, "Exploring the Magalloway," published in *Harper's*, November, 1864. This piece is a somewhat fictionalized account as to the character of the guide, called Gookin, who is a compound, with additions, of the less attractive traits of Lombard and Abbot. White, however, is barely disguised as "Brown"; and events and itinerary follow closely those of the journal, though with much fresh descriptive detail.

The reputation for roughness of the Magalloway range has not declined at the present day. The following is from a recent account of an attempt to climb Mt. Bosebuck, on the eastern side of the range. "The windfalls we encountered were such that I hope I never have to look even at fallen trees again, let alone climb up, over, around, and under them. . . . It was the worst collection [of blowdowns] that I'd ever seen." (Eunice Nelson Palmer, "Maine, Mountains, and Mammals," *Appalachia*, December, 1945.)

they stretched out on their pallets of spruce boughs. A light rain began to fall as Parkman was writing up his diary by the firelight, and the night was showery.

The next day they struggled on through the same dense growth up the second ridge, White all the time grumbling and lagging behind, though Abbot was now carrying his blanket. The guide cursed him to his face, "and said he never knew a fellow of so little pluck." As the weather, though still cloudy, had lifted a little, Parkman climbed a tree to take bearings. From the view he describes—Magalloway Mountain to the south, Connecticut Lake pale in the mist among its foothills to the west, a branch of the Dead Diamond River hidden from sight in a gorge directly below, and a long ridge opposite sloping away on the left to the Magalloway—the party had no doubt come up Stub Hill, which, as I have said, is the highest part of the range.

Still steering southeast they bushwhacked on down the mountain until they heard the sound of water and came out on a sheet of rock, "where the crisp mosses crackled under the foot," and a stream curvetted below over the boulders and granite shelves of its bed. This Parkman judged, as it proved correctly, to be a branch of the Little Magalloway. The change from the monotonous forest tracking gave everyone a lift, and the hardest part of the trip seemed to be over. White, his lameness mysteriously vanishing, dashed from rock to rock, pulling in a trout "from every deep hole and the foot of every waterfall." Parkman followed his example, while Abbot kindled a fire and cooked the fish as the boys caught them. In better spirits after this feast, they kept on down the course of the stream until they reached the valley bed, and the torrent leveled out into a little river navigable for canoes. Another mile brought them to the remains of an old camp site beside a waterfall where the stream plunged over a ledge into a deep basin. As it was getting dark they decided to camp here and feasted again on broiled trout, of which they caught a dozen in ten minutes from a rock in the middle of the falls. "The Magalloway trout," Parkman says, "are the noblest in appearance and the most delicious in taste I ever knew."

The next morning brought a council of war as to how to get down the river. "Abbot could make a raft, thought he could make a spruce canoe, and was certain he could make a log one, that is, a dugout." The party having decided in favor of the last, Abbot felled a pine and set to work, while White went back to sleep again, "after his established custom on all occasions," and Parkman, after building a smudge for Abbot, explored downstream to take the lay of the land. The mountain brook had brought them, as he had surmised, to the Little Magalloway, and he soon came on the familiar scene of his last year's camp site where the Little Magalloway joined the main stream. The water in the basin was running darker and deeper, and a hunter—Jerome, as he afterward found—had built a shack of split boards at the camping place. When he got back he found Abbot had changed his plans, the pine he had cut down to make a dugout having proved to be rotten, and was in the process of constructing a bark canoe, which Parkman helped him finish. It turned out to be a very doubtful affair indeed and leaked like a sieve as soon as they put it in the water, but they caulked it with spruce gum and bits of cloth, and hoped that with bailing it would do. "Had an Indian seen it he would have killed himself with laughing. We gazed upon it with pride; yet our pride was dashed with secret misgivings."

These misgivings were well founded. After another night at the falls and a breakfast of trout and rice, the three pushed off in the dubious craft. It negotiated one rapid successfully but the second brought disaster. A rock tore a four-foot gash in the side and water spouted in "like a stream from a pump." The experiment had turned out an utter failure. While the boys took to the woods, Abbot waded in the brook with the rickety craft to pilot the baggage down to the forks of the Magalloway, but it went to pieces in his hands in short order, and he barely managed to rescue the packs.

A driving rain had set in when after an hour's slogging through the woods the expedition arrived at the forks. Though the provisions they had brought with them were running short, there was an inexhaustible supply of trout in the pool, and common sense might have suggested holing up in Jerome's shelter till the weather broke. "We, however, were neither philosophers nor Leatherstockings, but a brace of restless collegians; and go ahead though the heavens fall must still be the word." Having failed with a canoe they decided to try a raft and in a couple of hours had knocked one together out of logs, and the boards of Jerome's shack, which they demolished for the purpose, the boys standing waist deep in the water to hold the timbers in place while Abbot withed them together with grapevine.

The raft fared as badly as the canoe. Because of the badness of the wood, it drew twice as much water as they had expected and was no match for the "rips" down which the river boiled, a little below the forks. "We pushed from shore in a deluge of rain. Like its luckless predecessor, the raft passed the first rapid in safety, only venting a groan or two as its logs encountered the stones beneath. . . . When it came on the second rapid the machine seemed to shiver in direful expectancy of its approaching destruction. Presently it grunted loud and dolefully. We set our poles and pushed it into the deepest part. For a while it bumped and blundered downward; at length there was a heavy shock, a crash, a boiling and rushing of many waters. The river spouted up between the logs . . . ; [the craft] would not budge; she was wedged fast on a sunken rock. The water broke over her; a grapevine snapped; the logs groaned and struggled under us. All was up with her. She was going to pieces, and we must abandon the wreck. The fir-trees on shore were dimly visible through the rain, with the river tumbling between, not more than three feet deep, but full of rocks and swift as a mill-race. Hooking our arms together and bracing ourselves with setting poles, we began our progress. Once or twice the current nearly took us off our legs; but, climbing over boulders and plunging through gullies, we reached land at last."

The expedition was now in a tight spot. Parkman, however, started the indefatigable Abbot to work on felling a tree for a dugout, while he and White made camp as best they could in the dripping forest. In the afternoon when the rain let up a little, Parkman went back to the basin to catch fish for supper, and by nightfall Abbot, plied with tea to keep his spirits up, had hewed out a log canoe in what seemed to Parkman an incredibly short space of time—"that day [Abbot] deserved, if he did not win, the honors of champion axman of New England." In the evening the rain began to pour down again, but by putting up White's saturated blanket for a cover, and spreading Parkman's on the ground underneath they achieved a shelter of sorts; and a huge bonfire which they managed to keep going in front dispelled some of the dampness. White, as usual, dropped off to sleep, but Parkman and Abbot talked till midnight. Abbot's colloquial powers were as impressive as his axmanship and the boy learned more from his conversation that evening about the manners and customs of the "semi-barbarians" Abbot lived among "than I could have done from a month's living among them." Abbot was indeed a phenomenon of the American backwoods democracy whose lineaments, the young Brahmin among other purposes, had come abroad to scan. "Our guide is a remarkably intelligent fellow; has astonishing information for one of his condition; is resolute and as independent as the wind. Unluckily, he is rather too conscious of his superiority in these respects, and likes too well to talk of his own achievements. He is coarse and matter-of-fact to a hopeless extremity, self-willed and self-confident as the devil; if any one would get respect or attention from him, he must meet him on his own ground in this matter." The boy could satisfy himself that he had. At least he found "that night in the rain, leagues from the dwellings of men . . . a very pleasant one."

The party woke to another day of rain. Abbot finished the dugout, while the boys got breakfast (White usually presided at these culinary operations, and, whatever his other failings, was an accomplished camp cook, as Parkman had noted with satisfaction their first night out on Lake George). Their "magnified horse trough" proved adequate, and the day was an uneventful grind in drizzle and shower with a short stop at noon to consume the last of their bread. Poor White went into a complete slump. "White paddled lazily and unskilfully, and showed much of that kind of resignation which consists in abandoning one's self to fate, instead of fighting with it. Abbot gave him something more than hints of what he thought of him; and when I proceeded, in a truly Christian spirit, to bestow on him a little friendly advice and exhortation, that he should be up and doing, he flung down his paddle, wrapped himself in his blanket, and sat down listlessly in the bottom of the canoe."

The party hoped to reach the rapids by nightfall, but as darkness drew on they saw a logger's hut on the left bank, from which a cart path seemed to lead to the settlements, which they knew were not far away. The hut was dry and snug, but they had only some rice left of their provisions and the thought of real supper and a real bed was too tempting. "Leaving the certain to pursue the uncertain good," they hurried along the path for a mile or so in the gathering dark, only to plunge up to their necks in a slough where the overgrown road ran out in a swamp, as lumber roads are apt to do. Covered with mud they had to take the back track. With straw beds and a good fire, however, they spent a tolerable night in the hut and woke late to find the sun out and the mist lifting. A three-mile paddle brought them to the carry, where Parkman and Slade had set out the year before, and that night they reached Captain Bragg's, not without difficulty on account of the swollen state of all the streams.

At Wilson's Parkman had seen his old friend Lombard and received from him the ears of the moose which he had shot and which Lombard had dried for him in his chimney. He also ran into Jerome—an encounter which had a paralyzing effect on White. "The first man we met was the Indian Jerome, who was cleaning a moose-hide in a field. He shook hands with me very fervently, probably expecting a donation for old acquaintance' sake, but the rascal was disappointed. Jerome is an outcast from his tribe for various misdeeds, too numerous and too gross to particularize. White, after muttering a salutation which Jerome did not hear, and half extending a hand which Jerome did not see—or pretended not to—stood fixed in awe and abhorrence at the sinister look of the fellow's face, the diabolical size of his mouth, the snaky glittering of his deep-set eyes, the hollowness of his cheeks, and the black marks dissipation has made on his countenance. Jerome is an admirable hunter. He killed more than twenty moose this spring."

After the luxury of a bed at Captain Bragg's and of watching the rain from the sheltered side of a window pane, Parkman and White reached Colebrook the next day, Abbot turning off homeward by a byroad to the north. From Colebrook the stage took them to Lancaster where White, reduced to his last quarter of a dollar, stopped to see his uncle and "borrow the needful," while Parkman kept on down through Franconia Notch to Plymouth and thence to Boston.

One wilderness venture of greater scope and danger than these two Magalloway trips lay before Parkman, but nothing else he ever undertook meant so much for his work. They were, so to speak, his Oregon Trail of the East. Here he first slept in the open and shot his first big game. Here for the first and only time he had the experience of forest river travel and learned its techniques. Here, too, on his second trip, across the rough country to the north, he learned all he was ever to learn at first hand of deep forest tracking. These few days—both Magalloway excursions came to less than two weeks —yielded an extraordinary harvest of impressions that was the life in epitome of his whole history: the great series of explorers' voyages from Champlain to La Salle that fills its first half; the innumerable woods marches of scouts, partisan bands, and armies that fill its second. The eastern forest, not the plains of the West, was his scene, and he here came closest to its heart. Vital for what he was to do as was Parkman's experience of Europe and the West, they lay on the circumference of a circle whose charmed center was this obscure river of the northern woods, which nowhere appears by name in his histories.

Parkman too had gone to this wilderness when it was still a novelty and a wonder. Forced back by the frontier of settlement, what was left of it was still in its primeval condition; the railroads had not yet reached it, or the pulp mills begun to chew it up. In fact he was very much of a pioneer in finding his way to it; it was not until four years later, in 1846, that Thoreau made his first Maine wilderness trip. Just as Parkman had launched himself single-handedly on his career of historian, so he had come to the woods without benefit of "summer camps," before the out-of-doors had become an institution in the upbringing of the sheltered classes, and he could see them and write about them with the fresh eyes of prime discovery. Indeed for the Boston of his day this native wilderness was almost more of an exotic than the paradisal islands of the South Seas or the fabled coasts of the orient.

Yet what he would make of it depended too on what he would make of its opposite; and events quickly combined to send him as far in the direction of civilization as he had gone in the direction of anti-civilization.

CHAPTER III

EUROPE

✿ ✿ ✿

Parkman's freshman and sophomore vacation journals are written with an *élan* that makes them on the whole his most effective writing of this kind. Here one sees him in the first possession of his literary powers, and in the first flush of his discovery of his subject and the wilderness world that was its scene. So, too, the bloom of health and animal spirits is on these pristine recordings. They are the product of Parkman's brief apogee of youth and well-being, before the early disordering of his constitution had overtaken him.

Yet signs of trouble are also patent enough. An entry in his 1842 journal is particularly indicative. "I woke this morning about as weak and spiritless as well could be," he writes after his first night's camp at Lake George. "All enterprise and activity was fairly gone; how I cannot tell, but . . . such has been the case with me, to a greater or lesser degree, for the last three or four weeks." Already the preternatural ardors and intensities to which the discovery of a life-engrossing purpose could excite an organism "highly irritable" by nature had begun to take their toll. All this, to be sure, strikes only a passing if ominous note in the general exhilaration of Parkman's Lake George–Magalloway journal; and for the time being, a day or so of boating and camping could put him back at the top of his form. But, giving full rein to his natural propensities, both in the study and in the field, spurring himself to action by main force when nature called quits, entering on his long course "with all the vehemence of one starting on a mile heat," he had already depleted to an alarming degree his reserves of resilience.

How much so is evident from the perfunctoriness of the record

66

of an excursion to Canada he made the summer of his junior year by way of Lake George, Lake Champlain, and the Richelieu River. He was apparently not up to a real wilderness trip; and recaptures a little the spirit of the year before only with a stop at Crawford's on the way home. For the rest, though he was seeing Montreal and Quebec for the first time, these sites that were to figure so largely in his history evoke only the scantiest of jottings in his notebook. Nor did he feel in the mood to keep more than brief notes of a visit he made immediately afterward to the colony of Abnaki Indians at Old Town in Maine, near Bangor. In the fall of 1843 he suffered his first serious breakdown.

The immediate cause of it he himself attributes to heart strain from overviolent exercise in the newly built college gymnasium. Likewise he speaks in his European journal of the "hellish beating" of his heart after he had scrambled up an Alpine valley near Andeer. But for the most part his trip was active enough, and organic heart trouble was not among the maladies of his later life. It is difficult to believe that this early heart complaint was more than a secondary symptom of a crisis of hypertension that had been in the making for several years, the spells of lassitude and prostration attendant on which he had attempted to counteract in the gymnasium by his usual methods. But, in any case, his condition was such that he had to leave college; and on November 12, 1843, two months after his twentieth birthday, he sailed for Gibraltar on the trading barque *Nautilus*. A sea voyage and foreign travel worked, temporarily at least, their expected effects. He was soon setting down his impressions of the voyage at length and with zest, and the very full journal he kept of the whole trip seldom shows him really out of sorts. The time-honored prescription of the grand tour was successful in staving off complete collapse for another two or three years.

The itinerary of Parkman's trip was a favorite route of early nineteenth century Boston travel and was very much that of Emerson's tour ten years or so earlier: first, Sicily and Italy by way of the Mediterranean; then the Alps and the Rhine; Paris, London, and the Scott country; and a return voyage from Liverpool. There is no need of following it in detail. The crossing to Gibraltar, though it took a month, was enlivened by a series of winter storms, which Parkman describes in his most spirited manner; one of these entries he later transferred almost verbatim to *Vassall Morton*. Among the officers and crew of the *Nautilus*—he himself was the only passenger—he was on particularly good terms with Mr. Hansen, the second mate. Hansen was a rough-and-ready frontiersman type who had been to the Rockies on one of Wyeth's expeditions and responded to Parkman's treats of brandy and water with stories of the West that were no doubt more inflammatory than brandy to the young man's imagination. Impatient as he became, like everyone else on board, at the headwinds and calms that kept the little ship off the Straits of Gibraltar for nearly a fortnight, it is apparent that he thoroughly enjoyed his first sea voyage.

And for Europe itself Parkman was in a singularly receptive frame of mind. If he was enough of a Puritan to have to be forced into a holiday of this sort by doctor's orders, he was enough of an anti-Puritan to take it in a holiday spirit and make the most of life as show and surface, which is the charm of travel, and not the least essential of its meanings. His journal does full justice to the Europe of romantic landscape, of the historic past, of exotic custom and spectacle —the carnival at Rome, and the pomps of Holy Week; Latin gaiety and Latin *savoir vivre;* the crowded outdoor life of southern cities; the franker southern recognition of *das ewig Weibliche*. "Few of the women had any regular beauty of features, but there was an expression of heart and spirit, and a loftiness beside, which did not shame their birth," this scion of Puritan divines writes at Rome at carnival time. "They flung their flowers at you with the freest and most graceful action imaginable. To battle with flowers against a laughing and conscious face—showering your ammunition thick as the carriage slowly passes the balcony—then straining your eyes to catch the last glance of the black-eyed witch and the last wave of her hand as the crowd closes around her—all this is no contemptible amusement." The end of the carnival brought him onto the Corso to take part himself with the Roman girls—"who fought like Amazons and had strong arms as I can testify"—in the game of putting out torches which then closed the festivities, a brilliant spectacle which he brilliantly depicts: the Corso as if on fire to the rooftops, the shouts of "*Senza moccolo*," the glittering forms of the maskers leaping into the air to guard their own lights, or put out those of others.

The journal does not often reach this, for a Bostonian at least, somewhat heady pitch, but enjoyment is one of its prevailing notes—the sheer pleasurable receptiveness to the richer European background of a gifted young American on the grand tour, an intelligently and discriminatingly impressionable young American, with a keen sense of history and an alert curiosity as to the diversities of human living. Nevertheless the crisis of health that had brought Parkman to Europe was likewise something of a crisis of spirit, and Europe also evoked from him a psychological response of a more intimate kind. It was not in his nature to dwell, even in the privacy of a journal, on the conflicts of his inner life, but amidst the eager and vivid recording of external details the European journal occasionally gives direct expression to a feeling of *Sturm und Drang*. Now on the threshold of maturity, spiritually and imaginatively at odds in many ways with the environment in which he had grown up, he was groping for alternatives. The lines along which Europe was bringing to a head these discontents are evident as he sums up his first impressions in an entry written on board the British troopship that took him from Gibraltar to Malta:

Here in this old world, I seem, thank heaven, to be carried about half a century backwards in time. As far as religion is concerned, there are the ceremonies of the Catholic Church; and the English litany, with rough soldiers and sailors making the responses. A becoming horror of dissenters, especially Unitarians, prevails everywhere. No one cants here of temperance reform, or of systems of diet—eat, drink, and be merry is the motto everywhere, and a stronger and hardier race of men than those around me now never laughed at the doctors. Above all there is no canting of peace. A wholesome system of coercion is manifest in all directions—thirty-two pounders looking over the bows—piles of balls on deck—muskets and cutlasses hung up below—the red jackets of marines—and the honest prayer that success should crown all these warlike preparations, yesterday responded to by fifty voices. There was none of the new-fangled suspicion that such belligerent petitions might be averse to the spirit of a religion that inculcates peace as its foundation. And I firmly believe that there was as much hearty faith and worship in many of those men as in any feeble consumptive wretch at home, who when smitten on one cheek literally turns the other likewise—instead of manfully kicking the offender into the gutter.

The immediate occasion of this outburst was the Anglican service he had just witnessed on the troopship and the spectacle from which he had freshly come of the might of the British *raj* at Gibraltar. He was no doubt reminded of another Episcopalian service he had listened to two years before at Lake George, when, as it happened, a young minister "with *Yankee ploughboy* stamped on every feature" had to the Harvard sophomore's astonishment and admiration preached a finely delivered sermon on the text from Exodus, "The Lord is a man of war." There were tracts of human nature that, to put it at the least, the Unitarian ethos very imperfectly comprehended. For Dr. Parkman's son, especially, reared in its bosom, its thin "preachments of the superiority of mind over matter" were calculated to provoke an emphatic rejection and a countermovement toward a more robust faith. "Any feeble consumptive wretch at home": so much for the Reverend William Ellery Channing, as one turned from the Boston ambience of "spirit," uplift, and peace societies towards the denser social realities of Europe.

It was not Anglicanism, however, but the "ceremonies of the Catholic Church" that were to be the focal point of Parkman's rebellion against his native Unitarianism. It is not surprising on several grounds that at this stage of his growth he should be attracted by the idea of Catholicism as a religion. For one thing, he shared the general inclination toward the medieval that was part of the literary tradition on which his imagination had nourished itself. "I . . . wished to get for a while out of the nineteenth century," as he put it in an article about his Roman sojourn he wrote for *Harper's* near the end of his life. There was also the persuasive personal example of his cousin Coolidge Shaw, whom he liked and admired, and who had shortly before become a Catholic convert. And finally, of course, there was the very special interest Catholicism held for him on account of the part it had played in his chosen field of Franco-American history. Aware that he needed for the purposes of his work to see something at first hand of Roman ecclesiasticism, he characteristically turned his European "cure" to account in this connection by taking every opportunity he could of acquainting himself with its ceremonies, its institutions, and, so far as possible, its inner life. The force of these influences combined to bring him to Rome—naturally the climax of his trip as far as a study of the church for historical purposes was concerned—in a state of mind in which he was not unwilling also to entertain the idea of Catholicism as a personal commitment. The idea, to be sure, did not take root, but abortive as, in the event, it proved, it was strong enough at the time to enhance in a most fruitful way his sympathies with certain aspects of historical Catholicism; and he could hardly have done justice to this phase of his subject without these first-hand impressions formed at such a particularly impressionable moment of his growing up.

This experience was the most important single aspect of his trip, and we shall return to it, but it would be a mistake to isolate it too much from its context of many-sided receptiveness to the general European scene. There were limits of course to Parkman's receptiveness. He was somewhat deficient in appreciation of the fine arts. At least music was almost a totally closed world to him; and, in spite of the pictorial character of his writing, he seems to have had little original feeling for painting, though he "did" the galleries conscientiously enough. In the field of the arts his one prime discovery was the Pulcinella theater in Naples, of which I have spoken, that popular drama that cast such a curious spell on him. Nor, except so far as he came a little within the sphere of the Catholic revival, does the turmoil of contemporary European intellectual and social movements find much of an echo in his journal. The only lion to whose haunts he made a special pilgrimage of homage was a dead lion, Sir Walter Scott. But within these limits and for his purposes, Europe yielded the young man a rich enough harvest, much richer indeed in the fundamentals of the physical and the visible than it had yielded his great transcendentalist contemporary eleven years before.

So one notes first of all the mere harvest of the eye—the sense of scene and setting, Parkman's responsiveness to which one hardly needs to underline and the record of which fills the bulk of his journal: night-pieces such as his description of the carnival at Rome or of the Easter illumination of St. Peter's; baroque grotesques like the scene of the mass among the mummies at Palermo (a forerunner of such masterly baroque passages in his histories as the description of the Huron Feast of the Dead); depictions of natural scenery, especially of the wilder sort; and genre pieces of street scenes, the interiors of inns, and the like; of both of which last his Sicilian travels and an outing in the Apennines with his classmate William Morris Hunt were particularly productive. Parkman of course was trying his hand in all this on more or less conventional tourist "subjects," and the journal form did not give scope for the incantatory rhythms and pregnant thematic repetitions of the descriptive writings in his histories. Yet in landscape, for instance, for a certain kind of painterliness and crispness of touch, he was not to surpass some of these pieces of his European journal. Possibly owing in part to the company of Hunt with his artist's eye, one or two of those evoked by the above-mentioned Apennine excursion show a particularly painterlike quality. The following, with its deep perspective and its fine discrimination of effects of light, is an example:

Leaving this place, we rode on toward Subiaco in a perfect amphitheatre of the mountains. Those on the right lay in dusky shadow, for the sun was setting behind them; but on the other side the enormous bare rocks were glaring in the light, with their tops still whiter than themselves with the snow. Grey villages, with light smoke hanging over them, were scattered thinly along their sides and summits, a thousand feet in the air. The air was beautifully clear, and the afternoon as still as death. Some of the distant Apennines were blue as the sky itself, and peculiarly shadowed in the oblique light.

Yet the whole journal is pictorial enough. As an example of portrait work, a little sketch like the following, struck off on the voyage
from Gibraltar to Malta, shows the same painterly suggestiveness
in its posing of the subject and its dramatic contrast of dark and
bright:

Polyphemus. There is a man on deck, with a face dark as a Negro or
mulatto, yet features unlike those races and very powerful—a beetling
brow, shaggy with hair, a swelling nostril, black strong beard—and an
expression as fierce and savage as I ever saw. He stands with folded arms,
a strange contrast to the light hair, florid faces, and military stiffness of
the Marines.

This is writing par excellence with one's "eye on the object"; but
for all its apparent externality it is also of course writing with an
imaginative effect beyond the merely graphic or pictorial. Though
the mode of these pieces is the familiar mode of the guidebook
picturesque, there is a creative compulsion, a sense of inner affinity,
behind the choice of theme, and nothing could carry Parkman's
signature more plainly than the enchanted mountain stillness of
the Apennines piece or the impression of savage force in the sketch
of the man on the *Polyphemus.* So even an offhand description of
the fountains of Palermo—hardly more than a listing—is informed
with his idiosyncratic feeling for running water with its obscure
sexual overtones, suggested by the emphasis on the fountain of the
nymphs at the close:

Palermo is full of beautiful fountains—water-gods—horses—serpents—
fishes—every imaginable variety of figure—pouring forth the pure water
of the mountains, into basins full of goldfish, or over rocks of marble
covered with a growth of water-plants. Sometimes a group of water-
nymphs are seen sporting together, flinging the water at each other.

So in the tunnel of the Anio—the "Grotto of the Syrens"—at Tivoli,
he notes the "calcarious depositions, which sometimes assume very
singular forms," one of them "precisely resembling the breast of a

woman"; and both passages are European analogues of the hidden stream of his American travel notes—the Flume at Franconia, the ravine at Garfield's, or a chasm near Crawford's he describes in his 1843 journal: "Nothing but great piles of damp mossy rocks . . . a stream is plunging somewhere underground, and breaking into a black pool among the moss."

But if its pictorial quality is the most noticeable trait of Parkman's journal, his apprehension was also alert enough to the social aspects of the scene—occupational traits, varieties of manners and customs, the differentia of regional and local patterns of life. He had consciously come to Europe as a "student of human nature," and it is not for nothing that he later gave Vassall Morton in his novel a bent for "ethnological inquiries," "an absorbing interest in tracing the distinctions, moral, intellectual, physical, of different races." At the moment he himself was attempting nothing on this score beyond the staple of what might be acquired in the ordinary range of tourist travel; nevertheless, one is impressed by the solidity of what he did acquire within this range and the sense his observations give of a relationship to a master purpose. Imaginatively, too, the receptiveness they show to the traits of the "Latin" temperament was particularly important in confirming his intuitive sympathy, on one side of his nature, with a civilization that was the counterimage of Boston and America. This early experience—and, as it happened, he was not to revisit southern Europe—was to aliment most creatively one of the ambivalences of feeling that give such force to his account of the struggle between Anglo-Saxon and Latin for mastery of the New World.

In the personal sense, likewise, the grand tour broadened valuably a social range limited by circumstances of birth and temperament. Travel "brings out" even the most diffident of New Englanders, and the student of human nature enlarged his view of that phenomenon with a sufficiently varied series of *amis de voyage*: Hansen and the rest of the crew of the *Nautilus;* a young American midshipman at Gibraltar, "frank and spirited . . . with a relishing spice of the devil in him"; old Lieutenant Sparks on the *Polyphemus,* with his memories of Napoleonic days; the Anglo-Sicilian Guiseppe Jackson, once a cook at Murdoch's Tavern in Cambridge; the admirable Luigi Rannesi, Parkman's guide on the muleback trip across Sicily, who "knew everybody from princes to beggars"; and various ecclesiastics such as Father Glover and other English Jesuits at Rome, and Padre Lucca at the Passionist convent. For the lighter side of things there was an elderly rake, the Spaniard Don Mateo Lopez, traveling in Sicily (an account of whose nocturnal diversions at Catania Parkman discreetly inked out of his journal), and at Paris, his own Uncle Sam, making the sybaritic most of his ostracism from Boston. Finally, for intellectual interest, there were two such extremes of American possibilities as Theodore Parker, the vanguard figure of New England radical transcendentalism, and the Virginian, St. Ives, a Catholic convert with a fervent dislike of democracy, a sort of forerunner in *Tendenz* (if hardly in character) of types like Melville's Ungar or James's Basil Ransom.

Parkman spent the greater part of his time in Sicily and Italy, neither of which, as I have said, he was to visit again. Sicily, with its mountain landscapes and its rich debris of civilizations, made a particularly deep impression on him, fresh from America as he was. Landing first at Syracuse and then at Messina, he made a trip from Messina down the eastern coast, enchanted by the views of Mt. Aetna and the sea and by the novelty of ruins—the remains of the Greek theater at Taormina, or the crumbling Saracen fortresses on the sea cliffs. As for Catholicism, the church of the Benedictine monastery in Catania moved him to set down in round terms the feelings that such monuments of the faith had begun to inspire in him:

The church of the Benedictines is the noblest edifice I have seen. This and others not unlike it have impressed me with new ideas of the Catholic religion. Not exactly, for I reverenced it before as the religion of generations of brave and great men—but now I honor it for itself. They are mistaken who sneer at its ceremonies as a mere mechanical farce: they have a powerful and salutary effect on the mind. Those who have witnessed the services in this Benedictine church, and deny what I say, must either be singularly stupid and insensible by nature, or rendered so by prejudice.

In western Sicily he made Palermo his base, where he spent a week, admiring the fountains and the gaiety of the inhabitants, and seeing "all the lions, which are numerous"—Monte Pellegrino, Monreale, the catacombs of the Capuchin convent, Santa Maria de Gesu with its panorama of the city and the mountains. On a muleback trip across the island to Girgenti, with its stops at the primitive, beggar-infested up-country inns, he saw something of Sicilian peasant poverty; likewise in the coast towns of the return route he had, through Luigi Rannesi, first-hand glimpses of the life of the Sicilian gentry—the modest establishment of a "baron" at Sciacca with girls spinning and hens cackling in the main room; or the salons of two or three wealthy *virtuosi* who shared Luigi's passion for antique coins and cameos. Parkman himself began to tire a little of classical antiquity, and the broken columns of Agrigentum left him apathetic. Nevertheless of all the Siclian sites he visited he dwells most enthusiastically on the temple of Segesta in its wild and lonely setting, a landscape, seen at sunset, of "unmatched sublimity and beauty." The cold, stormy weather of the last part of the trip also particularly gratified his taste for dramatic landscape by presenting a scene of snow-whitened mountains as he came out from the pass above the green plain of Palermo. All along his route, finally, he had made a point of stopping at convents and shrines; so now before descending to the city, he turned aside to visit the Benedictine monastery of San Martino, reserved for devotees of noble birth. Its luxurious appointments, however—including a game preserve and a billiard room—rather scandalized him, keyed as he was at the moment to a more heroic and austere mode of faith.

Naples was the next stop on his pilgrimage to Rome, notable chiefly for his discovery of the Pulcinella shows in the "little boxes" along the quay, and his meeting with Theodore Parker, who with his wife—"a pretty, timid, gentle little woman"—was staying at his hotel. Parker, then "about thirty-five years old, with a bald forehead, spectacles, a thick short nose, slightly suggestive of the busts of Socrates, and a large bucolic mouth" (as Parkman described him many years later) introduced himself at dinner one night; and Parkman recalled having seen him at a meeting of Unitarian ministers at his father's house. But as a Unitarian minister Parker was very much of a maverick. Indeed, his heresies had now put him under the ban of that Unitarian orthodoxy that numbered the Reverend Francis Parkman among its conspicuous lights—a fact that did not make him any less interesting to Dr. Parkman's son; and if the advanced cast of Parker's social opinions could hardly have been a common bond, his transcendental radicalism was ballasted by a very untranscendental solidity of intellect, a streak of boyish humor, and a warmth, spontaneity, and saliency of character that at once won the young Federalist. Both were rebels, if in different ways, against official Unitarianism; and Parkman, reserved as he was, would have found Parker a person to whom he could have opened himself as to his difficulties with his father over his choice of a career (which in fact he seems to have done; at least one gathers from a note of the following summer that Parker had been instrumental in persuading him to comply with his father's wish that he qualify himself for a recognized profession). Likewise, with his omnivorous erudition and his particular interest in history, Parker was also a person with whom the young man could have very profitably discussed the nature of the career he had chosen. A project such as Parkman's could not have failed to engage the older man's enthusiastic attention; and for Parkman a confirmation of his purposes from such a quarter —for among his other capacities Parker was an authoritative critical voice in New England letters—would, one surmises, have meant a great deal, coming just at that time. What excellent practical advice about historical writing Parker was capable of giving is evident from the long letter he sent his young friend seven years later on receiving from him a copy of *Pontiac*, the first fruit of his historical endeavors.

But if little of this appears directly in the journal, it is evident enough how congenial Parkman found the company of the Parkers during his stay at Naples and afterward at Rome, to which he traveled with them. Parker in action is the subject of several of the young man's liveliest sketches—dodging lava falls in the crater of Vesuvius, getting his spectacles broken by a sugarplum at the carnival in Naples, spouting passages from Vergil and Cicero on the diligence ride to Rome, starting up with "rather an untheological interjection" of excitement to identify the Colosseum as they entered the city. At Rome the Parkers took rooms in the Via Babuino; Parkman saw much of them there and made an expedition to Tivoli with them, together with his classmate Hunt and Hunt's freshman brother.

Parkman's Roman days with their climax in his stay at a Passionist convent were in a lesser way comparable to his Magalloway expeditions or, later, his sojourn among the Oglala Sioux. Each episode furnished him with concrete, living impressions of a cardinal aspect of his subject, without which, given the need of his type of imagination for the first-hand and the physically immediate, his history could hardly have been written. His Roman experience, however, was less direct in its bearings on what he was to do, and was not of a particularly dramatic cast. In so far as it was a drama of personal belief, indeed, it was something of an anticlimax. Parkman's conversion was undertaken shortly after his arrival at Rome by the Virginian convert St. Ives, mentioned above, who, to further the good work, introduced him to a group of English Jesuits. The only immediate result, however, was an irritated recoil on the young man's part. Circumstances and agent, it must be admitted, were not of the most propitious sort. The carnival was still in progress when Parkman arrived at Rome, and, as we have seen, he entered with zest into the spirit of it. His discovery of the Pulcinella shows at Naples, his meeting with Theodore Parker, and now the heady excitements of the carnival combined to put him in a state of overstimulation, and the double strain of a week of strenuous sightseeing that followed and the proselytization to which he was being subjected at the same time further set his nerves on edge. "A weary week of lionizing," he writes on February 27, "I would not give a damn for all the churches and ruins in Rome—at least such are my sentiments at present. . . . A Virginian named St. Ives, lately converted to Catholicism, has been trying to convert me, along with some of the Jesuits here. He has abandoned the attempt in disgust, telling me that I have not logic enough to be convinced of any thing, to which I replied by cursing logic and logicians." Chopping logic with Jesuits, one gathers from a later entry, was an exercise for which he found his Harvard training had not very well prepared him.

This is all Parkman has to say directly in his journal of St. Ives's efforts for his conversion, but the 1890 *Harper's* article gives further details. It was St. Ives, it there appears, who had in large part effected the conversion of Coolidge Shaw. Parkman met him at Theodore Parker's rooms, and St. Ives expressed a hope that Parkman would follow in his cousin's path. Parkman, however, took an immediate dislike to his cousin's mentor, though he was interested by him and willing to listen to him. The dislike was confirmed on further acquaintance, which revealed in his preceptor a marked strain of exhibitionism and aggressiveness. St. Ives, Parkman writes in his *Harper's* article (and it is obvious from a letter from his mother that he had written home a similarly unfavorable impression at the time) [1]— "hated democracy, and was fiercely arbitrary and domineering when he could be so unchecked, but was humble to those in high places. He had a keen intellect and a remarkably vivid imagination, to which he gave full rein. His vanity was great, and till he saw my incredulity, he entertained me with frequent stories of his adventures and exploits in his days of sin, always calling on me to observe the transformation wrought in him by his conversion. He was one of those to whom the imposing spectacle of organized power in the Roman Church appeals with fascination." St. Ives emerges as a very recognizable type in this little sketch, and it is not surprising that a few days' exposure to his histrionic personality left Parkman for the moment in a recalcitrant mood. If he had come to Rome with some half-formed intention of following Coolidge Shaw's example, it was pretty much dissipated by this experience, though it goes without saying, of

---

[1] "I am very much surprised," Mrs. Parkman answers, "at what you say of [Coolidge Shaw's] friend at Rome, of whom he speaks so highly, and has given the best character of to his family; how is it; is he deceived or you mistaken? However, no matter now—at any rate I infer you won't come home a Catholic and that's a comfort."

course, that more fundamental causes were at work in the failure
of his conversion than simply distaste for the agent who attempted it.

His recoil, furthermore, was by no means as yet a complete one.
The whole Roman section of his journal is marked by fluctuations of
feeling indicative of inner conflict. In fact, the very next journal
entry to the one quoted above—a passage he set apart with eight
stars—shows what an impression, in spite of St. Ives one might say,
his view of Catholicism at its center was making on him:

> I have now been three or four weeks in Rome—have been presented to
> his Holiness the Pope—have visited churches, convents, cemeteries, cata-
> combs, common sewers including the Cloaca Maxima, and ten thousand
> works of art. This will I say of Rome—that a place on every account more
> interesting—and which has a more vivifying and quickening influence on
> the faculties—could not be found on the face of the earth—or at least I
> should not wish to go to it if it could.

Annoyed as he had been at being worsted in argument, his Boston
self-sufficiency was shaken, and in the face of Catholic claims he
felt, for the moment at least, a certain provinciality of outlook. The
entry continues:

> It is as startling to a "son of Harvard" to see the astounding learning of
> these Jesuit fathers, and the appalling readiness and rapidity with which
> they pour forth their interminable streams of argument, as it would be to
> a Yankee parson to witness his whole congregation, with church, pulpit,
> and all, shut up within one of the great columns which support the dome
> of St. Peter's—a thing which assuredly might be done. The Catholics here
> boast that their church never stood at so high and happy a point as now—
> converts are pouring in—wisdom and sanctity abound.

The entry closes, finally, with a note of his visit to the studio of
the German artist Johann Overbeck, the leader of a band of painter
converts to Catholicism who lived like monks in the convent of San
Isidoro on the Pincian Hill and devoted themselves to an austere
and highly ideological revival of early Christian art (the sodality was
a forerunner of the Pre-Raphaelites and similar groups). The spirit
of their work fell in with Parkman's mood, and he writes of Overbeck

as "a man of wonderful genius," each face of whose drawings "speaks plainer than words the character of its author's mind: mild, earnest, and devout to enthusiasm."

Parkman's own enthusiasm for medieval Christianity was to be further inflamed shortly after by the little trip I have spoken of he made at this time into the hill country with Hunt, now in Europe to begin the art studies that were later to make him the leading American disciple and interpreter of the Barbizon School. The trip began with an outing at Tivoli with the Parkers; the next morning Parkman and Hunt started for Subiaco up the valley of the Anio for four days on muleback, visiting the Benedictine monasteries that clung to the savage precipices above the river, and stopping for the night at hill towns like Civatella with its Pelasgian fort, "older than the Bible," or Palestrina with its famous mosaic. At Palestrina too they found an equally remarkable *albergo* kept by two young sisters, "both handsome as the sun," and by no means displeased at the frank admiration of their American guests. "We spent the evening before the fire talking with them," the young man writes, "though Hunt, who does not speak a word of Italian, kept up his share of the conversation by signs. My Italian was not much better; but the girls were as intelligent as they were handsome, and, I think, as virtuous."

But of all that was *sehenswürdig* on this inspiriting little expedition it was of course the crag-built monasteries along the Anio that in relation to his main purpose most focused Parkman's attention and fired his imagination—St. Benedict, he thought, "must have had a peculiar taste for wild and lonely situations." The devotion that had hewn San Cosinato out of the rock of the cliff face seemed to him a most "admirable example of courage and enthusiasm," and he carried away a flower "as a memento of the gallant monks." At Sacro Speco, also partly built in the natural rock, over the famous cave on the mountainside above Subiaco which the saint had chosen for his hermitage—at those heights where it was still "cold as winter" and the Anio "twisted like a white thread among the rocks directly below"—he was "under strong temptation to beg the fathers to let me stay in their monastery for a few days." As Hunt was not similarly disposed he didn't make the request, but the visit clinched his determination to be admitted as a guest to a monastic establishment, and almost as soon as he got back to Rome he busied himself with efforts to that end. In the valley of the Anio, as he was no doubt aware, he had been treading ground that had seen the very beginnings of Western monasticism, for here St. Benedict had founded twelve convents before instituting his famous Rule at Monte Cassino; and here was the starting point of the movement that during the "Benedictine centuries" slowly reclaimed northern Europe from barbarism by a great civilizing enterprise, of which the Jesuit efforts in Canada and elsewhere, however dissimilar in spirit, were a kind of revival. At Sacro Speco Parkman was pursuing his "research" on the Church Missionary to one of its ultimate sources.

His first effort to see something of monastic life from the inside was at the convent of the Passionist Fathers at Rocca di Papa, overlooking Lake Albano—he had heard that the discipline of the Passionists was of the strictest—but he found that he would have to have permission from the superior of the order at Rome. This was apparently not forthcoming, but he finally did succeed in being admitted to a Passionist convent in the city, near the Colosseum, where a group of Italian layman were making a retreat in preparation for general confession at Easter. He seems to have been received under some misapprehension as to his status, for Padre Lucca, the director of the retreat, was a little startled to discover he was a Protestant. Nevertheless his heretical condition was taken in good part, with hopes for his conversion—St. Ives, it appeared, had also stayed at the convent—and from Friday through Palm Sunday the young Unitarian joined, as far as his Protestant conscience would allow him, in the exercises and devotions of the lay retreatants. The visit, it should be added, had also a spice of adventure—at least Theodore Parker seems to have felt some Maria Monkish apprehensions about the proceedings, and, according to the *Harper's* article, arranged with the American consul "to make the eagle scream" if Parkman did not reappear by a certain date.

Parkman's record of this experience is of course in large part simply factual; this was the key piece of the "research" he had made part of the program of his trip and he seized his opportunity by setting down in meticulous detail everything he could observe of the monks' regimen, religious observances, and so on. Emotionally the entries strike the same note of divided feeling that is evident through the rest of his Roman journal. He was amused at finding himself in such a situation, and amused at the attempts of Father Lucca's emissaries to convert him, the Passionists being hardly as adept in such matters as the Jesuits. And actually face-to-face with the "still living remnants of the thirteenth century" he found himself considerably less attracted by whatever notions in favor of asceticism he had been harboring. His impressions of the monks are almost entirely of dourness and uncouthness—their "thin scowling faces," or their "growling responses" after meals, when they "filed off through the galleries to their dens, looking like the living originals of the black pictures that hang along the whitewashed walls." He much preferred Father Lucca, plump, good-humored, well fed, "with a double chin like a bullfrog," who did not belong to the order but was in temporary residence to direct the retreat.

It was indeed this unexpected aspect of Catholic life—the institution of the retreat—rather than the monastic régime that engaged his sympathies during his stay with the Passionists. He became genuinely friendly with Father Lucca, and they parted with sentiments of mutual esteem: "Padre Lucca was unfeignedly sorry to have me go with unimpaired prospects of damnation. He said he still had hopes for me, and taking the kindest leave of me, gave me a book of Catholic devotions, which I shall certainly keep in remembrance of a very excellent man." It was perhaps particularly the recollection of Father Lucca that tempered an outbreak of anticlericalism that occurs in his journal two or three weeks later: "I used to like priests, and take off my hat and make a low bow, half in sport and half in earnest, whenever I met them—but I have got to despise the fellows. Yet I have met admirable men among them, and have always been treated by them all with the utmost civility and attention." As for the group of laymen at the convent, he noted what seemed to his

Protestant sense of the matter the very external and formalistic character of the exercises with which they were being prepared for general confession. At the same time, however, he was impressed with the genuineness and human tone of their religious feeling—the sense of community, the easy give-and-take of their relations with Father Lucca, the natural, unforced manner in which they talked of their faith:

There were among them men of every age, and of various condition—from the field laborer to the gentleman of good birth. . . .

As we [passed] the group of Italians, they took their hats off and kissed [Father Lucca's] hand reverently, and then immediately began to joke and laugh with him as if he were a familiar friend—as I suppose he was, as I have observed that many of the priests are to their parishioners. . . .

After supper tonight some of the Italians in the *Conversazione* expressed great sympathy for my miserable state of heresy—one of them, with true charity according to his light, said he would pray to the Virgin, who could do all things, to show me the truth. . . .

There is nothing gloomy or morose in the religion of these Italians here; no camp-meeting long faces. They talk and laugh gaily in the intervals allowed them for conversation; but when occasion calls it forth, they speak of religion with an earnestness, as well as a cheerfulness, that shows it has a hold on their hearts.

By the afternoon of Palm Sunday he was restless and ready to go, but he left the convent with a backward glance of a not altogether perfunctory sort: "When I got into the fresh air, I felt rather glad to be free of the gloomy galleries and cells—which nevertheless contain so much to be admired."

But whatever inclinations toward Catholicism may have been stirring in him, it was definitely a leave-taking. After the more intimate glimpses of the faith he had had at the retreat, he found the pomps and splendors of Holy Week—though he did not fail to take full note of them—something of an anticlimax, all in all "not worth seeing, were it not for the crowd of people they draw together."

On Tuesday after Easter he left Rome for Florence "with much regret and a hope to return." He was never to do so, however, literally or spiritually, though Coolidge Shaw (who followed Parkman to Rome to prepare himself for the career as a Jesuit missionary priest that was cut short by his early death in 1850) kept up for a while an ardently proselyting correspondence with him. A year later, according to the 1890 article, Shaw advised him to read as "sovereign against heresy" a book called, "if I remember rightly, *Mill's End of Controversy*." "I studied it from title-page to finis," Parkman goes on, "thought to myself: 'Is this all you have got to say?' and have remained ever since in solid disbelief as to the doctrines of Rome." [2]

But, it is hardly necessary to repeat, the episode left its residue. The bent of Parkman's temperament was fundamentally secular. His reckoning with the "nineteenth century" was to be along other lines, and in the sense of a personal commitment he had mistaken a little a strong imaginative sympathy for something more. He was to write in Scotland, as if in recoil from an emotionally false position, "I visited Abbotsford, Melrose and Dryburgh—and consider the day better spent than the whole four months I was in Sicily and Italy." But, imaginatively speaking, no part of his European trip was better spent, of course, than these four months under the spell of Catholicism Militant and Missionary, or had a more quickening influence on his historical dealings with the founding of Catholic Canada. At the same time they were equally formative in the clarification of attitudes they forced him to as to the nature of these dealings—the perception of the scope and force of his own commitment to the imperatives of the "nineteenth century," libertarian, Protestant ethos and the defining of that clean line of demarcation in his approach to his subject between what was to be made of it in the light of his own commitments and what was to be made of it as a counterimage of them in the light of a capacity for imaginative re-creation disengaged from questions of personal belief. In part an heir of the Enlightenment, nevertheless, unlike Gibbon, he was under no compulsion to dis-

[2] Parkman's own religious beliefs are discussed in Appendix A.

credit the reality of the forces that had attracted him to its opposite; and anticipating in part the medievalism of Henry Adams, he was under no compulsion to color it with the subtle sentimentality of displacement and alienation. Thus he achieved a unique kind of historical impartiality, in which dramatic objectiveness of presentation works to integral effect with positive, incisive, unequivocally stated canons of judgment.

But this was to be the result of a coalescence of elements of which his Catholic episode was only one. Likewise, important as this episode was, it does not engross, as I have said, the whole interest of his European trip as it bore upon the maturing of the work he had conceived. But these collateral aspects of the impact of Europe will appear from his own record of them as he turned them over in his mind on his return to his native scene. Meanwhile we need only indicate briefly the rest of his itinerary—his journey northward from Rome by way of Florence, Milan, Como, and the Splügen Pass to Andeer in the Grisons Alps; a fortnight at Paris under the auspices of his Uncle Samuel; a week in London, where his reading of Dickens made him feel as if he had been before; a hurried but fruitful visit to the Scott country; and passage homeward from Liverpool on the Cunarder *Acadia*, which brought him back to Boston in the middle of June, 1844.

CHAPTER IV

LAW AND LITERATURE

⚜ ⚜ ⚜

The young man's homecoming, however, was not the end of his vacation, for he still had the summer to kill before settling down as a law student in Cambridge. This last was the upshot of his father's wish that he prepare himself for a profession less anomalous than authorship in the eyes of respectable Boston for a young man of his position. As I have said, for such a young man—unless he went into business—law, medicine, and the ministry comprised the acceptable choices, of which unalluring prospects for this particular young man, the law ran least against the grain of his inclinations. No doubt he realized also the positive contribution a legal training could make to his own purposes. And though he had no intention of abandoning those purposes, we can not suppose he acceded to the idea in anything but good faith—we find him persisting with law work in a New York office during the complete breakdown of his health after the Oregon Trail trip until the state of his eyes compelled him to give it up. But from the start, of course, this adoption of a profession at the instance of his father, and in the face of such autonomous motions of spirit as his own, had an imposed character which could hardly fail to add its share to the complex of conflicts and tensions that led to his collapse.

But with his homecoming from Europe in June none of this was immediately imminent. The law could keep until fall; his Harvard commencement, as the custom then was, did not take place until late in August; and the summer was before him. So, still in a holiday mood, he set out in July for a walking trip in western Massachusetts, as if to digest his six months of Europe in the setting of his native wilderness for which he had had moments of acute homesickness. His glimpses of Berkshire scenery on his trip to Albany in 1842 had made him eager to visit the region; rich besides in associations with the French and Indian War, it offered another opportunity for a combination of research and pleasure trip before he turned, at his father's behest, to the legal grind. He climbed Monument Mountain; explored Bash-Bish Falls and the Hopper at Graylock; traced the site of Fort Massachusetts; sought out diaries and other documents of the colonial wars; and took down from their own lips the recollections of ancients like Dr. Partridge of Stockbridge or General Epaphras Hoyt of Deerfield, who had known in the flesh the generation that fought at Lake George, and abounded in vintage anecdotes of Amherst and Abercrombie, Rogers's Rangers and the redoubtable Colonel Williams. An incident of contemporary history also caught his attention, and he crossed the Taconics to Stephentown, New York, to watch a meeting of Anti-Renters. Stage-managed, with considerable help from the tavern bar, by agitators disguised as Indians, the spectacle did not fill him with elation. "The assembly," he wrote, "was of the very lowest kind . . . : I have never seen a viler concourse in America." Nevertheless he noted coolly enough that the Patroon's "feudal tenure, so strangely out of place in America, has probably lived its time."

Though historical matter is to the fore, it is naturally the reflections on America in the light of his European experience that particularly draw our attention among the fragmentary notes of this Berkshire expedition and of two or three little trips around Boston that preceded it—a Fourth of July celebration at Concord, a boat ride to Nahant, a visit to a Brook Farm gathering in West Roxbury. These show, for one thing, a somewhat broadened social outlook on the young traveler's part—or at least a Parkman who had discovered that the "students of H[arvard] do not on all occasions appear much better than their less favored country men, either in point of gentlemanly and *distingué* appearance or in conversation." So at Concord he noted the good nature of the crowd, the spontaneous "spirit of accommodation" which in Europe not "an hundred soldiers would . . . have ensured." This, he reflected in italics, was "*our low-*

est class"; if we lacked the polish of the European aristocracy, "the absence of their stupid and brutal peasantry is a fair offset." "No bowing" or "no English cringing" he writes approvingly of the independent Yankee landlords of the Berkshire inns.

On this level certainly Europe had not alienated him from his native New England; for him as for other figures of that earlier day, it was not necessary to cut one's local roots to become a citizen of the world. Still an incidental remark or two has a Jamesian turn. It was their naïveté, their American "innocence," for instance, with which the discussions of the "she-philosophers of W[est] Roxbury" most struck one "fresh from the manners of London and Paris—the entertainments and pleasures and working of passions which they in their retirement seem scarce to dream of." Again, a comment like the following is prophetic of a famous passage in *Notes of a Son and Brother:* "The simplicity and absence of forms—what an Englishman would call the *provincialism* of society here. A species of family —admits familiarities which could not be borne elsewhere." This is precisely, of course, the kernel of social observation from which, for James, the whole amazing floriation of the "international theme" took its growth.

For Parkman, however, these are simply notes by the way. Nevertheless he had of course comparisons between Europe and America to draw germane to his own purposes; and a stocktaking of his subject in its larger aspects was very much in his thoughts as the European experience fell into perspective. What, after Europe and its wealth of human associations, was the imagination to make of the bare American scene, these "dark, unstoried woods," to tell whose story he had committed himself? At Como he had drawn the classic American parallel with Lake George—as Cooper had already done in *The Last of the Mohicans*—and there was no question where his heart lay. "I have seen nothing more beautiful at home or abroad than this lake," he begins of Como, but inevitably the other picture displaces it—"that shaggy untamed aspect in the mountains," "those little islands, covered with rough and moss-grown pine trees"—and the passage closes on a note of acute nostalgia: "Even the wildest rocks seem softened in the air of Italy. Give me Lake George and the smell of the pine and fir!" In one sense Europe had only knit tighter the bond of the Fells, deepened the spell of the wilderness.

But Europe had induced doubts as well as affirmations. "The traveller in Europe," reads one note of the Berkshire journal—"The traveller in Europe. Art, nature, history combine. In America Art has done her best to destroy nature, association [has added] nothing." With England, and above all the Scotland of Sir Walter, fresh in one's mind, what, to repeat, was the imagination to make of the vast disproportion between the works of nature and the actions of man that the scene of the American past seemed to present? There had been the Indians, it is true, and a "day of struggle"; its "scenes of fear and blood are not without a horrid romance; and well does the rugged landscape recall them to mind." Yet was there not a poverty of suggestion, a lack of human depth in these wilderness scenes, if one thought of Scott's settings, a thousand associations clustering about their very names? "The breezes of the Tweed are an atmosphere of poetry and song, chivalry and romance. They kindle the spirit of the enthusiast into flame—the dullest feels that wonder and romance are around him—thus have the deeds and fancies of ages charmed that spot. And now turn thence to our dark unstoried woods! The poetic spark grows dull and dies, for there is nothing to fan it into life." The European past ran back through an endless vista of the human and the historic. The brief American past, on the contrary, brought one up with disconcerting suddenness before an appalling void of the nonhistoric. "For a thousand ages," the entry goes on, "her trees rose, flourished, and fell. In the autumn the vast continent glared at once with yellow and red and green; and when winter came, the ice of her waters groaned and cracked to the solitudes; and in the spring her savage streams burst their fetters, and bore down the refuse of the wilderness. It was half a world con-secrated to the operations of Nature!"

Yet in the very act of penning this vision of desolation he would seem to have come upon some element that fanned the "poetic spark" as glowingly as the breezes of the Tweed; and indeed the young historian was here setting down a preliminary version of several passages in his history—vast superterrestrial panoramas of the virgin continental expanse—that were to strike one of its most imaginative ground notes. Might there not be something in the very sense of omnipresent wildness and savagery these scenes conveyed, the startling juxtaposition of history and prehistory of which they were the setting, that would speak to the human condition, if not as variously, at least as deeply, as the storied European past that Scott had ransacked? "America in a state of transition," runs another note. "Her original state—her present—England's present . . . all peace and utilitarianism. . . . The child's journey, his associations—true elements of the romantic—but age dispels the fanciful illusion. . . . The heroes of our old wars, the farmers, etc. of our day. Matter of fact, universally prevalent." These were the conditions and this was the challenge: to confront "matter of fact" with the "true elements of the romantic," with aspects of feeling it had overlooked in its too shallow calculus of the heart. One could not, of course, do so on American grounds by reviving the heroisms of chivalry; but might not one confront it, precisely on these grounds, with something more fundamental it had omitted from its reckoning? The balance after all was not entirely in favor of Europe. The patina of history that gave so rich and various a coloring to the European past also veiled from sight its origins; in America history in large part was exactly a history of origins—a uniquely documented moment when civilized man came face to face with the conditions of his prehistoric beginnings. However obscurely, one sensed some current of central import that seemed to run between the fact of this immersion in the dark world of the forest—this experience of primeval nature and primeval savagery—and the working of human appetites and impulses in the full noon of "peace and utilitarianism." For the young man, at any rate, the die was long since cast; whatever questions Europe raised, he could only trust the instinct that had led him to "our dark unstoried woods" and abide the result:

England has her hedges and her smooth green hills, robed with a spirit of power and worth, strengthened and sanctioned by ages—but give me the rocky hill-side, the shaggy cedar and scrub-oak—the wide reach of un-cultivated landscape—the fiery glare of the sun among the evening clouds, flinging over all its wild and ruddy light.

Nevertheless Europe had made its mark. The wilderness was much; in a sense it was everything, the particularizing element in his ver-sion of the human drama. Yet the wilderness—the forest and the Indian—did not by themselves make up the sum of the equation; to have built his work on them alone, as he had once considered doing, would, for a multitude of reasons, have been to condemn himself to the marginal. "At one time," he wrote later in life to the Abbé Casgrain, "I thought of writing the history of the Indians, with the Iroquois as a central point; but on reflection I preferred the French colonies as equally suiting my purpose, while offering at once more unity and more variety, as well as more interest to civilized readers." He had no doubt reached this decision before he went to Europe; and it was, on one level, merely the most obvious common sense— no satisfactory history of the Indians has been written to this day, so great are the difficulties. But it was also a decision the more inward wisdom of which the European trip had strongly brought home, for it is of course the question of centrality that looms behind these comparisons of American and European landscape that preoccupied him in the Berkshires; the question of the higher interests of the "civilized reader." Blind at the moment as the "civilized reader"—or at least the Boston reader—might be to the possibilities of American themes, these interests were of course the young man's own. The problem, it would seem, was double, not single—to catch the spirit of the wilderness, certainly, but also to give it meaning in a wider context, to harmonize somehow the diverse claims upon him of Boston and the Fells, of Europe and the Iroquois, of civilization and anticivilization.

So at least one pieces together the train of reflections that dictated the detached entries of his Berkshire journal, as the young historian picked up again the thread of his investigations and meditated the larger aspects of his theme on this little excursion, the last of its kind, though he did not know it, that he was to make in his native New England.

His appetite whetted by this return to his subject, he threw himself as soon as he reached Cambridge into the prosecution of his interrupted schemes with all the "pernicious intensity" of which he speaks in his autobiographical sketches. He was, it is true, nominally a law student, a fact which added to the vexation of spirit evident in his journal almost from the moment of his return to Cambridge. Nevertheless the requirements of the law school in those primordial days were hardly exacting, and, if one can trust his own statement, left a wide enough margin for literary pursuits: "I am down at Divinity [Divinity Hall where he was rooming]," he writes his classmate Hale, "devoting one hour *per diem* to law, the rest to my own notions." So, pluming himself on avoiding the usual excesses of well-to-do young men, he plunged recklessly into what for him was the headiest of all excesses. Deceptively refreshed by his long holiday, he felt his intellectual faculties at their peak and gave them full rein. "Never, before or since," he was to recall, had he known "so great a facility of acquisition and comprehension." A year and a half later he was to find that he had again exhausted his capital of resilience, but in the meanwhile the process of burning the candle at both ends yielded its rewards as well as exacted its penalties.

Its penalties, the rapidly increasing tax it was levying on his nervous system, are obvious in the irritability and irascibility of the more personal entries of his journal at this period. The record of its rewards has for the most part to be read between the lines of an historian's notetaking—the items of bibliography and the like that begin to crowd out the personal matter, and, except for the Oregon Trail diary, make up the bulk of his later journals. One of the "notions" to which he was devoting himself, outside the hour a day he allotted to the law, was a remarkably comprehensive and thorough course of basic reading in European history, while the background was still fresh in his mind—a project that crammed two student notebooks with a sort of reference abstract of movements and de-

velopments from the barbarian invasions to the Reformation, compiled
from the pages of Gibbon, De Mably, Robertson, Sismondi, Guizot,
Macaulay, Michelet, Ranke, and a score of lesser luminaries. At the
same time he was pushing his work with equal vigor in the American
field. Here his immediate plans had crystallized around the idea of
a book on Pontiac's "conspiracy." In college, as we have seen, besides ranging generally in the literature of his subject, he had made
himself familiar with everything he could lay hands on relating
to the "operations at Lake George." This phase of the French and
Indian War had also preoccupied him during his Berkshire trip. Now,
however, he decided to lay aside the whole of his main history for
the time being and concentrate as a trial test of his powers on the
Indian rising against the victorious English that formed its afterpiece, an episode in which he could portray the "American forest
and the American Indian at the period when both received their
final doom." He plunged into the usual preliminaries of such work
with the intensity of application he brought to all his undertakings,
and by the summer of 1845 he was far enough advanced in his plans
for a field trip to the old Allegheny frontier and the Great Lakes,
which were the chief scenes of Pontiac's uprising.

Finally, with *Pontiac* thus in its incipient stages, he was also giving
himself to the excitements of actual composition, trying his hand not
for the moment at history itself, but more tentatively at quasi-his-
torical fiction. The result of this experiment was a series of sketches,
four in prose and one in verse, that appeared anonymously in the
1845 *Knickerbocker,* beginning with the February number. Un-
ambitious as these efforts are compared to what he was aiming at in
his historical preparations, he wrote them in part to test his ability
at handling the kind of wilderness material with which his histories
were to deal, and we shall need to scrutinize them.

For the content of these pieces he drew largely on his journals,
taking incidents of his American travels and recasting them in a
setting of eighteenth century frontier life. The poem need not detain us—nor in one sense need the rest of the pieces. They are examples of an archaic fictional genre, the sketch, that is, that hovers

uncertainly between incident and short story, and, except for "The Scalp-Hunter," where the narrative pattern is of the simplest flight-and-pursuit variety, their technique of construction is rudimentary. The incidents from the journals, moreover, rather lose their original sharpness of touch as Parkman reshapes them to the conventions of fiction and recasts them in a more formal literary English. But in terms of the problems he had set himself—the "rendering" of a bush fight, a canoe chase, a manhunt, a horseback ride: of such types of action as would form the elements of his history—this venture into the more exacting story form reveals all sorts of latent possibilities for which a journal hardly gave scope. Even a casual reader of these sketches would have realized that their familiar Cooperesque vein was being reworked to fresh and striking effect; and a more penetrating reader would not have been at fault who discerned in this modest debut powers suggestive of possibilities far beyond Cooper's range. "I must again cordially thank you for 'The Scalp-Hunter,' " Parkman's editor, Gaylord Clark, wrote him; "I am an 'old-stager' in matters of the sort; and it must be something *really* thrilling to keep me awake at night, after reading a proof sheet." "The Scalp-Hunter" would hardly keep us awake at night—fashions change in "matters of the sort"—but we are certainly aware in it, and in the rest of the sketches, of a narrative *élan*, an instinct for pace and dynamics, an immediacy of sensory perception, that touches off the shock of recognition.

As narrative, in the first place, the stories are alive with the first-hand discrimination of visual, auditory, or tactile impressions that is indispensable to dramatizing action pieces of this kind and heightening their tensions: "a patch of long grass near the shore bent and rose mournfully"; "all was quiet as death except the stream with its dull plunging"; "the heavy bullet, descending as it flew, came groaning solemnly through the air"; "there was a pause for an instant, and then came the clanging rattle of the barrel, as it bounded from side to side of the ravine, down the mountain"; "the sharp, quick crack of the New England rifles mingled with the louder and duller reports of the Indian guns"; "the afternoon sun was beating powerfully on the cliff where he sat, and filling the air with the resinous odors of the spruce and pine that grew around." Such details not only carry the stamp of first-hand perception, but are an integral part of the narrative fabric, an essential vivifying element that was to be one of Parkman's unfailing resources as an historical writer.

Not quite so much can be said of his handling of the longer atmospheric "set-pieces" that these stories gave him an opportunity to try his hand at. He was also to put pieces of this sort to memorable use in his later writing—and one finds already in "A Fragment of Family History" a trial version of the dead pine against the sunset that gives such effective coloring to the Lake Champlain chapter of *Pioneers*. Here, however, he tends to be a little too lavish with them and over-elaborates their details at the expense of the general effect. It was to take the longer lines of historical narrative with its wealth of thematic implications to charge these descriptive efforts with essential meanings, and an application of his friend Hunt's insistence in painting on the avoidance of clutter, to prune their occasional floridity. Nevertheless the instinct to make such scene-painting a dynamic contribution to the narrative instead of the static backdrop it too often is in his models, Scott and Cooper, is evident enough in these little pieces. "The Ranger's Adventure," for instance, is a very slight sketch, but scanty as the development is, Parkman's handling of the winter setting begins to add a third dimension to the story. "There had just been a heavy fall of snow: all the pines and hemlocks were loaded with it; and as the afternoon was still and clear, only occasional flakes or light masses dropped from the burdened boughs like feathers. These circumstances were stamped on the old man's mind, seeming like a constantly recurring dream." Then at the climax of the fight, when the ranger hears the "loud humming of a ball" that just misses him, "so alert and attentive were his faculties, that he observed where the bullet struck upon a loaded bough in front of him, scattering the glittering particles of snow." This is not as Stephen Crane would have done it—the touch is uncertain, the expression in places awkward and encumbered; but it looks forward to the sort of thing that Stephen Crane was to be celebrated for doing. And though historical writing did not allow this particular kind of subjectivity, it also looks forward to the interrelationship between setting, character, and theme that, by other means, Parkman was to establish time and again in his histories with such remarkable results for the inwardness and depth of his narrative.

But to return to the sketches themselves—there is a particular kind of sensory effect we notice in them that is not common in literature and is perhaps Parkman's most characteristic trait. This is the extraordinary degree of motor-mindedness his writing reveals, its uncanny sympathy with all forms of physical movement. In the examples quoted above it is as much this type of impression we feel as the visual or auditory: the motion of the wind in the dip and rise of the grass, the onward impetus of the groaning bullet, the physical plunge of the water in the stream, the bound and rebound of the gun barrel down the rocks. Material objects move with a bodily life, and bodily action takes on an aspect of hyperreality. "The Abenaki pitched forward to the ground, and his shaven head ploughed up the snow for yards by the impulse of his headlong pursuit"—such a sentence, in its context, starts at us from the page with an almost hallucinatory effect. So in the Doctor's ride in "Satan and Dr. Carver" the writing constantly suggests this quality of seeming itself to *be* the action it describes, from the full-arm downsweep of the Doctor's gun on Satan's flank at the start to the climax of runaway speed in the descent of the gulley, with its take-off in a whirl of unaccented syllables, its moment of galloping anapests, and its whirl of unaccented syllables again at the close: "There was a rushing like a gale; a chaos of vanishing rocks and trees; and in an instant he was at the bottom." One would hardly need to be told that the Doctor's gallop was based on its author's own experience, and Parkman was in fact taking lessons at the time from an ex-circus rider who had opened a riding school in Cambridge. "He chose the hardest horses," says Frothingham, "practiced riding in every form, with or without a saddle or stirrups; could run, leap, jump on a charger at full speed,— in short perform feats which only a 'professional' could execute." For this reason the story communicates perhaps more strikingly than any of the others the sheer exhilaration of physical activity, but the kinesthesia that pervades it is present everywhere in Parkman's writing, animating it even when he is not specifically describing objects in motion, so that his sentences themselves seem modes of motion or action. This kinesthetic energy is indeed the peculiar hallmark of his style.

If the young man's object was to re-create the "breathing reality" of the past, here then were some of the essential means. In so far as action was the life of history he could catch that life to the quick. Thus far his experiment should have been encouraging to its young author.

For the rest, one need not perhaps take these "blood and thunder chronicles of Indian squabbles"—to use his own phrase—more seriously than he himself professed to. Yet his attitude was serious enough for him to make one of them, "A Fragment of Family History," a sort of apologia for his own cravings for the tensions of physical adventure; and another, "The Scalp-Hunter," is unmistakably colored by intimations of the crack-up that, for him, life at any such level of tension, physical or mental, was bound to bring on. Both carry us a little beyond the mode of simple "blood and thunder" in which they were conceived.

"A Fragment of Family History" is indeed something of a conscious manifesto. "Reader, these scenes are rude and savage," runs one of its asides; "repulsive, no doubt, to the taste of literary epicures, and no less so to the transcendental 'spiritualists' who infest this city of Boston. Highly flattered should I be if my humble narrative should be honored with their condemnation. . . ." The first part of the story is based on an incident of Parkman's Berkshire trip, and the hero is more or less Parkman himself metamorphosed into an eighteenth century "Endicott Carver," night-bound, as Parkman had been, at a cabin at the head of Bash-Bish Falls. Here is the opening sentence of the story: "The chief passion of my ancestor was hunting, which he practiced incessantly, to the great disgust of his father, who was a farmer, and of his grand-father, who was a clergyman at Deerfield, Massachusetts." This is apocryphal as Parkman family history, but the parental disgust has a distinctly Bostonian and nineteenth century reference, and we sense that something more than the practice of hunting is at issue. "Passion"—a very un-Unitarian notion—is the keyword of the sentence; further on we read of the hero's "impetuous ardor that sometimes sleeps beneath the habitual coldness of New England"—another autobiographical touch; and in this context of passion, ardor, inwardness, the themes of hunting and fighting begin to emerge as emblems of a kind of moral demand on life.

The conception takes on further shades of meaning at the climax of the story: "The fight became already more than doubtful; for as the fierce impetuosity of the savages cooled at the unexpected check they had received, the deep Anglo-Saxon passion mounted higher in the breasts of the whites. Not that they gave vent to it, but it burned intensely within, rousing and concentrating all the faculties, and giving double strength and alertness to mind and sense. With foreheads knit, and lips pressed close together, they calculated the effect of every shot, and seized every advantage that offered." This is callow and melodramatic enough—we smile at passion mounting in the breast, knit foreheads, pressed lips, and so on; nevertheless we recognize an underlying seriousness of intention and are aware of tones of meaning in this wilderness bushfight not without pertinence to the condition of man in civilization. Again, it suggests an assertion of passion, or contained passion—depth and intensity of feeling—as a good; it affirmatively defines passion in action as a total engagement of the personality, an integral functioning of "mind and sense" at the limits of tension; it suggests finally the value of a discipline, so ingrained as to have become instinctive, that shapes this tension of passion to efficient ends ("they calculated the effect of every shot, and seized every advantage that offered").

This no doubt is putting it much too portentously; nevertheless these little adventure pieces have their "philosophy," and some such intimations make themselves felt in the telltale phrase that recurs at their moments of climax: "the white men pressed upon them with every faculty at its tension; hand, foot, and eye, on the alert" (again from "A Fragment of Family History"); "so alert and attentive were his faculties" ("The Ranger's Adventure"); "with every faculty at its utmost tension" ("The Scalp-Hunter") and, outside these fictions, in what Parkman recalled of his mental life at this period—"his faculties were stimulated to their best efficiency. Never before or since, has he known so great a facility of acquisition and comprehension." In its indirect way "A Fragment of Family History" is an attempt at a rationale of this moment of total engagement, an apologia for certain imperatives of human nature that Boston "spirit" —whether of the Unitarian or of the transcendental variety—had somewhat glaringly ignored in its view of things.

"The Scalp-Hunter," on the other hand, strikes the note of "A Fragment of Family History" in a very different key. Every counter-position runs the danger of its own partialities and excesses, and, though "The Scalp-Hunter" was the earlier published of the two stories, it is imprinted, as I have said, with a sense of the psychic perils the doctrine of "every faculty at its tension" involved for its author. In his letter to Ellis, after speaking of the pitch of efficiency he felt his mental faculties had reached, Parkman goes on: "Soon, however, he became conscious that the impelling force was growing beyond his control. Labor became a passion, and rest intolerable. . . . The stimulus rapidly increased. Despite of judgment and will, his mind turned constantly toward remote objects of pursuit, and strained vehemently to attain them. His condition was that . . . of a locomotive . . . under a head of steam too great for its strength . . . rushing on to the inevitable smash." With its theme of obsession and its atmosphere of disaster "The Scalp-Hunter" is plainly enough an unconscious projection of this condition.

Parkman devised the story to provide a setting for the climbing adventure on the Willey slide of his freshman vacation trip. After a massacre of a band of Indians by whites in search of the bounty on scalps, one of the whites, an old man, more greedy than the rest, sets out by himself to pursue the only Indian who has escaped. He tracks him to a ravine "in the Notch, close to the place where the unfortunate Willeys afterward met their fate." The Indian makes his way out of the ravine by a side wall before the steepest part is reached; but, in the passion of his pursuit, the old man does not notice this change of course and starts to scale the cliff. Obsessed with his purpose, he succeeds after a superhuman effort (losing his foothold halfway up, as Parkman had done, and dropping his gun down the rocks, as Parkman had dropped his stick) only to find himself trapped on a narrow shelf from which there is no escape. Two days later a storm sweeps him down to his death.

This too is a story of passion and engagement, and the recurrent emphasis appears at its central moment, as, in the gathering dusk, the old man "clenching his teeth together with eagerness and longing," makes his insensate way up the cliff: "with every faculty at its utmost tension, availing himself of every little point and crevice, he did what no man else could have done," But the crisis of tension, affirmed with such *élan* in "A Fragment of Family History," here takes on the quality of a nightmare, and passion and engagement figure as the agents of destruction. The cliff that Parkman had scaled in fact with boyish bravado reappears as fiction steeped in the colors of his growing psychic malaise. The passion of greed, to be sure, is too banal a conception to lift the story above melodrama. Nevertheless chase, cliff, and climb have the haunting reality of oneiric symbols, and the scalp-hunter himself in the obsession of his pursuit is a first, crude, and very unheroic version of the hero as victim of a leading passion and a fixed idea that took final shape in Parkman's portrait of La Salle, the character of his histories most deeply identified with himself. Indeed, dimly but unmistakably, one discerns in "A Fragment of Family History" and "The Scalp-Hunter," the germ of the whole great river cycle of *Pioneers* and *La Salle* with its double vision of Western man in the splendor and the tragedy of his unresting activism.

And if we turn back to the journals we find the same polarity of feeling that is apparent below the surface of these little adventure stories. Ambition, pride of self-sufficiency, a will unrelaxed in its pursuit of a remote goal—such for Parkman were the sources of achievement and of self-realization; but such too were, or might be, the sources of destruction; and under the forced draught of the impending crack-up a sense of this begins to make itself felt in his journal notes as well as in the *Knickerbocker* sketches. Possibly he began to harbor at this time the fear of insanity that haunted him at a later period. However that may be, the law school notebooks betray a feeling that some sort of nemesis, moral as well as psychic, was at hand. " 'Pride goeth before destruction and a haughty spirit before a fall,' " runs one entry, "—think of that!" Again, we read in his abstract of European history, "A man will sometimes believe himself a god"—a sentence quite unrelated to its context, inspired apparently by some example of classical hubris in Gibbon. Already Parkman was coming to a painful consciousness of that "Coriolanus-like" strain in himself that thirty years later he was to trace from such a depth of self-recognition in the character of La Salle.

So too the journal shows the crystallizing in self-knowledge of related aspects of what one might call the La Salle configuration—in particular, an equally painful consciousness of isolation. For Parkman this revolved especially around the rôle of leadership that his ego had conceived for itself and found itself blocked from exercising. "I would have given worlds for a companion, hardy, resolute, and enthusiastic; as it was, I was to all intents and purposes alone"; so, as we have seen, he wrote four years before, when the tragedy of La Salle and his mutinous followers had enacted itself in little for him on the banks of the Magalloway. This is an authentic *cri de cœur*, but it does not go beyond a boy's self-pity. Nor does an amusing echo in the law school journal of these Magalloway quarrels with Slade take us much further. "Ap. 23. D. D. S. on Fresh Pond—cross, childish, self-willed. He likes people whom he can direct, and who always yield to his selfish will. He is anxious to be treated with courtesy and consideration, yet he is himself often very offen[sive] by his childish obstinacy and self-will."

This is a little like the pot calling the kettle black, the bafflement of an ego with a decided penchant of its own for imposing its will. Nevertheless Parkman's failure with Slade and White in the psychology of command had begun to induce more mature and self-searching reflections than these on the subject of leadership. Externally Parkman's instinct for leadership was frustrated by the position of his class, exiled from national affairs by the Jacksonian Revolution. Embittered by this sense of exclusion, he is violent, as we have seen, in his rejection of attempts at social initiative on the part of any other class. Yet this state of being cut off also gave rise to doubts, if not of the qualifications, at least of the capacities, of his fellow-Brahmins and himself; a suspicion of the sort of inner flaw that, again, he was to trace in the character of La Salle—"too shy for society and too reserved for popularity, often unsympathetic and always seeming so, smothering emotions he could not utter, schooled to universal distrust," This is La Salle, not Parkman, yet it was also written from a depth of self-knowledge; and the law school journal shows him acutely aware of the incubus of diffidence that isolated him and thwarted the fruitful exercise of an instinctive habit of command. In one entry he asks, "Is a man a coward, because he feels less than himself in a crowd?" In another he notes "that remarkable constraint to which the presence of a person of inferior sense, acuteness, and energy will sometimes subject one far his superior" (a remark called forth, one might add, not by contact with the lower social orders, but by the behavior of his first cousin George Parkman at the Concord Fourth of July celebration). And—to look ahead a little—his sketch of young Cerré in St. Louis has a strongly autobiographical flavor, as of a man recognizing his own traits in another. "Young, silent through bashfulness, observing all, feeling all, and constantly in hostility to external influences—though resolute and determined, acting ever under the burden of constitutional diffidence. . . . How hostile is such a quality to a commanding character. . . . Some men have a sort of power from their very vanity. . . . Others there are who, with many of the internal qualities of command, can never assume its outward features—and fail in consequence." The figure of La Salle begins to take definite shape behind these reflections, where mere irritation at others for what thwarted and isolated him has given way to sober self-examination. The "qualities of command"

were very much on the young man's mind as he was about to set
out on an adventure which he knew would put his own to a stiffer
test than any to which he had yet put them.

Parkman's temperament was not one that gave itself gratuitously
to such dubieties and self-questionings; the dominant impression it
makes on us is always that of energy and positiveness. Nevertheless
his character is much more complex than is sometimes supposed. In
The Oregon Trail, the book by which he is best known, the persona
he creates for himself is that of the sportsman-ethnologist on a holiday. The portrait is real enough as far as it goes (though even here it
is apparent from his notebooks that he played down the seriousness
of his ethnological interests) but it is one that hardly comprehends
the range of his personality. The book barely hints, except by what
it lets appear of his illness, at the conflicts we have seen defining
themselves in his law school journal, and suggests only indirectly
the kind of perception, already maturing, that was to project from
these conflicts a companion in tragic destiny to Captain Ahab and
Ethan Brand. Here perhaps, crude as they are, the *Knickerbocker*
sketches are a better clue to the inner life that was to read itself
in the discordance of La Salle's "complex and painful nature" and
was to make of this heroic, solitary, and bleak-souled figure a master-
type of the duality at the heart of the individualist ethos, to the
imperatives of which Parkman himself was so deeply committed.

But to return to the more mundane level of Parkman's life during
these law school days. Here, as I have said, the wear and tear of
"every faculty at its tension" shows itself in the irritability that
begins to mark his journal entries almost as soon as he was back in
Cambridge. One of the first of them indeed is a major explosion of
bad temper. The occasion, one gathers, was a visit to Boston of the
spirited Pamela Prentiss with whom he had been so much taken at
Crawford's on his freshman vacation trip to the White Mountains.
This acquaintance had ripened into an adolescent love affair on later
visits to Keene, where two of his classmates conveniently lived;
echoes of it are heard in letters to him from other classmates and

in his European journal; and his attentions had apparently been marked enough to awaken matchmaking propensities in Boston. But if Pamela is the "Miss P" of his September, 1844, journal entry a rift had decidedly occurred by that time. At least the efforts of the amiable Dr. Bigelow to smooth what he supposed to be the path of young love drew down on him the following exasperated outburst:

Sunday, Sept. 21. Some men are fools—utter and inexpressible fools. I went over to Dr. B[igelow]'s last night to call on Miss ————. Heaven knows I am quite indifferent to her charms, and called merely out of politeness, not caring to have her think I slighted her. But the Dr., in the contemptible suspicion that he is full of, chose to interpret otherwise. William Train was there, whom I allowed to converse with Miss P. while I talked with the Dr's lady. The Dr. watched me, though I was not aware of it at the time, till happening to rise to take a bottle of Cologne, out of a mere whim, and applying some of it to my handkerchief; the idiot made a remark, in a meaning tone about *"long walks* in the evening" injuring me. He soon after asked me to take a glass of wine, saying it would make me *feel better.* He whispered in my ear that Train *would go soon,* and I better stay. What could I do or say? I longed to tell him the true state of my feelings, and above all what I thought of his suspicious impertinence. I left the house vexed beyond measure at being pitied as a jealous lover, when one object of my indifference to Miss ———— that evening was to prove, to her and the rest, how free I was from the influence of her attractions. Is it not hard for a man of sense to penetrate all the depths of a blockhead's folly? and to know what an interpretation such a fellow will put on his conduct? I sent him a letter which I think will trouble not a little his jealous and suspicious temper.

Dr. Jacob Bigelow, Professor of Materia Medica at Harvard, is the well known Boston figure whom we have already met as the friend of Parkman's Uncle George. Among his varied interests, he shared with his friend's nephew an enthusiasm for the White Mountains, where as a young man he had done pioneer botanical work while preparing his *Florula Bostoniensis,* and where Bigelow Lawn, on the col between Mt. Washington and Boott Spur, commemorates his name. It perhaps says something for the characters of both parties to this incident that it apparently left no lasting resentments, for six years later Dr. Bigelow's daughter Catherine became Parkman's wife. With Pamela too, according to Wheelwright, Parkman kept up a lifelong friendship; in 1859 she became the second wife of Judge Henry Flagg French of Exeter—later Assistant Secretary of the Treasury—and thus the stepmother of the future sculptor Daniel Chester French. Parkman drew on memories of her vivid and vivacious personality for traits both of Edith Leslie, the heroine of *Vassall Morton,* and of the dashing Fanny Euston by whom Vassall is transiently but disturbingly attracted, although Vassall's fictional imbroglio appears to be in the main the reflection of a later and different affair in its author's life. Nevertheless one surmises for this earlier involvement the same pattern of attraction and recoil that marks Vassall's relations with Fanny in the novel, and the same conflict in Parkman's feelings, as in Vassall's, of the higher and lower Eros, between the manifestations of which the protocol of the age drew such a remarkably clear-cut dividing line. However that may be, it is evident enough that a conflict of this sort, involving the violent repression of a powerful sexual drive, added its share for the young man to the mounting tensions of this law school period. He speaks himself in *Vassall Morton* of the "chivalresque instinct" that battled against "the urgency of vigorous blood" from which Vassall sought relief in constant physical exercise. On another level an entry in the Berkshire journal shows Vassall's creator in the throes of a struggle with such promptings: "Lee is full of factory girls. The very devil beset me there. I never suffered so much from certain longings which I resolved not to gratify, and which got me into such a nervous state that I scarcely slept all night."

But irritable as the young man's mood may have been, the sketches he sets down in his law school journal of friends, fellow students, Boston *nouveaux riches,* gatherings of come-outers, and so on are, like the scene of the evening at Dr. Bigelow's, sharply enough etched in their sarcastic or sardonic vein. If circumstances had forced Parkman to continue in this frustrated mood, one can imagine his turning into a sort of Cambridge St. Simon, distilling acid in some sedulously kept *journal intime*. Here, for instance, is a snapshot of President Quincy of Harvard at a meeting of the Massachusetts senate. "The Senate Chamber—the thin, large-nosed man, who tried to know everybody—took the Prex's cloak, with an 'how-de-do, Mr. Quincy,' and whom the Pres., with his usual felicity of manner, cut." Here is a sketch of a fellow law student: "Lyman—his silence, his oaths, his indecencies, his disgusting habits at table; windows broken and he will not mend them; goes to Brooks' room, looks into his drawers—'Hullo, you've got some gingerbread!'; invites himself to spend the evening there; stays till morning, and sleeps standing against the wall like a horse!! " Here, finally, is a boardinghouse scene, with a comic portrait of the above-mentioned Brooks and sardonic side thrusts at close friends like J. Peabody.

The theological controversy at Mrs. Sanders'. Brooks is a good-natured thoughtless, careless fellow, without either application, ambition, or any settled principle. He thought church-going was "horrid"—"such a damned bore to sit under a sermon 40 minutes—ministers ought to know better, damned if they hadn't," etc. Ritchie seriously and fervently upheld the Church of England, which seems in his eyes the receptacle of all holy and excellent things, while J. Peabody laughed at B's random heedless remarks, at the same time taking an occasional part in the discussion like one who had deep feelings on religious subjects—perhaps he thinks he has. J. G. also came in with his silly boyish observations, but was immediately snubbed. "Oh, *there!* that's enough," said Brooks, "stop now, that's good fellows—nothing I hate like talking religion, because it never comes to good—you can't convince one another—here, Watch, come here, old boy, and get your supper."

The raciness of these law school sketches—their sarcasm tempered to a finer edge of irony—finds its way into not a few portraits in Parkman's histories, particularly of types unsympathetic to him—the "character" of Archbishop Laval in *The Old Régime*, with its flavor of Gibbon and French memoir writing, is an example.

We have seen Parkman's curiosity, if not his sympathies, taking him across the Taconics to the Anti-Renter meeting in Stephentown; so we find him in the spring of 1845 at a notable gathering of Fourierites in Tremont Chapel, addressed by Ripley, "Horace Grant—the editor from N.Y." (by whom he meant Horace Greeley), Brisbane, Dana, and Channing—the flower of American reform, in short. Again, occasion and audience were scarcely calculated to arouse his enthusiasm: "most of them . . . rather a mean set of fellows—several foreigners—plenty of women, none pretty"; yet a touch or two catches authentically the perennial atmosphere of such gatherings —the "cordial shaking of hands and mutual congratulations before the meeting began"; the inevitable oldster, "looking like anything but an enthusiast," who "spoke with his hands in his pockets, and gave nothing but statistics, in a very dry, uninteresting manner." The young man stood as much of the speech-making as he could, and Greeley, in spite of his "weak, indecisive manner," made an impression on him with "some remarkable details . . . of the 'present system of society' as illustrated by the working classes of N.Y." But Brisbane and Dana followed in a couple of "windy speeches," and as Channing—the nephew of his *bête noir*, the great William Ellery Channing—was starting another in the same vein he came away. "They say that there is a system of laws by which the world is to be governed 'harmoniously,' and that they have discovered those laws," is his succinct summing-up; so much, one gathers, for utopia. The fall before he had gone out to Watertown to a meeting of Millerites, those prophets of an immediate Second Coming whose activities in the back country along the Canadian border he had seen something of on his 1842 trip. The fanaticism of the sectaries he had found only less antipathetic than he was to find the utopianism of the reformers; and these two experiments seem to have satisfied his curiosity as to the new religious and social lights of his time. At least if he was present again at a conventicle of come-outers the circumstance is not on record. In the event, it would be hard to maintain that for him, at least, Henry Chatillon and the Sioux were any less pertinent guides to a comprehension of the age than Tremont Chapel.

For the rest, one must not exaggerate of course the prevailingly atrabilious tone of his journal, which, as is often the case, served as an escape valve for fits of spleen. Absorbed as he was in his projects, he was by no means a recluse by nature, and the "keen appetite for social enjoyment" he says he felt at the time is evident enough in a lively correspondence with his classmates; the social enjoyments which are its subject ranging from the decorous pleasures of the Salem Assembly to a "war-dance with scalp-yells" in the middle of the Cambridge Common. This last was the finale of a drinking spree at Peabody's rooms, an occasion on which Parkman succeeded, "without perceptibly annoying the rest," in raising his notably untuneful voice in the chorus of "Yankee Doodle." In these letters, too, classmates and law students appear in a genial enough light as compared with the journal; "Old Snow," for instance, established at Graduates Hall "with two pianos, Shelley, and a half-cask of ale"; or sprawled in a rocking chair at Peabody's party, "with one foot on the table, and other on his neighbor's shoulder, laughing and making execrable puns." [1] In general, he wrote Hale at Keene, "we have here in the Law School a sprinkling of fine fellows from north, south, east, and west—some in the quiet studying line, some in the *all Hell* style, and some a judicious combination of both."

His own manner of living he describes in a letter to another classmate, the epicurean Cary:

Here am I, down in Divinity Hall (!) enjoying to my heart's content that *otium cum dignitate* which you so affectionately admire. . . . Do you not envy me my literary ease?—a sea-coal fire—a dressing-gown—slippers —a favorite author; all set off by an occasional bottle of champagne, or a bowl of stewed oysters at Washburn's? This is the cream of existence. To lay abed in the morning, till the sun has half melted away the trees and castles on the window-panes, and Nigger Lewis's fire is almost burnt out, listening meanwhile to the steps of the starved Divinities as they rush

[1] Charles B. Snow of Fitchburg, a classmate and friend, of whom Parkman gives a character sketch in his Berkshire journal:

" 'Old Snow'—his careless abandonment—his tobacco chewing—his admiration of George [Cary]—his hatreds—his indifference and laziness —his want of foresight—his violent expressions of friendship.

"A ship without a rudder—a good fellow, but on the way to wreck and worthlessness."

shivering and panting to their prayers and recitations—then to get up to a fashionable breakfast at eleven—then go to lecture —find it a little too late, and adjourn to Joe Peabody's room, for a novel, conversation, and a morning glass of madeira. . . . After all, man *was* made to be happy; ambition is a humbug—a dream of youth; and exertion another. . . . I think the morbid tendency to unnecessary action passes away as manhood comes on; at any rate, I have never been half so quiescent as since I was qualified to vote against Polk and Dallas.

From a young man whose passion for work and whose secretly nutured ambitions had already begun the final ruin of his health, his letter, to say the least, has to be taken with as many grains of salt as his almost mendacious evasions of inquiries about his writing for the *Knickerbocker*, rumors of which had reached his classmates. Still, he had no new-fangled scruples as to the amenities of life that birth and wealth put in his way, and if these letters to Hale, Perry, and Cary conceal as much of Parkman's nature as they reveal, their mood is a genuine enough one. Admired by his friends, highly attractive to women, he cuts a striking figure in a daguerreotype of the time, the now sturdy shoulders and the face, with its combination of strength and sensitiveness and its direct, half-challenging expression, handsomely set off by black dress coat, white waistcoat, stiff shirt, and rakishly knotted plaid cravat. Whatever was not well within, to the outer eye the high-mettled, high-strung young thoroughbred that looks at us from this picture seems more than adequate to carrying off with éclat the diverse rôles—wilderness ranger, crack shot, crack rider, historical student, writer, traveler, *homme du monde*—which he had conceived for himself in the pride of life.

Nevertheless all was far from well within, as was very apparent when the young man came back from the historical trip, already mentioned, that he made to Pennsylvania and the Great Lakes in the summer of 1845. Like "social enjoyment," however, travel and the exhilaration of the historical chase could still for the moment the growing sense of malaise; and the bristle of disgruntlement with which, as usual, the notes of this expedition open gives way soon enough to the excitement of digging up material on the "Paxton boys" at Lancaster or of viewing at first hand the classic sites of the Old Northwest, which were the focal points of Pontiac's War.

Mackinaw Island was the western terminus of his trip, from which he made excursions to the Sault and to the ruins of Fort Michilimackinac on the mainland, the scene of perhaps the grimmest event of Pontiac's rising. At Mackinaw too he met old Robert Stuart of Astoria fame, who cast a critical light for him on the Indian lore of Schoolcraft's recently published *Algic Researches;* and who also no doubt, like the mate of the *Nautilus*, further whetted his appetite for the Far West with memories of the overland return from Astoria in 1812. For the rest, the island, with its white rock spires and pellucid waters, was a living remnant of old Canada. Indians still resorted to its beaches, where at night one heard the mournful singing from their lodges as they fuddled themselves on rum; half-breed children in barbaric moccasins and leggings stared at one from the boat landing; and the easy-going ways of habitant and voyageur set the tone of life. Once again a counterimage of the "nineteenth century" exercised its compulsive spell.

On the way back "*six trunks* of old McDougall's papers"—Lieutenant McDougall who had been captured on an embassy to Pontiac in 1763—took the young historian to Palmer, Michigan, for an overhauling of these relics; and Detroit, of course, the center and highwater mark of Pontiac's effort, was a stopping place for investigations. Here indeed he came on some of his richest historical ore in the recollections of ancients like François Baby whom he sought out in the Canadian environs of the little city; gleaning from them such graphic details for his account of the famous siege as the incident of Pontiac's visit to M. Baby's father or the boy's view, from a housetop along the route, of Dalzell's brigade on its ill-fated sortie to Bloody Bridge. Likewise, at the Devil's Hole at Niagara—the scene of a notable Indian ambush—the journal vibrates with the *frisson historique,* as the future narrator of the episode verifies the details of topography and sketches the extraordinary setting of river and gorge: the "immense . . . gully . . . with sheer, savage lime-stone fencing it on three sides," over the edge of which the Indians precipitated the whites.

Finally, at Syracuse, Parkman broke his railway journey to go out on horseback to Onondaga Castle, the council house of the Five Nations, a tranquil scene of cornfields, intervale, and groves, answering in most respects to John Bartram's description of a century before. From its living inhabitants, however, he could gather little that bore on the lost glories of their ancestral Iroquoia; and here, as all along, the trip, so fruitful in other respects, indicated that he would have to cast his net wider. He had caught tantalizing glimpses of Indian life on the upper Lakes, where Chippewa canoes still plied those remote waters. But the fragments of tribes he had seen at Mackinaw were far gone on white man's liquor, and discussions of folklore with Robert Stuart or Joseph Gurnae, the "very intelligent" half-breed who paddled him down the rapids at the Sault, offered only collateral guides to what he needed. As he had taken himself to Rome for light on the life and spirit of Catholicism, so it was the more urgent to make contact with Indian culture as a living organism. Here, it was evident, there was nothing for it but to push his quest beyond the frontier, to that West of the wild tribes, where on so many other counts, his inclinations had been pointing him.

Meanwhile, if the past preoccupied him on the Lakes, the present and its portents did not escape his eye. If Mackinaw was still the "picture of an ancient Canadian settlement," the day of the fur companies was over, as he noted, and the "voyageurs' occupation's gone." The tavern talk at Palmer was all of mines and steamboats; copper speculators were thronging into the primitive scene of the Sault; and Norwegian immigrants crowded the wharves at Buffalo. These portents, to be sure, were not viewed entirely with elation. His cousin Quincy Shaw was later to turn a very pretty penny indeed from Lake Superior copper; but the spectacle of non-Brahmins making money was a different matter, and a pair of such vulgarians, a certain Mr. and Mrs. Jones at the Sault "grown elevated by prospects of wealth," are the subjects of an acrid little sketch. As for the Norwegian immigrants, he could make less of them than of the Senecas he had seen stalking in the streets of Buffalo: "very diminutive," he found them, "very ugly—very stupid and brutal in appearance—and very dirty. They appear to me less intelligent [than] and as ignorant as the Indians." Certainly, to repeat, the afflatus of American destiny, the whisper of the American dream, do not inform the pen of the young patrician as he glances at the future in the making. Nevertheless the elements of the picture come sharply into focus, and these by-notes of a search for the historical past are a vivid record of the Upper Lakes on the verge of transition from one epoch to another.

But revivifying as this little expedition had been, its effect was transient and already on the homeward journey the familiar symptoms begin to be evident. At Niagara Parkman speaks of an attack of indigestion; the spectacle of the falls left him apathetic; and the crowd of sightseers with their fatuous questions seemed intolerable. That evening, to be sure, he had recovered enough to be able to "sympathize with the species" again, and the next day's trip to the Devil's Hole put him for the moment at the top of his form. But the exhilaration quickly spent itself, and the journal closes, as it opened, in a tangle of irascibility: "The noisy and vulgar party of girls, who sat on the backs of the seats and filled the cars with their cackling. The old fool of a woman, their mother. . . . Is not a *half-*educated, vulgar, weak woman a disgusting animal? . . . The half-and-half genteel—damn them!"

Yet, snapping nerves and exacerbated caste feeling apart, what *was* one to make, fresh from Mackinaw, of such appurtenances of progress and civilization, and of the generally ascendant hubbub of that Manifest Destiny that was making such short work of the Mackinaw scheme of things? He had watched one morning at the island a group of Indians still drunk and singing in the ruins of a tumbledown lodge—among them a "remarkably handsome squaw," and beside her a good-looking young buck, "with his leggins and bare thighs." The scene is set down without comment in compellingly painterlike strokes. A drunken squaw, it is evident, was somehow a less unedifying spectacle than an American *mère des filles* "doing" Niagara; and on this homeward journey even Boston perhaps might have been conceived to have its reckoning to make with the Mackinaw scheme of things.

Nevertheless, to Boston one came back; to the task of finishing law school, that token of the paternal sense of the Bostonian scheme of things; and above all to the recurrent bouts of indigestion and insomnia, and the persistent, ominously increasing eyestrain that had now begun, intermittently at least, to make reading impossible. The young man took his law degree in January, partly by dint of having his sister read Blackstone aloud to him in bed, then set out for a month of documentary research on Pontiac in New York, Philadelphia, Baltimore, and Harrisburg. But his favorite prescription of "taking the devil by the horns," of throwing himself the more vehemently into his work the worse he felt, was losing its efficacy. He was now in no state for this kind of purely mental application, and by the end of the winter his condition was so alarming that his father's consent was quickly gained to Quincy Shaw's proposal of a joint hunting expedition on the Oregon Trail. As there was historical field work to be done on the way, he arranged to meet Shaw in St. Louis and left Boston for Pittsburgh on March 28. His health soon began to show signs of improvement.

Crossing Pennsylvania by stagecoach, he stopped to explore the scenes of Bouquet's operations in Pontiac's War, visited the site of Braddock's defeat, and then surrendered to the relaxing charms of the midland spring—rich with "a hundred shades of green" and the bloom of peach trees—as the steamboat took him down the Ohio on that enchanted river voyage of mid-nineteenth century American travel. At St. Louis there was Cahokia to be visited, the little French settlement across the river, where Pontiac had been assassinated; and there were patriarchs of the fur trade to be interviewed for historical recollections, such as the elder Cerré or the already legendary Pierre Chouteau, who had been brought as a child to the frontier outpost of which his half-brother was a founder, who was a boy grown at the time of Pontiac's death, and who had spanned in his eighty-eight years the whole rise of the wilderness post to the roaring metropolis of the forties. Finally, for information on the Western Indians, Parkman talked at St. Louis with Thomas Fitzpatrick, as preeminent among mountain men as Pierre Chouteau among the executives of the fur trade, and a highly intelligent observer of Indian life who had supplied the material on the Western tribes for Albert Gallatin's famous *Synopsis*. But here Parkman's luckiest stroke was his engagement as guide, through the Chouteau company, of their hunter Henry Chatillon, who had just come back from four years in the wilderness. In character Henry was the fine flower of the Franco-American mountain man, and, besides his other assets, he had a squaw wife among the Sioux—a daughter, in fact, of the powerful Oglala chief Bull Bear. This connection and the intimate knowledge of the Sioux it had given Henry did more than anything else for the success of the young man's chief object on his trip.

Shaw, in the meanwhile, had arrived in St. Louis, and by the end of April the pair were making their final preparations at Westport. On May 9, 1846, the little party of four—Henry, the two sahibs, and an *engagé* named Deslauriers—set off for whatever adventures awaited them beyond that outpost of civilization.

CHAPTER V

THE WEST

❖ ❖ ❖

Parkman's Western expedition is the best known episode of his life, and it is not perhaps necessary to retrace its itinerary in detail. The first part of it was over the Westport–Fort Laramie section of the Oregon Trail, the last part over the Santa Fe Trail, both of which by 1846 had become major highways of American travel. The rest was adventure off the beaten track in pursuit of a band of Oglala Sioux with whom he spent three weeks in a fastness of the Rocky Mountains to the south of Fort Laramie. The account he wrote of his trip and the recently recovered journal on which this account is based make together a document of some importance for the history of the Western movement in that "year of decision" that saw the winning by the United States of Oregon, California, and Santa Fe. His description of the Oglala Sioux is likewise an important contribution to ethnology; it is in fact the best firsthand description extant of the culture of the Plains Indians while it was still in an intact state. For the general reader, finally, his book remains, and justly, in spite of certain limitations, the classic American account of the "wild" West—the West of the fur trade, the Indian, and the buffalo, which he observed just before it began to vanish from the scene.

The worth of this achievement has been evaluated from diverse points of view; which is to say that as a book on the West—and particularly a book on the West by an Easterner—*The Oregon Trail* has naturally figured in the controversies that have sprung up over the interpretation of American history and culture in terms of the frontier, or of a polarity between East and West. For a Westernizer like Parrington, for instance, Parkman took on stature, because of

The Oregon Trail, as the only New England man of letters who displayed any kind of vital interest at all in the West and the frontier. For Bernard De Voto, on the other hand, Parkman is, regrettably, too much of an Easterner; sympathetic enough to the wild West, he failed to respond to Manifest Destiny and the emigration, and "one aches for the book that might have been added to our literature if God had a little thawed the Brahmin snobberies." Professor Henry Nash Smith, in the process of subverting the whole frontier hypothesis, closes the circle. Of all "myths" of the West, he finds that of the wild West the least serious, and he can account for the interest of a man like Parkman, the "product of a complex social order," in such primtive social beings as Indians and trappers only as a "paradoxical rejection of organized society," an example of "the slightly decadent cult of wildness and savagery which the early nineteenth century took over from Byron." [1]

Actually, when we examine Parkman's Western experience as a phase of his education—in Henry Adams's sense of the word—and in the light of what his education meant, this context of reference seems not a little irrelevant, though his experience has seldom been examined in any other. In fact, the question of the rôle of the West in American history has hardly more bearing on what fundamentally *The Oregon Trail* is about than the question of the rôle of the South Seas in American history has on what *Typee* and *Omoo* are about. For all the difference in temperament and circumstances, Parkman went to the West under the impulsion of very much the same drives that

[1] Since my position is one of general dissent from their interpretation of Parkman's Western experience, I should express here my indebtedness in other respects to Mr. De Voto and Professor Smith. Though we are both of course ultimately drawing on Parkman himself, any reader of Mr. De Voto's *Year of Decision* will be aware of how unblushingly I have made use, when it suits my purposes, of his reconstruction of Parkman's crossing to Laramie and stay among the Sioux. My obligations to Professor Smith are of a more personal kind. To his share of a correspondence— to which he patiently gave his time—over his remarks on Parkman in *Virgin Land,* I owe the very special kind of stimulus to a clarification of ideas that one can only owe to friendly criticism from a point of view different from one's own.

took Melville to the South Seas, and the result was formative in very much the same way. Both men were the "product of a complex social order," both felt sharply the imbalances and discordances of that order, both were impelled to put to the test of reality a fantasy of life on other levels, and both came back from the experience with a deepened perception of the meaning of the social order from which they had fled—the meaning, that is, of that nineteenth century civilization with which their maturity was to deal. The experience, in short, was a familiar one that repeated itself fruitfully during the whole expansionist phase of European culture, as its "radiation" on a world-wide scale brought it into contact—usually destructive— with cultures of a different nature and induced a more searching scrutiny of its own values. Like Melville's South Seas of the whale chase, the Marquesans, and Queequeg, it is to some such background as this that Parkman's West of the buffalo hunt, the Oglala, and Henry Chatillon relates itself; and its attraction for him, far from implying a "paradoxical rejection of organized society," is authenticated precisely by the relevance to the life of "organized society" —for which this transitory Western order of things was preparing the way—of the drives that sent him on his quest.

That the West in the end provided no solution for the ills of civilization of which these drives were a reflex is beside the point. Education consists precisely in such trial and error, such tempering by experience of the appetences that shape one's demands on life. Its aim of course is not solutions, but sharpened perceptions in terms of self-knowledge and knowledge of the world. Here for a young man whose birthright was the upper level of American society in its most complex and highly developed form and who had explored the denser, more fixed complexities of the European center, the Western periphery, with its aspects of strangeness and danger, with the drift of uprooted, atomized life along its trails, with its microcosm of utter social otherness in the lodges of the Oglala, offered the best of schools for completing his initiation into the varieties and possibilities of the human condition and orienting himself among them. The chief meaning of the West for Parkman, in short, was, to a fuller measure, the meaning for him of "backward" Sicily, of Catholic Rome, of French Mackinaw—the meaning that is, of everything that the very legitimate impulse "to get for a while out of the nineteenth century," could contribute, by way of focus and perspective, to a comprehension of the nineteenth century.

Parkman's three weeks among the Oglala was the Ultima Thule of his voyagings outward from his own day. It forms the core of his Western experience, and the chapters describing it and the events that led up to it are the most compelling of his book. Nevertheless, other aspects of the West, and above all the human comedy of the life that crowded its trails, could not fail to leave their mark and evoke their response. If this was a more feral wilderness than any the young man had yet known, it was also, at least along its two tenuous lines of passage, a far more populous wilderness than the New England backwoods of his boyhood forays. The winds of Manifest Destiny that hardly stirred those pristine solitudes and whose side gusts he had felt on the upper Lakes, he found blowing full gale across the illimitable spaces of the plains. Its agents, high and low, were on the march that fateful summer when the farther West had become ripe for the plucking from Britain and Mexico. His outward journey was along the route of the emigration, the solid core of expansionism, Oregon bound in slow-moving, familial oxcarts, its trickle of four years earlier now swollen to a freshet of some twenty-five hundred souls. The segments of one large and historic band in particular he watched converge at Westport, ran into on the trail, and saw break into new combinations at Fort Laramie, one of which, diverging from the beaten way, was to achieve as the "Donner party" the most celebrated of emigrant disasters. Meanwhile, the fur trade, the precursor of empire, which had pioneered the trail to Oregon, still, even in its decline, dominated the mountain wilderness from its entrepôt at Laramie, where the old Astor company held chief sway, fleecing impartially the emigrants and its own employees, and filling the trail a hundred miles east and west of the post with the comings and goings of its motley personnel. To the south, along his return route, displacing its usual traffic in merchandise and silver with the outposts of Mexico, moved the rear guard and supply trains of General Kearney's Army of the West. Already, as the Mexican War gathered momentum during the young man's sojourn in the mountains, it had occupied Santa Fe and was preparing for its march to the Pacific. Finally, swelling the press of life on both routes, was a miscellaneous array of strays, adventurers, and sightseers like himself, such as the British sportsmen with whom he and Shaw made part of the journey to Laramie, or the derelict from Kearney's army, the disgruntled emigrant, the Iowa horse trader, and the sailor off a California hide ship, with whom they joined forces for the trip back to the settlements.

Whiggishly cool as Parkman was to all this as an upsurge of the triumphant democracy—unresponsive to what his commentators call the "profound social forces at work in the West," and sadly deficient in the sentiments which have hallowed for us the saga of the Covered Wagon—he was, nevertheless, anything but indifferent to what he was seeing simply in its essential qualities as human spectacle. Here indeed his trip assumes for us something of the aspect of a Chaucerian pilgrimage, and already in the preparatory bustle of St. Louis we find him reflecting on the "strange variety of human character" he had seen, and the infinite diversity of human nature, "the contemplation [of which] grows more absorbing as its features disclose themselves to view." With all conditions of man on the move and put to stresses that brought nakedly to light the innate springs of character, the West here offered this observer of his kind a field for observation unique in his time—or equalled only on the other, maritime frontier of America. In spite of the "Brahmin snobberies," he brought to his observations an instinct for the qualities of character, for the color and style of personality, that helps us to define the meaning of the spectacle perhaps as importantly as a grasp of those somewhat questionably profound "social forces" in which he has been held so reprehensibly unversed.

What Parkman made of the West, humanly speaking, is bound up with the conflict of isolative and outward-going attitudes toward the American world at large that one follows through his earlier journals and watches reach its climax on his Western trip—that little drama of human relationships that comes to its felicitous issue in his friendship with Henry Chatillon. As usual, the negative forces were particularly in the ascendant at the beginning of his trip, when he was working off an accumulated charge of spleen. The slightest of pretexts, or none at all, stirs up the rankling grudge of his social class, scanning the Jacksonian scene for confirmation of its cherished doctrines of inequality. "Is it not true, that the lower you descend in education and social position, the more vicious men become?" he asks at Harrisburg at the sight of a man "lounging" by the river bank. A boorish stage driver on the ride to Pittsburgh provokes similar reflections, hardly less preposterous in the triviality of their cause. Could this individual, the young man wonders, actually belong to the same species as "certain female friends" to whom his thoughts recur? " 'Human nature is the same everywhere'—so says everybody, but does not education make most essential distinctions?" What could "a Wordsworth, for instance," find in common with one's "brutish clods" of fellow-passengers? What sympathies could any "ordinary man of high education . . . have with such"?

This ideological mood, to be sure, largely dissipated itself in the genialities of the springtime river voyage, but the young man's hypersensitiveness on the score of manners remained a sufficiently formidable barrier to intercourse. He had his share of "offishness"— to use his own phrase—that repelled casual familiarity; an inborn diffidence, fostered in his case almost to the point of morbidity by a protective social code, the cornerstone of which was respect for reticences and privacies. "Reserve . . . seems to be no part of the western character . . . ," he writes at Louisville, in the comparatively amenable social atmosphere of the river steamer. "I observe this trait [of reserve or "offishness"] in myself—today, for instance, when a young fellow expressed satisfaction that he should accompany me to St. Louis, I felt rather inclined to shake him off, though he had made himself agreeable enough." The tone of this observation is sufficiently detached and even self-critical, but such detachment did not survive the conditions of the trail, when Parkman found himself exposed to a full fire of inquisitiveness and intrusiveness from the rank-and-file of the emigration. To the end of the chapter such encounters hardly ever fail to record themselves in accents of acute personal outrage that, again, strike us as comically disproportionate to the circumstances, as if criminality were somehow to be imputed to the uncouth "movers" for their lack of the social *mesure* of Beacon Hill. Perhaps the climactic instance was an invasion of his quarters at Fort Laramie—an instance the more piquant in that he and Shaw had sustained with entire complaisance an equally unsolicited visitation the night before from the Indians of the fort. "The emigrant's party passed the upper ford," he writes in his journal the next day, "and a troop of women came into the fort, invading our room without scruple or reserve. Yankee curiosity and questioning is nothing to those of these people." So the journal, and the young man's shock at this breach of manners was unabated a year later when he elaborated the incident in his book. He and Shaw, we learn, dismayed at the incursion of these "cadaverous faces and long lank figures . . . withdrew in all speed [to their room], vainly hoping it might prove a sanctuary," and had to repel a "numerous deputation" who appeared at the door, "but found no encouragement to remain."

This is not of course the only note Parkman strikes in regard to the emigration. In fact a visit the next day to the camp of this same group was the occasion for a very discerning passage on emigrant hardships—the demoralization that set in at Laramie, as, cheated by the people at the fort ("a set of mean swindlers"), blackmailed by the Indians, quarreling among themselves, the movers began to show the effects of the disintegrating anxiety of this journey into strangeness they had undertaken, the worst part of which was still to come. These tough frontiersmen, he realized, were at home in "the *forest*," but totally out of their element on the plains, and an appreciation of the workaday heroism of their venture communicates itself. Nevertheless the object and circumstances of Parkman's trip made his contacts with the emigration somewhat tangential ones; and certainly if the meaning of the West is to be comprised in a prescience of what the emigration was to become for American folk legend, no one could have drawn a more complete blank. "I have often perplexed myself to divine the motives that gave impulse to this migration," he wrote in a much quoted passage of *The Oregon Trail;* "but whatever they may be, whether an insane hope of a better condition in life, or a desire of shaking off restraints of law and society, or mere restlessness, certain it is that multitudes bitterly resent the journey, and, after they have reached the land of promise, are happy enough to escape from it."

But make what we will of such negations, we should be very much blinded by our own social bias if they formed our final impression of Parkman's dealings with humanity on his Western trip. As always, these blocks to communication gave way before his responsiveness to style in personality at any level of life; and it was precisely in this bracing frontier air, in this least hothouse of social atmospheres, that such recognitions and acceptances came to their richest flowering. If the young man's grounds of response are not patterned to our own ideological specifications, they are grounds that no view can afford to overlook, and in fact, in the event, they led to perceptions that our own view can turn to significant enough account.

A few examples will make clear the traits that drew Parkman to people and the quality of his responses. Thus, among the emigration, a party of Virginia mountaineers, boarding the steamer with their goods and chattels at Paducah, won instant approval. Though "apparently not much educated" they were admirably "good-looking and hardy," "manly . . . and agreeable in their manners," "intelligent and open" to talk to, the women—also "remarkably good-looking"—without any of "that detestable, starched, lackadaisical expression common in vulgar Yankee women." Again, at St. Louis he struck up an acquaintance with some of the Russell-Boggs-Donner party, already mentioned, and found spirits among them to admire: Ewing, for instance, "the impulsive, unobserving, ardent Kentuckian," and his companion, the "quiet, sedate, and manly Jacobs." And on the trail itself, his exasperation at the "raw, noisy, western way" was by no means an insuperable barrier to affirmative responses. A party, "chiefly Missourians," with whom he spent an evening by the Platte he found a "very good set of men." He visits the camp of a group whose inquisitiveness had particularly outraged him and notes that, nevertheless, they were "fine-looking fellows, with an air of frankness, generosity, and even courtesy." Of the group he traveled with briefly and got to know best, he writes—in spite of his annoyance at the arrangement, which was the doing of his British trail-mates and slowed the pace of the party—"the men . . . were all that could be desired, rude indeed in manners, but frank, manly, and intelligent." He also remarks the good bearing and intelligence of one of them with whom he shared guard duty; and he was on the best of terms with their leader, a representative enough specimen—like the rest—of the general human run of the emigration. This is hardly to say, of course, that all his impressions once he got beyond his initial irritations were favorable ones, but good or bad, they bear the unmistakable stamp of authenticity. Whatever generalities about the emigration his presuppositions compelled him to, in the sum of concrete cases and individual instances his instinct for character tells its own story.

So much for what he made on his outward journey of this America he saw on march along the trails. On his return journey—to pass over here his relations with the trapping fraternity in the mountains—we find these beginnings of reciprocity coming to full flower in his comradeship with two of the quartet already mentioned, who were his trail companions from Fort Bent to the settlements. This pair—Munroe, the horse trader, and Jim Gurney, the sailor—had already joined forces en route from California, Jim representing, as Parkman puts it, "the extraordinary phenomenon of a sailor who understood how to manage a horse." Munroe, "tall [and] well-formed . . . with a face and manner such as inspire confidence at once," he describes as "an excellent fellow, open, warm-hearted, and intelligent." Gurney was a dark, curly-bearded, stocky little man, whose energy, competence, humor, and gift for profanity equally won his admiration. Both were characteristic products of the same general American run of things as the emigration; and nothing could have a pleasanter flavor of recognitions, reciprocities, and mutual amity than Parkman's account of his trip back in their company, as, with the ridiculous Hodgeman, quondam steamer clerk and misplaced army volunteer, filling the rôle of court jester, the party crept at their ease along the banks of the Arkansas, "happy and careless as so many beggars" (a state of mutuality, one might add, that was decidedly not achieved in respect to the Britishers of his own class and background with whom, in preference to the "movers," he began his trip, so much to the scandal of his commentators).

Finally, rounding out the sum of affirmations, we come to the figure of Henry Chatillon, Parkman's friendship with whom illuminates the whole record of his journey. Henry, who had made his living as a hunter since he was fifteen and as far as "education" went, could neither read nor write, was, Parkman says, a "proof of what unaided nature will sometimes do." Given Henry's French Canadian origins, this is a statement to which we may take exception. Nature, one surmises, shared no little of the credit for Henry's shaping with a tradition notable for the stamp of *gentilesse* it succeeds in imprinting on its offspring at all levels of life; and there is at least a hint of such childhood influences in the extra day Henry stipulated for at St. Louis to visit his mother before he went back to the wilderness where he had just spent four years. Yet if Henry's French *gentilesse* sets him somewhat apart in the tale of Parkman's human discoveries in the West, it only gives a special coloring to traits we have seen him responding to and underscoring in the most various connections: good physical presence, good natural manners, "openness," "frankness," competence, intelligence, positiveness and saliency of character. In short, taking Henry and the sum of instances that Henry fills out, *The Oregon Trail*, we realize, affirms on this score what Melville and Whitman so momentously affirmed: the emergence on the American scene of a distinctive democratic style in personality. In his review of Parkman's book, Melville's divination was not at fault when he greeted the portrait of Henry with the clearest sense of its kinship to his own types of the "kingly commons."

That, in Parkman's case, we have to do with something quite different from an affirmation of democracy or the "common man" as such hardly needs saying. What is suggested, however, is a quality of perception that took him well beyond the range of the "Brahmin snobberies" that are supposed to have circumscribed his view of the West. How far, even on the conceptual level these perceptions took him, may be gathered from some remarks on the American character he had occasion to make five years later, in the course of an essay on Cooper. The gist of them is precisely a complaint at the lack among the "educated and polished classes" in America of the idiosyncrasy of character to be found, not alone, as Europeans believed, among the "backwoodsmen of the West," but among "the whole merchant marine, from captains to cabin-boys, the lumbermen of Maine, the farmers of New England, and indeed all the laboring population of the country. . . ." "It is a matter of common remark," he bluntly concludes, "that the most highly educated classes among us are far from being the most efficient either in thought or action. The vigorous life of the nation springs from the deep rich soil at the bottom of society."

Such, in set terms, was Parkman's recognition of the pre–Civil War America which his early travels, and particularly this culminating Western trip, had revealed to him, and *The Oregon Trail* is quickened by the discoveries and perceptions on which this recognition was based; perceptions, as I have said, perhaps more germane to a reading of the West than the topicalities of Manifest Destiny.

But what the West had to show here was only a special display, so to speak, of what America at large had to show. For all their busyness its pilgrimage ways were merely imprecise tracks across an utterly alien world of sun, dust, alkali, and sagebrush, woodless and waterless, the haunt of the Indian, the buffalo, and a primal loneliness ferally ready to take over at the least break in the tenuous links of the human chain that now spanned it. For the young Brahmin and the most workaday of his fellow travelers alike, the compulsion of this strangeness and this danger was the essence of their journey, and here if anywhere the peculiar secrets of the West were to be scanned. We return then to the young man's quest of them, as he set out from Westport in middle May through the lush prairie country of the journey's beginning.

Except for the smallness of the party, the first stage of his journey —the traverse to Laramie on the Oregon Trail—followed the pattern of most such crossings. Its main incidents were chiefly disagreements with his trail companions, the English sportsmen already spoken of: a certain Captain Chandler, fussy and fearful; his younger brother Jack; and an inept and officious Mr. Romaine, who took command of the joint party (and promptly proceeded to lose the trail) by virtue of an earlier trip to the West from which he had apparently profited nothing. As the forks of the Platte, the young men, fed up with Romaine's bungling arrogance and the "old womanism of the Capt.," decided to push on by themselves, and reached Laramie in good order on June 15.

Parkman had been out more than a month now, and in spite of the British ineptitudes and occasional days when he reports himself feeling "hipped," his journey so far could hardly have had a more liberating and revivifying effect. Quickly expert in the techniques of plains travel and plains hunting under Henry's tutelage, he was leading once more the open-air life of his boyhood expeditions, for which he had had moments of acute nostalgia in Europe. Once again the vision that had been the moose incorporated itself in more awesome form, as he watched spellbound the declivities of the Platte darken with buffalo, as far as eye could reach. Once again he could give himself over to the ecstasies of the chase, the wilder now for being on horseback and demanding more complex skills. And, a few days before Laramie, all the chances of the trip seemed turning in his favor, when Henry discerned Old Smoke's village of Oglala pouring down a distant bluff; and a tall warrior, with bow and dogskin quiver, naked to the waist on his high-bowed saddle, rode over to exchange signals of amity.

As on his earlier forays his health and spirits had promptly improved. Yet it was not to come off scot-free that he had engaged to immerse himself in the destructive element. The first payment on the account was exacted at Laramie when dysentery from the alkali water attacked him full force, to recur, with delusive intermissions, through the rest of the trip. From Laramie on, a quality of phantasmagoria displaces the holiday mood of the narrative, as he tried to stop the ravages of the violent diarrhea that racked him by a starvation diet of a biscuit a day, or, hardly able to walk without reeling, forced himself into the saddle at Bull Bear's village, convinced of the probability that he would "never leave those deserts." The whole central episode of his journey comes to us heightened by the almost hallucinative perceptions of nerves in a state of hyperesthesia from illness and exhaustion.

Meanwhile at Laramie, in spite of the ravages of dysentery, there were the social amenities of the post to be observed and plans to be made for the party's next move. These last revolved around the project of a grand confederated Sioux war expedition against the Snakes, set on foot by Tunica, an aspirant for leadership in the village to which Bear Robe, Henry's squaw, belonged, and over which—as over the rest of the Oglala Sioux—her father Bull Bear had exercised potent sway until his assassination a few years earlier. But Tunica was far from possessing Bull Bear's abilities, and given the difficulty at best of organizing Indians for such large-scale enterprises, the prospect of the war party's actually materializing was doubtful, as Parkman realized. Still, when he and Shaw arrived at the fort, bands were gathering from three hundred miles about, and obviously the chance of attaching himself to such an expedition was not to be overlooked. So, with this idea in mind, the party set out on June 20 to wait at the mouth of the Chugwater, seventeen miles up Laramie Creek, where Tunica's village was expected to pass. Besides the original four—Parkman, Shaw, Henry, and Deslauriers—there was another hand, Raymond, whom they had engaged at the fort, and keeping them company, a trader named Reynal, his enormous squaw Margot, also from Tunica's village, and her Indian nephews, His Horses and the Hail Storm.

At Chugwater their wait lengthened to a fortnight, as the village made its dilatory way, stopping to hunt north of the Platte. In the meanwhile grave news of his squaw came to Henry, which took him to her brothers' lodges, where he found she was dying. Shaw went with him, while Parkman made a trip to the fort. But for the most part he had to contain his impatience as best he could in the monotony of the camp, reading or dozing through the heat-ridden hours under the shade of an ancient cottonwood, while the scene before him etched itself on his memory like a daguerreotype: the trim tent; Reynal's battered lodge; the steep white buttes byond the river; the further landscape of arid, sun-steeped plain and distant mountains. With the arrival, however, of four trappers on the 30th to graze their horses, the tempo of events began to quicken. Scattered Indians also appeared—among them young Bull Bear, Henry's brother-in-law—and finally on July 3 the rest of the village poured over the butte in a disorderly array of horses, dogs, mules, *traineaux*, warriors, squaws, and children, until a hundred and fifty lodges had sprung up on the flats by the river.

Here was a chance for observation the young man made the most of, irksome as he, in his condition, found the pertinacity of Sioux hospitality. But this eagerly awaited event, as he had half foreseen, proved to be an anticlimax. Instead of taking the warpath, the volatile Tunica, talked out of his intentions by the officials at the fort, now proposed to cut lodge poles in the mountains. After some days of vacillation the village agreed to this plan and trailed off up Laramie Creek on July 6, though their nominal chief later changed his mind again and did not pass the mountains with them. Parkman was thus faced with a dilemma. Should he go after the village or take his dwindling chances on the possibility of a war party? He chose the latter course and pushed on to the rendezvous, sixty miles to the west, only to find he had made the wrong choice. No Indians were to be seen, and it was evident that Tunica's grand scheme had entirely fallen through.

His position was now really critical. Shaw was averse to his idea of trying to rejoin Tunica's village, and there was nothing for it but to take Raymond—who had turned out to be not very bright— and chance it on his own. Considering the precarious state of his health, the uncertainty of the village's exact whereabouts, and its five days' head start over country that was the abomination of desolation, the gamble was a sufficiently desperate one.

Disaster almost struck the day after they left Shaw, when Raymond let their horses escape and had to spend four hours catching them. The next day they came across the trail of the village, lost it again on the flinty hardpan of the plain, and picked it up beyond their night's encampment where Laramie Creek broke from the hills. The trail was now plain enough through the narrow defiles, but in the meanwhile another piece of bad luck had overtaken them. Parkman's little mare Pauline fell ill in her turn, and was scarcely able to carry her rider, who was himself scarcely able to sit upright in the saddle. "Man and horse were helpless alike." That day and the next only sheer will power kept him going, crawling up a steep pitch on his hands and knees, the trail rope wrapped round his arm, when he was too weak to lead Pauline on foot; or forcing himself from the lethargy of exhaustion at the top to the almost impossible effort of remounting.

Nevertheless they were gaining on the village and had passed three of its camp sites before they bivouacked a little beyond the third. The mountain country too had a compelling beauty, strange, yet oddly familiar. Images of a New England boyhood started up at the z-ing of a locust in a stand of pine; one rock-needled defile made him think of Dixville; and the trees along the clear stream that ran through it were "all alive with birds like Mt. Auburn." Thus, in his extremity, the days of strength and wholeness, of a boy's pride of life, rose like a mirage before the mind's eye. And so too, in his extremity, he felt himself stirred by an unwonted consciousness of kind. At one of the village camp sites Raymond was able to distinguish the traces of Reynal's lodge, and pointed them out to him. Between the brutish Reynal and himself he was aware of "hardly a feeling in common," no bond except the "precarious one of a kindred race." Yet he found himself staring at the place with the intensest interest, moved, and perplexed to understand what moved him.

In spite of their progress, the next day promised to be worse. They were now down to a little flour for food, and in their over-anxiousness missed easy shots at antelope around a water hole.

Furthermore, as they had topped the last of the foothills, the levels of the Laramie Basin had opened before them for a dozen miles without a sign of Indians. Raymond, who had brought up the subject the day before, again urged turning back, and when they lost the trail on the sun-baked flats, Parkman himself had the gloomiest forebodings of failure, for he knew he was at the end of his strength. But he stipulated with Raymond to go on for at least the rest of the day, and this time he was not to be balked by mutiny, as on his New England forays. When they emerged at noon from a gap in a ridge of low swells that had bounded the view, the sight he had been looking for met his eyes. There, a mile or so beyond, a circle of tall lodges rose by the naked creek bank, and the plain was dotted with dark spots that resolved themselves into human figures. The Indians, who were in debatable hunting grounds and were on the watch, had also seen him and Raymond. Reynal came out to meet them, and Parkman was soon installed in the lodge of Kongra-Tonka (Big Crow), one of the village warriors. "Never," he wrote, "did the heart of wanderer more gladden at the sight of home"; or, as the journal has it, "Thanked God that my enterprise was not defeated."

For the next three weeks—or nineteen days, to be exact—Parkman lived with this band of Sioux as they drifted by leisurely stages around the Laramie Basin, procuring hides and poles for new tepees. The buffalo, which supplied them with housing as well as food and clothing, were most plentiful in the western part of the basin, toward the Medicine Bow Range. Here, in some danger from hostile Snakes and Utahs, they made a great "surround" and camped for five days, while the squaws fashioned the skins of the cows into robes and new lodge covers. Then, circling back again, they made an incursion into the Laramie Mountains to cut pine saplings for the poles. This business finished, they recrossed the range to safer territory, where Parkman left them on August 2, near his old Chugwater camp site.

Such was the surface pattern of events during these three momentous weeks. Here what he had come to see at such risk was prosaic enough—merely the Sioux making provision for themselves in the matter of housing. Actually it was the revelation of the whole life style of a great primitive culture; and Parkman's record of it is a classic document of such explorations into the "backward and abysm" of human experience.

What, in its broadest aspects, he was seeing was a society and a community for which the basic antimonies of "civilization" did not exist, the standing conflicts of flesh and spirit, heart and head, instinct and conscience, that sharpened steadily, decade by decade, as the nineteenth century ran its course. So much is true, of course, of all archaic cultures to which men, harried by such imbalances, have turned for images of integration. For the rest, the life style of this particular culture was a reflex of the young man's particular discontents: it was as inevitable that Parkman, a child of Unitarianism, should turn to the fierce strenuousness of the hunting Sioux for a counterimage of human possibilities, as that Melville, a child of Calvinism, should turn to the relaxed sensuousness, the cult of

> . . . beauté
> Luxe, calme, et volupté,

that shaped the pattern of Marquesan existence.

But on this point, if we look for a parallel in Melville, the whaling phase of his South Seas experience is in a sense perhaps more apposite than the vale of Typee. At any rate, as with all the Plains Indians, the culture of the Sioux was one patterned to give a central place to the instincts of the chase and the kill. Hunting and fighting were not here marginal pursuits, but integral to the life of the group and the individual: the village literally existed by that moment of total engagement, of "every faculty at its tension," that the young man had celebrated in his early stories. So he saw this appetite for the chase come to its functional climax in the great five-day "surround" of buffalo that provided the village with hides and meat; so he watched the young Hail Storm, Reynal's nephew, put on manhood by virtue of his nascent prowess as a hunter; so he heard from Big Crow, the mature warrior who had counted his fourteen *coups* in battle, tales of this most honorific Sioux form of the chase. He was not to see the Sioux on the warpath, but he took part in their buffalo hunting. With their amazing horsemanship and their skill in the use of the bow, they had brought the art around which their lives revolved to one of its peaks of perfection, and the spectacle was unforgettable: the superb figures of the hunters, stripped to cincture and moccasins, charging, saddleless and stirrupless, on the mass of shaggy beasts; the dust, the trampling, the yells, at the moment of impact, as arrow followed arrow into their lumbering and plunging bodies; the dark carcasses falling, or the wounded bristling up "like gigantic cats," as the riders galloped by to fresh kills. So through the "surround" the hunters killed, skinned, and gorged with the rest—as did Parkman himself—on the raw liver and tripes; the carcasses piled up before the lodges; the squaws worked the hides into covers; meat abounded in the village; and life fulfilled itself in these primordial rhythms of tension and release of tension.

Or, again, one day, he watched the Hail Storm, on his little pony, running a gigantic bull buffalo—a lithe-limbed, handsome, smooth-faced boy, pitting himself with superb skill and mastery against the fury of his monstrous antagonist. At Chugwater a few weeks earlier, the Hail Storm had been a mere youngster, still bashful and backward with the girl squaws, his aspirations just whetted by the kill of his first deer. Now Parkman saw him in the full process of coming of age, already talked of as a hunter, making his conquests among the squaws, and hot for the fleshing of his "maiden scalping-knife" that would stamp him a full-fledged brave. So in brute valor and act the Hail Storm put on manhood—ran his buffalo, and closed for the death, turning to laugh from sheer joy of mastery, as the eyes of the great beast glared through its mane and the blood froth began to stream from its mouth and nostrils. Again, life fulfilled itself in the moment's *agon*, and Parkman watched, a sick man on a sick horse.

One could respond less whole-mindedly, to be sure, to Big Crow's impassively recited incidents of the human chase among the Sioux. The "civilized" instincts had, after all, their own deep roots, and some of these tales could not be heard without repulsion. One, in particular, narrated, Parkman says, with "an air of earnest simplicity," as of a child telling its mother some anecdote of the day's doings, illustrated the "worst features of Indian character." It concerned the fate of a hostile Snake, captured by Big Crow and his young men in the Medicine Bow mountains. Chasing their victim up the mountainside, they surrounded and caught him, and, while two of the younger braves held him pinioned, Big Crow scalped him alive. Then, kindling a great bonfire and cutting the tendons of their captive's wrists and ankles, they threw him into the flames, and kept him there with long poles until he was burnt to death. This was revolting enough, and there were further particulars "much too revolting to mention." Yet Sioux life had woven even these extremes of the human range into a coherent and harmonious pattern; and as, in illness and weakness, one listened to Big Crow at ease in his lodge, master of his functions as hunter and warrior, his body—back, arms, and breast—scarred with wounds from these guerrilla encounters or from the ritual torture of the Sun Dance, some secret place of the imagination stirred at the thought of inflicting or enduring such cruelties, and a hidden will to violence tasted the Sioux exaltation of such extremes of violence.

There was no doubt a touch of pathology in Parkman's response to all this, as witness the occasional overdwelling on scenes of torture in his histories. But the pathology of one culture is the normality of another; and the Sioux, like all the Plains Indians, had made a strikingly viable affair of their cult of excess, of the intoxications of hunting and fighting. Perhaps, in the infancy of ethnology, only an observer with velleities like Parkman's could have come so close to their psychology and motivations.

And in the meanwhile the imagination stirred less ambiguously to other aspects of Sioux life: the stamp of style it set on bearing, equipment, and ceremonial; its instinctive expression in accent and color; the verve and drama of its most ordinary activities. For one thing, the Sioux were magnificent physical specimens. "Superb naked forms stood silently gazing at us," Parkman wrote of his arrival at the village; and his first sight of it at Chugwater made him realize what Benjamin West had meant when he exclaimed of the Apollo Belvedere, "By God, a Mohawk!" Thus the Sioux shamed an overclothed and hypochondriac generation with the glory of the flesh. And they likewise shamed a drably clothed generation by their frank pleasure in the adornment of it. The Hail Storm, assuming the *toga virilis*, vermilioned his face, hung shell pendants in his ears, and wore his red blanket with a knowing dash; White Shield, a proved brave, posed in his magnificent feather war bonnet "perfectly conscious of the gallant air which it gave to his dark face and his vigorous, graceful figure."

Or take the sight of the village on the march, a routine enough aspect of Sioux existence. Yet nothing left a more ineffaceable impression, and familiarity never dulled the fascination of this spectacle, as the lodges came down and the disorderly procession, strung out a mile or more over the plain, took its way to the glitter of lance points in the pellucid air and strident vibrancies of color from trappings and equipment. Braves in paint and feathers galloped their mounts along the flanks; files of sturdy elders stalked magnificent in white buffalo robes; withered crones, ugly as Macbeth's witches, screamed at the pack horses; dogs and naked children scampered underfoot; young squaws grinned from gaudily caparisoned mules; and for the watching "meneaska" the whole Sioux scheme of things spoke its reproach in color and *élan* to the pall of tonelessness that, at one's back, the "nineteenth century" spread like a blight over men's ways.

Yet there was another side to the coin. These warriors and elders who made such a brave show of things under the sun were also, one perceived, boasters, liars, gluttons, and shameless beggars. With a fine flair for mimicry and pantomime, for storytelling and speechmaking, their ordinary talk was a gabble of obscenities and irrationalities, childish beyond description. They could bear wounds with the utmost fortitude, but illness left them helpless. On the other hand, if warlike ardor evaporated at the touch of a cold or sore throat, they were liable to unexpected outbreaks of aimless ferocity, and their splendid physiques were too often marred by facial expressions of a repellently fierce and malignant cast. They had, to be sure, their domestic affections, chiefly an extravagant fondness for children, but one was not safe among them; except for old Red Water, the Nestor of the village, and the Panther, an untypically companionable younger brave, who gave him lessons in Oglala, Parkman would have trusted himself alone with none of the band. Admirable as one found their way of life, one could discover "very few points of sympathy" in character; and there were moods when like the frontiersmen, one regarded them simply as a "troublesome and dangerous species of wild beast."

This intractability could be set down to the nature of their particular culture. Habituated to extremes, they were unfitted for the mean of the human gamut. But one came in the final count to a more impassable gulf than this. "They merely vegetate," runs one of the notebook entries, and, whatever their achievements, they lived in a void of mind, a vast vacuity of spirit, that at the last one simply could not transcend. Masters of the moment, they had, one perceived, no purposes or conceptions beyond the moment, no curiosity beyond the purview of custom, no inkling even of the doom that was already palpably upon them; wayward, changeable, and impatient of restraint as children, they were children in mind and selfhood, and survivals of the world's childhood. They were, in short, savages—marvelously gifted savages who had achieved an integration and wholeness of life that a civilized man could envy, but on a level to which no civilized man could go back. Face to face with them, one plumbed at last the finality of that commitment to Mind, Consciousness, and Will which their inviolate world had never known.

Thus disenchantment kept pace even as enchantment grew, and the round of hunting, dog feasts, gambling, "medicine" ritual, and mere *far niente* that filled the cycle of Sioux days began to seem second nature. One surrendered even to the listless inactivity—so oppressive at first—that alternated with the bouts of fierce excitement in the rhythm of their hunting life; and, as the young man had given himself to the frenzy of the chase, so he knew the spell of endless, breathless afternoons, dozed away with the rest in "a profound lethargy, the very spirit of indolence," while the sun filled the bowl of the plains, or, as the band moved into the hills, pines and running water again revived memories of New England. But enough was enough. When the village had finished its stint in the mountains, he knew that he had had as much as he would ever have of what he had come for, and it was time to go. On August 2 he and Raymond started back through the range with Hail Storm as guide, but stopped on the way to hunt black-tailed deer, and were overtaken by the village. He rode with it the rest of the day through intense heat and a pall of smoke from forest fires in the mountains, watched it for the last time as it straggled in colorful array down a rocky gorge to the plain, smoked a last pipe with Reynal, bivouacked that night at Chugwater, and rejoined Shaw and Henry at Laramie the next day, August 3. It was like a "new phase of existence" to be eating a civilized meal once more, and after three weeks of the Sioux, Shaw and Henry took on the quality of apparitions from another world.

Yet he had been "half unwilling" to leave the village, and it was no simple dialectic of illusion and disillusion to which the inner drama of his Indian weeks played itself out. In one sense, it is true, he had harbored a fantasy which the touch of reality had dispelled. It was apparent enough, for instance, that Indians in the flesh were different beings from Indians in the pages of Cooper, and whatever notions of the "noble savage" variety he may have entertained received their quietus. And in a more inward sense the journey was a clarification of the possible and impossible issue of things—a last return to the world of the Fells, the unfallen world of boyhood with its oneness of flesh and spirit, a return to this world and an emergence from it to adult recognition of the ineluctable dualities of life and the knowledge that, whatever their imbalance, it was not to be redressed on these terms. Yet in the deepest sense his journey was the exploration of a world that is never left behind, a world of powers and virtues from which civilization itself springs and draws its vitality, and with which it loses contact only at its peril. Mind and Consciousness were one's destiny, but Mind and Consciousness were no more the whole of the equation that this mindless world of drift, drive, and appetence he saw objectified and organized in the patterns of Sioux culture, and nothing could have been more fruitful or creative than the instinct that impelled him to steep himself in it. His journey backward in time was likewise a journey to the depths of self, the exploration of a hinterland where Unitarianism preferred not to venture, which Transcendentalism mistook the nature of, and which Utilitarianism simply ignored; a spanning, in sum, of the dissociations of his age in the full range of their polarity. To his dying day, the physical trophies of this journey—lance, feather war bonnet, medicine pouch, pipe, bow and arrow—hung on the wall of his Boston study; and the fact is symbolically meaningful enough.

But, in the meanwhile, the Sioux had not exhausted the possibilities of the West for the young man. Despite recurring bouts of illness, two months of carefree vagabondage remained to him, and, as the party made its leisurely way south to Bent's Fort, then home over the Santa Fe Trail—the Omoo phase, one might say, of his Western experience—another image of the West, the West of Henry and the "mountain man," confirmed the spell it had cast on him from the beginning. Here Cooper had not been at fault; fact, one discovered, authenticated fiction, and Henry was Leatherstocking to the letter, or at least Leatherstocking in a Franco-American guise. Here, in short, savagery had wedded itself to civilization, and, with such examples as Henry at least, what could seem a happier, a more viable resolution of polarities than the results? "There is something admirably felicitous," Parkman later wrote of Leatherstocking, "in the conception of this hybrid . . . in whom . . . the truest moral perceptions are joined with the wandering instincts and hatred of restraint which stamp the Indian or the Bedouin." To live the life of the Sioux and at the same time to preserve one's identity as a civilized being—with this most accessible of all versions of the Fells before the mind's eye, it is small wonder that, in the misery of the next year, "the desire was intense to return to the prairie."

One did not, of course. For the moment, the image of Leatherstocking, autonomous in his wilderness setting, figured large in the national mythology, an innocent projection, unshadowed by darker contradictions, of the age's famous ideal of "self-reliance." Yet, to use figuratively a phrase of Balzac's, Leatherstocking, in relation to the real dynamics of self-reliance, was only "*ce grand eunuque*"; and as much could be said of Henry—he "had not the restless energy of the Anglo-American," Parkman wrote, and was "content to take things as he found them." It was a refreshing, an amiable enough fault; but, on a nonmaterial plane at least, the young man was committed to nothing more deeply than the central imperatives of this "energy." The difference was there and one's destiny was precisely to confront, for better or worse, the full sum of contradictions and discordances in the ethos of self-reliance that Henry's way passed by.

Yet Henry was perfect in his time and place, and if his time was brief and his place peripheral, such images of integration have a lasting validity. Civilization needs them to keep it sweet and to temper the impact of its own specific drives by the reminder of counter-qualities, which it is always in danger of crushing out; just as, for the wholeness of maturity, an adult must keep, to quote Ortega y Gasset, "a certain well-spring of youthfulness and even of childishness." Thus, of the residue of meanings that the West has left behind, perhaps the myth of the Indian and the mountain man is after all the most "serious," the most richly symbolic. Not to have responded as Parkman did to Henry and Henry's way of life would have been as much a failure of apprehension on his part, at that particular American turn of time, as not to have transcended that response.

And, at the last, we come back to what we began with, to Henry, not as myth or symbol, but simply as the very vernacular figure who, with other children of the time, completed the young man's education of the heart. Here, in this flowering of human recognitions, lay perhaps the truest acquisition of experience on his Western trip, whatever its immediate purposes. "For this Henry Chatillon we feel a fresh and unbounded love," Melville wrote in his review—with a *Schwärmerei* foreign to Parkman's temperament (as was, for what the statement is worth, the erotic bias toward the masculine that partly colored Melville's feeling). Yet Parkman's own more low-keyed way of putting the case strikes as deeply authentic a note of fraternity: "I have never, in the city or in the wilderness, met a better man than my true-hearted friend, Henry Chatillon."

CHAPTER VI

THE OREGON TRAIL

✤ ✤ ✤

Parkman returned from the West in October of 1846, and with the collapse that followed, one phase of his life came to a full stop. Fate had dealt him out during his early youth the exact measure, neither more nor less, of what he needed for what he was to do; and, broadly speaking, everything his work owes to the intake of external experience was to be drawn from this capital accumulated in his first twenty-three years. From this point on, what counts in the relation of his life to his work is the inward change, the slow reeducation of the ego and the will, wrought by the sufferings of the shadowed years ahead—indeed, for the human tone of his work, nothing perhaps counts more. But such a history does not record itself in outward events, and the tale of these now becomes of secondary interest. For the young man, with his air castles in ruins about him, everything soon contracted to the stark question of whether he would be able to resume his work at all, the main body of which, as he had conceived it, did not even begin to see the light for another seventeen years. The essential biographical "fact" of these years is this silent struggle of the creative spirit against physical ills and the torments of the mind.

The first phase of the long-drawn-out contest takes us from Parkman's breakdown in 1846–1847 to a time of partial recovery around 1850, the year of his marriage and of his completion of *Pontiac*. The dysentery that had afflicted him in the West disappeared with his return to civilization, but a suite of new disorders— or rather aggravations of old disorders—followed, until within a year "all collapsed, but the tenacious strength of muscles hardened by long activity." Besides the indigestion, the sleeplessness, and the weakness of sight, the symptoms he speaks of at this time were a stoppage of circulation in the extremities, and, above all, a shattering condition of hyperstimulation at any attempt at mental effort, a "wild whirl" that possessed the brain, together with a "universal turmoil of the nervous system." This indeed, all his life, was to be the chief manifestation of "the enemy"—as he called the varying complex of disorders that afflicted him—and the most formidable of the hurdles in his path, not excepting partial blindness. "My eyes I don't mind," he wrote, with characteristic understatement, to E. G. Squier in 1849. "I can get along without them, but to have one's brain stirred up in a mush may be regarded as a decided obstacle to intellectual achievements." Parkman, however, gives more explicit details of these cerebral attacks when they later renewed themselves with increased severity, and we shall return to them in due course. For the rest, at this distance of time, a precise diagnosis of his "case" in a modern clinical sense is perhaps not possible, but the cause of his disorders is obviously to be looked for in the underlying stresses that the interplay of temperament and Boston-American circumstance had put upon the psyche, and the general nature of these stresses is clear enough.

But the etiology of a "whirl" in the brain was beyond the purview of medical science of the time, and for the moment the young man's chief concern was treatment of his eyes. For this purpose he went to New York about a month after his homecoming to put himself in the hands of Dr. S. R. Elliott of Staten Island, who, the year before, had successfully treated his sister Caroline. Except for two visits to a hydropathic spa at Brattleboro, Vermont—on the first of which, in the fall of 1847, he managed to finish by dictation *The Oregon Trail*, begun shortly after his return from the West, then dropped as his disorders increased—he lived in New York or Staten Island for the next two years, submitting, with the best grace he could, to the "rest cure" that was the basis of Dr. Elliott's system. The doctor's establishment seems to have been a forerunner of the

modern sanitarium, and a good many high-strung New Englanders
—among them Longfellow, Lowell, and, in Parkman's time, the
actor Levi Thaxter, the future husband of the poetess Celia Thaxter
—resorted to it for the endemic eyestrain of the period. In Parkman's case, the cure, as it happened, did little for his eyes, but it
had no doubt a certain therapeutic effect on his general condition.

Its lessons of a sanative idleness were not, however, easily enforced. "Patience, I suppose, is the only medicine," the young man
wrote Norton; "and a most hateful one to me it is." Now condemned to "total inaction" he had at last to face squarely the detestable fact of invalidism and school his spirit to meet it—to embrace the opposite of everything that had seemed to make life
worth living, to learn the cold virtues of patience and passive endurance, to substitute for the exhilaration of the frontal assault the
tedious strategies of indirection. The voices of the world called,
and, in the heyday of one's youth, one could not respond. As we
have seen, there were times when the impulse to go back to the
West and "settle squarely the question to be or not to be" was almost irresistible; and the Mexican War, with classmates who had
enlisted passing through New York, was another turn of the screw.
Forty years later Parkman could recall in all their freshness the feelings of "envious bitterness" awakened by the sight in a shop window
of a battle print of officers and men serving a field battery at
Buena Vista. As for the life of action, so—the crowning humiliation—for the half-despised life of mind. What answer, even here,
was one to make to the promptings of ambition, what figure was
one to cut in the race for achievement, when the least effort to put
forth one's gifts set up an intolerable hurly-burly in the brain from
which the only relief was to stretch flat on one's back "without
thought or motion"? Middle age, if it survives at all a crack-up
like Parkman's, can resign itself to such a taking in of sail as faced
the young man with a certain philosophy, if not with a positive
sense of relief. But at twenty-four, with his energies quick within
him and his craving for action unstilled, this change to flat stagna-

tion could well claim, as he wrote, "a place, not of the meanest, in that legion of mental tortures which makes the torments of the Inferno seem endurable."

And indeed Dr. Elliott's prescription of complete idleness, therapeutic up to a point as it undoubtedly was, nevertheless threatened in the end to become a remedy worse than the disease. By the spring of 1848, when his condition was again at its worst, Parkman realized that if anything like effort on the old headlong scale was barred, it was imperative for his sanity that he at least have something to occupy him. Dr. Elliott felt that brainwork would be "poison," but in homeopathic doses, might it not prove beneficial? The difficulty, to be sure, "was so near the impossible that the line of distinction often disappeared"; nevertheless the young man decided to try, and, with infinite precautions, started on the composition of *Pontiac*. The necessary books and documents were sent down from Boston and read aloud to him at such times as he could listen, "the length of each reading never, without injury, much exceeding half an hour." In the meanwhile he had had a wire writing frame constructed, by means of which and a black crayon he could take fairly legible notes with his eyes closed. His notes in turn were deciphered and read back to him, and finally the actual text was dictated at a rate which "for the first half year . . . averaged about six lines a day." The whole snail-like process was of course interrupted by days and weeks when he was not able to work at all.

Nevertheless a start had been made, a technique for circumventing "the enemy" had been worked out, and, in spite of his physician's warnings, his health showed fluctuating signs of improvement—a condition of affairs to which the sucess of *The Oregon Trail*, appearing serially in the *Knickerbocker*, no doubt also contributed (Clark, in fact, by skipping numbers, spun out the serialization to keep the new subscribers the story had won for the magazine). In the fall of 1848 Parkman made a second visit to Dr. Wesselhoeft's spa at Brattleboro. Here—perhaps, as we shall see, on account of emotional complications—his eyes, he wrote Norton, "relapsed into a state quite as bad certainly as they have been," and he had to leave "post-haste" for Staten Island. But a month more of Dr. Elliott's rest cure was now all that he could stand; he had learned well enough how to apply its lessons himself, and at the end of the year he went back to Boston. Though his eyes remained as troublesome as ever, the attacks of the "cerebral devil" became for the time being less importunate; composing in his mind as he paced the darkened garret of the Bowdoin Square house—the only exercise that the condition of his eyes permitted him on sunshiny days—he was able to push steadily enough his work on *Pontiac*, and, with relatives for readers and amanuenses, finished it in the winter of 1850–1851. Dreary as he might find his situation, compared with the imaginings of adolescence, the first shock of the catastrophe had worn off and a *modus vivendi* had been reached with "the enemy" —or so for the time it illusively seemed.

In the meanwhile, the struggle with invalidism had not precluded two stimulating friendships that date from this period, to say nothing of a stormy love affair apparently connected with the young man's visit to Brattleboro in the fall of 1848, and finally, his engagement to Catherine Bigelow in the spring of the next year.

The friends who figure most largely in Parkman's correspondence at this time are his cousin Charles Eliot Norton, then interested in ethnology, and Ephraim George Squier, a pioneer figure in anthropology and Indian archaeology. Apart from the specialized interests they shared in common with Parkman, the two men were of utterly contrasting types: Norton hiding an extraordinary, almost feminine talent for intimacy under an exterior of Boston gentility; Squier—though with his own warm gift of sympathy—an "original" of the saltiest kind, outgoing and exuberant, with a vein of iron like Parkman's own. Both, however, in their different ways, played a fortifying rôle in the young man's struggle against the demons of frustration and despair. To Norton, possessed, as I have said, of a talent for friendship that was to make him the confidant of so many spirits more forceful than himself, Parkman revealed as much of his anguish in its quick as he revealed to anyone at the time—

letters where the shaky pencil scrawl perhaps tells us even more than the words themselves. Squier, on the contrary, evoked some of the most characteristic expressions of the iron determination with which the young man faced the paralysis of his energies. "From a complete and ample experience of both," he wrote Squier in 1849, "I can bear witness that no amount of physical pain is so intolerable as the position of being stranded and doomed to lie rotting for year after year. However, I have not abandoned any plan which I have ever formed and I have no intention of abandoning any until I am made cold meat of." No sentence Parkman wrote has a more idiosyncratic ring.

In lesser ways, too, Squier's personality evoked from Parkman a freedom of reference for which the general run of his correspondence did not give the same scope. It is hard to suppose, for instance, his writing to Norton in quite the vein of his acknowledgment of Squier's book, *The Serpent Symbol and the Worship of the Reciprocal Principles of Nature in America*, a study of the sexual element in Indian religions: "Many thanks for it. Thus far I know nothing of its interior except the very captivating pictures of snakes, and unseemly phallic emblems which impress me with a desire for further information. . . . The reader, however [a high-school girl], will soon resume her labors, when I propose to enlighten her mind by a contemplation of the reciprocal powers of nature and the superstitions thereto belonging." And Parkman nowhere else expresses so sharply as in another letter, concerning Squier's ethnological activities in Central America, the importunings of the Mackinaw mood that Boston was perhaps peculiarly calculated to inspire: "I owe you a grudge, as [your narrative] kindled in me a burning desire to get among fevers and volcanoes, niggers, Indians and other outcasts of humanity, a restless fit which is apt to seize me at intervals and which you unmercifully exaggerate."

Masculine friendship, however, tonic as it might be, hardly answered the passional needs of Parkman's nature; and it is not surprising to find him in his mid-twenties again involved in a somewhat exacting affair of the heart—or this time, rather, a double affair of the heart.

What we can gather of this affair has to be pieced together from later references in Parkman's correspondence with Mary Dwight Parkman and from the "New Baden" episode in *Vassall Norton*. Though Fanny Euston in the novel, like the heroine, Edith Leslie, is modeled in part on Parkman's first love, Pamela Prentiss, it is apparent from his letters that in the New Baden episode Fanny is mainly intended to represent someone else, referred to in the letters as "B" or "Miss B": a woman—or girl, rather, as she is in the book —of rich emotional resources, but reckless and headstrong, to whom Parkman seems to have been strongly attracted not long before his engagement to Catherine Bigelow. Other links between the letters and the novel show that the whole episode in the novel is thinly disguised autobiography, and that it was devised, among other reasons, to give Parkman's version of circumstances, which, involving an abrupt break with one lady followed speedily by an engagement to another, gave rise at the time to a certain amount of unfavorable comment. "I have come to think," he wrote Mary Parkman in 1853, "that you have endeavored to place a friendly interpretation on circumstances of my past life, which seemed to justify and even to demand an unfavorable construction. Believe me, the kinder view is the more correct."

Briefly, the situation in the novel is as follows. Vassall, on a visit to a New England watering-place, recognizable as Brattleboro of the 1840's, is strongly drawn to the dashing and vivacious Fanny. While he is not exactly in love with the "handsome, dare-devil" girl, he finds himself "greatly troubled in regard to her—shaken and tossed with a variety of conflicting emotions." In spite of her wildness and waywardness, she also reveals "a deep vein of womanly tenderness," and the "multiplied and constantly changing phases of her character" all conspire to "keep [Vassall's] interest somewhat painfully excited." The situation, however, threatens to get out of hand. Interested as he is in Fanny, and responsive as she is to his interest, Vassall realizes that he does not wish to marry her, and feeling in danger of committing himself further than he intends, he decides to leave New Baden at once (as Parkman himself left Brattleboro "post-haste")—a decision, as the book gallantly puts it, "for which he was entitled to no little credit, if its merit is to be measured by the effort it cost him."

The dénouement of the episode takes place during Vassall's return to Boston, when he accidentally falls in with Edith Leslie, the heroine of the novel, to whom he has long been attached. On the rebound from the painful agitation of the affair with Fanny, Vassall is deeply moved by the encounter; "it seemed as if Fanny had kindled within him a flame which could not fix itself upon her, yet must needs find fuel somewhere," and he proposes to Edith. This somewhat abrupt shift of amatory interest is explained in a long apologue of a storm at sea, where "the wind came from every point of the compass" and "blew hot and cold by fits," until Vassall suddenly finds himself "safe on shore" in a scene "full of repose, and tranquil, graceful power," of which Edith Leslie is the personification. In the 1853 letter already quoted, Parkman speaks in exactly the same terms of his own marriage to Catherine Bigelow: "The change from then to now is a change from tempest to calm. Out of that tempest I saw a harbor of refuge; and looking for peace and rest, I found happiness."

Allowing for fictional heightenings and foreshortenings, and for the composite sources from which the portrait of Fanny was drawn, this New Baden episode of *Vassall Morton* may be taken in its essentials as Parkman's version of the circumstances that led to his own marriage. For the rest, it is not too indirectly hinted in the novel that one of the reasons for Vassall's retreat from New Baden was the disturbing nature of the erotic impulses that the affair aroused in him. After his first meeting with Fanny, for instance, he feels that whatever he had known of love before "was no more like this than a draught from a clear spring is like a draught of spiced wine"; and his apprehension that Fanny's "wayward will . . . may carry her, God knows whither" is matched by his fear in the allegory of the storm that he himself was about to "lose [his] reckoning altogether, and be blown away, body and soul." Couched in "period" novelese, all this has a slightly ridiculous air, but one can be sure that it is an expression in an alien medium of a perfectly authentic life style and the record of a perfectly autonomous choice. Parkman was hardly a George Apley. If the author of the *Knickerbocker* sketches now strikes the note of *mesure,* it was not from any deficiency of passion for which the appearance of *mesure* is a substitute.

As to Catherine Bigelow, her early death has left her a rather shadowy figure. She was, it appears, of a lively turn of mind, witty and entertaining to talk to; though fond of poetry, "more practical than intellectual" in her interests; and of an equable disposition, with a large fund, like Parkman himself, of inward warmth. The couple's married life of eight years, though marked by severe trials, and at the end by harrowing ones, was obviously based on a deep reciprocity of feeling, and if the marriage had hardly been entered upon in the spirit of a grand passion, it nevertheless brought Parkman a very positive sort of felicity. "Looking for peace and rest, I found happiness," he wrote Mary Parkman in 1853, as we have seen, and the letter goes on, "I owe unbounded gratitude to the source of that happiness, and I feel far more than gratitude." In a different key, a letter to Norton, the first summer of his marriage, strikes the same note: "Then . . . I was handsomely used up, soul and body on the rack. . . . You may judge whether my present condition is a more favorable one. I detest being spoony, but if you want to understand the thing, take a jump out of hellfire to the opposite extreme."

Shadows were to fall soon enough over this domestic idyll, as over the beginnings of achievement and public recognition that accompanied it. Nevertheless, in spite of all obstacles, *The Oregon Trail* and *Pontiac* were before the world, and the talents that had showed themselves tentatively in the *Knickerbocker* sketches of a few years earlier had now put forth their signal first fruits. *The Oregon Trail* is the most considerable by-product of the historical quest that records itself in the remarkable journals of Parkman's *Wanderjahre;* it also of course claims our attention in its own right as a narrative of travel and adventure. With *Pontiac* Parkman turns to the more exacting, and—for him—more deeply imaginative task for which all this was preparation, and we see him for the first time working in his most characteristic medium and in his most characteristic vein. He is not yet, to be sure, working to his best effect, but this maiden effort already displays his essential manner and method as an historian.

The Oregon Trail has had a curious literary life. It has always attracted readers and made its way on its own merits. After Parkman's death, however, extraneous circumstances—its use for many years in high school English courses, repeated allusion to it in the profuse literature of the Western movement, and a comparative lack of attention to the rest of Parkman's writings—combined to give it a somewhat factitious public fame. (It is indeed by far Parkman's best known book: a situation much as if Melville should figure for us almost exclusively as the author of *Typee* or *Omoo*.) More recently, with the recovery of the original journals on which it was based, the book has been correspondingly undervalued. The fresh material and the more colloquial style of the journals have given rise to extravagant claims; and indeed the eye of a passionate Western antiquarianism has discerned in them the elements of a great lost sociohistoric work on the West, of which the actual *Oregon Trail* is only an abortion; a work which Parkman was deflected from writing by the "Brahmin snobberies," an overaddiction to Cooper, the purely sporting interests of Quincy Shaw, and the squeamishness of Charles Eliot Norton (who prepared the magazine version for book publication and did in fact bowdlerize some of Parkman's references to sex and liquor).

Impressive as the journals are, they hardly support such a claim, and there is no evidence that Parkman had any intention of writing a book different in kind from the book he actually did write: of a kind, that is to say, in which, for good reasons, the age particularly abounded, and of which Melville's *Typee* and *Omoo* are specimens, or Dana's *Two Years Before the Mast*, or Stephens's account of the lost Maya cities, or, to confine ourselves to the American West, books like Ruxton's *Adventures in Mexico and the Rocky Mountains* or Garrard's *Wah-to-Yah*. Whether or not Parkman should have written a different kind of book is another question, but the journals, to repeat, can hardly be said to reveal any major distortion of emphasis between the day-to-day records of the experience and their final reworking in the shape of a narrative of travel.

Naturally in such a reworking very real questions of loss or gain arise. For one thing, Parkman rather plays down in the book the professional and technical aspects of his search for the Indian, and does not reproduce seriatim as they appear in the journal the ethnological data he gathered from continual questioning of Henry Chatillon, Reynal, and others. Nevertheless, in the manner of his histories, he incorporated most of this material—or as much of it as he had tested by actual observation—unobtrusively but to striking effect in the account of his stay with the Oglala, and the deletion of the notes in their original undigested form is hardly to be regretted.

More serious for the general reader is the omission from the book, which opens with Parkman and Shaw on their way from St. Louis to Westport, of all the preliminaries of the trip—the voyage down the Ohio, the talks at St. Louis with Fitzpatrick and the elders of the fur trade, the visit to Cahokia, the glimpse of Henry Clay in the lobby of the Planters' House, exercising those arts "by which politicians—even the best of them—thrive," and so on. Not only is all this material omitted, but the book itself gets under way somewhat tentatively as far as the writing is concerned, and the opening chapters are certainly inferior in interest and liveliness to the journal entries. If one hardly discerns here the elements of a different book from the one Parkman actually wrote, one nevertheless feels that the book he did write would have been somewhat richer on its own grounds for the sort of prologue to the central episode that the journals give.

Further than this it is difficult to go with Parkman's westernizing commentators. Once the book hits its stride, its relation to the journal is the perfectly normal one of developed narrative to brief field notes, with all the advantages the more complexly organized form offers for rendering the subject that is central to both—Parkman's stay with the Oglala, that is to say, and the events that led up to it. This experience was the core at once of trip, journal, and book; the book is planned and executed to set it in relief; and no better medium could be found for doing so than the one Parkman chose, the narrative of travel, that is, as it flourished in the first half of the nineteenth century. It is, we feel, fundamentally the nature of Parkman's experience itself with which his commentators quarrel; and the phantom of a great lost work on the West conjured up from the journals is the projection of an a priori judgment as to the aspects of the West Parkman ought to have emphasized. Since the journals show that Parkman took in, sociohistorically speaking, more of the background of the "Western movement" than might be gathered from the book, and since this Western movement of the historians is what Parkman should mainly have concerned himself with, rather than with Indians, *ergo*, compared to the journals, *The Oregon Trail* is a miscarriage of literary effort. But enough has perhaps been said already as to the essential seriousness, validity, and import of Parkman's central theme, and the irrelevance of viewing it solely in the context of the Western movement. In regard to theme and content at least, the journals do not greatly modify our conception of the book that was fashioned from them.

When we turn from matter to manner, to be sure, the question of gains and losses becomes more acute. The prose of the journals is a crisp, incisive vernacular of a distinctly modern cast. The prose of the book, on the other hand, is basically the public prose of Parkman's time, the—from our point of view—somewhat formal, "mandarin" English that, with whatever individual modifications, served the purposes of his contemporaries from Hawthorne and Melville to Bayard Taylor. This is a prose that precludes certain effects— precisely, of course, those that depend on a simpler syntactical structure and a more colloquial diction—and Parkman by no means always manages it to its own best effect. Yet, by and large, the prose of *The Oregon Trail* hardly strikes us as deficient in expressiveness or as "dated" in more than the superficial sense in which we would say that the prose of *Typee* or *Our Old Home* is dated. The experience as Parkman felt it called for a depth and roundness of presentation beyond the scope of the journal style—just as it called for a kind of narrative continuity beyond the scope of the journal form—and such a presentation could only have been achieved through some such denser, more complex verbal medium as the one Parkman adopted. We can regret that much of the vernacular quality of the journal was lost in the process, but, again, the quarrel of Parkman's latter-day commentators with the style of *The Oregon Trail* is, we feel, fundamentally a quarrel with the nature of Parkman's experience itself, or his mode of apprehending it, rather than with his manner of presenting it. It is a quarrel, that is to say, with an imagination that in the end looked for the reality of things to their inwardness of meaning, and worked more congenially through the recollected and re-created impression than through the immediate impression, however vigorous and sharp.

Nevertheless the prose of the journal is unexceptionable within its limits and for its purposes, while the prose of the book, if it attempts something more exacting and on the whole achieves it, is not a perfectly mastered instrument. "Yesterday rode down with Paul Dorion . . . to Richard's fort," we read in the journal. "Found there Russell's or Bogg's comp'y, engaged in drinking and refitting, and a host of Canadians besides. Russell drunk as a pigeon." Parkman, with reason, wanted to make more of this incident in the book and elaborated it. We see Russell, for instance, "haranguing the company in the style of a stump orator," while "with one hand he sawed the air, and with the other clutched firmly a brown jug of whiskey, which he applied every moment to his lips, forgetting that he had drained the contents long ago." But compared to the journal this is of course depressing; the effect is labored, and the drop in expressiveness from the vernacular of "drunk as a pigeon" a stylistic fiasco.

Sometimes, too, descriptive passages are done in the journal with a painterly crispness of touch, for the loss of which little in the more elaborated book version compensates. The scene of Old Smoke's village crossing the creek at Laramie is an example. The journal

entry, for instance, closes as follows: "—dogs barking, horses breaking loose, children laughing and shouting—squaws thrusting into
the ground the lance and shield of the master of the lodge—naked
and splendidly formed men passing and repassing through the swift
water." In the book this becomes: "As each horse gained the bank he
scrambled up as he could. Stray horses and colts came among the
rest, often breaking away at full speed through the crowd, followed
by old hags screaming after their fashion on all occasions of excitement. Buxom young squaws, blooming in all the charms of vermilion,
stood here and there on the bank, holding aloft their master's lance,
as a signal to collect the scattered portions of his household." This
again, with its wordiness and its tawdry "buxom" and "blooming,"
is a sad falling off from the prose of the journal, and Parkman's retouching only blurs the tellingly painterlike strokes he had originally
achieved.

In such passages Parkman made the mistake of not letting well
enough alone. As might be expected, the book is most successful,
compared to the journal, when Parkman uses the journal simply as
a starting point, and taking some brief, factual entry, re-creates scene
or incident freshly in his mind from the recall of it which the journal
reference evokes. Once by the Platte he got lost on a buffalo hunt.
"Got separated from the others—" the journal runs, "rode for hours
westwardly over the prairie—saw the hills dotted with thousands of
buffalo. Antelopes—prairie-dogs—burrowing owls—wild geese—
wolves, etc. Finding my course wrong, followed a buffalo-track
northward, and about noon came out on the road. Awkward feeling,
being lost on the prairie." This is succinct and incisive, but it is
quick with unrealized potentialities that demand a different kind of
treatment, and only when we turn to Parkman's development of
the passage in the book does a full sense of the experience com-
municate itself.

But in the meantime my ride had been by no means a solitary one. The
face of the country was dotted far and wide with countless hundreds of
buffalo. They trooped along in files and columns, bulls, cows, and calves,
on the green faces of the declivities in front. They scrambled away over

the hills to the right and left; and far off, the pale blue swells in the extreme distance were dotted with innumerable specks. Sometimes I surprised shaggy old bulls grazing alone, or sleeping behind the ridges I ascended. They would leap up at my approach, stare stupidly at me through their tangled manes, and then gallop heavily away. The antelope were very numerous; and as they are always bold when in the neighborhood of buffalo, they would approach to look at me, gaze intensely with their great round eyes, then suddenly leap aside, and stretch lightly away over the prairie, as swiftly as a race-horse. Squalid, ruffian-like wolves sneaked through the hollows and sandy ravines. Several times I passed through villages of prairie-dogs, who sat, each at the mouth of his burrow, holding his paws before him in a supplicating attitude, and yelping away most vehemently, whisking his little tail with every squeaking cry he uttered. Prairie-dogs are not fastidious in their choice of companions; various long checkered snakes were sunning themselves in the midst of the village, and demure little gray owls, with a large white ring around each eye, were perched side by side with the rightful inhabitants. The prairie teemed with life. Again and again I looked toward the crowded hillsides, and was sure I saw horsemen; and riding near, with a mixture of hope and dread, for Indians were abroad, I found them transformed into a group of buffalo. There was nothing in human shape amid all this vast congregation of brute forms.

When I turned down the buffalo path, the prairie seemed changed; only a wolf or two glided by at intervals, like conscious felons, never looking to the right or left. Being now free from anxiety, I was at leisure to observe minutely the objects around me; and here, for the first time, I noticed insects wholly different from any of the varieties found farther to the eastward. Gaudy butterflies fluttered about my horse's head; strangely formed beetles, glittering with metallic lustre, were crawling upon plants that I had never seen before; multitudes of lizards, too, were darting like lightning over the sand.

There are, to be sure, dubious touches in this, such as the somewhat theatrical wolves, gliding by like "conscious felons"; and there are places where we could wish the prose were tighter knit. But, taken as a whole, how preponderately the balance of gains and losses lies in favor of the book! Here terseness and sharpness of statement are barriers to communication: the greater complexity of detail and structure of the book version is the means to a positive release of imaginative force, manifesting itself in rhythm and cadence, and a sustained movement from sentence to sentence; and the experience hardly exists until it thus unfolds itself touch by touch from the germ of the journal note.

So in the opening, for instance, a sense of illimitable space is evoked by the incantatory echoing of "far" in "far and wide" and "far off," and by the lingering vowels and liquids of "pale blue swells" that slow up the movement for a moment at a climax, when the eye reaches the verge of the horizon. At the same time there is an equally kinesthetic force of a different kind in the "files and columns, bulls, cows, and calves" of the second sentence, where the words troop along like the buffalo themselves: or, a sentence or two below, in "gaze intensely with their great round eyes, then leap suddenly aside, and stretch lightly away over the prairie," where, in the same way, the syllabic pattern shapes itself to the antelope's movement of pause and flight. So stroke by stroke this land vision of buffalo herds and teeming animal life builds itself up for us to somewhat the same imaginative effect—in kind, at least, if not here in degree—as the sea visions of a slightly elder contemporary, re-creating what he had seen a little before this of vast whale herds swarming in the depths of the Pacific. The elements of the passage indeed recur with haunting persistency through Parkman's work. We shall find evocations of boundless space marking crucial passages of *Pontiac* and *Pioneers*, and the vision of pullulating animal life, which had already begun to take shape in the little ms. narrative of his 1841 Magalloway trip, reappears in various settings with thematic enrichments and increasing imaginative force until Parkman achieves his culminating version of it in the 1885 revision of *Pioneers*. But intimations of what he was to make of it are evident enough in this Western setting of it; and what he does here with the journal entry becomes prevailingly what he does with the journal as the book reaches its central episode and his theme begins fully to engage his imagination.

For all this the verbal medium of the book achieves—by and large, and whatever the occasional flaws in Parkman's handling of it—the authentic congruence of matter and manner that makes us feel that the subject was to be treated in the way it is treated and not in another way; that makes us feel that *this* and not something else was the ultimate meaning of the experience. The journal indeed, because of the conditions under which it was kept, becomes more and more meager and abbreviated after the opening phase of the trip, and one has only to test the richer, more expressive effect of the book by supposing the book to have remained *perdu* and the journal to have been the only public version of the venture. In such a case, for one thing, we should probably be as much struck by the fresh material to be found in the book as we now are by what was omitted from it. Incidents like that of Parkman's leading Pauline up the pass on his hands and knees do not appear at all in the journal, nor a wealth of incidents, scenes, and characterizing details of Indian life, particularly of Indian domestic life, like the inimitable scene of Big Crow's singing to his baby son, for instance, or disposing of his erring concubine.

But more importantly, it is only from the book that we become aware of the reach of perception and expressive power which here both exhibits the Indian world to the life as a functioning cultural organism and makes of the individuals that compose it the only really plausible Indians in the whole literature of the subject—a realism that was a shock to some of Parkman's contemporaries, including Melville, who did not know Indians at first hand. However sharp an observer the journal shows Parkman to have been, without the book we should scarcely surmise the gifts that could integrate these observations into an organized whole, and, as in his histories, make a "breathing reality" from such raw material of documentation; the gifts that here span the gap of cultural otherness as in his histories they span the gap of past time.

Finally, quickened as the journal is by the inwardness of the impulsions that sent Parkman on his quest, the very sharpness of his immediate impressions as he sets them down obscures for us the peculiarly compelling quality of this inwardness—the truth of vision, as well as the truth of fact—which sets *The Oregon Trail* apart from any other book on the West. Only some less cursory manner than that of the journal could have succeeded in communicating this quality, and, again, it is only from the book that we realize the force of conception, which, as for analogous matter in the histories, lifts to a quasi-symbolic level its account of the perilous passage of the mountains, the sojourn in the hidden fastness beyond, the sickness of the sojourner, and the life of the lost world he seeks to retrieve—the whole episode, in short, that was the reason for the journey. In sum, if, as I have said, the book rather than the journal had been recovered from the limbo of Parkman's work desk, our regrets at the loss of stylistic sharpness and vernacular flavor would be quite swallowed up in the revelation of what the writing of the book does for the experience by way of imparting roundness and fullness and psychological depth, and we should hardly cavil at a manner so effectively expressive of what the experience had come to mean when time had a little distanced it and put it in perspective, and the task of re-creating it had unlocked the more fundamental resources of Parkman's imagination.

Disengaging *The Oregon Trail*, then, from a priori notions of what it should have been about and how it should have been written, we can view it for what it is. Here, as I have suggested, its closest affinities are with Melville's *Typee*. There is, of course, a world of difference between the books, as between the temperaments and talents of their authors. In a documentary sense *The Oregon Trail* is the solider of the two, and Parkman's portrayal of the Sioux is better informed, more rounded, and more lifelike than Melville's portrayal of the Marquesans. On the other hand, though *Typee* does not surpass *The Oregon Trail* in *depth* of imaginative response to their kindred theme, it is the product of an imagination vastly more ductile and wide-ranging than Parkman's, and more directly expressive of the play of personality. But it is the fundamental similarities, rather than the differences, that concern us here—the common impulse behind both books, and the common import that both books, though ostensibly written to "amuse," impart to the quest that is their theme; and it is only by some such collocation that one places *The Oregon Trail* in the context of reference that best explains it. Except for *Typee*, no other American book is so deeply stamped with the seriousness which the experience that each describes could have in the conditions of the time or grasps so compellingly the peculiar opportunity offered by the time for putting to the test of actuality the recurrent archetypal fantasy which in each is the motive of this experience. Here, as I have said, the West spoke to the human condition with perhaps its richest meaning; and *The Oregon Trail* owes its preeminence as a book on the West precisely to what it makes of the West in this sense, to its discrimination, among other possible meanings, of this meaning.

Nevertheless there are limits to our interest in *The Oregon Trail*. However fruitful and formative, and however deeply felt, the experience was after all a peripheral one; and the mode of personal narrative, however useful for Parkman's immediate ends, only partly engaged his special powers. The book, indeed, most awakens our responsiveness in the degree to which it suggests the manner of his histories, and rises to its most expressive level when it confronts a task of creation similar to that of his histories. In *Pontiac* where the ground of treatment shifts altogether from the direct presentation of personal experience to the interfusing in the imagination of the data of such experience with the *données* of historic circumstance, we realize how native the historical mode is to Parkman's talents and bent of temperament, and see him, as I have said, working for the first time in the medium most congenial to him. *Pontiac*, to be sure, confronted him with the problem of vivifying the Indian theme at two removes—of now spanning at once both the gap of historic time as well as the gap of cultural otherness. For reasons which will be apparent, the double problem proved insoluble even for him, at least on the level of actualization his conception of historical writing demanded. But if *Pontiac* is a partial failure in a sense in which *The Oregon Trail* is not, the scope of the theme that underlies both books is immensely enhanced when the historical mode itself provides the kind of distancing necessary to the best exercise of Parkman's gift of vivification; when an actual historical conflict becomes the objective equivalent for the inner conflicts that drew him to the theme; and when, instead of through the "I" of personal narrative, his dramatizing instincts can work through a given cast of historical characters.

CHAPTER VII

PONTIAC AND HISTORY: THE FABRIC OF STYLE

⚜ ⚜ ⚜

As the preface states, Parkman's aim in *Pontiac* was "to portray the American forest and the American Indian at the period when both received their final doom"; a doom implicit in the overthrow of New France and spelled out by the failure of the Indian rising under Pontiac that followed—the most formidable of its kind in American annals. The subject of the book is thus the close of the first phase of a portentous episode in the extraordinary raying out from Europe of Western civilization on which the modern world is founded, and the earlier steps of which on the North American continent—the primary exploration of the interior by the French and the clash for hegemony with the English—the main body of Parkman's history was to trace. In this afterpiece to his main history he deals particularly with the subversion or extinction of indigenous peoples and indigenous cultures that everywhere was the reverse side of the process of Western expansion. Less spectacular than some of its analogues like the Spanish conquests of Mexico and Peru, the North American struggle was nevertheless uniquely decisive in its import for the future: its obscure brush fights sealed the doom of "the forest and the Indian" on a wider than local scale and with a more than literal finality, and its outcome signalized an irrevocable shift in the balance of the world. Both as fact and symbol, then, the downfall of the forest had its central bearing on the "nineteenth century," on the urbanized, industrialized, mechanized culture that was shaping itself beneath the surface of the untrammeled Jacksonian time when Parkman's histories were conceived; and the thematic strength

161

of *Pontiac*, as of the rest of his histories, derives from the perception it embodies of this filiation and the intuition that informs them of the main drift and trend of latter-day Western civilization, as it was to unfold itself on American grounds, no less, or precisely even more, ambiguously for the human condition than elsewhere. The theme of the forest and the Indian, to be sure, was hardly a novel one in American letters, and with Cooper had begun notably to haunt the American imagination. But if Parkman's manner of handling the theme in *Pontiac* still shows traces of Cooper's influence, the quality of his feeling for it is closer to D. H. Lawrence than to Cooper, and just as his sense of it is conditioned by a more complex and exacting commitment than Cooper's to the imperatives of "civilization," so his treatment of it in *Pontiac* raises it from the level of fantasy on which Cooper approached it to the level of genuine tragedy—at least in conception, if here not altogether successfully in execution.

The partial failure of Parkman's intention in *Pontiac* arises most obviously from his attempt to make its titular hero a living character in the sense that the "white" actors in the drama are living characters, a tragic protagonist whose figure is meant to dominate the book. This is a conception Parkman lacked the materials to realize. More importantly, however, there is a certain confusion in the book as to which of its elements is actually the main focus of tragic emphasis. That is to say, what emerges is not so much the tragedy of the Indian, the ostensible subject, but the tragedy, or the possibility of tragedy, latent in the ethos of the conquering West itself. Likewise, we have to note in *Pontiac*, as in *The Oregon Trail*, an as yet imperfect mastery of the medium of expression, an occasional over-rhetorical quality of style, which in his later years indeed gave Parkman himself a distaste for the book.[1] But we shall return to these

[1] The standard edition of *Pontiac* is the revised version of 1870, incorporating new material that had come to light during the nineteen years since the first publication of the book. So far as historical interpretation is concerned, the most important difference is the decidedly less favorable view Parkman took of Lord Amherst as commander-in-chief of the British forces in America. The revision also comprised extensive verbal changes making for greater sobriety of style, such as the entire omission of a

points presently. For the moment we are concerned with the aspects of *Pontiac* that already make sufficiently evident Parkman's characteristic traits as an historian.

These are, to put the matter baldly, a grasp of theme that invests a remote and—at first view—minor historical subject with central relevance and the tensions of tragedy; a gift for dramatic narrative that at once vivifies the subject in detail and organizes its elements into a thematically expressive structural whole; and, finally, a sense of fact and relationships, and a thoroughness and judgment in determining them, that make of this whole in the highest degree a specifically *historical* structure.

These are traits that are rarely found combined in historical writing, at least in such harmonious balance; and it is of course our sense of their felicitous interplay—of a fusion at the highest level of the subjective and objective elements essential to greatness in historical writing—that underlies our satisfaction with Parkman as an historian. To emphasize one set of elements at the expense of another, as the scope of this book largely compels us to do, is inevitably to risk a degree of falsification. Even the lay reader is aware of how deeply the imaginative effect of Parkman's work is rooted in its impeccable factuality—in the minuteness and exhaustiveness of research, the perfect mastery of the historical *données*, the famous "methodology" which set a standard in these matters still unsuperseded; and, speaking merely on aesthetic grounds, we can hardly afford to overlook this basic quality of truth to fact—of literal and certifiable authenticity—without our thorough conviction of which the writing of history fails to move us, or moves us imperfectly, no matter what its other qualities.[2] So, again, of Parkman's sense of relationships: if

---

highly overcolored sunset piece that occurs in the original account of Detroit on the eve of the siege. The passages I quote for discussion, however, remain unchanged in the later version.

[2] To quote once more from an often-quoted passage in G. M. Trevelyan's *History of England:* "In the realm of History, the moment we have reason to think we are being given fiction instead of fact, be the fiction never so brilliant, our interest collapses like a pricked balloon. To hold

at a first reading of Parkman we are perhaps struck most of all by the sheer momentum of the narrative and its almost hallucinatory effect of actuality, we are equally struck on a second reading by its discrimination of the causes and conditions underlying the surface pattern of events, Parkman's grasp of which essentials has left his work, of all great nineteenth century histories, perhaps the least open to reconsideration in the light of later shifts of emphasis and points of view. Here, again speaking merely on aesthetic grounds, we can hardly afford to overlook an element so indispensable to the effect of the work as a whole and without a fundamental tincture of which no brilliance of narrative in historical writing is redeemed from thinness.

In short, whatever analogies his work suggests with other forms of literature, Parkman writing history is radically and quintessentially an historian, and not a poet or dramatist or novelist *manqué;* and his work is indefeasibly history, and not, as to some extent we feel even with Carlyle, a straining beyond the limits of historical writing toward some other medium of expression—as we might say of *The French Revolution,* in certain respects at least, that it is less properly history than an amazing anticipation of the art of the cinema. The point might seem too obvious to insist on; unless we insist on it, however, we are in some danger, as has been said, of supposing the effectiveness of Parkman's writing to be bought at the cost of the specific qualities that differentiate the historic mode from other modes of writing; or, if we wish to look at the matter in the light of the history of historical writing, of seeming to approach him in terms of a once common—and misleading—antithesis between the "scientific" and the "literary" historian. Parkman was, of course, conspicuously both, and here, as everywhere in his work, we have to do with an organic fusion of apparent opposites: scientific method and artistic sensibility; rational judgment and imaginative insight; factual realism and the evocativeness of poetry. To

---

our interest [the historian] must tell us something we believe to be true about the men who once walked the earth. It is the fact about the past that is poetic; just because it really happened, it gathers round it all the inscrutable mystery of life and death and time."

isolate and emphasize one term of these pairs to the neglect of the other, one must reiterate, is to risk giving a distorted impression of the whole.

Nevertheless, all critical analysis involves some such isolating process; and, after all, historical writing as a work of art and imagination was paramount in Parkman's own conception of what he was doing, of what he called "the task of rekindling [the life of his subject], calling out of the dust the soul and body of it and making it a breathing reality." Parkman here defines—or perhaps paraphrases Michelet in defining—the task of vivification, of truth to imaginative actuality (together in Parkman's case with the new standards of research, of literal and exhaustive truth to fact, insisted on by Ranke) that is the most striking aspect of history writing in the first half of the nineteenth century: *"la condition nouvelle imposée à l'histoire,"* as Michelet put it, *"non plus de raconter seulement ou juger, mais d'évoquer, refaire, ressuciter les âges. Avoir assez de flamme pour réchauffer des cendres refroidies si longtemps, c'était le premier point. . . . Le second . . . c'était d'être en commerce avec ces morts ressucités, qui sait? d'être enfin un des leurs."* [3] This

[3] The passage is from the preface to Michelet's *Histoire de France.* Besides the corresponding passage from Parkman's 1886 letter to Martin Brimmer quoted above, one should also cite the following from his Introduction to *Pioneers* (1865) with its emphasis at the end on Michelet's second point—*"d'être en commerce avec ces morts ressucités . . . d'être enfin un des leurs."*

"Faithfulness to the truth of history involves far more than a research, however patient and scrupulous, into special facts . . . The narrator must seek to imbue himself with the life and spirit of the time. He must study events in their bearings near and remote; in the character, habits, and manners of those who took part in them. He must himself be, as it were, a sharer or spectator of the action he describes."

As we have noted, Michelet is among the writers Parkman drew on for the abstract of European history in which he summarized the intensive reading of his law school years. Later, the records of the Boston Athenaeum show him borrowing volumes of the *Histoire de France* during the 1850's and 1860's, particularly the marvelous second volume, on the Middle Ages, which he had out three times.

He apparently did not read German, and would not have known at first hand—though he no doubt did through secondary sources—Ranke's essay on historical method in his *Geschichte römanischen und germanischen*

conception of historical writing itself takes its cue from literature. Except perhaps for Chateaubriand, it was of course Sir Walter Scott, as much as any single individual, who laid on history the obligation of "evoking, recreating, revivifying" the past that Michelet defines as the historian's primary task; and this task called for literary ability in the historian of a new and special kind: an imagination, sensibility, and expressive power, in short, parallel to that of the novelist, that could invest reality with the illusion of imaginative invention, as the novelist invests imaginative invention with the illusion of reality. Thus, distinguish as we must between the aspects of life that are the special provinces of history and fiction, we have to do with an approach to history that is at one with fiction in its creative aim and shares many of its means. To conjure up from the inchoate data of the historical record a world like the novelist's of living action and living human beings was for Parkman of the essence of the matter; and, providing we remember that the most scrupulous fidelity to the data of the historical record was also of the essence of the matter, we do no great violence to Parkman's achievement if we subordinate other considerations to a view of him as writer and artist.

But, finally and emphatically, there is also a sense in which, if we are to understand Parkman *as an historian*, we not only may but *must* approach him on the side of literature. Though the task that Scott had imposed on history of re-creating the past in its characteristic colors as a living entity added a whole new dimension to historical writing, such vivfication of and for its own sake takes an historian only so far. There still remains, for one thing, the necessity already mentioned, of interpreting the facts as well as of

---

Völker (1824) which opened the way to the "scientific" study of modern history and in which occurs the celebrated—if highly ambiguous—dictum that historical writing was not a matter of judging the past or instructing the future but simply a laboratory demonstration of how things actually happened (*"wie es eigentlich gewesen"*). It is evident from Parkman's law school notebooks that he knew S. Austin's translation (1840, revised editions 1841 and 1847) of Ranke's *History of the Papacy*.

determining them accurately and of bringing them to life—the necessity, that is to say, of relating the foreground play of events to the conditions that shape them and are shaped by them, of evaluating the actions of the human agents through whom events come to pass in the light of these relationships. If revivification of the past is the most distinctive aspect of the "new" history of the early nineteenth century as Michelet envisages it, he did not conceive that it dispensed the historian from his obligation of "judging" or interpreting.

But I have already touched on this point; and our concern here is with "interpretation" in a deeper or more inward sense: the kind of traffic between the historian and his subject that establishes the ultimate pattern of meaning in the interest of which (perhaps largely unconsciously) he discriminates the elements of his subject and, as the case may be, moralizes them or philosophizes them or deploys his arts of vivification to bring them home to us—the apprehension, say, of what it was to be a citizen of a Greek *polis* that pervades Thucydides; the image of the Age of Reason which Antonine Rome reflected back to Gibbon; the feeling for the ambiguities of nineteenth century civilization that shapes Parkman's vision of the forest. Beyond individual differences of temperament and of modes of seeing life, this is the final, the indispensable element of subjectiveness in an historian, and thus in some sense it is always a matter of "literature": a matter of accent and emphasis that makes itself felt through the medium of words. But here, again, in Parkman's case, we have to do with literature in a considerably more limited sense, the sense, that is, in which his manner as an artist relates him to contemporaries like Hawthorne and Melville and derives from the revolution in sensibility that first revealed itself conspicuously in English in the "new" poetry of the century's beginning. To reach his essential meaning as an historian, we must bring to bear on our reading of him, to repeat, the same kind of responsiveness we bring to bear on the reading of such prose and such poetry, where suggestion, symbol, and evocation are the heart of the matter.

Having said so much, one is at once impelled to qualify. If Parkman's forest, for instance, has profound affinities with the forest of

The Scarlet Letter, or with the sea of *Moby Dick,* there is an essential aspect of his work that is reflected in his fondness for writers like La Rochefoucauld and the Duc de Saint Simon, or in the fact that Jane Austen was the favorite novelist of his maturity; and the strain of social and psychological realism that such tastes indicate is fundamental to the effect of his work as a whole—fundamental indeed to its mere being as history. Parkman is as much a master of this mode as he is of the mode of imaginative suggestiveness, of evocation and symbol, that relates him to Hawthorne and Melville; and, again, it is the harmonious blending of these diverse strains that conditions our response to him. Nevertheless—and necessarily so—it is the more inward mode that is the organizing principle, that, interfusing the solid realism of Parkman's presentation of character and event, establishes the controlling thematic pattern and forces us in reading him to attend above all to what is conveyed through evocative rhythm and cadence, through an instinct for sensory detail that creates an almost hallucinatory atmosphere of immediacy, through meaningful gradations in the degree of intensity with which this power of hallucinatory vividness makes itself felt, and through the heightening of tone—by these and other means—that charges certain elements of the subject with symbolic values; through an artistry, in short, which, if it underlines, amplifies, intensifies what comes to us by way of overt comment, works on us finally in ways and to effects of meaning beyond the reach of overt comment and explicit statement.

But this is to look beyond *Pontiac* to the writings of Parkman's maturity where this aspect of his historical art—and it is its most distinctive aspect—achieves its consummation. *Pontiac,* as I have said, displays this artistry of evocation and suggestion in characteristic if not always fully perfected form, and we shall trace the pattern of theme it establishes. For the moment, however, we must dwell a little more particularly on the countermode of factuality and realism, already alluded to, which is as integral as its opposite to the final effect; or at least we shall examine the texture of Parkman's prose as it adapts itself on the one hand to this realistic strain, and, on the other, to the complementary strain of imaginative vision.

In so far as both concern style and manner, the question is one of that sober ground, against which, in the Baconian adage, lively colors show best; of a comparatively neutral, if expressive, medium of discourse, from which and back to which the writer can modulate for the elements of his subject that more deeply engage his imagination, but which in the meanwhile dispatches with a maximum of effectiveness the more ordinary historical business that authenticates for us these moments of intenser emphasis. One might illustrate with passages that show Parkman engaged in the more specialized forms of such business—evaluation of evidence, analysis of causes and conditions, mooting of controversial points, and so on—but in *Pontiac* his stylistic touch in this expository kind, though evident enough, is relatively less certain than in his later work, and its vigor is bought at a certain cost of overheightened or overelaborate rhetorical emphasis. Instead, we shall choose a paragraph of simple narrative, where we have to do with an achieved piece of prose. Here then is Parkman actualizing the siege of Detroit for us, not at its moments of crisis, but in its everyday activities—or lack of activity.

Time passed on, and brought little change and no relief to the harassed and endangered garrison. Day after day the Indians continued their attacks, until their war-cries and the rattle of their guns became familiar sounds. For many weeks, no man lay down to sleep, except in his clothes, and with his weapons by his side. Parties sallied, from time to time, to burn the outbuildings, which gave shelter to the enemy. They cut down orchard trees, and levelled fences, until the ground about the fort was clear and open, and the enemy had no cover left whence to fire. The two vessels in the river, sweeping the northern and southern curtains of the works with their fire, deterred the Indians from approaching those points, and gave material aid to the garrison. Still, worming their way through the grass, sheltering themselves behind every rising ground, the pertinacious savages would crawl close to the palisade, and shoot arrows, tipped with burning tow, upon the roofs of the houses; but cisterns and tanks of water were everywhere provided against such an emergency, and these attempts proved abortive. The little church, which stood near the palisade, was particularly exposed, and would probably have been set on fire, had not the priest of the settlement threatened Pontiac with the vengeance of the Great Spirit, should he be guilty of such sacrilege. Pontiac, who was filled with eagerness to get possession of the garrison, neglected no expedient that his savage tactics could supply. He went farther, and begged the French inhabitants to teach him the European method of attacking a fortified place by regular approaches; but the rude Canadians knew as little of the matter as he; or, if, by chance, a few were better informed, they wisely preferred to conceal their knowledge. Soon after the first attack, the Ottawa chief had sent in to Gladwyn a summons to surrender, assuring him that, if the place were at once given up, he might embark on board the vessels, with all his men; but that, if he persisted in his defence, he would treat him as Indians treat each other; that is, he would burn him alive. To this Gladwyn made answer that he cared nothing for his threats. The attacks were now renewed with increased activity, and the assailants were soon after inspired with fresh ardor by the arrival of a hundred and twenty Ojibwa warriors from Grand River. Every man in the fort, officers, soldiers, traders, and *engagés*, now slept upon the ramparts; even in stormy weather none were allowed to withdraw to their quarters; yet a spirit of confidence and cheerfulness still prevailed among the weary garrison.

Two things strike us about the prose of this passage. On the one hand, we note the nonconnotative, almost baldly factual quality of its diction—the lack of visionary evocativeness, which distinguishes it from the *Oregon Trail* passage I have discussed. On the other hand, we note the pervasive Parkmanian kinesthesia, which, if here adapted to different ends, it shares with that passage, and which turns the low-keyed monochromatic quality of its verbal coloring to positive effect; emphasizing the unemphatic, so to speak, so that when we come to the more spectacular events that follow, the routine, quotidian aspects of the siege remain a fundamental element in our apprehension of the whole.

Thus—to look at details—throughout the first part of the paragraph, the grouping and structure of the opening sentences themselves remarkably reinforce the explicit indications of routine and repetitive action in phrases like "time passed on," "day after day," and so on, which establish the general tone of the paragraph. We have, that is, a block of four successive sentences of almost identical length—sixteen to twenty words—and, together with the next sentence, a block of five sentences of almost identical structure and rhythmic pattern: "Time passed on, and. . . . Day after day the Indians continued their attacks, until. . . . For many weeks no man lay down to sleep, except. . . . Parties sallied, from time to time, to burn. . . . They cut down orchard trees, and levelled fences, until. . . ." Unless offset by some coloring of diction, or other emphasis, which is absent here, this pattern of subject and verb at the beginning, trailed by modifying clauses or phrases, is the most anticlimactic, the least dramatic of sentence patterns; and the fivefold recurrence of it in successive sentences at the start creates an effect of repetitiveness and stasis that pervades the whole paragraph and informs with the same effect every other sentence of similar pattern. In short, simply through its verbal structure, the paragraph itself *is* that state of "little change and no relief" it sets out to describe.

So much for fundamental tone. But if this writing creates an atmosphere of monotony which the subject matter indicates, it is not of course monotonous writing. For one thing, there are distinctions to be made among the kinds of repetitive action described, some being more striking than others. Thus, after the first four sentences, the movement begins to point to a minor climax. The fifth sentence, as I have said—"They cut down orchard trees," etc.—follows the pattern of the first four, but now with a notable increase in length, to twenty-eight words, which here by itself has an intensive effect. Then with the sentence that follows, on the daily bombardment by the vessels, the change of movement becomes more marked. A relatively long and emphatic participial phrase—"sweeping the northern and southern curtains . . ."—interposes between subject and verb; and the falling rhythm of the opening sentences begins to give way to a rising one. With the attempts of the Indian to set the fort on fire, the most arresting of these more or less routine events, the movement completes itself. A longer, more emphatic, and now double-membered participial phrase—"worming their way . . . , sheltering themselves"—suspends the entrance of both subject and verb; this "periodic" structure in turn brings to a crest the rising rhythm of the sentence before; and we ride this rhythmic crest with the flight of the fire arrows, so to speak, until the sentence piles up against the semicolon. Yet the effect of all this, of course, is relative only and subordinated to the dominant tone of the paragraph. So, in keeping with the abortiveness of the Indians' incendiary efforts, the rhythmic impetus quickly levels off and ebbs through the rest of the climax sentence, making it as a whole an anticlimactic one; and the factual subject-verb opening of the sentence that follows—"the little church . . . was particularly exposed" (the interposed *which* clause being merely a neutral place indicator) reestablishes the prevailing pattern.

For the rest, the last part of the paragraph, which brings a series of nonrepetitive but equally abortive incidents into the general scheme, also has its minor climax in Pontiac's two moves, the most important of these incidents. Here a certain tension is created by the emphatic position of "burn him alive." But, for the most part, what has weight here is simply the amount of space given to Pontiac's doings—three sentences, two of which are notably longer than the average of the paragraph. This makes the Pontiac material stand out as a subunit of the paragraph, but again, without giving it an emphasis that counteracts the general effect. Then at the end, to be sure, we do have a heightening of tone that definitely breaks the stasis and advances the action from one stage to another. If we wind up with what we began with—that is, the garrison on watch, presented in a low-keyed way at the beginning of the paragraph—we return to it in a triple-membered sentence, with the added emphasis of fresh detail and the rising rhythm of the enumeration after "every man in the fort"—"officers, soldiers, traders, and *engagés*." But even so, in the sentence before, which conveys the information responsible for this heightening of tone, we note Parkman's instinctive use of the less forceful passive voice of the verb—"were now renewed . . . were soon after inspired . . ."—to keep the movement within the tonal limits of the paragraph as a whole.

But one could hardly cite a paragraph of Parkman's, no matter how factual in tone or low-keyed in diction, without some trace of this kinetic leaven, this inner vitality of movement, which, as his first biographer put it, "animates the reader much as music does, independently of specific aims." Here indeed one touches the secret principle that gives unity of effect to Parkman's writing from its least to its most highly charged moments; and one lingers over the point simply because his strongly colored passages may obscure from us this more fundamental source of his powers. But also one could hardly cite a paragraph of Parkman's, no matter how highly colored in phrasing or evocative in tone, where our response is not also conditioned by the substratum of realism that expresses itself in the bare factuality of statement, the objectiveness of approach, the neutral, low-keyed vocabulary of the passage I have quoted.

Yet this passage is, of course, elaborated for a special effect, and nowhere in *Pontiac* does the staple of Parkman's prose quite attain the stripped succinctness of his later histories—the clipper-ship quality that makes his writing seem an ultimate in functional craftsmanship. For an example at a moment of climax one might cite the passage in *Frontenac* where the audacious governor's quarrel with Versailles over a matter of fundamental policy reaches its decisive point of action:

In the question of Fort Frontenac, as in every thing else, the opposition to the governor, always busy and vehement, found its chief representative in the intendant, who told the minister that the policy of Frontenac was all wrong; that the public good was not its object; that he disobeyed or evaded the orders of the king; and that he suffered the Iroquois to delude him by false overtures of peace. The representations of the intendant and his faction had such effect, that Pontchartrain wrote to the governor that the plan of re-establishing Fort Frontenac "must absolutely be abandoned." Frontenac, bent on accomplishing his purpose, and doubly so because his enemies opposed it, had anticipated the orders of the minister, and sent seven hundred men to Lake Ontario to repair the fort. The day after they left Montreal, the letter of Pontchartrain arrived. The intendant demanded their recall. Frontenac refused. The fort was repaired, garrisoned, and victualled for a year.

This passage, more than the one I have quoted from *Pontiac*, depends for its effect on its context—the expository passages in which Parkman sets forth the general limitations of the French effort in America, and, in turn, Frontenac's perception of the possibilities to be achieved within these limits; the previous narration of the vicissitudes of Fort Frontenac, the abandonment or retention of which was the key to these crucial issues of policy; and above all the richly colored, highly evocative description in *La Salle* of Frontenac's original establishment of the post, during his first governorship. Nevertheless, even taken by itself, the passage can be seen to gain its effect by the same kinesthetic means. Again, though we are now dealing with a decisive moment of action instead of with inaction, the verbal coloring is wholly neutral and denotative; the tone even more baldly factual; and the tensions of climax which the writing now creates likewise derive entirely from the implication of the action itself in the structure, rhythm, and movement of phrase and sentence. Thus we have three relatively long and complexly ordered sentences, one for each of the three parties to the controversy, setting forth the precedent conditions; then the sudden retracting of the sentence span and stripping off of modifiers when we come to the immediate circumstances of the action; and finally, the driving home of this movement through the quick, sharp counterchange of short sentences that reaches its climax of expressive terseness in the two-word unit: "Frontenac refused."

And, of course, behind this kinetic quality of Parkman's prose, even at its plainest and most factual, lies a feeling for history in which the primacy of the event is paramount; no other historical work could more fittingly take for its motto, in the profoundest sense, Goethe's *Am Anfang war die Tat.* Thus when we come to Parkman's expository manner—his passages, that is to say, of explicit analytical discourse—we are struck both by the relative infrequency of such passages and their extreme incisiveness of effect. To the greatest degree, a sense of the causes and conditions from which events spring is conveyed by Parkman's handling of events themselves; and what explicit examination of their origins or significance is called for is set down with a trenchant economy of expression that only such handling could make possible. Though *Pontiac* already exhibits these characteristics of Parkman's expository writing, the rhetorical pointing, as I have said, is still a little too obtrusive. Nor is there space here to illustrate by examples involving major questions of historical interpretation. Nevertheless, the following passage from a later work, dealing with a minor point of the kind, makes sufficiently evident his way of relating the foreground train of events to its background and setting it in its broader historical context.

The passage is from *The Old Régime in Canada* and has to do with the quarrels over protocol that marked Bishop Laval's ascendancy in the colony's affairs, as they were later to mark Frontenac's:

The above incidents are set down in the private journal of the superior of the Jesuits, which was not meant for the public eye. The bishop, it will be seen, was, by the showing of his friends, in most cases the aggressor. The disputes in question, though of a nature to provoke a smile on irreverent lips, were by no means so puerile as they appear. It is difficult in a modern democratic society to conceive the substantial importance of the signs and symbols of dignity and authority at a time and among a people where they were adjusted with the most scrupulous precision, and accepted by all classes as exponents of relative degrees in the social and political scale. Whether the bishop or the governor should sit in the higher seat at table thus became a political question, for it defined to the popular understanding the position of Church and State in their relations to government.

The effectiveness of the passage depends partly on the incisive verbal exactness of its generalizations: "exponents of relative degrees in the social and political scale"; "defined . . . the position of Church and State in their relations to government"; and partly on the return to the specific—"whether the bishop or the governor should sit in the higher seat at table"—which keeps these generalized statements close to the concrete phenomena whose significance they indicate. But what perhaps most of all fixes the point in the reader's mind is the rhythmic swell of the pleonastic doublets with which the main part of the passage opens: "signs and symbols of dignity and authority at a time and among a people." By means of this unobtrusive rhetorical heightening, these abstractions present themselves for the purposes of analytical discourse with the pomp and circumstance of their phenomenal manifestations on the external scene; and the processes of intellection that place the action in its context of conditions are implicated in the structure of Parkman's prose as kinetically as with his presentation of action itself. At any rate, this moment of apparent redundance of phrase combines with the extreme conciseness and trenchancy of the rest to achieve a maximum of effect in a minimum of space that drives the point home once and for all and establishes at a stroke the frame of reference for every other action of the sort which Parkman has occasion to narrate.

But we still have to do here with functional, denotative prose; and, as I have said, Parkman has another string to his bow both for narrative and interpretation. For a passage of this verbally connotative, highly charged sort, we find an example to hand at the end of Chapter II of *Pontiac*, where Parkman surveys the French and English systems in North America on the eve of their final clash. This chapter, part narrative, part exposition, is in fact a preliminary sketch of his main history up to *Montcalm and Wolfe*, and a preliminary formulation of the terms in which he interpreted the struggle that was its subject. The concluding paragraph, with its sudden transition to the mode of ultrarational imaginative cognition, is likewise a first, momentary unfolding of the deeper thematic implications underlying these conceptual formulations.

Thus far secure in the west, France next essayed to gain foothold upon the sources of the Ohio; and about the year 1748, the sagacious Count Galissonière proposed to bring over ten thousand peasants from France, and plant them in the valley of the beautiful river, and on the lakes. But while at Quebec, in the Castle of St. Louis, soldiers and statesmen were revolving schemes like this, the slowly-moving power of England bore on with silent progress from the east. Already the British settlements were creeping along the valley of the Mohawk, and ascending the eastern slopes of the

Alleghanies. Forests crashing to the axe, dark spires of smoke ascending from autumnal fires, were heralds of the advancing host; and while, on one side of the mountains, Celeron de Bienville was burying plates of lead, engraved with the arms of France, the ploughs and axes of Virginian woodsmen were enforcing a surer title on the other. The adverse powers were drawing near. The hour of collision was at hand.

We cannot linger here over the syntactical and rhythmic structure of this passage, except to remark in general how integral it is to the effect of the now highly charged and connotative phrasing, just as we have found the same principle of vitality animating the verbally low-keyed type of passage we have been discussing. Here, however, structure and phrasing combine to put the passage on a qualitatively different plane of discourse and to establish new levels of meaning and relevance for the subject matter of the chapter of which it is the thematic recapitulation.

We note, for one thing, the gain in depth and perspective achieved by this vivification of historical process in its palpable immediacy. The material of the chapter, which has been clarified for us at the conceptual level, takes on a wholly new dimension, though the concluding paragraph adds nothing whatever to it by way of explicit ideation.

Here, for what it does add, one might look first at the concealed image of an oncoming tide, with which, after the low-keyed opening, the more highly charged part of the passage begins—"the slowly-moving power of England," and so on. Parkman picks up this metaphor from a sentence occurring a couple of paragraphs earlier in the chapter, where it appears without connotative effect, simply as a conventional counter of speech: "And now it remained for France . . . to entrench herself west of the Alleghanies before the swelling tide of British colonization could overflow these mountain barriers." Now, however, the dead metaphor is kindled to life, and if not explicitly reintroduced, exerts a cumulatively suggestive power through the series of phrases derived from it: "slowly-moving," "bore on," "silent progress," "creeping," "ascending," "advancing." At the same time, the geographical indications, which, in the earlier passage, are merely denotative items in informative or analytical discourse, now take on a measure of physical actualization. A spatial vision, as if from some superterrestrial point of view, begins to shape itself; we at once see and feel along its length the thrust of this human tide against the mountain wall; and shadowy perspectives begin to open out around the subject of all that historical memory is stirred to bring to it of the migrations of peoples and the age-old *Drang nach Westen,* of which this is the culminating phase.

With the climatic heightening of tone produced by the key phrases of the whole passage—"forests crashing to the axe," and so on—the sense of physical actualization reaches its maximum, and with it the sense of implicit historical meanings. This part of the passage is also, as far as its overt content of thought is concerned, simply a reworking, with fresh detail, of a sentence that occurs earlier in the chapter: "The court and army supplied the main springs of her vital action, and the hands that planted the lilies of France in the heart of the wilderness had never guided the plough-share or wielded the spade." Here, however, Parkman discards completely the metaphor—or complex of metaphors—which is the germ of this somewhat dubious flower of rhetoric, and gains his effect entirely by specifying and concretizing. The indefinite "hands" take shape as specific actors in the drama: Celeron de Bienville and Virginian woodsmen; the metonymic "lilies" become what they literally and materially were, "plates of lead, engraved with the arms of France"; and the plows and axes, freed from the quasi-abstraction of "hands," now do their work in all the concrete immediacy that the preceding evocation of tree-felling and brush-burning—the first acts of the homesteading pioneer—has given them.

At the same time, this climax of vivification continues to open out horizons around the subject, horizons that now become more precisely defined and project themselves toward the future as well as toward the past. The lead plates with the armorial bearings not only epitomize the "court and army," but take us through the whole range of Feudalism and Royal Absolutism, the once viable but now archaic forms in which the spirit of the West has incarnated itself. Similarly, the plows and axes are prepotent with intimations of the consequences, material-mechanical and social-political, implicit in this change of phase we seem to see taking place before our eyes: the French Revolution, the Industrial Revolution, the Jacksonian Revolution, the emergence of the Third Estate, the emergence of the Fourth Estate—or however far or variously we wish to extend the sequence. In a sense, and in an important sense, all this rests of course on conceptual formulations in the body of the chapter, pointing the contrasts between the rival cultures: "Feudalism . . . arrayed against Democracy; Popery against Protestantism; the sword against the ploughshare"; "war and adventure, not trade or tillage"; "feudal exactions, a ruinous system of monopoly, and the inter-meddlings or arbitrary power," as opposed to laissez-faire enterprise. But now, with the whole sequence of the development of the West from its beginnings shadowed forth for its setting, the material of the chapter shows in full historical depth and perspective, and gains immensely in reach of reference by a presentation which, in not limiting itself to any particular set of formulations, suggests the whole gamut of possible formulations, and incites us to apprehend the historical forces in play as dynamic process and in their integral wholeness of effect.

But most of all this closing passage incites us to an inward, interpretative conception of the play of these forces, thus vivified in their external manifestations. Over and above the flat contrasts with which the chapter ostensibly deals—the question of which subspecies of Western civilization, the more "backward" or the more "advanced," was to master the new continent—the question of the Western ethos itself begins to emerge, and the question of its latter-day meaning for humanity.

Here we return to the most highly charged phrases of the passage—"forests crashing to the axe, dark spires of smoke ascending from autumnal fires"—phrases we have seen functioning secondarily in the passage to heighten Parkman's vivification of its ideational content. In themselves however, they take us altogether beyond the range of ideation and intellection; and represent the kind of writing in Parkman that is usually set down—admiringly or condescendingly—to his flair for the "picturesque" or to his "feeling for nature." But how short a way this brings us is evident from the telltale signs of some more significant and inward traffic between the writer and his material to which any sensitive reading of the passage in its context compels our attention.

So we note the markedly rhythmic character of the lines, and their incantatory effect, heightened by the clanging assonance of "crash"—"axe," and the full rhyme of "spires"—"fires." So too we note their high potential of sensory evocativeness: visual; auditory; and above all, of course, kinesthetic. Thus we feel the very impetus and impact of an ax stroke in the first phrase, with its harsh assonance, and its run of unstressed syllables after "crash" driving home the final syllable against its resistant consonant frame. Likewise, the lazy upcoiling of smoke in still air seems itself implicated in the retarded rhythmical movement of the second phrase, with its spondaic opening, and its full, lingering vowel sounds: "dark," "spires," "smoke," "ascend," "fires." This is the forest, one might say, in the very act of giving up the ghost. And finally, in spite of the contrast in tone of the paired phrases, we feel a symbiotic relationship between them—a filiation of ax and forest beyond that of mere circumstantial contingency—marked rhetorically, for one thing, by the frame of assonance and rhyme that at once differentiates the parts and sets off the whole as an integral subunit of the paragraph.

At the same time, as for the rest of the passage, only now at an ultimate level of meaning, the very immediacy with which the phrases invest the physical acts they describe charges them with symbolic intimations. So behind the ax blow, nerving and implementing it from some deep source of personal identification, we feel the whole complex of psychic imperatives—of practical activism, energy, and will—peculiar to the West, as on this most signal of its latter-day ventures, it reshapes the forest world of the new continent to its own pattern. So too, and from an equally profound vein of alienation, the counterimage of the forest is eloquent of the reverse side of the venture, and we sense clustering round it all the aspects of psychic life the triumph of these imperatives can thwart, stunt, or blight, and at the expense of which these achievements of the West are bought.[4] And finally, in the totality of effect of the paired phrases we recognize the fusion to an integral response at the same deep level of both the vein of identification and the vein of alienation which transmutes these images of ax and forest to emblems of an inner drama—a drama, the protagonist of which, so to speak, is the ethos of the West itself, apprehended in its full duality of creativeness and destructiveness, as it seemed to come to unchecked dominance in Parkman's own nineteenth century, and apprehended with a tragic sense of the precarious balance between the rewards and exactions of the human commitment to it which Parkman himself so deeply shared. Passingly but unmistakably, the passage announces the quintessential theme we shall find unfolding through the body of Parkman's work, ordering its structure and determining the incidence of its factual *données*.

[4] Cf. Lowell's unfinished essay on Parkman, his last piece of writing, printed posthumously in the November, 1892, *Century:*

"We forget ourselves . . . to thread those expectant solitudes of forest (*insuetum nemus*) that seem listening with stayed breath for the inevitable ax. . . . The world into which we are led touches the imagination with pathetic interest. It is mainly a world of silence and expectation, awaiting the masters who are to subdue it and to fill it with the tumult of human life, and of almost more than human energy."

CHAPTER VIII

PONTIAC AND HISTORY: THE FABRIC OF STRUCTURE

⚜ ⚜ ⚜

Turning, then, to the ordering of the larger units, we find that the passage we have just discussed is a pattern in little of the characteristic architecture of Parkman's histories, considered as wholes. So in *Pontiac*, always given the groundwork of factuality and realism which supports this structure, we note a key episode corresponding in function and implication to the core of climactically charged phrases we have examined above, and a corresponding presentation of the rest of the material at graduated levels of vivification that relate it thematically to this central episode.

In *Pontiac* this episode in Bouquet's march to the Ohio country, with the ensuing capitulation of the forest tribes at the council of the Muskingum, and their surrender of their white "captives." Merely at its face value of course—as the decisive military action of the war, and as the first official thrust of English power into the trans-Appalachian heartland of the continent—the episode demands the emphasis that Parkman gives it. As he treats it, however, it takes on the peculiar coloration with which he always imbues such decisive turns in the advance of civilization.

Thus the positive implications of the episode are deepened and affirmed by the heightening of sensory preception through the book which comes to a climax with the evocations of the natural setting of Bouquet's march and with the brilliantly narrated scenes of the council that follow. At the same time the closing scenes add a dimension of meaning of a different sort. These have to do with the fact that, as was usual on such occasions, a large number of the white "captives"—actually adopted members of the tribe—whom Bouquet had awed the Indians into surrendering, were extremely unwilling to return to civilization. This was a phenomenon on which Parkman could hardly fail to dwell, and the long passage he devotes to explaining it is the most eloquent and highly wrought of the book. Unlike the key passages of the later histories, its mode, to be sure, is that of explicit analysis rather than of implicit suggestion, and it is less effective thematically, invoking as it does a set of ideas, on which, more than with most matters of the sort in Parkman's work, time has rather heavily laid its hand. Nevertheless what Parkman makes of this curious countereddy in the advance of civilization and what he makes of that advance itself as Bouquet's expedition heralds it is characteristic in the play of dualities it sets up; and prefigures clearly enough the richer devolepments of the sort he was to achieve with the less limited material of *Pioneers* and *La Salle*.

But we can discuss more cogently what Parkman already achieves in *Pontiac* if we look at the climactic scenes in their setting, as the gradations of intensity in the vivification of the rest of the material focus the lines of the narrative on this most pregnant of its episodes. Here the *données* of the book suggest first of all a simple movement of flux and reflux, an elemental pattern of challenge and response, as the groundwork for the more complex developments the material yields at Parkman's hands. In this basic scheme, obviously enough, the moments of intenser emphasis associate themselves through the first part of the book with the Indian counterthrust against encroaching civilization and, conversely, through the last of the book with the victorious *riposte* of civilization to this challenge.

Thus the book opens with an expository survey of the northern Indians and their culture—a projection backward in time to the world of savagery in its pristine state—which lays the thematic basis of the whole, so far as the "doom" of the Indian is concerned. Following this, a sketch, still largely expository and analytical, of French-English rivalry in America, and of the relations of the Indians to the rival powers, traces the lines of historical causation to their converging point and brings us to the immediate circumstances of the uprising. The book then mounts sharply at the close of this introductory section to a first climax of vividness and immediacy in the scenes of Indian preparation for the war—the dream-vigils of the chiefs; the campfires in the clearings; the war dances around them; the departure of the war parties; and so on.

The main action to which these scenes are a prelude follows the eastward driving thrust of the Indian world at bay from its remote wilderness origins to its repercussions in the world of civil society behind the frontier. This action subdivides itself into three more or less simultaneous phases, which Parkman treats in order, as above. First, that is, we have the reconquest by the Indians of the wilderness posts except for Detroit and Pittsburgh; next, the devastation of the frontier and Bouquet's relief of Pittsburgh at Bushy Run; and, finally, the internal crisis behind the frontier, as the differences between borderer and town-dwelling Quaker over the Indian question sharpen to the point of quasi-civil war.

For the first phase of the action—the war in the wilderness—the siege of Detroit is naturally the focal point of the narrative; and the fate of the other forest garrisons and of the attempts to relieve the main post, are presented "off-stage," so to speak, as the news of them reaches the fort. As with the Indian preparations for the war at the close of the introductory section, so now, when the full impact of the war begins to make itself felt, a sharp heightening of tone marks the start of this catalogue of disasters: the scene, that is, of the bodies of the relief detachment drifting by the fort, which confirms for the garrison the rumor of their rout. With this scene the narrative reaches a second and intensified climax of immediacy, the level of which is maintained by various means through the rest of this phase of the action: the device of the "messenger's speech" itself, which gives a dramatic focus to our point of view by keeping it that of the beleaguered garrison; the evocations of the natural setting in the separately narrated accounts of the capture of Mackinaw and the ambuscade of the Devil's Hole; or, for the siege of Detroit itself, such detail as Parkman had gathered from the recollections of living eyewitnesses on his Lakes trip—the boy on the rooftop, for instance, watching Dazell's troops file by in the summer night to their repulse at Bloody Ridge. And, finally, with the atmosphere of the narrative thus charged and heightened, Parkman can dispense with immediacy of effect of this kind where a writer of less artistic tact would have been most tempted to deploy it—that is in the chapters that follow on the devastation of the frontier, which he treats in his barer, factual manner, letting citations from contemporary accounts convey the actuality of events.

Similarly, the mode of social realism prevails for the third main episode of this part of the narrative—the civil wars of borderer and Quaker that the tensions of the Indian onslaught bring to a head. In its discrimination of the underlying forces at work behind these dissensions, and in its incisive but finely shaded moral chiaroscuro, Parkman's handling of this episode is characteristic of the occasions in his histories when the circumstances of his narrative take him from the wilderness to the complexities of organized society. Here, however, we can only stop to note the elements of the episode Parkman turns to chief thematic account in the context of the book: the play of ironic contradictions that marks the position of all parties in the colony on the Indian question. Thus, the frontiersmen march on Philadelphia to wrest protection from the Quaker Assembly against havoc their own fierce, Presbyterian "Indian-hating" has largely incited, with the blood on their hands of the lynching in Lancaster jail of the Christianized Conestogas. Thus, again, faced by this threat, the Quakers, compromising their humanitarian sentiments and their high principles of nonresistance, promptly authorize in their own behalf a resort to the detested "carnal weapon" which, safe themselves from Indian attack, they had refused the harassed borderers. Yet the heat of these civil commotions dissipates itself in a battle of pamphlets, as the Assembly, bowing to the logic of events, passes the measures necessary for the prosecution of the war; and hints of a larger irony develop, when we contemplate the situation of the Moravian converts whom the Quakers shelter in the city, or the condition to which Christian kindness has reduced the Conestogas before Christian hate disposes of the wretched remnants of the tribe. Thus the doom of the Indian is spelled out through the whole range of the white world's moral gamut, as all parties compose their differences in face of the enterprise to which all parties, willy-nilly, are committed.

But this hint of ambiguities is as yet hardly more than an undernote in the movement of reflux that now begins and that brings the book to its climax with Bouquet's thrust to the heart of the Indian country. After the account of Bradford's parallel but mismanaged campaign on the Lakes, the narrative resumes the mode of its earlier scenes; the vividness of effect that there marks the stages of the Indian drive against the colonies now associates itself with the victorious counterthrust of civilization; and the book reaches its culminating level in immediacy of rendering and in richness of implication.

Already, earlier in the book, when Bouquet crosses the Alleghanies to relieve Fort Pitt by his action at Bushy Run, the writing has taken on this coloring and quickens to impressions of the oxen, their tongues lolling from their jaws, straining with the baggage wagons up the forested ridges in the July heat; of the sultry air impregnated by the resinous smell of sun-scorched pines; of the vast sweep of forest and mountain that discloses itself at the summit of the main ridge. So now, when Bouquet pushes beyond the limits of his previous advance, into the Ohio country which no English force had yet penetrated, such images, more and more deeply interfused with Parkman's own wilderness memories, are invoked again with incremental effect. Thus he re-creates from his youthful expeditions the gloom of primeval woods, "where the black soil oozed beneath the tread . . . and the carcasses of prostrate trees green with the decay of a century, sank into pulp at the lightest pressure of the foot." Or, again, we see the troops defiling through forest of a fresher growth, while "the restless leaves of young maples and basswood shook down spots of sunlight on the marching columns." And finally, at the end of the passage, a sudden shift to a superterrestrial point of view again evokes with deepened implications, a vast spatial vision, as the army begins to encounter the oases of open meadow, which are the "precursors of the prairies," and which, "growing wider and more frequent as one advances westward, expand at last into the boundless plains beyond the Mississippi."

With the kinetic verbal movement we find in the passages taken as wholes; with their appeal to the "deeper" sensory perceptions, the olfactory and tactile, as well as visual—their emphasis on the smell of the pine pitch, for instance, or the feel to the foot of the spongy soil or the rotten tree trunks; and with the concluding spatial vision that suddenly evokes the geography of the whole continental heartland into which the reflux of civilization now carries us, this sequence, as I have said, brings the narrative to its maximum level of immediacy of presentation, and at the same time charges the whole episode—the march itself, the incidents of the council that follow, the closing scenes of the liberation of the white captives— with Parkman's peculiarly idiosyncratic sense of such turns in the "advance" of the West, of which this vividness and immediacy of presentation is the reflex. So, in this context, the recurring spatial vision conjures up for us from the mere physical geography the whole portentous development of which this midland region was to be the scene. So, again, the tensions of perception we have felt mounting through the book, now breathe the very spirit of Western energy and will that here begin to lay the foundations of the achievement. And, finally, the depth of identification these passages achieve with the workings of the Western ethos as they implement the venture gives the sharpest dramatic focus to the thematic counterpointing of the closing scenes, which in turn bring to a climax the hint of ambiguities behind the venture; involving us, with their intimations of secret disaffection, in a contradiction engendered at the heart of the latter-day West itself by the very dynamism of its own specific drives. Or at least one may so interpret the *matter* of the long passage I have spoken of, where Parkman attempts to account for the defection from civilization of those white captives who had come to prefer the savage state; though, as I have said, the passage itself, for all its eloquence, fails to articulate theme and material on the plane of direct imaginative apprehension which gives conviction to the rest of the episode.[1] Nevertheless, making what abatements we must on this score and on others, the germ of implications we have noted in the passage at the end of Chapter II now unfolds itself to the extent that the relatively limited scope of *Pontiac* allows; and the essential Parkmanian manner and theme announce themselves unmistakably.

Thus the conflict of savagery and civilization—the doom of the forest and the Indian—projects itself as the image of a conflict within the ethos of civilization itself. Nevertheless the doom of the Indian remains to be consummated in literal fact on the external scene, and in the closing section of the book we follow the reflux of civilization into the wilderness to its ultimate consequences for the Indian—at least so far as the fate of the Indian is personified in the fate of Pontiac—as in the first part of the book we follow the impact of the Indian drive against civilization to its remoter repercussions behind the pale of the frontier.

The matter of this epilogue comprises Pontiac's abortive attempt

---

[1] The passage, running to four and a half pages, is too long to quote. The following shows how deeply imprinted it is with Parkman's own experience:

"Among the captives brought in for delivery were some fast bound to prevent their escape; and many others, who, amid the general tumult of joy and sorrow, sat sullen and scowling, angry that they were forced to abandon the wild license of the forest for the irksome restraints of society. Thus to look back with fond longing to inhospitable deserts, where men, beasts, and Nature herself, seem arrayed in arms, and where ease, security, and all that civilization reckons among the goods of life, are alike cut off, may appear to argue some strange perversity or moral malformation. Yet such has been the experience of many a sound and healthful mind. To him who has once tasted the reckless independence, the haughty self-reliance, the sense of irresponsible freedom, which the forest life engenders, civilization thenceforth seems flat and stale. Its pleasures are insipid, its pursuits wearisome, its conventionalities, duties, and mutual dependence alike tedious and disgusting. The entrapped wanderer grows fierce and restless, and pants for breathing-room. . . . The wilderness, rough, harsh, and inexorable, has charms more potent in their seductive influence than all the lures of luxury and sloth. And often he on whom it has cast its magic finds no heart to dissolve the spell, and remains a wanderer and an Ishmaelite to the hour of his death."

to rekindle the war in the further wilderness of the Illinois, his realization of the delusiveness of the promises of aid from France on which he had relied, his peace mission to Sir William Johnson, and his assassination at Cahokia at the hands of an Illinois Indian bribed by an English trader. As the emphasis of the first part of the book fell on scenes of savagery, so now, as civilization begins a new encroachment on the wilderness, the emphasis is reversed.

Thus, the introductory chapter—a descriptive and historical sketch of the Illinois country, which now becomes the scene of action —opens with another version, in this different setting, of the vision of foisoning natural life we have found in *The Oregon Trail*. Then answering it and dominant to the end, the more highly charged passages are impressions, gathered on Parkman's own Lakes trip and Oregon Trail trip, of the civilization that in a brief span of time was to reshape this teeming midland wilderness to its own image. So the tide of progress sweeps over the handful of French settlers— content to take the wilderness and the Indian as they found them— to bedevil them with "the intolerable burden of self-government." So the single lifetime of old Pierre Chouteau in St. Louis has witnessed the change to the booming metropolis of the forties, with its spreading miles of roofs and its steamer-crowded levee, from the scene of primeval solitude where he had come as a child and where he had looked on Pontiac in the flesh. So again the bustling cities of the Lakes and their commerce rise on the mind's eye while Pontiac makes his way across those as yet solitary waters to the council with Johnson, the scanty material apparatus of his culture soon to become "the wonder of schoolboys, and the prized relics of the antiquary's cabinet." So, finally, in the last sentence of the book, the theme works itself out to the conclusion implicit from the beginning, and these closing projections of the future—balancing the backward projection, with which the book opens, of the Indian world before the white man—culminate in the full diapason of the white man's "nineteenth century" going about its multifarious business over the ruin of the forest and the Indian, and quite literally over Pontiac's dead body. "Meanwhile the murdered chief lay on the spot where he had fallen, until St. Ange, mindful of former friendship, sent to claim the body, and buried it with warlike honors, near his fort of St. Louis. . . . Neither mound nor tablet marked the burial-place of Pontiac. For a mausoleum, a city has risen above the forest hero; and the race whom he hated with such burning rancor trample with unceasing footsteps over his forgotten grave."

Yet this is not quite all. The play of inner conflicts which has enriched the climatic scenes of the book also makes itself felt in this closing section; and we must scrutinize a little more closely the image of the wilderness and the image of the city which frame it and fill out the thematic pattern.

The first, as I have said, is an evocation of the natural life of the land similar to the passage in *The Oregon Trail* we have already examined. Though it has its imperfections—especially the sustained and frigid conceit of the "marriage" of the Missouri to the Mississippi which introduces it—the passage is charged with a symbolic force that is only rudimentarily present in the *Oregon Trail* passage, and gathers to itself the symbolic intimations in other wilderness passages of *Pontiac*.

One aspect of these is obvious enough. Here, as everywhere else in Parkman, the image of the wilderness imbues itself, among other things, with a sense of forces at the roots of psychic life which "nineteenth century" civilization ignores or drives underground. The fecund, teeming wilderness that was; the faceless, depersonalized city crowd that is—this is a palpable enough reflex of a protest of the human condition against the exactions of latter-day civilization, and relates itself palpably enough to similar intimations in the climactic scene of the white captives we have discussed; or to the ruin of the forest by steel and fire of the earlier passage with which this main sequence of the book begins. In sum, we might seem to have to do here merely with a familiar Romantic dissociation of nature and civilization, a flat contrast of opposites in which the emotional tone inclines the balance to a rejection of civilization. And up to a point this is true: at least an opposition of contraries of which these terms are the poles is a fundamental element in the book; and we shall return to what Parkman makes of it. Nevertheless, we find already in the passage a reading of nature itself which reflects the antitheses of Parkman's reading of civilization and sets up an interplay between the image of the wilderness and the image of the city that complements their opposition.

Here, first of all, we may best examine the passage in its more immediate reference to the American enterprise of civilization-building and to a prevailing American conception of the meaning and direction of the enterprise. The reference is perhaps too palpably evident in the theological metaphor on which the passage turns: "Yet this western paradise is not free from the primal curse"; or, as the conclusion puts it, is a "land prodigal of good and evil." Here, one might say, the passage becomes a historical parable, and restores to its authentic form the primordial myth of nature, a pleasingly emasculated version of which the American spirit, dazzled from the start by the paradisal aspects of nature in the new world, was particularly inclined to invoke.

Thus, in the first part of the passage, if the wilderness is "Nature" in opposition to the blighting or destructive aspects of civilization, it is also, in the general American sense, Nature in accord with the creative aspects of civilization—the new world of fabulous natural richness, the end of which is its adaptation to man's use. The Western imperatives of energy and will that bring about this transformation have their own deep psychic roots; and we have felt an emblematic rightness in the clustering of wilderness images, at their maximum intensity of effect, around the account of Bouquet's expedition, which nevertheless spells the conquest and disappearance of the wilderness. So, now, when we view more closely this midland wilderness which civilization is to transform, the description quickens—up to a point—with an affirmative sense of things to come. This wilderness in its pristine state, to be sure, is a "paradise" of game: as in the *Oregon Trail* passage, evocations of its swarming animal life—the deer grazing on its prairies, the elk trooping in herds, the "countless bison . . . filing in grave procession to drink at the rivers," the woods inhabited by wildcat, raccoon, and opossum—

strike the groundnote of contrast; yet the fecund soil, the alimenting streams, the beauty of the midland spring also bespeak the transmutation to a seeming paradise of man.

Then, with the metaphor of the "primal curse" I have quoted, Nature itself is cited to refute this paradisal conception, and the idyllic mood of the passage abruptly gives way to a catalogue of the horrors that lurk in the bosom of this smiling Eden—the pestilence-breeding swamp from which "the beneficent sun, which kindles into life so many forms of loveliness . . . fails not to engender venom and death"; the water snake, "winding his checkered length of loathsome beauty" across its pools, "where the hot and lifeless water reeks with exhalations"; the moccasin, thrusting his head from under the carcass of some fallen tree in the depths of the forest; the rattlesnake coiled on the sun-scorched surface of the prairie, ready to strike in the full light of day. Here, again, we detect the groundnote of contrast; this wilderness is still Nature in opposition to civilization: a symbol of forces benign or malign which civilization, or at least the nineteenth century version of it, tends to overlook in its calculus of the human spirit. Yet this wilderness, as a metaphor of human nature, is also a metaphor of civilization itself, which misconceives its own meaning if it ignores these dualities. In the end, as we have seen, the wilderness is neither a paradise nor an inferno, but a "land prodigal of good and evil." But if its "good" is no illusion, and the feat of turning its good to human use no vain feat, neither is its evil to be exorcised by exterminating the Indian, draining the swamp, and felling the forest; and civilization in taming the wilderness nevertheless inherits the pain, cost, and conflict inherent, precisely, in the nature of things.

Thus it is patent enough that what, among other things, the passage has to do with, is the famous American myth of the "garden of the world"; the simplistic and idyllic conception of America as an innocent Eden, excepted from the Fall, exempt from the contradictions and disaccords of older societies, at once beyond the scope of history and civilization and the ultimate flowering of history and civilization; a conception to which the frontier-agrarian phase of American experience gave a transitory color of reality, and which came to posthumous life in the "frontier hypothesis" of American history that dominated the thinking of the academy after Parkman's day. To repeat, Nature itself, in Parkman's more authentic version of the myth, refutes this idyllic conception; and the image of the wilderness, as it were, reinforces the image of the city as a measure of what the American enterprise of mastering the wilderness is in the end committed to: a commitment which the book affirms, but now in terms of the fullest recognition of its exactions and ambiguities—of everything the closing image of the city suggests, in Parkman's context, of the complex, problematic, urbanized, mechanized world that under the surface of the Jacksonian time the "nineteenth century" was establishing itself as the norm of the human condition, on American grounds as well as elsewhere.

Yet the sense of contrast between Nature and civilization of course still strikes us, and profoundly so, though we cannot explain it in quite the way our earlier statement of it seemed to indicate. It is evident, in other words, that Parkman's Nature is not to be contained by the naïve Rousseauistic conception which his preoccupation with the wilderness and the Indian might at first suggest—or the hardly less naïve revision of this structure that substituted the "savage savage" for the "noble savage" as the West viewed more closely the condition of man in his "natural" state. What sort of Nature then are we dealing with in Parkman?

Here we must anticipate a little and look for a moment at two other passages—one at the beginning of *Pioneers* and the other in *The Old Régime in Canada*—which, together with the present passage, are crucial for the question from the position and emphasis Parkman gives them. In the *Pontiac* passage, as we have noted, the controlling image of Eden and the primal curse is borrowed from theology, and we have a postlapsarian Nature of intermingled good and evil. In the passage, or rather suite of passages, from *Pioneers*— another version, this time in a Florida setting, of the same vision of teeming life—the controlling metaphor is drawn from science, but works to the same effect. The passage turns on the Darwinian concept of the struggle for existence, and we have a Nature of fabulous richness and beauty, and at the same time—and each conditioned on the other—a Nature of murderous internecine strife.

But it is to the third passage I have spoken of—although it contains no explicit reference at all of the foregoing kind—that we may best look for Parkman's "philosophy" of Nature. This passage is a vision analogous to the other two, the setting of which is now Parkman's own Northern forest; and if, unlike the second passage, it is imperfectly articulated with its immediate context, it is perhaps the most highly charged of all Parkman's forest pieces. Though it gathers to itself a whole complex of symbolic elements in his treatment of the forest, the same feeling of intermingled beauty and horror runs through it, and its culminating point again strikes the note of the interdependent strife of opposites, here in its most primordial form of death giving birth to life and life indissolubly linked to death—a vision of "fallen trunks, bent in the impotence of rottenness . . . while around, and on and through them springs the young growth that battens on their decay—the forest devouring its own dead." In this passage there is no reference, as with the other two passages, to point its bearings, but—since for the moment we are considering the matter on the conceptual level—it is not difficult to supply one, and one that from the fundamental drift of all the passages we may take as the master conception. For, whether or not Parkman knew Lucretius at first hand, his Nature suggests nothing more closely than the Lucretian *Natura*, where, precisely, as in the last passage, nothing comes to birth except through the death of something else, and the essence of which likewise is the symbiotic strife of adverse forces, the unending oppositions and conjunctions of Venus and Mars. In some such conception at any rate we find the groundwork of what Parkman makes of the familiar Romantic counterposing of Nature and civilization.

Here, as I have said, Parkman's wilderness does not affirm a state of primal peace and innocence from which civilization is a falling away; and does affirm a state of primal savagery and malignance only in proportion as the particular enterprise of civilization in relation to which his version of the wilderness is conceived has nurtured illusions on this score. His Nature, to repeat, is a Nature of good and evil; and man's second, self-created Nature of culture and civilization necessarily embodies the principle of good and evil, of conflict and contradiction, inherent in the general frame of things. Nevertheless if this primary Nature is a Nature of strife and conflict, it also achieves harmony of a kind: its symbiosis of opposing elements is an organic one; imbalances automatically correct themselves; though subject to perpetual change, the whole remains in perfect articulation with the parts; and the entire process, so to speak, is stylized. Thus Nature becomes the counterimage of civilization to the degree that, as man transcends the automatism of Nature, the symbiosis of opposites tends to become mechanical rather than organic; imbalances compound themselves; and wholeness is achieved only fitfully, partially, or precariously, and on more and more exacting terms. These discordances, coeval with civilization itself, are the price of the intervention of Mind and Will in the primary order of Nature, as man reshapes it to his own scale; and the price rises as man's perennial "conquest" of Nature takes a qualitatively novel turn with the coming to dominance of a civilization that commits man to Mind and Will—to rational intellection and pragmatic voluntarism—in a way, and to a point of imbalance, that no other civilization had done.

To this degree, then, Parkman's image of Nature is fashioned from the usual Romantic opposition of Nature to civilization; and is infused with the responsiveness to the forms of external nature in which Romanticism found a symbolic vocabulary for its most authentic insight—its perception of and insistence on the rôle of the subliminal and the nonrational in the human scheme of things; its assertion of all that, symbolically and inwardly speaking, was a reflex of the latter-day human condition in such a phrase of Parkman's as this "world of woods which the nineteenth century is fast civilizing out of existence."

Yet the principle of discordance at the heart of civilization is also at the heart of Parkman's Nature itself; and if his Nature affirms, in a sort, a norm of wholeness and harmony, it is not in the usual Romantic terms of a rejection of civilization, but, on the contrary, in terms of the most exacting commitment to its imperatives: in terms of all that the image of the city at the close of *Pontiac* suggests—at least in the context of Parkman's work as a whole—of an individualism that at once unlocks prodigious resources of spirit and creates an unparalled desolation of spirit; of a pratical activism that similarly spreads bane and blessing in the outer world; of a literate rationalism that answers one set of psychic needs by stunting and starving others; and so through the whole complex of dualities resulting from the Industrial Revolution, the rise of democracy, the rise of science, the spread of education, the gospel of utilitarianism, the gospel of self-reliance, and so on, that constitutes Parkman's "nineteenth century." By furnishing grounds for encompassing these dualities, and at the same time by comprehending what was valid in the Romantic discrimination of the particular imbalances in which they resulted, Parkman's reading of Nature transmutes the usual Romantic myth of Nature, resting on a sense of alienation alone, into the essential stuff of Tragedy, fashioned from the same deeply-felt counterposing of the elements of alienation and identification which give rise to his tragic vision of the latter-day West itself. In sum, Parkman's treatment of his wilderness scene is not merely a surplus to the serious business of his histories, to be taken or let alone according to taste, but an essential expression of his attitude toward his theme.

It is perhaps a measure of the degree to which this is already evident in *Pontiac* that the book has been interpreted in two diametrically opposed senses. On the one hand, it has figured as an essay in Romantic primitivism, a reclamation of Nature, and especially savage Nature, based on a sentimental rejection of "progress" and civilization. On the other hand, it has been read as an essay in the apologetics of progress and civilization, a reclamation of the American conquest of Nature, based on a rationalization of its cost to the savage on the score of his intractable savagery. Actually, when we grasp the essential movement of the book, we find it supports neither interpretation; or rather points to a synthesis that comprehends the grounds of both—a tragic version of the advance of the West, in which figure equally an affirmation of the venture and a sense of its inner costs and deprivations, of which the "doom" of the forest and the Indian on the external scene is a symbol.

Nevertheless, this is to look well beyond what *Pontiac* itself achieves by way of tragic synthesis; and it must be admitted that the book leaves us with the sense of an unresolved discordance between its elements: the hint of inner tragedy in the triumph of the West that is actually its main thematic leaven; and the tragedy of the Indian that Parkman intended to make the focus of emphasis. This last was a conception that, in any case, given the kind of vivification demanded by Parkman's approach to historical writing, was bound to involve him in difficulties. The most immediately apparent of these is indicated by his comparative failure with Pontiac himself in the rôle of tragic protagonist. As Theodore Parker, in a letter acknowledging a presentation copy of the book, justly put it: "The title indicates that the *conspiracy of Pontiac* is the chief theme. But in the book itself it seems to me this is not exactly so. . . . The picture of Pontiac is not adequate to his important place in the history."

Here, to be sure, because of the fact that, though Pontiac was the chief fomenter of the uprising, his actual part in it was confined to the operations at Detroit, the material of the historic record itself was an obstacle to making him the dominant figure in the book Parkman meant him to be. But even if this were not so, Parkman's failure with Pontiac, to express it paradoxically, was implicit in the very gift for characterization which makes his non-Indian figures such living actors in the drama. What the logic of his approach called for was a figure at least as individually distinct and as realistically drawn as, say, Bouquet on the English side—who, as the book turned out, is actually its most prominent character. What was lacking, on the other hand, was precisely the basis necessary for such a portrait—not only the kind of personal documentation which Parkman draws on for his portrait of Bouquet, but above all a ground of reference for appraisal and judgment, common alike to the world of the author, the reader, and the author's characters.

To illustrate, we may take Parkman's attempt to actualize Pontiac for us at a crucial moment of his activities, when he had set in motion his ruse for the capture of Detroit.

His cabin was a small, oven-shaped structure of bark and rushes. Here he dwelt, with his squaws and children; and here, doubtless, he might often have been seen, lounging, half-naked, on a rush mat, or a bearskin, like any ordinary warrior. We may fancy the current of his thoughts, the turmoil of his uncurbed passions, as he revolved the treacheries which, to his savage mind, seemed fair and honorable. At one moment, his fierce heart would burn with the anticipation of vengeance on the detested English; at another, he would meditate how he best might turn the approaching tumults to the furtherance of his own ambitious schemes. Yet we may believe that Pontiac was not a stranger to the high emotion of the patriot hero, the champion not merely of his nation's rights, but of the very existence of his race.

This, one need hardly say, is unconvincing as a piece of portraiture. We do not have the particular traits of a particular Indian, in their habit as they were, but an alien's guess—however informed—as to what they might have been. On the level of the intellect, we can credit Pontiac with thoughts and feelings approximating those Parkman ascribes to him; but on the artistic level we are painfully conscious that Parkman's presentation of them is an approximation only—a translation, so to speak, into our own cultural vocabulary of another cultural language, of which only the rudiments are decipherable, or for which we lack equivalent terms. The high coloring of "uncurbed passions," "treacheries," "fierce heart," "patriot hero," and so on, does not disguise the fundamental uncertainty conveyed by "we may fancy" or "we may believe," and, creditable as these qualifying phrases are to Parkman's sense of historic candor, the note seems forced, and what was intended for drama falls into melodrama. And one can say as much for what Parkman makes of Pontiac through the book as as whole. Impeccable as to costume and gesture, no doubt, he nevertheless stalks through its pages like a waxwork figure on a stage of flesh-and-blood actors.

Here, one feels, the gifts which, with livings models before him, enabled Parkman to achieve the convincing Indian characterizations of *The Oregon Trail* by something just short of a *tour de force*, were being set to a really impossible task. Some of his difficulties with Pontiac, however, can be laid to his own "culture-bound" response to certain manifestations of the Indian ethos—a reflection, in part, at least, of the rudimentary state in his time of the sciences of anthropology and ethnology to which he looked for collateral light on his subject.

This is particularly evident in his handling of the Indian use of "treachery" in warfare. He did not, to be sure, fail to recognize, after a fashion, the famous question of moral relativism—already posed by anthropology—that was involved here. It is hinted at in the passage quoted above, and in another place Parkman explicitly cautions us that "all savages are prone to treachery" and that the "ancestors of our own . . . race are no less obnoxious to the charge." But anthropology had as yet hardly begun to realize in practice the relativistic approach implicit in its postulates; and Parkman likewise, when he comes to concrete instances, can only appraise them in terms of the moral standards and feelings of his own culture. Thus at the beginning of the very paragraph from which I have just quoted he speaks of Pontiac's conduct as "here and elsewhere . . . marked with the blackest treachery," and goes on to lament that such a "commanding and magnanimous nature should be stained with the odious vice of cowards and traitors." So, in another connection, we read of Pontiac's "dastardly treachery," and of the Indians' "dastardly purpose of interposing Captain Campbell as a screen"; and we find the Grand Santeur, who, in approved Indian fashion, had captured Michilimackinac and massacred the garrison by the ruse of a mock lacrosse game, "expiating his evil deeds by a bloody death." Again, we feel that Theodore Parker's strictures on this point are firmly enough grounded. "You evidently have a fondness for the Indian," he writes, "—not a romantic fondness, but one that has been tempered by sight of the fact. Yet I do not think you do the Indian quite justice. . . . The treachery which you criticize in the Indian was to him no more a violation of any sentiment or idea that he felt or knew than it was for a Briton to fight with powder and balls."

And likewise, as I have said, we are also acutely aware of the inadequate stock of anthropological insights on which an historian of Parkman's day might draw, in the key passage, several times referred to, where he tries to explain the preference of the white "captives" for the Indian life from which they were being reluctantly liberated. This eloquent passage strikes us with its force of feeling and its richness of intimations; but it does not impress us equally by its conceptual relevance to the matter in hand. The ideas Parkman appeals to for an explanation of the phenomenon he is discussing are, briefly, the idea of liberty and the idea of closeness to Nature; to Nature here, that is, in the purely Wordsworthian or Wordsworthian-Byronic sense. To say that these conceptions are altogether invalid in such a context would be an exaggeration. Nevertheless the development of anthropology and depth psychology has of course altered, qualified, and refined them beyond recognition; and here as elsewhere in *Pontiac* we are conscious of a strain of obsolescence in the conceptual apparatus at Parkman's command in regard to his Indian material.

But this point aside, Parkman's conception of his Indian material in the mode of tragedy is imperfectly realized, because any conception in the mode of tragedy is perhaps bound to be when a writer attempts to realize it in the framework of a culture so alien to his own. As we have seen, the actual weight of tragic incidence in *Pontiac* falls elsewhere; though to a degree the "doom" of the Indian, which is the ostensible subject of the book, stands, like the doom of the wilderness, in effective symbolic relationship to what is actually its central theme. But, unlike the wilderness, which, as a nonhuman element in the drama, lends itself, without distracting claims, to symbolic treatment, the Indian, as a human actor in the drama, resists such treatment; and, given the claim to our attention in his own right which Parkman's approach awakens but is not altogether able to satisfy, the tragedy of the Indian remains somewhat intractable to the historian's art both as fact and symbol.

But if time has laid a somewhat heavier hand on *Pontiac* than on the rest of Parkman's work, our final impression of the book is emphatically not of its weaknesses. *Pontiac* appeared in 1851, in that marvelous half-decade of American letters that saw the publication of *Representative Men, Walden, White-Jacket, Moby-Dick, The Scarlet Letter, The House of the Seven Gables,* and *Leaves of Grass.* Even as a maiden work among maturer productions it makes its mark in this company; and if in part it looks forward to a new age of realism in literature and meticulous factuality in scholarship, it is predominantly an expression of the deeper imaginative spirit of that pre–Civil War flowering, of which Parkman, one might say, was to be the last voice. As to its specific qualities, they were perhaps best divined by a forgotten contemporary of Parkman's of whom one would like to know more. The book was well received by reviewers, and as a make-weight to their not altogether informed praise, drew from Theodore Parker the friendly, detailed, and intelligent analysis of the book's faults, from which I have quoted— a letter its author never would have troubled to write if he had not also been inspired with the liveliest sense of the book's virtues, both as promise and performance. But it remained for Brantz Mayer of Baltimore—an antiquarian delver in Parkman's field, but much else besides—to define these virtues in a few pregnant phrases as posterity might judge them. "I am doubly indebted to you for your beautiful gift," he writes, "and the kind allusion in your preface, which I hardly deserved. . . . Although I have not quite finished [the book], I can no longer ungraciously delay the expression of my delight and gratitude. Your work has, in truth, impressed me as the first history of North American events, pertaining to our race, which combines *perfectly* a philosophical spirit of investigation with a dramatic power of narrative. Especially have I been charmed with your grouping of Indian Nations, tribes and characteristics . . . which is the key of the splendid Tragedy."

Here, to be sure, we must abate a little Mayer's "perfectly" if only in view of what was to follow *Pontiac;* we would also prefer to read "our culture" or "our civilization" for "our race"; and in the context of *Pontiac* itself we must give a somewhat different reference to "tragedy" from what Mayer intends. Nevertheless, in this cluster of phrases—"our race" in North America, "philosophical spirit of investigation," "dramatic power of narrative," and "splendid Tragedy"—Mayer has put his finger on the qualities already evident in *Pontiac*—on the centrality of theme and the capacity to envisage it in the most profound of artistic modes; on the almost unique combination of imaginative insight, intellectual penetration, and mastery of technique—that announce the arrival of an historian of the first rank. And, we feel, it is as much prophetic intuition as mere friendly hyperbole that led Mayer to risk, merely on the strength of the first version of *Pontiac* alone, the comparison with which he closes. "I think you may tread as proudly and confidently of enduring remembrance in the History and Literature of the English Race as Gibbon did on that memorable night when he laid down his pen after writing the last lines of the *Decline and Fall.*"

CHAPTER IX

THE DARK YEARS:
ECLIPSE AND RECOVERY

⚜ ⚜ ⚜

With *Pontiac* and *The Oregon Trail* behind him, with his disorders apparently under control, happily married, and possessed of private means on the death of his father in 1852, Parkman at the age of twenty-nine might well have supposed himself in comparatively smooth waters. Indeed, with *Pontiac* off the stocks, he seems to have turned at once to the main project of which his first two books were collateral offshoots; and we find him writing to Jared Sparks in 1852 that he was busy with the composition of a "chapter on Cartier's voyages." This chapter, however, was not destined to see the light of print for another thirteen years. In the same year of his letter to Sparks "the enemy" struck again with redoubled force; and the shadows of the darkest and most trying period of his life closed round him.

Besides an aggravation of his old disorders—the eyestrain, the bouts of indigestion and insomnia, the paralyzing "whirl" in the brain attendant on mental effort, the depressive spells that followed —"the enemy" now brought to bear a new weapon in the shape of a crippling arthritis of the knee which for a while deprived Parkman entirely of physical exercise and from which he suffered for the rest of his life. At the onset of these attacks, indeed, he was unable to walk at all and had to be carried about, "forwarded like a crate of brittle China," as he wrote to Mary Parkman of an abortive trip to Northampton to try a water cure. With a state of complete physical inaction intensifying the effects of the mental inaction to which the attacks of "the enemy" had always reduced him, only the naked will to endure saw him through the years of gloomy confinement that followed.

There were intermittances of course in the grip of his disorders, and some signs of partial recovery during the middle fifties. At least in 1856 we find him making a scholarly pilgrimage to Montreal, Ottawa, and Quebec; and the same year saw the publication of his novel *Vassall Morton*. But whatever promise might have been augured from this betterment was dashed by a series of domestic calamities which brought on the worst breakdown of his life. In 1857 his four-year-old son died; and his wife, who never rallied from the shock and fell into a state of blank melancholia, herself died the next year in childbirth of a second daughter (an older daughter had been born to the couple in 1851). With these tensions and the shattering of his domestic happiness, his condition became so alarming that his family feared for his sanity—fears by which he himself was haunted—and in the winter of 1858–1859 he went to Paris to consult the eminent brain specialist Brown-Séquard, who, as he put it, had "fixed Sumner's head."

Travel, as always, brought him some relief. Brown-Séquard, to be sure, could do little for his cerebral attacks, but was able to allay his apprehensions of insanity and, Parkman felt, had also helped his arthritis. At least if walking for any distance was out of the question, he could get about enough to haul himself to the top decks of the omnibuses that threaded the Paris of the Second Empire; and, like many persons after him, discovered the therapeutic charm of random exploration to which this novelty of urban transport invited. And, finally, he was able to turn even the gloomy circumstances of this trip to historical account by a scrutiny of the French colonial archives, to select at first hand the documents of which he wanted transcripts—a proceeding necessitated, in part, by an unhappy experience a few years earlier with a copyist, the antiquary and journalist Ben Perley Poore, who took advantage of his incapacities to foist on him as copies of otherwise unavailable Paris originals duplicates of transcripts Poore had already made for the Massachusetts State archives. But even this sort of mental application had its dangers;

exploring Paris by bus could hardly be a lasting palliative for his troubles; and, again, whatever promise of betterment the trip might have held out must have seemed illusory enough when he came back to Boston in worse plight than when he had left—in such a state, in fact, that for a time he was unable even to sign his name. For anything he had reason to suppose, he was condemned to some such game of cat-and-mouse with "the enemy," to some such "death-in-life" of incapacitation, for the rest of his days.

Nevertheless, this black year proved to be the nadir of his fortunes; and during the early sixties the tide began to turn, little by little at first, then fairly rapidly. So, by July of 1863, we find the *Atlantic* beginning to publish advance chapters of the Florida episode of *Pioneers;* the book itself was ready for the press by January of 1865; and thereafter, though Parkman was to be afflicted with a complex of physical and nervous ills to the end of his life, he was able to continue steadily enough with the great series he had planned and finally to complete it. This of course is to put the matter much too summarily—or even, one might say, callously, as if in our concern with Parkman's achievement we could disregard the very thin margin of difference in cost and suffering that made it possible. Nevertheless, the only intimately personal record we have of this period of eclipse and recovery—his letters, that is, to Mary Parkman —shows an unmistakable change of tone during this time, an increasingly marked ground note of confidence that replaces the accents of despair which even his iron stoicism could not conceal in his letters of the fifties. Whatever else he had to suffer, the dreadful feeling of impotence, which was the darkest shadow of his life, had begun to loose its hold; and if this time of revival was not without its checks and setbacks, he meets them with a resilience that surprises even himself.

His letters to Mary Parkman dwell particularly on two adverse events of this period of comparative recovery: one momentously public; the other, though connected with the first, of a highly private character. The Civil War stirred Parkman deeply and at various levels of response; so much so, on one level, that he took upon himself a forensic rôle in the shape of a series of letters to the Boston *Daily Advertiser* dealing with the questions of leadership in a democracy so sharply posed by the national crisis—letters which show, among other things, some significant modifications in his own attitude toward democracy. But it will be more convenient to look at these letters in connection with a second appearance Parkman made as commentator on public questions during the 1870's; and we have only to note here the peculiarly personal way in which, as may be imagined, the war struck home to one who had bemused his boyhood with fancies of "a life of action and a death in battle," and set such store by the qualities of character he conceived the martial career to put to an ultimate test. "Having been inclined to look with slight esteem on invalidism," he wrote in his 1886 letter to Martin Brimmer, "the plight in which I found myself was mortifying; but I may fairly say that I never called on others to bear the burden of it and always kept up a show of equanimity and good humor. The worst strain on these was when the Civil War broke out and I was doomed to sit an idle looker on." But a letter, written at the time, to Mary Parkman, then living in Europe, conveys to us in the quick the ignominy he felt at this rôle of spectator to which his situation condemned him. In an atmosphere charged with the gloom of Union losses at Antietam and Cedar Mountain, he had just made a visit to the camp of the 44th Massachusetts Infantry at Readville, a regiment in which several of his classmates or college mates were officers. "We are in the midst of war, I begin to feel it," he writes, "Wilder Dwight [a cousin of Mary Parkman's, fatally wounded at Antietam] was buried yesterday, and everybody is bidding goodbye to some friend or other. I spent a day and night at the camp at Readville. . . . The regiment is a picked corps. When I left them I was sick of life—but I will not utter what lies at my heart, even to you. . . . I thought I had known what deprivation is, but I had not."

And the Civil War also affected Parkman's private life in a different but equally ignominious way, that left him, so far as the affair was known to unfriendly critics, in the position of an assiduous and unsuccessful suitor of a girl fourteen years his junior, and left him outdistanced by a rival who had played in reality, in the ordeal of battle, a part that had been the most cherished projection of his own image of himself. In 1860 his cousin Quincy Shaw had married Pauline Agassiz, a daughter of the scientist Louis Agassiz; and a little later Parkman himself fell deeply in love with her next older sister Ida, a girl of twenty-four or twenty-five at the time, teaching French and German in the school her stepmother had opened in Cambridge to eke out the professor's salary. Now a widower, entering his forties, it had been for some time past, he wrote Mary Parkman in 1863, his "dearest wish" to make Ida his wife; but, doubting whether his health and circumstances justified his proposing to her, he had kept the relationship on a basis of friendship until he could feel they did so. This effort to hide his real feelings was only too successful. Ida, with "characteristic unconsciousness," took the relationship at its face value; and, according to Parkman's letter, on the very day when he had decided the time was ripe to declare himself, he received a note from her telling him of her engagement to young Henry Higginson—the future banker and founder of the Boston Symphony—whom she had rejected the year before, and who went off to war, "reckless, possibly, of his life, came back wounded, moved her compassion, and gained his wish." The stroke was not softened by accidentally encountering Ida, for the first time after he had received her note, at the bedside of the wounded Higginson, on whom he had gone to call at her request. Nor, on a more superficial level, was it tempered by other aspects of the affair: for if Parkman had succeeded in concealing his intentions from Ida he had not from Cambridge gossip, which put it about that he "was moving heaven and earth to marry Miss Agassiz." Indeed a rumor to this effect had reached the mysterious "Miss B" of his Brattleboro days, who reappeared in Boston at this juncture, and whose pique, Parkman felt, threatened damage to his courtship which he had been at considerable pains to forestall.[1]

[1] Parkman gives an account of this imbroglio in his letters to Mary Parkman and asks her help in straightening it out. The traits of "Miss B" that

But if the miscarriage of his courtship seems to have written finis to hopes and prospects of one kind, this unhappy reverse—"one of the most painful of my life"—did little to set back the revival of his creative forces that was now taking place. Though it was more than a month before he had "a tolerable night's sleep," the effect of the shock he found not so serious as at first he thought it would prove; and "thanks to long preparation," he got through the wedding which he had "dreaded more than death," without the expected torture. So his sister Lizzie writes to Mary Parkman shortly before Ida's marriage, "I have not said anything of Frank, for I suppose you hear from him sometimes. He has had a better year than any for a long time I should think." As we have noted, the opening chapters of *Pioneers* had already appeared in print in this same year.

Meanwhile we must look a little at the temporary change of direction to which Parkman chiefly attributed the betterment such activity signalized. This was the pursuit of horticulture into which, to the exclusion of everything else, he threw his energies for two or three years after his return from Europe in the desperate condition we have seen. The tranquilizing effects of gardening on harried nerves have been noteworthy since gardens were; and its therapeutic value for Parkman in this sense is obvious enough in what it offered, for instance, by way of fresh air and exercise; or by way of outlet for a strain of "handedness" in his make-up for which education and environment had done little. So it brought him into the open, even when he could not use his legs, to direct operations from a wheel chair, which he propelled with characteristic vigor, and from which he contrived to hoe or prune himself. Likewise, in the skills demanded

---

here emerge with Parkman's flair for characterizing strokes make it evident, as I have said, that she was in large part the model for Fanny Euston in *Vassall Morton* and that Vassall's situation as regards Fanny reflects those "circumstances of my past life, which seemed to justify . . . an unfavorable construction" Parkman speaks of in his 1853 letter to Mary Parkman and alludes to again in the present letters.

Complete texts of the letters to Mary Parkman are now available in Wilbur Jacobs's admirably edited *Letters of Francis Parkman* (2 vols.).

by the art of hybridizing, which soon engaged him, it gave expression to a manipulatory instinct that recalls the chemical experiments of his boyhood. But, fond of it for its own sake as he was, horticulture could hardly have been beneficial to Parkman simply as a pastime; and it chiefly served its turn for him in a very Parkmanian fashion, as a means of exacting and tangible achievement, and a challenge to competitive excellence. At any rate he brought to it the same thoroughness and energy of application he brought to his histories, and quickly became notably successful at it; winning over three hundred awards from the Massachusetts Horticultural Society between 1859 and 1884, the period of his active interest in gardening; holding various offices in the Society up to president; and serving for a year in 1871 as Professor of Horticulture at the Bussey Institute. He also for a while made a business of his avocation, forming a partnership in 1862 with a nurseryman named Spooner, though he gave this up after a year, presumably because of his return to historical writing.

The scene of his horticultural operations was the summer place he acquired on the shores of Jamaica Pond in Brookline, after the death of his father—three acres of land, and a cottage, which he made his warm weather home for the rest of his life. Already in 1861, only a year or so after he had started gardening, his success was notable enough to put him in possession of a unique collection, his development of which, together with his work as a rosarian, gave him a permanent name in the annals of American horticulture. This was a collection of Japanese plants—the first of its kind to arrive in America—made in Yokohama by the botanist George B. Hall, and turned over to Parkman by his college mate and neighbor, Francis Lee, on Lee's departure for the war. Among other specimens, the collection contained the double-blossomed apple, now known as the Parkman crab, and bulbs of the *Lilium auratum*, which he was the first person in America or Europe to bring to flowering outside Japan. With such material to work on, he devoted himself particularly to the hybridization of lilies, his chief triumph in this field being the *Lilium parkmani*, a crossing of *L. auratum* with another

Japanese stock, which he sold in 1876 to an English florist for one thousand dollars. But, as I have noted, he was also among the foremost of American rose-growers. He is said to have had at one time over a thousand varieties in his garden; and *The Book of Roses*, which he published in 1866, was for many years a standard manual of the subject.

Here, however, we are chiefly concerned with Parkman's pursuit of horticulture as a second circumvention of "the enemy," a more elaborate flanking movement, one might say, suited to the more desperate circumstances of the fifties, that rescued him from the demons of frustration and restored the functioning of his higher energies by deploying them temporarily in a secondary field of action, just as the devising of a new tactic of approach to his central task itself had worked a restoration of his powers in the earlier crisis of the forties. Yet if we can give all the credit that Parkman himself gives to horticulture on this score, we have to note, too, influences of another kind that helped to sustain him through his dreadful years of eclipse and prepared the way for the happier turn of affairs to which his new pursuit was the immediate means. Even his iron self-discipline was not proof against the need for emotional release in human relationships; and the most vital of such relationships in his life, outside marriage, was born of the desperate exigency of this need during the protracted crisis of the fifties.

Here, to be sure, as with Norton and Squier during the forties, masculine friendship played its part. So we find Parkman confiding something of his troubles to Professor Child of English and Scottish ballad fame, and a singularly winning spirit, who was his fellow passenger on the dark crossing to Paris in 1859. But there were limits to Parkman's responsiveness in this kind; and it was inevitable that for the deeper needs of communication he should turn to the opposite sex. " 'But you have male friends; very old and intimate ones,' " Fanny Euston says to the hero in *Vassall Morton*. " 'Excellent in their way,' " Vassall answers, " 'But I would as soon confess to my horse. Find me a woman of sense, with a brain to discern, a heart to feel, passion to feel vehemently, and principle to feel rightly, and I will show her my mind; or, if not, I will show it to no one.' " The paragon thus described by Vassall had already appeared in Parkman's own life. It would seem that as early as 1853 some shadow had begun to fall on Catherine Bigelow which, he felt, prevented his turning to her to fulfill such a rôle in that year of disaster. At least, writing to Mary Parkman of his breakdown, he says in the letter I have already quoted in a different connection: "I know but one other person to whom I would use this kind of language, and she has too much sorrow of her own, for me to increase it by my complaints. Before her I am bound to assume what pretense of cheerfulness I can." But, whatever the circumstances, it was, as may have been surmised, this same Mary Dwight Parkman whom he made his confessor under the stress of these renewed attacks of "the enemy" and whose gift of understanding evoked the series of letters which, to use his own phrase of the remarkable 1853 letter, were the "most communicative" he ever penned. Three years later she was to figure herself in *Vassall Morton* as the Mrs. Ashland whose "presence disarmed [Vassall], in great degree, of his usual reserve" and before whom "he was not scrupulous to wear a mask"; and to her, as much as to anyone in his life, Parkman revealed in the quick the emotions hidden by this integument of diffidence and self-repression.

This confidante of the two greatest of American historians—for later in life, as we shall see, she was also a particular intimate of Henry Adams—has led a curiously occulted and fragmentary posthumous existence. Letters to her from her sisters Ellen (Mrs. Edward Twisleton) and Lizzy [2] have been published, or at least

---

[2] The wife of J. Eliot Cabot—the memorialist of Emerson—and a born and inveterate letter-writer in an age of letter-writing, whose correspondence is a mine of Boston social history. Thus she duly records for Mary Parkman Ida Agassiz's engagement, of which she did not take a very exalted view. "Before this you have heard of Ida's engagement, for which I know you have long been prepared as I have, because from the nature of things it must come. I went through a year of disappointment to find that the Phoenix was not to come who *seems* fit for such a darling as she is, but now I am gradually reviving, hoping that he is a Phoenix though under the name of Higginson. Certain it is that 'the girls' who have always

privately printed, but no collection of her own letters; as a contributor to Godkin's *Nation*, she herself appeared in print during her lifetime, but anonymously; Henry James evokes her memory in *William Wetmore Story and His Friends*, but likewise without naming her; Parkman's letters to her—the sole known record of this friendship, except as they clarify *Vassall Morton*—have only recently come to light; and if she appears in her own person in Henry Cabot Lodge's *Early Memories*, where Lodge records his boyhood admiration of her and his later friendship with her, posterity has not shown a consuming interest in Lodge's friendships, at least apart from his relations with Henry Adams. And, finally, if the curiosity of the general reader may have been piqued by Adams's own references to a "Mrs. Parkman" in letters to Lodge at the time of her death in 1879, such curiosity would be completely baffled by an editorial footnote which mistakenly identifies her as Catherine Scollay Bigelow, Francis Parkman's wife, then twenty-one years dead. Yet, as one may judge, she was a personality of mark in her time and place, as were other members of her family; and it is worth while piecing together a little the scattered information we have about her.

Parkman had first known her as the sister of his friend and classmate, Edmund Dwight; and in 1849 she had become a relation-in-law by her marriage to his first cousin, young Dr. Sam Parkman, though she was no doubt also blood kin in a more remote degree through the ramifications of the Eliot clan, to which her mother belonged. Her father, the elder Edmund Dwight, had made himself a pioneer figure in the industrialization of New England by his development of water-power sites at Holyoke and Chicopee on the Connecticut; and, through his position on the State Board of Education, was an important supporter of Horace Mann's campaign for the reform of the Massachusetts school system. In private life, how-

---

howled before at the idea of Ida's marrying him, now rejoice and declare that the war has exerted a transforming, strengthening and elevating power upon him unknown in the annals of human development hitherto. At present, I am believing all this as hard as ever I can."

ever, he seems to have been a type of Victorian domestic tyrant, somewhat on the order of Elizabeth Barrett Browning's father. Even his official eulogist speaks of the unamiableness of his social manner; and the few letters of Mary Parkman's own to be found among her papers—an early sheaf to her friend Sarah Perkins Cleveland—are, in part, the record of what was obviously a harrowing girlhood experience, as she watched her father's harshness and insensibility reduce her mother to a state of chronic invalidism. Nor was her maturer life unacquainted with adversity. In 1854, six years after they were married, her husband died of typhoid fever contracted on a visit to a poor patient; and three years later she was left in very straitened financial circumstances by the panic of 1857, which, temporarily at least, swept away a large part of the Dwight wealth. This crisis she met by opening a private school in Boston, where, it appears from letters from Paris after the death of his wife, Parkman's daughter Grace was a pupil, as was also young Cabot Lodge.

In the early sixties, as we have noted, she was in Europe, where she had been called by the illness of her strikingly beautiful younger sister Ellen, who died in 1862, and who had been a girlhood friend of Catherine Bigelow's. As we shall find, Henry James saw in Ellen's romantic marriage ten years before to the Englishman Edward Twisleton (later Lord Saye and Sele) the "rosy dawn" of that social phenomenon which he himself turned to such striking literary account.

During the seventies, letters to Mary Parkman from Wendell Phillips Garrison show that she did considerable writing for the *Nation*. In fact, in 1878, Garrison asked her to "assume entire control of our fiction," though adding that she might "occasionally collide with H. James, jr., who, however, chiefly devotes himself to foreign novels—French and Turgeneff's." For a year and a half before her death she seems to have written regularly, if anonymously, the *Nation*'s omnibus reviews of novels. Finally, during this time, when she lived much at Beverly Farms, she became, as I have said, a close friend of Henry Adams and his wife. Adams wrote to her daughter after her death: "Your mother was not a mere society

friend whose house, in common with fifty others, I enjoyed visiting; she was one of the two or three confidential companions I had
in the world, and I do not know where to turn for another to take
her place. Her opinions and advice have been weighty with me in
very serious matters; her society was the greatest social charm of our
summers; and I think she must have thought of this in her last advice
to me not to abandon Massachusetts for nothing was more likely to
reconcile us to our absence than the loss of her." As the reader of
Adams's collected letters knows, he expresses similar sentiments in
letters to Lodge.

So much for external circumstance. We come to a harder task
when we try to grasp more closely individual traits of character
and personality. Unhappily for our present purpose, James, who
might, one surmises, have given us much here, evokes the figure of
Mary Parkman in his *William Wetmore Story* only collectively
with that of her sister Lizzy, and evokes both as a marginal gloss,
so to speak, to his main text, which is the fair and stricken Ellen.
Still the passage must be quoted for what it gives of the general
Dwight aura—if not simply for what it gives of James himself in
such moods of reminiscence. Going through the Story correspondence of the fifties, he pauses over a letter to Mrs. Story from Mrs.
Gaskell, who in the autumn of 1856, "inquires as to the identity of
'a very agreeable American Kennedy, whom I met a good deal in
London this year, and a charming Mrs. Edward Twisleton and a
Miss Dwight, her sister' "—names at which for James "the faint
echoes begin more or less to sound and the dim scene to people itself." "The very agreeable Kennedy eludes us," he goes on, "but we
recognize the rosy dawn of the 'international' marriage, destined
subsequently so to flourish, in the writer's other reference. Images
of fair and elegant girls transplanted to English soil, briefly and
charmingly blooming there, then early extinguished and long
mourned, peep again through the closed window—with clever
Boston sisters, eminent and trenchant, and reserved, in their time,
for happier fates, but now at last, shadows as well, looking at us
also, if we like, through the clouded pane."

In this last, like the plural "fair and elegant girls" for the indubitably singular Ellen, James's reference is ostensibly to Lizzy—the "Miss Dwight" of Mrs. Gaskell's 1856 letter, who shortly became Mrs. Cabot and whose death at the time he was at work on *Story and His Friends* no doubt imbued the passage with its particular nostalgia. Nevertheless, it is hard not to suppose an awareness on James's part of a literalness of plurality in "clever Boston sisters" which gives a shading to this turn of phrase different from his generalization of Ellen earlier in the sentence. At any rate, his adjectives apply equally well to Mary, in her time, as to Elizabeth, and if we so take them, "clever," "eminent," and "trenchant" combine with other hints to suggest a certain formidableness of manner; or at least to suggest that the secret of Mary Parkman's gift is not to be looked for in a facile affability. For the rest, we must turn from James's tantalizing half-glimpse, to make what we can of the unevocative, if unambiguous, Lodge. Though a benighted generation can perhaps make little of his statement that Mary Parkman was "a well-bred woman in the fullest sense," we find that she was also, "what was rarer in those days, a woman of the world in the best sense," witty and humorous, widely and deeply read in men and books, with a taste for genuine learning, and—filling out for us James's "trenchant"—though "not intentionally intolerant or unfair," a person of "intense beliefs, as well as strong likes and dislikes." But if all this takes us so far, we can only guess from its effects at the main and most important—the secret of a *mana*, perhaps undefinable in any event, a power of evoking communication at the deepest level, that left an indelible impression on those who were capable of feeling it. So Parkman writes in his 1853 letter: "There is something about you which attracts confidence"; and so, as we have seen, Henry Adams, at the end of the chapter: "Your mother . . . was one of the two or three confidential companions I had in the world."

But in Parkman's case we have to do with a profounder if narrower vein of emotional capacity than with Adams and an intenser will to emotional repression that made his friendship with Mary

Parkman unique in his life. What it meant to him, in the circumstances of the fifties, must be judged from all that is implied in the context of the 1853 letter by the simple phrase, "expression is a relief," as he unburdens himself of the sense of "reiterated and protracted disaster" that oppresses him; or sets down the nightmare prospect that haunts him of a spectral "death in life" of paralyzed energies, aborted purposes, and mere "passive endurance, where courage and determination avail nothing"; or as he turns to those circumstances of his past life, already alluded to, of which he feels he must speak, not "doubting in general the fulness of your sympathies," but "doubting whether in such a case they would be extended to me"; and so to the end of this remarkable confession, which he calls "the longest letter I have written with my own hand for seven years and"—justly—"by far the most communicative I ever wrote." Likewise, the desperate exigency of this need for communication finds expression in the scene from *Vassall Morton* where Mrs. Ashland discerns Vassall's secret; a scene that—though Vassall's "secret" is a novelistic one, and not Parkman's own—becomes an almost embarrassingly personal revelation in the light of the 1853 letter, whether or not the manner of Vassall's emotional release is a literal transcript of reality. To quote the closing sentences:

Morton did not look up; but an undefined expression passed over his face, like the shadow of a black cloud. When, a moment after, he raised his eyes, he saw those of [his friend] fixed upon him with the same earnest gaze as before. Such a scrutiny from another would have been intolerable to him; but in her it gave him no uneasiness. . . . Morton looked up till he met her eyes. The surprise, the sudden consciousness that she was privy to his grief, the warm and heartfelt woman's sympathy that he read in every line of her face, were too much for his manhood, and he burst into tears.

Finally we may add the little language, so to speak—even more revealing in a sense—of letters written during the sixties under less intensity of emotional stress. "Do not take the length of my notes as the measure of my regard. I do not get used to your absence, and miss you, if possible, more and more." "Having had a friend to whom one has been accustomed to speak himself freely, it is not easy to reconcile oneself to the loss—so, as I leave the stable every morning, I look across the Public Garden to your window with a fresh feeling of regret." "If I wrote as often as I think of you, you would have a letter daily, to say no more." "It will be more pleasure than I can tell you to see you again."

That, for once, the need for communication, the need to speak and to share, was overmastering enough to break through in this way the tough integument of self-containment and self-repression that guarded Parkman's emotions, says much for a certain strain in his work that we would be rather at a loss to account for without some such ground of personal immediacy—the particular shading of tragic pity, for instance, with which the reiterated word "voiceless" in the descriptions of the scenes of his actions invests Parkman's portrayal of the utterly solitary and heart-locked La Salle, the archhero and archvictim, one might say, of a "self-reliance" that has become monomania. But Parkman's own experience of the human limits of self-reliance—the discovery, reached at such cost for a person of his temperament, that "expression is a relief"—is also directly responsible for the turn to autobiographical writing which dictated the main productions that need concern us here of the period we are considering: that is to say, his novel *Vassall Morton*—the only production in fact of his years of occultation during the fifties [3]—and the autobiographical sketch he composed in 1864 and later sent to George Ellis, endorsed, "Not to be used during my life." These, too, are somewhat inexplicable without the basis of human intercourse we find in his friendship with Mary Parkman, and their origins must be referred to it. His 1853 letter is obviously the germ of *Vassall Morton*—some of Vassall's speeches and solil-

[3] One should note, however, two slightly earlier pieces: his review of Squier's *Serpent Symbol* in the *Christian Examiner* (July, 1851); and his essay on Cooper in the *North American Review* (January, 1852).

oquies indeed reproduce the phrasing of the letter almost verbatim [4]—and if the 1864 apologia is pitched in a significantly different key, it is a product of the same impulse to "confession."

Neither of them, however, need detain us at any great length, for their nature and bearing have already been sufficiently indicated. Fictionally speaking, indeed, *Vassall Morton*, with its stage soliloquies, its wildly melodramatic plot, and its sketchy, undeveloped scenes, need detain us even less than Parkman's youthful *Knickerbocker* pieces. As George William Curtis said in reviewing it—though he found it the best of recent American novels—"Mr. Parkman's literary position provokes a demand, not of comparative, but of positive, excellence in any work he undertakes, and his novel does not satisfy that demand." Its odd mingling of social realism and extravagant melodrama reminds us in a certain way of Melville's *Pierre;* and the prison-fortress of the Ehrenberg, where Vassall supposes himself to be immured for life, is an expressive enough symbol of Parkman's own "dungeon of the spirit." Nevertheless, for the present-day reader the chief interest of the book lies in its incidental scenes and dialogues, and the character it largely has of an autobiographical *roman-à-clef*.

Thus Vassall's prison soliloquies develop Parkman's sentiments as to his own predicament we find expressed in the 1853 letter. So, too, as we have seen, those "circumstances of my past life," to which he feels compelled to revert in the letter, have their novelistic surrogate in Vassall's imbroglio with Fanny Euston and his subsequent engagement to Edith Leslie. Likewise the White Mountain meeting and the

---

[4] Compare, for instance, Vassall's soliloquy in prison (Chapter XXXIX):

"There are those in these vaults . . . who have passed a score of years in this living death. And canting fools would console them with saying that "all is for the best." I will sooner believe the world is governed by devils. . . . It is folly to cheat myself with hope. . . . Abroad in the free world, fortitude will count for much . . . here, it is but bare and blank endurance. Yet it is something that I can still find heart to face my doom; that there are still moments when I dare meet this death-in-life, this slow-consuming horror, face to face."

visits to Keene of his earlier attachment to Pamela Prentiss find their place in the book; and, as I have said, Vassall's friendship with Mrs. Ashland memorializes the crucial friendship of his creator's own life. No doubt actuality also supplied the material for two incidental episodes that illustrate less pleasing aspects of the feminine character: that of Mr. Leslie's enslavement to his second wife, the instruments of whose tyranny are "nerves" and hypochondria; and the even more ruinous liaison of a young Southerner, a Harvard classmate of Vassall's, with a rather vividly realized cannibal of hearts, somewhat on the order of Becky Sharp—perhaps an echo of an affair alluded to in one of Parkman's letters to Norton. At any rate, these reflections of Parkman's diverse responses to the *ewig Weibliche* provide one of the more animating elements of the book. But his sense of the feminineness of the feminine, or rather of the principle it embodies and of its formative influence on character—pervasive enough in the book—is perhaps more strikingly expressed by what is surely a highly autobiographical passage in one of his antisuffrage articles of the seventies:

Many men of the higher sort recall as an epoch in their lives that wonderful awakening of energies, ambitions, and aspirations which comes with the first consciousness of the other sex. Sometimes the change amounts to a revolution in character, and the young man can hardly recognize himself in the boy of two or three years before. The influence that begins the awakening is powerful to maintain it. Hunger, thirst, the instinct of self-preservation, malice, envy, and other of the lower motive forces, are self-sustaining. But, excepting those that belong to the province of religion, the nobler desires and energies draw impulse and aliment from the principle of sex. Truth itself would seem hardly worth the pursuit if women were not in the world.

Another strain of interest in the book is the purpose it serves as a medium for the expression of its author's social and political views. Two prominent elements of these indeed—his distrust of democracy, and his dislike of Puritanism—announce themselves in the double defiance of the choice of name for his hero which gives the book its title: Vassall, from a leading Tory family of Cambridge, ejected at the Revolution; and Morton, as recalling of course Morton of Merrymount, that thorn in the side of the New England theocracy, who was also a lover of the New England wilderness. Much of such matter appears in the college conversations of the earlier chapters of the book, where traits of Parkman's classmates are recognizable among the interlocutors.[5] So Dan Slade figures as Meredith, the companion of Vassall's backwoods wanderings; and the Laodicean Cary as Chester, who chaffs Vassall on his very "American" craving for activity. But it would be more interesting to know the original of Dick Rosny, the exponent of democracy in these exchanges—a breezy, likable Westerner, with his way to make in the world, for whom the Jacksonian time is his oyster, and whose vitality evokes a sympathetic response from Vassall that sweetens their differences of opinion (though Parkman, to be sure, tips the scales a little here by providing Rosny with Huguenot forebears, in whom he takes the same sort of pride that Parkman himself took in his own strain of Huguenot blood). Later in the book, gambling his chances on the paths to glory of the Mexican War, Rosny meets a hero's death in battle.

But the substance of these topical conversations is more pointedly articulated in Parkman's Civil War letters and *North American* pieces of the 1870's, and can be left in abeyance for the moment. For the rest, besides the glimpses the book gives us of Parkman's insight into other aspects of his "education," we note the particular emphasis it lays on the uses of adversity, which is, in fact, its central theme. This lesson of *pathei mathos*, of learning by suffering, is perhaps too insistently underscored for the novelistic good of the book, but it is revealing enough in what it shows of Parkman's awareness of the humanizing influence on him of his own trials, and of the rather special need his own nature stood in of some such chastening experience. Nevertheless, at the time when he wrote the

[5] As are those of Henry Chatillon in the figure of Max Kubitski, the soldier-guard who befriends Vassall, effects his escape from the Ehrenberg, guides him through the forest, and is killed in the pursuit when the fugitives are recognized.

book, he had not yet reached the vantage point from which he could resolve all this to the best effect. The worst of his ordeal was still before him, and the anguish of what he had already endured was still close enough to make his sense of it—expressed particularly in Vassall's prison soliloquies—the predominant note of the book. This somewhat overwrought emotional tone is no doubt one of the reasons—besides his consciousness of having put something less than his best effort into its composition—why in later life Parkman disliked hearing the book mentioned and never referred to it himself.

As I have said, the 1864 letter to Ellis, or rather apologia to posterity, of which he entrusted a second version to Martin Brimmer in 1886, strikes a significantly different note, a note of confident, if cautious, mastery which, in the immediate circumstances of his life, is a measure of his recovery and of the revival of his powers. With the worst of his troubles now behind him, he was able to examine clinically and objectively their causes, symptoms, and effects; and the result is a remarkably perceptive essay in self-analysis. Yet one must not exaggerate the degree of betterment that all this indicates. Though his great project now seemed at last actually in the process of realization, Parkman had no means of knowing that twenty productive years lay ahead of him, and one of the objects of the letter, certainly, was to put on record for posterity the conditions against which he had had and still had to contend, in case he did not live to finish the task to which he had pledged himself, or, what was worse, in case a new onset of "the enemy" should consign him irrevocably to that death-in-life which already, at least by his own exacting standards of achievement, had made such a blank of his prime. "The enemy," after all, is a cardinal fact of Parkman's biography, and, in a certain sense, was a cardinal influence on his writing; and we cannot leave this period of his life without considering a little more closely some aspects of its workings.

Assuming—which is not necessarily the case—that his various ills were all parts of a single complex, we need only mention again their more purely "somatic" manifestations: the eyestrain and hypersensitiveness to light, which was one of his earliest symptoms, and the arthritis which appeared during the fifties; and from both of which, together with a persistent insomnia, he was never to be altogether free. But the central and most peculiar feature of his case is of course the shattering effect of cerebral effort or excitement on his system, and the paralyzing kind of chain reaction it set off. This is the "whirl" in the brain, or the "brain in a mush" of the forties, but we first get a detailed description of the condition in his 1864 letter to Ellis.

Among the symptoms Parkman speaks of here, the most definite is the sensation of an iron band contracting around the head at attempts to "concentrate the thoughts, listen to reading, or, at times, to engage in conversation." The more drastic and less endurable forms of attack he finds harder to describe "from want of analogous sensations by which to convey the requisite impressions," though he later suggests a comparison with the effects on the victim of the water torture once used in prisons. But to put the matter in his own words:

All the irritability of the system centered in the head. . . . The brain was stimulated to a restless activity, impelling through it a headlong current of thought which, however, must be arrested and the irritated organ held in quiescence on a penalty to avert which no degree of exertion was too costly. The whirl, the confusion, and strange undefined torture attending this condition are only to be conceived by one who has felt them. . . . Sleep, of course, was banished during the periods of attack, and in its place was demanded, for the exclusion of thought, an effort more severe than the writer has ever put forth in any other cause. In a few hours, however, a condition of exhaustion would ensue; and both patient and disease being spent, the latter fell into a dull lethargic state far more supportable. . . . Influences tending to depress the mind have at all times proved far less injurious than those tending to excite or even pleasureably exhilarate, and a lively conversation has often been the cause of serious mischief. A cautious vigilance has been necessary from the first, and this cerebral devil has perhaps had his uses as a teacher of philosophy.

Parkman speaks of these as the "extreme conditions" of the disorder, but since its appearance, there had not been a "waking hour" when the patient was not "in some degree conscious of the presence of the malady."

All this of course takes us only a certain distance. If the indications of severe neurosis are forcefully enough conveyed—the sense of being impelled toward some undefined catastrophe, or the sense of unique and incommunicable suffering—its particular elements, as latter-day psychology might try to envisage them, are probably beyond our grasp, or at least traceable only in a very tentative fashion. In a narrower range of view, and taking the matter at the level on which Parkman himself presents it of overresponsiveness to cerebral stimulation, it is obvious that one chief immediate cause of his troubles was an exaggeration to a paralyzing degree of the intense inner excitement that any writer worth his salt feels in the presence of his subject—if also, one surmises, though more obscurely, of those "unpleasant doubts as to his ability to realize it" that were the corollary of this excitement when he first conceived his project at the age of eighteen. It is likewise obvious that if Parkman's occultations suggest on the surface what is currently termed a "writing-block," they were in actuality, as his first biographer noted, the precise opposite of that phenomenon, at least in its usual form. His problem, that is to say, was one of restraining a too vehement application of his faculties rather than of spurring them to action from stagnation or disgust; and when he could write at all, the evidence goes to show that he wrote, or dictated, rapidly and *con amore*, and after *Pontiac*, at least, with very little correction. And, finally, it is obvious that, whatever its ultimate nature, Parkman's case was not the "hollow man" configuration of our own time, involving, in spite of external achievement, the sense of a disintegration and collapse of the grounds of selfhood; just as, in a minor way, it is perhaps significant that his "crack-up" made itself manifest in youth rather than with the onset of middle age, and had taken its severest toll before he was forty.

Thus, pathologically speaking, it is difficult to read Parkman's work by the light of his illness, except in so far as it is patently, in part, a surrogate for participation in a life of action from which he had been cut off; and his writing is not, in the usual sense at least, an exploitation of his neurosis, or the writing of a sick man. Nevertheless it is impossible to conceive of his work's being what it is without the conditions for its creation which his illness imposed upon him. Here, for one thing, we seem plainly to have to do with a fundamental ambiguity in his attitude toward the adoption of the career of letters as a vocation which the realization of his project entailed: a commitment against which not only his own inborn craving for activity strongly militated, but also every external influence of his environment, both American at large, and Boston-Brahmin-Puritan in particular. "I . . . conceived literary ambitions, and, at the same time, began to despise a literary life," he tells us in his letter to Martin Brimmer; and however inflexible he was on one level in pursuit of his chosen task, one senses a resistance to the "calling" of authorship—to his rôle of artist and creator—which some subconscious mechanism of the psyche like illness was required to overcome. At any rate there is something almost uncanny in the way his complex of maladies shaped his life to the best deployment of his powers, and ruthlessly fitted its lines to a profounder realization of his purpose than he could have otherwise achieved.

Thus we note the first drastic intervention of "the enemy" at the precise moment when he had acquired exactly the modicum of external experience necessary for his work and when a division or dissipation of creative energy would almost certainly have resulted if his proclivities for a life of action had been given further range. Again, we note the delay imposed by "the enemy" on the realization of his main project until the years between forty and sixty, when his powers were at their ripest; when the initial ardor and passion of his conception, the more potent for keeping, could still quicken the work and at the same time he could bring to it the maturity of feeling and judgment that waits on middle age. And finally—to anticipate—we note the epilogue of this drama of binding and loosing: the period of quasi occulation after *Montcalm and Wolfe* and the third release of his faculties that allowed him to complete his work, just before his death, exactly as he had planned it to the last jot and tittle, yet as if a ghostly hand were setting its signature to what had been literally and figuratively a *life* work in a manner which its creator could never have consciously willed. In this respect at least, it is difficult not to see the complex of forces that Parkman objectified and externalized under the name of "the enemy" as, in reality, the expression of a profound inner compulsion, the secret working, so to speak, of daemon or muse, remorselessly bending to their purpose a prodigious energy of spirit, so that it should be brought to bear and brought to bear alone, at times and seasons of their own choosing, on the one thing of all things its possessor was born to do.

And, finally, something similar may be predicated of what Parkman's illness meant for the human tone of his work—this answer to his youthful impulse to test himself to the limits of endurance, granted not in any shape he had envisaged, but in the shape of what he had most dreaded and hated. This of course is the only kind of answer to such wishes that deeply "counts"; and as we have noted, Parkman was aware enough of the formative influence on his character of his struggle with "the enemy." In one of the later scenes of his novel, he puts into the mouth of Fanny Euston, now sobered and tempered by an ordeal through which she herself had passed, some of his perceptions on this score: " 'Tell me,' " Vassall asks her:

"Tell me what effect you think any long and severe suffering ought to have on a man—something, I mean, that would bring him to the brink of despair, and keep him there for months and years."
"What kind of man do you mean?"
"Suppose one given over to pleasure, ambition, or any other engrossing pursuit not too disinterested."
"Such suffering, rightly taken, would strip life of its disguises, and show it in its naked truth. It would teach the man to know himself and to know others. It would awaken his sympathies, enlarge his mind, and greatly expand his sphere of vision."

Yet we have to do of course in Parkman's case with more special demands than can be set down simply to any "engrossing pursuit not too disinterested," and we note again, in the moral and human sense, the daemonic quality of his illness, as of something shunned and sought, which makes it seem as specific a preparation for his work as everything on which he could bring to bear his formidable resources of conscious will power—the mere determination not to abandon a project to which he had set his hand until he was "made cold meat of," or the preliminary labors of documentation and the like which, without abating in the slightest the standard of thoroughness he had set himself in such matters, he managed to carry on in the teeth of "the enemy" except during the very worst phases of his times of occultation. The "cerebral devil" had indeed his "uses as a teacher of philosophy"; and nothing could be more intrinsic to the moral impression Parkman's work makes on us than this experience which authenticated by a knowledge of its ultimate exactions a "self-reliance" that had owed a little too much to outer circumstance, and which tempered to its essential humanity, in the common crucible of pain and suffering, a spirit a little too prone to take itself from the side of its differentiations.

Nor, as I said, must we think of the experience as something over and done with, when we come to the great productive years of Parkman's life. As the project had been conceived and the material for it ingested in the shadow of "the enemy," so was the work written; and the margin of remittance that allowed it to see the light at all was just sufficient, and no more. Nevertheless it was sufficient. With the publication of *Pioneers* in 1865, the secret transactions between Parkman and his muse had come to their destined issue; and the series—except for *A Half Century of Conflict* and the Acadian chapters of *The Old Régime*—appeared at steady enough intervals over the next two decades: *Pioneers of France in the New World* in 1865; *The Jesuits in North America* in 1867; the first version of *La Salle (The Discovery of the Great West)* in 1869; a revised version of *Pontiac* in 1870; *The Old Régime in Canada* in 1874; *Count Frontenac and New France Under Louis XIV* in 1877; the revised *La Salle* in 1879; the two volumes of *Montcalm and Wolfe* in 1884; and the revised *Pioneers* in 1885.

CHAPTER X

THE CYCLE OF EXPLORATION: *PIONEERS*

⚜ ⚜ ⚜

Parkman composed his history of the rise and fall of New France in separate volumes, intended to be complete in themselves, and which, except in two instances, actually are so. Nevertheless the volumes of course also form a connected series, falling into sub-divisions transcending the limits of the individual parts. Thus the main subject of the first three volumes—*Pioneers, Jesuits,* and *La Salle*—is the feat of primary exploration that took the French through the heart of the continent from the mouth of the St. Lawrence to the mouth of the Mississippi; while, in a kindred spirit of enterprise, the Jesuit missionaries abortively attempted to effect their own nonsecular version of this conquest of the wilderness. But French secular colonization failed likewise to consolidate the gains of exploration; and the fourth volume of the series, *The Old Régime in Canada* examines the reasons for this failure, as well as the sources of French strength, in a survey of the economic, social, civil, and religious life of the colony, which constitutes in fact something of a pioneer American essay in the history of institutions. The last three volumes—*Frontenac, A Half Century of Conflict,* and *Mont-calm and Wolfe*—set forth the achievements and ultimate collapse of this régime in its struggle with the English for the hegemony of the continent, where, geographically and militarily speaking, it held such a commanding position. *Pontiac,* finally, the first written of Parkman's histories, forms an epilogue to the whole, tracing the ruin of the forest and the Indian, which was a concomitant result of the ruin of New France, and left the field clear for the now para-

227

mount "Anglo-Saxon" version of Western culture to work out its destiny unchecked.

Within the groupings of this formal scheme, and with the vastly wider range of reference that his material now affords him, Parkman, as I have said, develops through their whole gamut of implications the thematic elements we have found in embryo in *Pontiac*. Before beginning to trace these developments, however, we must consider one or two collateral aspects of Parkman's manner of organizing his material. We may note, first, that in order to achieve the groupings I have indicated he sacrifices a certain unity of effect in the case of two of the individual volumes. Thus, though the main part of *The Old Régime* consists of an institutional analysis of early Canada, the book is also something of a catch-all for other matter: a narrative of events between the close of *Jesuits* and the beginning of *La Salle*, which he had passed over in order to treat the cycle of exploration as a unit; and finally, added just before his death, an opening section on Acadian affairs, for which the material had not been available when he first wrote the book. Likewise, *A Half Century of Conflict* gives a certain impression of heterogeneity. From the lack of any central figure in the action, Parkman himself frankly conceived it as a transition volume, and did not attempt to make it a self-subsistent unit. But even here, the book, written later than the rest, leaves a certain gap in continuity by its failure to deal with the internal history of the colony between the second governorship of Frontenac and the state of affairs under Vaudrevil at the time of the English conquest, vividly set forth in *Montcalm and Wolfe*. These, however, are minor flaws in the totality of effect that Parkman's main groupings achieve for the series as a whole.

The other question we have to discuss is not, properly taken, a matter of flaws or blemishes at all—on the contrary it concerns an element of Parkman's work that is one of its most conspicuous strengths: namely, as indicated above in reference to *A Half Century of Conflict*, the fact that his preferred approach to his material was the biographical one. Nevertheless this fact has given rise to a serious misconception of Parkman's attitude toward historical writing; and too many of his commentators have set him down too hastily—and too patronizingly—as an exponent of the "great man" theory of history. We cannot examine the question here at length, but a few considerations will show how far from actuality this assumption is, at least in the unqualified and simplistic form that the usual statement of it takes.

To begin with, we might scan with more attention than has apparently been given them the very first sentences of Parkman's preface to the first volume of his history. "The springs of American civilization, unlike those of the elder world, lie revealed in the clear light of History. In appearance they are feeble; in reality, copious and full of force. Acting at the sources of life, instruments otherwise weak become mighty for good and evil, and men, lost elsewhere in the crowd, stand forth as agents of Destiny." The basis of this, obviously, is not an a priori, generalized conception of the paramount rôle of the individual in history, but an empirical estimate of the rôle of the individual in the particular circumstances of the particular historical situation with which the writer is dealing. "Instruments, *otherwise weak*" or "men, *lost elsewhere in the crowd*" are terms of a relative view; and unless we can gainsay the enhanced scope of individual action in the particular circumstances of Parkman's history, we have no quarrel with a presentation that emphasizes it. To take an analogous example from American history: we would hardly be prepared to condemn out of hand as an undue magnification of the individual a treatment of the early history of the Supreme Court that took the form of a biography of John Marshall.

But even in his particular historical context—to turn from theory to practice—we by no means find the kind of emphasis on the "great man" some of his commentators lead us to suppose. Indeed, one of the most striking traits of his histories is the subtly modulated balance they achieve in this respect—the fineness of shading with which they discriminate the varying relationship between the actions of individuals and the "conditions" that shape them and are shaped by them. Thus Wolfe and La Salle are the two figures of his histories whose achievements and whose intrinsic qualities of character perhaps most attracted Parkman; yet, incisively as he portrays both of them, Wolfe is never allowed to dominate the narrative as La Salle does—the explorer on his own in the wilderness—and Parkman's emphasis is carefully proportioned to the socially denser and vastly more complex web of conditions that determines the reach of Wolfe's actions. But, more fundamentally for our present point, one also notes that he allows to none of his heroes the kind of indispensability in the chain of historical causation implied by the "great man" conception, and more or less explicitly disavows it. Thus, after enumerating the series of coincidences that made possible Wolfe's victory at Quebec, he goes on: "But for these conspiring circumstances New France might have lived a little longer, and the fruitless heroism of Wolfe would have passed, with countless other heroisms, into oblivion." In other words, if Wolfe had not taken Quebec, someone else would have, and, for a multiplicity of reasons, which Parkman sets forth elsewhere, New France was apparently fated to collapse, sooner or later, in any case. Again, Parkman's view of La Salle as an "agent of Destiny" is certainly not one that magnifies the historical bearings of his hero's actual achievements. In the closing paragraph of the volume that recounts them, and the feats of others which made them possible, Parkman writes: "Here ends the wild and mournful story of the explorers of the Mississippi. Of all their toil and sacrifice, no fruit remained but a great geographical discovery, and a grand type of incarnate energy and will." La Salle's exploits, that is to say, are only the culminating phase of a general effort, itself finally abortive in relation to the historical purposes it aimed to subserve; and even as a type of character Parkman nowhere credits his most conspicuous hero with any preeminent influence of an historically formative or normative kind. Even so, this of course is hardly history as the automatic play of impersonal forces, but it is equally far from being history as the "lengthened shadow of a man." Indeed, in a certain nondeterministic sense, we may say that the individual figures for Parkman as the lengthened shadow of history.

Nevertheless, the biographical emphasis of his work is not a gratuitous one, valid simply as a particularly viable approach to his particular subject matter. Here as elsewhere we must ultimately refer our sense of the peculiar *rightness* of his emphasis to the same cause that transforms every other element of his histories into elements of a great drama of the Western ethos and gives central relevance to material which would otherwise constitute what he himself once characterized it, in a certain sense, as constituting, not a history, but an episode. Thus La Salle takes primary place in Parkman's galaxy of characters, not simply as a type of "energy and will" in general, but specifically of neo-Western energy and will, a type par excellence of "modern practical enterprise" and of nineteenth century individualism in its most unmodulated form. So, in varying degrees of complement or contrast, the other main characters group themselves around this central figure. And so, finally, this whole element of portraiture relates itself to other aspects of Parkman's work and is polarized by the same currents that give essential significance to his descriptions of the wilderness; or to his reconstruction of forms or modes of civilization destined to succumb in the struggle for mastery of the wilderness; or to his evocations—beginning with the "axe and plough" passage of *Pontiac*—of the master form, which brings a sense of its largely "off-stage" workings into the very heart of the drama—and for which, precisely, the figure of La Salle is the on-stage nexus. In sum, if individuals "count" deeply for Parkman in their own right, and their personalities bulk large in his work, it is not because he envisages them as autonomous agents "making history" independently of circumstances and conditions. On the contrary, it is because they project for him various aspects of the interplay between the perennial *fonds* of human nature and the special circumstances and conditions of the historical situation in the light of which he viewed them—that ambiguous drama of the coming to dominance of the latter-day West, which comprehended both their day and his, and which is the ultimate ground of reference of his whole work.

It is thus apparent—to return to our immediate point—that the

French play a double rôle in this drama; and the two main sub-
divisions of Parkman's history I have indicated serve as the structural
framework of this double emphasis. Through the later volumes,
that is, the quasi-feudal character of the French régime, its tolerance
of the wilderness and the Indian, and its partial amalgamation to their
modes of life stand in obvious contrast to the social forms and inner
spirit of its rival; and here, as an archaic type of Western culture
in losing conflict with a more advanced one, the French venture
ranges itself toward the wilderness pole in Parkman's fundamental
dialectic of wilderness and civilization. Nevertheless, as we have
seen, we do not have to do in Parkman with a merely elegiac re-
vulsion from the present to the past. The locus of his drama is the
Western ethos itself in its most central and dynamic aspects, and
here one phase of the French venture provided the exact correlative
he needed for a projection of its workings. Through the first three
volumes, that is—or through the cycle of voyages that is their main
subject—the French, as primary explorers of the wilderness, are
vanguard figures in the advance of the West; in this respect the
French venture, as Parkman treats it, gathers to itself everything
that the literal fact of exploration suggests or symbolizes in the
development of Western man; and this peculiarly Western complex of the will to knowledge and the will to pragmatic achievement
finally incarnates itself in the figure who, as I have said, is the key
figure of Parkman's history—the type to whom the future belongs,
engendered, as it were, from the first major contact of wilderness
and civilization on the new continent, and embodying in its naked-
est form the pattern of human drives, that, diffused through a
whole social organism, and canalized to appropriate workaday
ends, was to complete the conquest of the wilderness to which New
France itself was unequal. Thus the significance of the drama which
is consummated on the external scene through the rest of the history is freighted with its full weight of implications by this inward,
psychological-symbolic presentation of it that Parkman fashions
from the main subject of his opening volumes.

This tale of exploration, in its mode of conception, begins as apotheosis and ends as tragedy. Its inner movement is the movement of a double response to the complex of drives of which, as I have said, the figure of the explorer setting off for the unknown is the literal and symbolical representative in the development of the West and the culminating form of which is the "atomic" individualism of Parkman's own nineteenth century. In *Pioneers* we find this complex presented in its most attractive guise, and, so to speak, under its most innocent aspect.

The leading motif of the book is the passion for knowledge, the Western *libido sciendi* by which, and by the will and courage to implement which, its hero, Samuel de Champlain, is possessed to the full. From duty, loyalty, and force of circumstance, rather than from natural inclination, Champlain is also an empire builder and founder of colonies—"the Aeneas of a destined people"—but for him, as Parkman notes, "settlements were important chiefly as a base of discovery." The keynote of his character and of the book is his avowal, in the narrative of his 1615 voyage, of this leading passion, the *"extrême affection . . . aux découvertes,"* which has pricked him on ever more insistently to win as complete a knowledge as he could (*"une parfaite connaissance"*) of the new country. At the same time this passion does not become obsessive with Champlain. Just as he is moved by no ulterior design on the new world his explorations bring to light—or by none beyond an earnest desire for the conversion of its inhabitants to Christianity—so his masterdrives leave the balance of his psyche unwarped; and, with his feeling for amenities—he was a lover of gardens, for instance, and cultivated roses at Quebec—with his affection for his girl wife, with his ardent but unbigoted Catholic faith, this child of Renaissance Christian humanism, for all his vein of iron, is a model of the sanity and harmony of spirit that were its ideals. In sum, as I have said, what we have to do with in *Pioneers* is the *libido sciendi* of Western man under its fairest aspect—a glowing, disinterested love of knowledge for its own sake, predominant over instrumental considerations, in harmony with nature and with human nature. All this is underlined and amplified by other elements of the book: by Parkman's treatment of the natural setting, which makes the scheme of the book itself an extraordinary dramatization of the act of cognition; and, finally, in its culminating episode of the Ottawa voyage, when Champlain strikes his boldest stroke to the heart of the unknown, by the invocation of the mythic figure, who, more than Aeneas, is the tutelary genius of the explorer—that "wanderer of the Odyssey," who, "could he have urged his pilgrimage so far," might have beheld these "ancient wilds" as Champlain beheld them. Champlain's voyage as Parkman records it, is impeccably a matter of fact and record, but we are also embarked, we realize, on another voyage: the voyage of the Dantean Ulysses in the splendor of its brave and innocent beginnings.

Even at its beginnings, to be sure, the venture is not without its hints of ambiguity. The first part of *Pioneers,* dealing with the isolated Huguenot attempt at colonization in Florida, cut short by Menendez—an episode actually subsequent in time to the first phase of French activity to the north—embodies in its opening chapters the same equivocal vision of the wilderness, the midland version of which we have found in *Pontiac;* or rather now develops it with a surer hand, through a longer, more richly textured sequence of passages, and to a more inclusive range of implications. Starting with the idyllic mood of the colonists' own first impressions—a classic rendering, steeped in golden light, of the conception of the New World as an earthly paradise—the sequence moves through heightening tensions of perception to the revelation of a wilderness as rich and teeming, indeed, as at the explorers' first view, or even more so as its details emerge with hallucinatory reality from the golden haze of the fabulous through which it is first seen; but also a wilderness whose beauty and fecund plenitude are bought at a cost, a wilderness with a heart of darkness, where, in the luxuriant depths of the forest, the carnivores of its fauna prey on the herbivores; where, by the stream side, "the rattlesnake suns himself on the sandy bank," or the moccasin "lurks under the water-lilies"; where through openings in the "bewildering monotony of the pine barrens" a feral sun throws "spots and streaks of yellow light"; and where, for the finale of the sequence, Spanish moss strangles the cypresses in the "black and root-encumbered slough," "wrapping its victims like a drapery of tattered cobwebs, and slowly draining away their life, for even plants devour each other, and play their silent parts in the universal tragedy of nature." In sum, to repeat, we have again, now pointed up by this Darwinian turn, the vision of interdependent beauty and horror, of symbiotic good and evil, that is Parkman's most tellingly recurrent version of the wilderness. With the emphasis that makes it here, from its initial position, a sort of prologue to the whole history, and articulated as it now is with complete artistic mastery, it has of course its own comment to make on the remoter meanings of that "conquest" of nature, which in its primary phase, shows so fairly through the rest of the book.[1]

So, likewise, has another, utterly different version of nature which haunts the opening chapters of both parts of the book, as, amid false starts and setbacks, a few bridgeheads of civilization tentatively establish themselves on the fringes of the continent—a nature of elusive vastnesses and immensities which, by their dwarfing of the human scale, suggest the ironies of disparity involved in the ultimate success of the venture, even as they throw into relief the apparent feebleness of its beginnings. And so finally, even in the culminating chapters of the book, when the venture is fairly launched and has taken on its character of historical irreversibility, an undernote hints at the ambiguities latent in the pattern of human responses that the

[1] This sequence is also closely integrated with its immediate context and counterpoints strikingly the demoralization of the French venture under the influence of dreams of very material gold that mingle with illusions of the Golden Age; until, with the appearance of Menendez, the rest of the episode plays itself out in a concatenation of massacre and counter-massacre, in which man's inhumanity to man more than matches the *bellum omnium contra omnes* that rages in the depths of the wilderness.

The effectiveness of these passages as we now have them was not, however, achieved at a single stroke. See Appendix B.

implementing of this attack on the wilderness calls forth or brings to dominance; and, for a moment, as with the foregoing passages, the writing foreshadows the tone and atmosphere of *La Salle*.

Nevertheless, all this remains merely a foreshadowing in *Pioneers*, deepening our response to the book by its indications of a wider context of reference, but subordinated to the particular emphasis that Parkman here gives his theme. Even in the first part of the book the key passages are those that dramatize the process of apprehension, the movement of the perceiving mind as it converts the unknown to the known; similar passages recur with augmented effect in the second part as we begin again the invasion of the unknown from a more important quarter; and all the lines of the narrative, in turn, are brought to focus on the series of exploits, culminating in Champlain's Ottawa voyage, that were a major step in unveiling for the European consciousness the secrets of the continental interior.

Thus our first engagement with the continental hinterland as a challenge to cognition, so to speak, comes in Parkman's account of Ribaut's Florida landfall. The bare, neutral-toned prose quickens to incantatory cadences as the voyagers first discern "the long, low line where the wilderness of waves met the wilderness of woods"; and then, with a sudden shift to a superterrestrial point of view, the outline of a vast spatial vision of the whole begins to form for a moment as they turn to coast "the fringes of that waste of verdure which rolled in shadowy undulation far to the unknown West."

Then, after the preliminary scenes I have spoken of, conceived in the idyllic mood of Ribaut's May Day landing at the mouth of the St. John's, the narrative reaches its first climax of apperception with Ottigny's ascent of the river the next year.

As the expedition starts, the prose again takes on an incantatory tone, but the shadowy vision of Ribaut's landfall now begins to concretize itself in the most immediate sensory detail, and with the familiar Parkmanian implication of the reader in the totality of the physical process that releases its wider range of meanings. "Having nearly finished the fort, Laudonnière . . . sent his lieutenant, Ottigny, to spy out the secrets of the interior. . . . The lazy waters of the St. John's, tinged to coffee-color by the exudations of the swamps, curled before the prow of Ottigny's sail-boat as he advanced into the prolific wilderness which no European eye had ever yet beheld." With the highly specific detail of the color of the water, and the propellant rhythm—breaking for a moment before "curled" like the bow-wave itself—that communicates the onward movement of the boat, everything in the sentence combines to give the maximum of resonance to the closing phrase; and the dominant motif of the book is firmly established, as, with startling immediacy, the sequence of passages thus introduced brings into our ken a first enclave of that unknown adumbrated for a moment in its whole vast, shadowy expanse in the vision of Ribaut's landfall. This particular epiphany of the unknown, like the rest of the Florida episode, is hardly, of course, of the first historical importance, but what Parkman makes of it links thematically the two parts of the book and sets the pattern for his handling of the major train of events he groups together in the second part.

Thus again we have first a vague, vast vision of the whole continental expanse; a movement of increasing vividness of presentation through the intermediate action; and a second and main climax of perceptual intensity with the start of the series of voyages that constitute the most momentous of early revelations of the continental interior.

The passages in the second part of the book that articulate this scheme and correspond to those in the first part we have just discussed occur in connection with Cartier's arrival at the site of Montreal on his discoverer's voyage of 1535; and with Champlain's arrival at the mouth of the St. Lawrence on his 1608 voyage. Both "moments" have, of course, their literal significance. The site of Montreal was the *ne plus ultra* of discovery for Europeans in a European ship, the transition point from the familiar ocean world to the world of the forest, the canoe, and the forest stream; and Cartier's expeditions to it remained in fact the farthest European penetration of the interior in this direction for three quarters of a century. Champlain's 1608 voyage, in turn, saw the founding of

Quebec and led to the series of expeditions that took the French for the first time beyond Cartier's mark and, almost in one bound, to the Great Lakes and the continental heartland.

Again, then, with Cartier's landing in 1535 and ascent of the Mountain of Montreal the writing takes on an incantatory quality, and the actual panorama of the explorer's view expands to spatial dimensions even more preternatural in their sweep than those of Ribaut's Florida landfall.

East, west, and south, the mantling forest was over all, and the broad blue ribbon of the great river glistened amid a realm of verdure. Beyond, to the bounds of Mexico, stretched a leafy desert, and the vast hive of industry, the mighty battle-ground of later centuries, lay sunk in savage torpor, wrapped in illimitable woods.

The horizon of this view seems to emerge across the body of the continent with the horizon of the earlier passage; a shadowy vision of history—the Industrial Revolution, the Civil War—expanded, like the horizon, to the continental scale, now begins to shape itself from the vision of prehistory; and once more, with augmented effect, the whole vast continental mass presents its secular inertia to the dynamism of conscious apperception, the act of primary cognition, to be consummated by Champlain's disruption of this "savage torpor" which Cartier, "first of white men," now gazes on.

But, as we have noted, a long interval of time elapses before the French resume Cartier's line of march toward the interior. In the meanwhile coastal exploration comes to the fore; and Parkman's dramatization of the natural setting shapes itself accordingly, as the intricate northern seaboard (the seaboard of Acadia, that is, in the older, broader French sense of the word) little by little reveals itself to us. We see it first, before Cartier discovers the St. Lawrence, when Verrezano's pioneer coasting of the continent lands him briefly on the shores of Maine—a glimpse of "surf-beaten rocks, the pine-tree and the fir, the shadows and the gloom of mighty forests." Then this vague, generalized impression begins to define itself with heightened immediacy of effect as Cartier, on his last St. Lawrence expedition, revisits the coastal scene for the third time, and, "passing in safety the tempestuous Atlantic, the fog-banks of Newfoundland, the island rocks clouded with screaming sea-fowl, and the forests breathing piny odors from the shore," casts anchor at the site of Quebec. The beholding of the eye is now reinforced by details like the cry of the birds and the smell of the pines that evoke more primordial sensory responses; and the passage establishes the intermediate level of vivification at which the next phase of the action is presented: the lateral southward thrust along the Acadian coast that, after the period of latency following Cartier's voyages, signalized the renewal of French effort in the new world and was a preliminary to the reoccupation of the valley of the St. Lawrence. These chapters likewise see the appearance of the chief actor in the drama; not yet, to be sure, in his chief rôle, but nevertheless playing the congenial part of navigator, geographer, and map maker. Indeed, besides the precarious settlement at Port Royal, the main tangible result of this Acadian sortie of the French was Champlain's achievement in these fields—"the light that [he] threw into the dark places of American geography, and the order that he brought out of the chaos of American cartography." Now tensed by the energy of intellect that thus converts the unknown to the known on the plane of scientific abstraction and rationality, the narrative counterpoints the process, so to speak, in terms of the energy of perception that provides the data for the workings of the process; and Champlain's maps take living shape before our eyes, as the spare, nervous prose quickens to evocations of their physical elements: beach, bar, and dune; shoals at low tide, "dark with the swash of sea-weed"; "reefs and surf-washed islands, rocky headlands, and deep embosomed bays."

But French energy has also turned again to the area of Cartier's exploits; and after tracing the Acadian episode to its melancholy upshot in Argall's sack of Port Royal in 1613, the narrative goes back to the more important enterprise on which the French in the meanwhile have been engaged, and of which Champlain's 1608 voyage is the effectual beginning. The chapter opens epic-fashion *in medias res*, with Champlain's ship entering the St. Lawrence. Again we have the highly concrete detail and the kinetic rendering of the movement of the boat that associates the passage with the Ottigny passage of the first part of the book; and similarly, but now to augmented effect, Parkman at one stroke brings his main narrative to a new level of perceptual intensity:

A lonely ship sailed up the St. Lawrence. The white whales foundering in the Bay of Tadoussac, and the wild duck diving as the foaming prow drew near—there was no life but these in all that watery solitude, twenty miles from shore to shore. The ship was from Honfleur, and was commanded by Samuel de Champlain. He was the Aeneas of a destined people, and in her womb lay the embryo life of Canada.

Yet, as we have seen, the founding of a colony and the establishment of French ascendancy, strongly as these considerations moved Champlain, were not what lay nearest his heart; and, as Parkman takes us back to France to explain the circumstances of his appearance at the mouth of the St. Lawrence, another passage puts us at the source of the current of volition that impels the ship and urges the voyage. The passage is Parkman's setting of the explorer's own avowal, already mentioned, of his passion for discovery, translating into terms of specific sensory perception the generalized statements of the original, and charging the whole with the immediacy of those moments of nostalgia for the new world scene that Parkman himself had felt in Europe ("Give me Lake George, and the smell of the pine and fir").

Champlain was, at the time, in Paris; but his unquiet thoughts turned westward. . . . As explorers of Arctic seas have pined in their repose for polar ice and snow, so did his restless thoughts revert to the fog-wrapped coasts, the piny odors of forests, the noise of waters, the sharp and piercing sunlight. . . . He longed to unveil the mystery of that boundless wilderness, and plant the Catholic faith and the power of France amid its ancient barbarism.[2]

[2] "L'extréme affection que i'ay tousiours euë aux descouuertes de la nouuelle France, m'a rendu desireux de plus en plus à trauerser les terres,

The motif that we first heard in the account of Ottigny's voyage
—"which no European eye had ever yet beheld"—sounds again with
all the increment of effect that Parkman's highly inward presentation of it at this particular conjunction of character and circumstance now gives it; and likewise, but to similarly augmented effect,
a sequence of passages follows, which if not yet the further plunge
into the unknown to which the chapter leads, consolidates for us,
so to speak, the earlier winnings of exploration at a pitch of vivification that the writing up to this point had reached only in the
Florida chapters. Thus, with Champlain's establishment of a post
at Quebec, the more important St. Lawrence scene, with which we
are familiar from Cartier's voyages, now emerges for the first time
in the full concreteness and immediacy of effect that Parkman's
writing is capable of imparting. Here, for instance, is his recording
of such characteristic and—for Europeans—novel phenomena as
the strong sunlight, or the advent of the New World autumn and
spring.

Here the citadel now stands; then the fierce sun fell on the bald, baking
rock, with its crisped mosses and parched lichens.

. . . the yellow and scarlet of the maples, the deep purple of the ash, the
garnet hue of young oaks, the crimson of the tupelo at the water's edge,
and the golden plumage of birch saplings in the fissures of the cliff.

. . . the clamor of the wild geese was heard; the bluebirds appeared in the
naked woods . . . the shad-bush seemed a wreath of snow; the white stars
of the bloodroot gleamed among dank, fallen leaves; and in the young
grass of the wet meadows the marsh-marigolds shone like spots of gold.

The controlled intensification through the narrative of the dynamics of perception these passages illustrate may be measured by

pour en fin auoir vne parfaicte cognoissance du pays, par le moyeu des
fleuues, lacs, & riuieres, qui y sont en grand nombre & aussi recognoistre
les peuples qui y habitent, à dessein de les amener à la cognoissance de
Dieu" (*The Works of Samuel de Champlain*, H. P. Biggar, ed. III, 13).

comparing the second of them with Parkman's low-keyed treatment of the same phenomenon of the American autumn in his earlier account of Cartier on the St. Lawrence: "walls of verdure brightened in the autumnal sun," for instance, or "forests painted by the early frosts." Indeed it can be seen that all the far-flung train of events of the book present themselves as elements of a single continuum in the mind's process of converting the unknown to the known; and the inner scheme of the whole is a dramatization of its leading theme as a single, ideal act of cognition—begun in the Florida chapters, abruptly broken off, then begun again in the main narrative—conceived in its primary terms of sense perception. So, finally, with the responses of the eye and the other senses now heightened to the pitch of intensity we have noted, we move to the culmination of this epiphany of the unknown, as Champlain pushes beyond Cartier's mark and awakens to the life of percipience that "savage torpor" we have glimpsed for a moment in all its vast unviolated entirety in the initial vision of Cartier's panorama.

Thus, as the explorer thrusts to the south up the Richelieu in 1609 to discover the lake that bears his name, we have the scene of the wilderness sunset that Parkman fashions from his memory of "what a roving student of this generation" had seen "on those same shores, at that same hour"—the Adirondacks, "darkly piled in mist and shadow," under a burning afterglow; in the foreground, a dead pine black against the fiery light, a crow perched on its top; and above "the nighthawk, circling in his flight, and, with a strange whirring sound, diving through the air each moment for the insects he makes his prey."

Likewise, finally, we have the climactic sequence, threaded through the account of Champlain's crowning exploit: his exploration in 1613, that is, of the Ottawa route to Lake Huron, which was the vital link in the early advance of the French to the heart of the continent. The sequence opens with a sunrise piece, matching the Adirondack sunset of the Lake Champlain chapter, as Parkman, drawing again on memories of his own boyhood wilderness expeditions, reworks the fumbling impression of a Magalloway dawn we find in his "Sept. 1841" ms. into a marvel of characteristic tone coloring and kinesthesia.

Day dawned. The east glowed with tranquil fire, that pierced with eyes of flame the fir-trees whose jagged tops stood drawn in black against the burning heaven. Beneath, the glossy river slept in shadow, or spread far and wide in sheets of burnished bronze; and the white moon, paling in the face of day, hung like a disk of silver in the western sky. Now a fervid light touched the dead top of the hemlock, and creeping downward bathed the mossy beard of the patriarchal cedar, unstirred in the breathless air; now a fiercer spark beamed from the east; and now, half risen on the sight, a dome of crimson fire, the sun blazed with floods of radiance across the awakened wilderness.[3]

[3] Compare "Sept. 1841" ms., 20:
"It was after sunrise when I again awoke. . . . The scenery of this spot, apart from the excitement and interest of its solitude, was worth much toil to look upon. The forest rose from the water's edge in a mass so dense that it was like a wall encircling the dark still basin. The trees were not of a uniform height. Tall pines and hemlocks stretched upwards far above the ordinary level of the tree-tops, and the upper limbs of these giants were just now tinged with the rays of the rising sun, while masses of vapor were entangled amid the thick foliage below. Huge old trees leaned forward over the water with the white moss hanging in festoons from their leafless boughs, like, as Audubon or somebody else says most appropriately, the floating beard of a tottering old man."
In the first version of *Pioneers* the sunrise passage that retrieves this abortive effort was preceded by a long description, running to over a page, of Champlain's "evening bivouac," which Parkman deleted entirely in his 1885 revision. This, likewise, was based closely on details of his own Magalloway encampments. The sleeper waking to stir the fire is an example:

Perhaps, as the night wore on, chilled by the river-damps, some slumberer woke, rose, kneeled by the sunken fire, spread his numbed hands over the dull embers, and stirred them with a half-consumed brand. Then the sparks, streaming upward, roamed like fireflies among the dusky boughs. The	In the middle of the night I rose. . . . The fire had sunk to a dull red heap of coals and I was chilled through with the cold mists of the river. . . . Our fire was quickly replenished. . . . I lay long watching the bright sparks that flew up from the fire before I fell into a gentle doze. ("Sept. 1841" ms., 19)

We may note of this passage, for one thing, the particular authenticity of visual detail like the "eyes of flame" of sunrise light through pine branches, which is as telltale a witness to the closeness of personal experience from which the passage is written as the feel to the climber's hand of lichens on sunbaked rock conveyed by the Quebec passage quoted above. So, indeed, through the whole of these climactic chapters, from the "moment" of Champlain's nostalgia in Paris, the data of vivification are drawn from a constantly deepening personal source.

But even more characteristic perhaps, is, again, the involvement, so to speak, of the process described, the augmentation of light, in the very structure of the passage itself. Thus—after the two bare monosyllables of the opening "Day dawned"—we have a strikingly incremental effect simply from the progressive lengthening of the span of the sentences, here in an almost exact ratio, as it happens, of fifteen syllables (an increase, that is, from thirty to forty-five to sixty-three syllables, to give the total count; the main syntactical units follow the same pattern in the order of one to two to three; and, likewise, the main rhythmic units—though the determination of these is necessarily a more subjective matter—in the order of four to six to eight). All this in turn is subtly heightened

---

scared owl screamed, and the watcher turned quick glances into the dark. . . . As he lay once more by the replenished fire, sounds stole upon his ear, faint, mysterious, startling to the awakened fancy,— the whispering fall of a leaf, the creaking of a bough, the stir of some night insect, the soft footfall of some prowling beast, from the far-off shore the mournful howl of a lonely wolf, or the leaping of a fish where, athwart the pines, the weird moon gleamed on the midnight river. (*Pioneers*, 1865, Chap. XII)

All at once a long hideous shriek came ringing over the forest . . . then all was still as death again but the roar and crackling of our fire. This startling interruption proceeded from the owls. . . . We had some faint hope of a concert from the wolves, but these delightful musicians declined to gratify us. ("Sept. 1841" ms., 17) Soon the moon came up and glistened on the still river. (*Journals*, 28)

by the increasing relative incidence of polysyllables in the highly monosyllabic verbal pattern set by the opening sentence—with all that it makes for quickness of pace—so that the longest continuous run of polysyllables coincides with the closing phrasal group, "floods of *radiance across* the *awakened wilderness.*" Likewise, a similar crescendo brings to predominance the main vowel sound of *radiance*, as it repeats itself through the paragraph, from the opening *day;* through *flame* in the next sentence; *paling, face, day* in the third; *bathed* in the fourth; to the emphatically clustered group at the end: *blazed, radiance, awakened.* And, finally, of course, we have the dramatically repeated, incremental "now's" of the triple-membered climax sentence, an obvious enough rhetorical device, but so integrated here with every other element of the passage that Parkman can deploy it to an effect as far from banal as the deployment of conventional cadence formulae in the music of Haydn or Mozart.

And in this charged atmosphere we come to the finale of the sequence in a paragraph which completes our introduction to the northern forest of the voyageur and this novel world for European eyes of the canoe and the forest stream. For the material of the opening section of the paragraph, with its specific local topography, Parkman draws in part perhaps on impressions gathered on his trip to Ottawa in 1856 (as he certainly does for the material of the preceding paragraphs, where Champlain passes the falls at the site of the city) and in part paraphrases Champlain's account, fitting the explorer's loose-strung prose to his own succinct patterns of rhythm and cadence. Rhetorically, this part of the paragraph follows the incremental scheme of repeated "now's," here implicating in its structure the onward movement of the canoe—and the response of desire and will to the ardors of the upstream voyage that impels it.

Day by day brought a renewal of their toils. Hour by hour, they moved prosperously up the long windings of the solitary stream; then in quick succession, rapid followed rapid, till the bed of the Ottawa seemed a slope of foam[*la rapidité du courant est si grande, qu'elle faict vn bruit effroy-able, & descendant de degré en degré, faict vne escume si blanche par tout que l'eau ne paroist aucunement*]. Now, like a wall bristling at the top with woody islets, the Falls of the Chats faced them with the sheer plunge of their sixteen cataracts; now they glided beneath overhanging cliffs, where, seeing but unseen, the crouched wildcat eyed them from the thicket; now through the maze of water-girded rocks [*quantité de petites isles que ne sent que rochers aspres & difficiles*], which the white cedar and the spruce clasped with serpent-like roots, or among islands where old hemlocks darkened the water with deep green shadow.

For the rest of the paragraph our feeling of closeness to the action and of immediacy of vision becomes almost uncanny, as Parkman's Magalloway reminiscences again fill the scene, and the apparition of the moose at the close completes this reconstruction of Champlain's voyage with what was the climactic event of the historian's own first wilderness expedition:

Here, too, the rock-maple reared its verdant masses, the beech its glisten-ing leaves and clean, smooth stem, and behind, stiff and sombre, rose the balsam-fir. Here in the tortuous channels the muskrat swam and plunged, and the splashing wild duck dived beneath the alders or among the red and matted roots of thirsty water-willows. Aloft, the white-pine towered above a sea of verdure; old fir-trees, hoary and grim, shaggy with pendant mosses, leaned above the stream, and beneath, dead and submerged, some fallen oak thrust from the current its bare, bleached limbs, like the skele-ton of a drowned giant. In the weedy cove stood the moose, neck-deep in water to escape the flies, wading shoreward, with glistening sides, as the canoes drew near, shaking his broad antlers and writhing his hideous nos-tril, as with clumsy trot he vanished in the woods.

Almost all of this passage can be documented from the narrative of his first Magalloway expedition that Parkman rewrote from his journal after he got home, or from the journal itself;[4] and it is

---

[4] Thus we have the wild duck he had watched among the alders of the Magalloway: "Whole broods of duck would start from the alders by the bank, and rush, hurrying and splashing, beyond the reach of danger" ("Sept. 1841" ms., 17); the fir-trees he had seen leaning above its surface:

evident that the core of his account of Champlain's most momentous exploring voyage is his own miniature boyhood expedition into the same wilderness, undertaken under the impulse of the same drives, effected with no small share of the same force of initiative and will, and calling forth the same pristine response of vision. The effect of identification with action and character that is always present in Parkman's work is here hardly surprising: in his generic rôle of explorer, Champlain on the Ottawa, as the historian re-creates his voyage, is literally one with the young Parkman on the Magalloway.

Yet we hardly need the literal certification of authenticity that an anatomizing of the content of these passages gives us—revealing as it is of the very specific, or one might say specifically historical, kind of grounding in certifiable actuality that underlies Parkman's most imaginative passages, as it underlies his most matter-of-fact— we hardly need all this, of course, to be aware that the narrative in these climactic chapters is alimented from *some* more and more inward personal source. The point is important only as this inwardness broadens as well as deepens; and the physical, perceptual, and psychological immediacy of presentation which it authenticates opens out plane after plane of meaning around the subject of the book. Re-creation and interpretation fuse in a totality that, from the hidden springs of Parkman's Magalloway days, embraces the literal significance of the voyage for the first phase of the conquest of

---

"From the high banks huge old pines stooped forward over the water, the moss hanging from their aged branches" (*Journals*, 29); and especially the moose he had seen crossing the river on the last day of his trip, and had chased and shot. Actually, to produce the closing picture of the above passage, Parkman fused together two reminiscences of moose on the Magalloway. Going through a marshy tract on the upstream journey, he had noticed fresh tracks on the bank and had followed them—with no success, as it happened—to one of the pools, where, he was told, "in the heat of the day, [the moose] may be seen standing up to his neck in the water to enjoy the coolness and avoid the attacks of the flies" ("Sept. 1841" ms., 18). The next day, on the return trip, the party "had gone five or six miles . . . when a moose sprang from the woods at a distance before us, splashed through the river, shook the water from his sides, gazed at us an instant, and was gone" ("Sept. 1841" ms., 21).

Nature to which the New World challenges Western man, and
reaches a culminating level of comprehensiveness with the following invocation I have mentioned of the "wanderer of the Odyssey,"
the mythic prototype of the volitions that implement the venture
and the larger venture of the Western ethos of which it is a part.

Yet the ends of things are in their beginnings; and even in the
midst of this apotheosis of the explorer, and of the whole Western
complex of spirit, of which the explorer on his own in the wilderness is the literal and symbolic image, a different undernote begins
to sound, and the ambiguities of a latter-day individualism begin
to suggest themselves. To some such effect, at least, we find recurring through the narrative, and particularly at three crucial points,
a word that prefigures the whole tone and tenor of *La Salle*—first
in the magistral sentence that opens the main sequence of episodes:
"A lonely ship sailed up the St. Lawrence"; again, as Champlain
starts up the Richelieu for the discovery of Lake Champlain, past
the cliffs of Belœil, "aloft in the lonely air"; and again, when Parkman indicates the personal sources he is drawing on for his account
of Champlain's Ottawa voyage: "He who now . . . would see the
evening bivouac of Champlain, has but to encamp, with Indian
guides, on the . . . borders of some lonely river . . . of Maine."

In the meanwhile, however, we turn to an attempt at a conquest of Nature of very different kind, inspired, in reverse to
the vision of the wilderness as an earthly paradise with which *Pioneers* opens, by a vision of the wilderness as embodied evil, as,
literally, the domain of Satan, a "realm of the powers of night,
blasted beneath the sceptre of hell."

CHAPTER XI

THE CYCLE OF EXPLORATION: *JESUITS, LA SALLE*

⚜ ⚜ ⚜

The Jesuit venture in Canada was an attempt to realize the only motive of Champlain's explorations that deeply engaged him, beyond the impulse to exploration for its own sake. Though the venture came to grief, its failure, as Parkman saw it, was less from inherent flaws in its conception, than from the combination of circumstances that pitted the Iroquois against the Hurons—shrewdly chosen by the Jesuits as their first main field of missionary endeavor, because of their populousness, the relatively advanced stage of their culture, and their key position in Indian trade—at a time when the Iroquois were in a phase of violent aggressiveness, and when the morale of the Hurons had been undermined by plague and famine. At the end of the book Parkman estimates the chances of this project of a "Northern Paraguay" and unfolds its possibilities. If the Jesuits had been able to curb or control the Iroquois, he finds,

it is little less than certain that their dream would have become a reality. Savages tamed—not civilized, for that was scarcely possible—would have been distributed in communities through the valleys of the Great Lakes and the Mississippi, ruled by priests in the interest of Catholicity and of France. Their habits of agriculture would have been developed, and their instincts of mutual slaughter repressed. The swift decline of the Indian population would have been arrested; and it would have been made, through the fur-trade, a source of prosperity to New France. . . . She would have occupied the West with traders, settlers, and garrisons, and cut up the virgin wilderness into fiefs . . . and when at last the great conflict came, England and Liberty would have been confronted, not by a

249

depleted antagonist, still feeble from the exhaustion of a starved and per-
secuted infancy, but by an athletic champion of the principles of Richelieu
and Loyola.

Indeed, given the fatal weakness, inherent in the policy of ex-
cluding Huguenots, that dogged all subsequent French effort by
cutting it off from sources of dynamic incentive to colonization,
the Indian-centered Jesuit venture, envisaging only a limited and
localized kind of "white" settlement, was alone inspired by the combination of moral idealism and practical command of means in relation to ends that might have produced results for the French in
the New World commensurate with their response to the challenge
of primary exploration. Parkman's expressed attitude toward these
possibilities is emphatically and unequivocally a negative one. In
the Preface to *Jesuits* he writes, "it will be seen . . . that civil and
religious liberty found strange allies in this Western World"; and
he develops the point at the end, very much in the strain of Bancroft:

Liberty may thank the Iroquois, that, by their insensate fury, the plans of
her adversary were brought to nought. . . . Not that they changed the
destinies [of New France]. The contest on this continent between Liberty
and Absolutism was never doubtful; but the triumph of the one would
have been dearly bought, and the downfall of the other incomplete. Popu-
lations formed in the ideas and habits of a feudal monarchy, and controlled
by a hierarchy profoundly hostile to freedom of thought, would have remained a hindrance and a stumbling-block in the way of that majestic
experiment of which America is the field.

Indeed, the passage closes, still in Bancroft's vein, with a view of
the Iroquois as instruments of divine interposition on behalf of
the "majestic experiment":

The Jesuits saw their hopes struck down; and their faith, though not
shaken, was sorely tried. The Providence of God seemed in their eyes dark
and inexplicable; but, from the stand-point of Liberty, that Providence is
clear as the sun at noon.

But whatever the "majestic experiment" owed to the Iroquois, Parkman, elsewhere in the book, also adduces more intrinsic reasons for the failure of the counterexperiment. The occasion for the passage is the embassy of Father Druilletes to New England in 1650-1651, and his impressions of "the thrift and vigor of these sturdy young colonies, and the strength of their population." After noting, in contrast, such factors as the exclusion of the Huguenots, and the adverseness to increase of population of the fur trade and missionary activity, the "vital forces of New France," Parkman indicates "behind all this" an element in the religious ideals of the rival colonies "which alone would have gone far to produce the contrast in material growth."

To the mind of the Puritan, heaven was God's throne; but no less was the earth His footstool: and each in its degree and kind had its demand on man. He held it a duty to labor and to multiply; and, building on the Old Testament quite as much as on the New, thought that a reward on earth as well as in heaven awaited those who were faithful to the law. Doubtless, such a belief is widely open to abuse, and it would be folly to pretend that it escaped abuse in New England; but there was in it an element manly, healthful, and invigorating. On the other hand, those who shaped the character, and in great measure the destiny, of New France had always on their lips the nothingness and the vanity of life. For them, time was nothing but a preparation for eternity, and the highest virtue consisted in a renunciation of all the cares, toils, and interests of earth. That such a doctrine has often been joined to an intense worldliness, all history proclaims; but with this we have at present nothing to do. If all mankind acted on it in good faith the world would sink into decrepitude. It is the monastic idea carried into the wide field of active life.

These passages are characteristic of Parkman's manner of setting forth the grounds of his historical judgments and dealing with the *ultimata* of historical causation. In the dialectic of challenge and response presented to Western civilization by the New World, the fundamental challenge is the pragmatic one of peopling it and turning its resources to man's use—"strength of population" and "material growth." Libertarianism, laissez faire, and the Puritan gospel of mundane works—"to labor and to multiply"—are both the efficient means to the end, and, whatever Parkman's quarrel with some of their manifestations, greater goods in themselves than their opposites. Such, summarily, is the frame of judgment against which he measured the Jesuit experiment, and, with further ramifications, New France in general. The manner is as trenchant as the judgment is summary; and the more trenchant as Parkman touches on ultimate issues over which disagreement is bound to be perennial. Thus the question broached in the passage just quoted is of course the famous question of the "Protestant ethic" which, after his death, was to be explored from every possible angle by an international corpus of scholars in a prolonged and voluminous historical debate. Here it is disposed of in eight sentences, decisively and *sans phrase.* And so throughout. Parkman, to be sure, is exceedingly sparing of historical generalizations: his sense of his task was to present his material in such a way that it spoke for itself with a minimum of explicit comment. But when generalization is called for, it takes the same incisive form as in the above passages, and articulates in the same clean-cut way the complex of commitments which determines the writer's view of the wider issues raised by his subject.

Yet if this were all, little would be left. In the total context of Parkman's histories, this frank taking of a stand is actually a technique of impartiality, disengaging the historical imagination from "ideology," so to speak, for its task of re-creation, and drawing a clear-cut line of demarcation between what may be made of the historical data in the light of the writer's own commitments and what may be made of them in the light of any commitment, as his dramatizing power revivifies them in their existential immediacy. How successfully *Jesuits* achieves this kind of objectiveness is attested by the Abbé Casgrain in a sketch of Parkman's work first published in 1872:

His history is a reparation and a work of justice which our enemies have too long refused us. . . . He has gone to the very sources of our history; he has studied them with a care, a love, worthy of all praise; he has told the story, just as he has found it, and said: "Accept or reject my conclusions; but here are the facts." We can scarcely hope more of an impartial enemy. The eloquence of the facts, told truthfully and loyally, triumphs over erroneous interpretations.

Indeed *Jesuits* was to prove a more signal act of "reparation" than the Abbé could be aware of: for the heretic-agnostic-rationalist historian's evocation from the dust of the missionary martyrs of Canada furnished the impetus for a movement that led, in our own century, to their canonization by the Catholic Church.

Nor, on the positive side, in spite of his clearly avowed limitations of sympathy, did Parkman lack personal sources of identification on which to draw for his reconstruction of the Jesuit venture. We have seen the appeal the relics in Italy of the Church Militant and Missionary had made to his instincts of self-dedication; and here he had grounds of unqualified response to what was the leading note of the venture in terms of volition and motivation among its participants. So he speaks in one place of that "principle of self-abnegation which is the life of true religion, and which is vital, no less, to the highest forms of heroism"; and he sums up the venture in this sense in as forthrightly affirmative a way as he rejects its implicit social and political tendencies: "a fervor more intense, a self-abnegation more complete, a self-devotion more constant and enduring will scarcely find its record on the page of human history." Strongly as his own sense of fitness would have deprecated the comparison, no one knew better the springs of the radical kind of self-commitment that prompted alike to do and suffer robust spirits such as the peasant-born Chaumonot, inured to hardship, or the leonine Brébeuf, "the Ajax of the mission," whose "deep nature, like a furnace white hot, glowed with the still intensity of his enthusiasm"; and on the other hand, *âmes sensibles* like Jogues or Garnier, bred to learning and refinement, and constitutionally frail, but kindled by the same inner fire to the same or greater prodigies of fortitude.

So, too, Parkman was equally responsive to the core of human warmth that underlay the fervid supernaturalism of the venture, and kept it from the harshness of fanaticism—a humaneness of spirit particularly evident of course in the unique relationship of Jesuit and Indian, which, whatever the historian's view of the ultimate possibilities of the Jesuit experiment, he signalized as the groundwork of perhaps the only viable adaptation of white to Indian culture that European civilization could have attempted in its invasion of the continent. The more thaumaturgic aspects of Jesuit supernaturalism were of course no barrier to this achievement; and often enough, as with the rivalries of priest and medicine man, inspire Parkman to comedy. Nevertheless, he pays eloquent tribute to the real transformation of the Indian ethos that Jesuit influence, so far as it went, was able to effect without a root-and-branch eradication of Indian culture. Thus, speaking of the Good Friday prayers of the Montagnais converts who were with Father Druilletes on his mission to the Abnakis, he writes:

What was their prayer? It was a petition for the forgiveness and conversion of their enemies, the Iroquois. Those who know the intensity and tenacity of an Indian's hatred will see in this something more than a change from one superstition to another. An idea had been presented to the mind of the savage, to which he had previously been an utter stranger. This is the most remarkable record of success in the whole body of the Jesuit *Relations;* but it is very far from being the only evidence, that, in teaching the dogmas and observances of the Roman Church, the missionaries taught also the morals of Christianity. When we look for the results of these missions, we soon become aware that the influence of the French and the Jesuits extended far beyond the circle of converts. . . . As for the religion which the Jesuits taught [the Indians], however Protestants may carp at it, it was the only form of Christianity likely to take root in their . . . nature.

And, finally, if Parkman brings to such aspects of the Jesuit venture—its fervor and glow, its heroisms and humanities, its disinterestedness and single-heartedness (at least in its earlier, primarily nonpolitical phase) its cultural creativeness as it affected the Indian —if Parkman brings to all this a fullness of sympathy which was part of his general feeling for history, he also brings to his presentation of it an innate flair for its particular historical coloring, for the distinctive *style* in character and atmosphere that made it, in the field of human action, one of the masterpieces, so to speak, of Counter Reformation baroque. We have already noted the instinctive feeling for the mode of the baroque to be found in passages of Parkman's journals, and we occasionally come across other passages of the sort throughout his histories. In *Jesuits*, however, this vein is predominant and gives to the book a turn of vivification peculiar to itself.

To look first at the details of setting and tone coloring. Here we find in *Jesuits* comparatively little emphasis on the natural background—the features of which, in any case, are for the most part familiar to us from *Pioneers*—and, if a sense of omnipresent forest and wilderness is evoked throughout, we apprehend the wilderness most particularly in its drearier or grimmer aspects. So we see the Fathers on the innumerable portages of the Ottawa struggling through the tangle of rocks, roots, and underbrush, "damp with perpetual shade, and redolent of decayed leaves and mouldering wood"; or on their rounds of plague-ridden villages in the gloom of February, "wading through sodden snow, under the bare and dripping forests, drenched with incessant rains." Or if this somber coloring is relieved, it is mainly by scenes of high winter, beautiful but feral: the flicker of the aurora overhead, and the snapping of frost-riven branches, as Father Le Jeune, gnawed to the bone by cold, reads his breviary in the moonlit forest; or the dazzle and glare by day, and the "vast white desert" by moonlight, of the snow-buried St. Lawrence, up which Father Anne De Nouë journeys to his death in a blizzard.

Yet the most striking detail of the first of these scenes is the firelit lodge, the miniature Indian Inferno, which Le Jeune has just left, shooting forth from "chink and crevice . . . long streams of light athwart the twisted boughs." Likewise, the feral beauty of the winter river serves for the most part to set off the scene of the pit in the snow where De Nouë's body was discovered, frozen to death in an attitude of prayer—a posture imitated, as a footnote tells us, by one of the Indians who made the discovery, on meeting his own death, three years later, at the hands of the Iroquois:

[De Nouë] had dug a circular excavation in the snow, and was kneeling in it on the earth. His head was bare, his eyes open and turned upwards, and his hands clasped on his breast. His hat and snowshoes lay at his side. The body was leaning slightly forward, resting against the bank of snow before it, and frozen to the hardness of marble.

Here the rendering of external nature is subordinated to the achievement of a certain tonality to an effect somewhat as if a Canadian El Greco had set himself to illustrate the *Relations;* and so, throughout, the main focus of perception in *Jesuits* is the Indian world, seen through the Fathers' eyes, rather than the wilderness itself. The characteristic settings are interiors of long house, lodge, or mission station, or the circle of the torture fire; and, pictorially speaking, the characteristic mode of presentation, as I have said, is that of baroque art, with its melodramatic contrasts, its high lights and deep shadows, its effects of violent movement, and its predilection in subject matter for the macabre, the bizarre, the fantastic, or the grotesque. For more obvious specimens of the kind, one may illustrate from Parkman's account, taken from Brébeuf, of the Huron Feast of the Dead and the torture of an Iroquois captive that followed—the climactic scenes of the opening chapters of the book:

One of the bundles of bones, tied to a pole on the scaffold, had chanced to fall into the grave. This accident had precipitated the closing act, and perhaps increased its frenzy. Guided by the unearthly din, and the broad glare of flames fed with heaps of fat pine logs, the priests soon reached the spot, and saw what seemed, in their eyes, an image of Hell. All around blazed countless fires, and the air resounded with discordant outcries. The naked multitude, on, under, and around the scaffold, were flinging the remains of their dead, discharged from their envelopments of skins, pell-mell into the pit, where Brébeuf discerned men, who, as the ghastly shower fell around them, arranged the bones in their places with long poles.

The priests were soon to witness another and more terrible rite. . . . It took place in the lodge of the great war-chief, Atsen. Eleven fires blazed on the ground of this capacious dwelling. The platforms on each side were closely packed with spectators; and betwixt these and the fires, the young warriors stood in lines, each bearing lighted pine-knots or rolls of birch-bark. The heat, the smoke, the glare of flames, the wild yells, contorted visages, and furious gestures of these human devils, as their victim, goaded by their torches, bounded through the fires again and again, from end to end of the house, transfixed the priests with horror.

The image of Hell on earth which makes its first appearance in these passages is the central, organizing image of the book, literally and constantly present to the Jesuit imagination as the figure par excellence of the circumstances of the Canadian mission, and set forth by Parkman above all in the scenes of torture, burning, and violent death, which are such a prominent feature of the book, as they were of Jesuit experience, in their capacity both as witnesses and victims. Thus, beginning with the passage quoted above, we have the torturings of Father Jogues as an envoy to the Mohawks, or of Father Bressani, as their prisoner; or the burning by the Hurons of the Oneida chief, Ononkwaya (a particularly lurid example of the kind); or, for the culmination of the sequence and the book, the martyrdoms in quick succession of Brébeuf, Lalemant, Garnier, and Chabanel, when the storm of Iroquois destruction finally sweeps over the Hurons, to blast the promise of the mission in the bud.

But, if scenes like these receive their due emphasis, Parkman's instinct for the baroque is deployed no less effectively in rendering the everyday life of a missionary in an Indian lodge—a matter, for the rest, which the Jesuits also subsumed under the figure of a terrestrial Inferno. Among these "little images of Hell," perhaps the most striking are the genre-pieces in the account of Father Le Jeune's mission to the Montagnais, with their painterly emphasis—among other elements of vivification—on grotesqueries of attitude or equally grotesque effects of sudden movement, like the rush of dogs at the close of the following:

Put aside the bear-skin, and enter the hut. Here, in a space some thirteen feet square, were packed nineteen savages, men, women, and children, with their dogs, crouched, squatted, coiled like hedgehogs, or lying on their backs, with knees drawn up perpendicularly to keep their feet out of the fire. . . . During a snowstorm, and often at other times, the wigwam was filled with fumes so dense, stifling, and acrid, that all its inmates were forced to lie flat on their faces, breathing through mouths in contact with the cold earth. . . . The dogs were not an unmixed evil, for by sleeping on and around [Le Jeune] they kept him warm at night; but, as an offset to this good service, they walked, ran, and jumped over him as he lay, snatched the food from his birchen dish, or, in a mad rush at some bone or discarded morsel, now and then overset both dish and missionary.

Likewise, scenes that stand in profoundest contrast to these images of Hell, and signalize the achievements and triumphs of the counter powers, are conceived in variations of the same general mode. Such, for instance, with its atmosphere of miracle and fantasy, is the scene of the elevation of the Host and of the altar afterward in the darkling meadow, festooned with strings of fireflies, which closes the account of the founding of Montreal (a lay enterprise, to be sure, under Sulpician rather than Jesuit auspices, but a product of the same fervors of Canadamania in France that inspired the missionaries to their martyrdoms). Again, for another triumph of the faith, and potentially perhaps an even more significant one, we have Parkman's rendering of the scene in the newly built mission house at Ossossané that marked the turning of the tide of Jesuit proselytizing among the Hurons—their first baptism, that is, instead of infants or of dying adults, of a warrior "in full health and manhood, respected and influential in his tribe." This is another interior piece in the predominant mode of the book, the grotesque or bizarre details which it accents here composed to an effect that is peculiarly suggestive of the cultural fruitfulness the encounter of Jesuit and Indian seemed to promise.

Thus, for vivification in the more strictly pictorial sense of the word, the book has a particular stamp of its own. Indeed, in this strict sense, it is perhaps the most painterly of all Parkman's histories, or at least the most literally scenic—consisting, of one thing, as it largely does, of action within a limited frame of view that presents itself naturally as a stage picture, and of action, furthermore, including the scenes of torture, that in itself is literally drama: that is to say, the enactment of ritual. But the book also incorporates in its very conception a certain element of illusionism or theatricality, intrinsic to the mood of the venture, with its play of visionary lights and shadows, its startling contrasts, its preternatural tensions of spirit, and its flamboyant counteraccenting of the aspects of Catholicism that the movement against which it was reacting particularly stigmatized as "superstition."

Nevertheless, if Parkman's handling of all this gives the book its predominant tonality, we have also to reckon, for the final effect, with the spare, factual, relatively uncolored kind of writing which in *Jesuits,* as everywhere else, forms the substratum of his presentation of his material, and, turned to various uses, keeps the more evocative and imaginatively immediate passages from imposing their special tone at the expense of the many-sidedness of historical actuality. For one thing, of course, Parkman has the Jesuits to deal with in other capacities than as missionaries and martyrs. So we note, on these less intense levels of action, his handling of Father Druilletes's embassy to New England to negotiate for joint action against the Iroquois—an account which deftly underlines both the humor and the humanity in this exchange of amenities between Jesuit and Puritan (though the ambassador's proposals were politely rejected), and makes Druilletes's shrewd observations the occasion for the passage I have quoted on the difference in religious character of the rival theocracies.

Furthermore, even in connection with the missionary activities of the Fathers, Parkman deploys a plain matter-of-factness in presentation which, by emphasizing the prosaic side of the venture, sets in more striking relief its central strain of apostolic ardor. Here we may cite his description of Ste. Marie, the main post of the Huron mission, and his re-creation of its everyday life and of one of the general councils of the missionaries of which it was the scene—the whole forming a particularly effective chapter of the book. Through it, to

be sure, we feel the current of force Parkman has already set in
motion in the ornately wrought scene of the baptismal mass mentioned above, and which here charges the low-keyed and merely
factual-seeming allusions to scenes of a similar kind.

On every alternate Saturday, as well as on feast-days, the converts came
in crowds from the farthest villages. They were entertained during Saturday, Sunday, and a part of Monday; and the rites of the church were
celebrated before them with all possible solemnity and pomp.

Again, at the close, we feel at once the *frisson* of the supernatural
and the premonition of martyrdom in an allusion, underscored with
only a slight apparent heightening of tone, to the empty chair of
Father Daniel,

never more to be filled by him,—never at least in the flesh, for Chaumonot
averred, that not long since, when the Fathers were met in council, he had
seen their dead companion seated in their midst, as of old, with a countenance radiant and majestic. They believed his story,—no doubt he believed it himself. . . . Daniel's station had been at St. Joseph; but the mission and the missionary had alike ceased to exist.

But, for the most part, reference, as well as manner, keep us in the
barest and most factual, if highly concretized, way to the signs of
the remarkable practical sagacity and organizing ability, of which,
as well as of proselytizing zeal, Ste. Marie was the fruit—the layout
and construction of the buildings, the arrangements for accommo-
dating the Indians, the highly successful agriculture, the "method,
discipline, and subordination" of daily life responsible for these
achievements. Juxtaposed as the chapter is to the closing scenes of
blood and fire, this plain matter-of-factness and objectiveness of
treatment bring out all the more the possibilities of the venture, so
soon to be rendered abortive, and clothe with a somber eloquence
Parkman's bald summarizing of Jesuit activity at this command post
of the mission: "Everything indicates a fixed resolve on the part of
the Fathers to build up a solid and permanent establishment."

Finally, for literalness and factuality of another kind, we may note the skill with which Parkman makes use in *Jesuits* of the peculiarly rich opportunity for directness of effect offered him by his sources. Indeed, in their minuteness, intimacy, first-handedness, and transparent sincerity of intention, the *Relations* (and cognate material) on which the book is based, are themselves a record which an historian could hardly help letting speak for itself, though there is of course no less of art in Parkman's selection and deployment of such material than in the construction of his more pictorial and highly wrought passages. So, for paraphrase, we have, for instance, the bare, unadorned, but wholly moving account of Jogues's search for the body of Goupil; or, for literal translation, such touches as that from Jogues's letter on his departure for the second, fatal Mohawk mission—the utterly simple and naked sentence in which he foretells his martyrdom: "I shall go, and shall not return." ["*Ibo et non redibo.*"]

But all this is simply to emphasize again the telling, incisive factuality which is the basis of Parkman's writing, and the ground of modulation to his more highly colored and immediately arresting passages. But here, likewise, we note the essential nature of such passages for inwardness of presentation, and we note their organic relation to the subject matter. In *Jesuits*, as I have said, they establish the peculiar tonality which is expressive of the spirit of the venture, and organize the narrative around the image of Hell, in its major and minor manifestations, which the course and upshot of the venture necessarily make the predominant image of the book—counterpointed, nevertheless as its recurrence is, by scenes charged with an emphasis of the opposite sort, and relieved by relatively low-keyed narrative and description of Jesuit activity in its more mundane phases. Likewise, Parkman's articulation of this baroque, neomedieval vision of Nature and the New World, not as an earthly paradise, but as a domain of the Nether Powers, gives the book its resonance in the series as a whole, so that the venture, in spite of the circumstances that cut it short, takes its place as a major representative—and the most alien to actual developments—of the competing forms of Western culture that strove to set their imprint on the conquest of the continent. But here the book ranges itself with the later volume of the series; and the point is one to which we shall return. Meanwhile we turn back to heroes of the will of a different stamp and follow the tale of exploration, begun in *Pioneers*, to its conclusion with La Salle in the valley of the Mississippi.

In *La Salle* we have again the highly organic treatment of the natural setting that we found in *Pioneers*; and the implications of the descriptive writing in the earlier volume are worked out as the cycle of voyages completes itself with La Salle's arrival at the mouth of the Mississippi, the nuclear scene of the book. *Pioneers*, as we have noted, moves to its climax, in the account of the Ottawa voyage, through a suite of increasingly detailed and richly colored passages; whereas in *La Salle*, on the other hand, the movement of the book is precisely the reverse, from richness to bareness and bleakness of effect, until it reaches a climax of elemental abstraction that in its denuded brevity is the polar opposite of the expanding, more and more sensorily evocative sequence in which *Pioneers* culminates. Nevertheless *Pioneers* and *La Salle* stand in the closest thematic relationship, composing an entity of movement and countermovement; and indeed Parkman so manages his emphases that the whole substance of the cycle seems contained in one vast parataxis formed by the opening sentences of the climactic passages of both books: "A lonely ship sailed up the St. Lawrence. . . . And now they neared their journey's end."

Pioneers, as we have seen, is an apotheosis of the explorer and of the explorer's passion, the Western *"volonté de la découverte,"* which the very structure of the book underlines on plane after plane of meaning in the richest accord of human drives and external nature. In *La Salle* we find a different configuration of these drives and passions. The *libido sciendi* motivates its hero as strongly as it motivates Champlain, but unlike Champlain—except so far as circumstances forced him to play the part—La Salle is also, for one thing, a type par excellence of the entrepreneur and empire builder as well as of explorer: the will to knowledge is now subsumed under instrumental considerations, and the relationship of man and nature shows nakedly as the Western drive to the "conquest" of nature. But even this instrumentalism is secondary with La Salle to something else—the goal is less than the pursuit of it, and he is above all an incarnation of the will itself, the unresting, insatiable activism and voluntarism of Western man that is the most distinctive trait of his culture, and in La Salle is predominant over every other aspect of psychic life to the point of monomania. If *Pioneers*, in its broadest reference, is an apotheosis of the Western spirit at its most creative, *La Salle* adumbrates the possible nemesis of this creativity and spells out the tragedy of defects of virtues, of one-sided integration that threatens disintegration, of distinctive choices in the gamut of human possibilities pushed beyond the human range, which, if it is in some form a perennial tragedy of all culture and civilization, seems latent in the ethos of the West beyond any other. At least, taking both books together in the most general way, it is some such implication that, by his handling of the interplay of action, character, and setting, the linked movement and countermovement Parkman fashions for both collaborates to suggest.

On this ultimate plane of tragic meaning, however, *La Salle* comprehends other elements of tragedy, and in its most immediate and overt aspect is a tragedy of leadership in the Shakesperian vein, projected from Parkman's sense of temperamental kinship with his hero, his feelings of class frustration in the face of triumphant Jacksonism, and his secret doubts, involved with his own boyhood failures in the mana of command, as to the sources of this frustration. Here La Salle figures as a latter-day Coriolanus, the leader deposed by the average man who cannot rise to the demands of his leadership —a note, naturally, that is struck above all in Parkman's account of La Salle's assassination at the hands of his mutinous followers:

At that moment, a shot was fired from the grass, instantly followed by another; and pierced through the brain, La Salle dropped dead. . . . The murderers now came forward, and with wild looks gathered about their victim. "There thou liest, great Bashaw! There thou liest!" [*"Te voilà grand Bacha, te voilà!"*] exclaimed the surgeon Liotot, in base exultation over the unconscious corpse. With mockery and insult they stripped it naked, dragged it into the bushes, and left it there, a prey to the buzzards and the wolves.

Yet, if the commons are not to be excused, this dénouement would hardly have its tragic resonance, except for what Parkman has made of the flaw of character that collaborates with circumstance to bring it about—the discordances of La Salle's "complex and painful nature," in which are to be found at once the "springs of his triumphs, his failures, and his death." No one as steeped as Parkman in the Puritan-individualist ethos of personal accountability, or as deeply responsive to the Shakesperian conception of character as destiny, could have interpreted otherwise a case, that, literally and symbolically, touched himself and his situation so close to home.

The fatal flaw in La Salle's qualifications for leadership was of course the burden of constitutional diffidence, the complex of pride, shyness, and reserve, that cut him off from men and prevented him from communicating to his followers the inner warmth of enthusiasm that nourished his own energies. "Hiding his shyness under a cold reserve"; unable "to express, and much less to simulate feeling, —a trait sometimes seen in those with whom feeling is most deep"; he lacks, in fine, "that sympathetic power, the inestimable gift of the true leader of men, in which lies the difference between a willing and a constrained obedience." As one need hardly point out, this strain of diffidence in La Salle, at odds with a native instinct of command, was a trait of character that struck home to Parkman in the most inward way and the ramifications of which he traces with a psychological sureness born of the most intimate kind of recognition. Parkman, one must repeat, was not La Salle; and there is no blurring of objectiveness in this masterpiece of historical portraiture. Nevertheless there is equally no mistaking the elements of temperamental kinship that guide Parkman to the tragic flaw in his hero's endowments, and the polarizing around what he makes of it of his own preoccupation with the problems of leadership, personal and public —the blockage of mana and the resort to a "constrained obedience" that provoked the mutinies in little of his boyhood expeditions; the autobiographic touches in his portrait of the younger Cerré at St. Louis, when he was about to put his powers of leadership to a severer (and this time successful) test; and, on a broader plane, the ambiguities of feeling, evident in his early travel journals, as to the sources of the defeat of his own class and caste by the Jacksonian democracy, to view the workings of which at first hand was one of the motives of these journeys. Or rather—and what is more to the point—it is some such stuff of Federalist obsolescence and personal frustration which Parkman objectifies in his portrayal of La Salle, purges of its personal and local character, and transmutes to a work of tragic art, a rendering, sure, superb, unsentimental, of the uncommon man as leader, brought down by the failure of rapport to which his leadership is perennially liable.

Yet, as I have said, in our final impression of the book, a more comprehensive nemesis hangs over the figure of La Salle, and its implications of tragedy take a wider range. For one thing, if La Salle is the protagonist of a tragedy of leadership, he is so, in part, not because he exemplifies the archaic and the obsolete, but because he is a man ahead of his time, attempting to work his works in a social context unprepared for them. If he is a type of the uncommon man, he is so, in his most central aspect, simply by virtue, as forerunner, of his representative character, by the manifestation in him to a more than ordinary degree and in their most unmodulated form of the predominant traits, or what were to become such, of a whole culture—namely, in the broadest sense, Parkman's own. Here again we have to reckon with the duality of Parkman's attitude toward the forces in play on the American scene of his time: on the one hand, the grudge of class and caste that set him at odds with Jacksonian democracy; and, on the other, his profound reponsiveness to the prevailing ethos of individualism and "self-reliance" that cut paradoxically across the grain both of Jacksonian equalitarianism and Federalist inequalitarianism. At any rate, above all else, La Salle is a projection for Parkman of this latter-day configuration of Western dynamism, and of his sense, in the most inward way, of the human commitment to its imperatives, and of the exactions of that commitment. It is perhaps hardly necessary to cite chapter and verse for what Parkman makes in this respect, simply as an individual, of this figure "cast in iron," this "grand type of incarnate energy and will"; the staple of whose character is an "invincible determination of purpose"; in whom "the cravings of a deep ambition, the hunger of an insatiable intellect, the intense longing for action and achievement, subdued all other passions"; who, "by a necessity of his nature, could obey no initiative but his own"; who "trusted himself, and learned more and more to trust no others." Again, Parkman is not La Salle, if only by the narrow but decisive margin that kept the iron of his own personality from rigidifying in this temperamental mold. Nevertheless, as with the discordant strain of diffidence in La Salle, there is no mistaking the *fonds* of self-recognition on which Parkman draws to re-create the dominant traits of his hero; and, equally, there is no mistaking the mode of these traits, the specific pulsations of the particular iron string to which every fiber of La Salle's being vibrates. This is a point, too, on which Parkman himself is perfectly explicit. Throughout, he places La Salle in a nineteenth century context, and underscores the representative quality, the historical and cultural typicality— in kind at least, if not in degree—of his hero's pattern of psyche, as it foreshadows the ethos of nineteenth century Western man. So, coming back to La Salle's activities from his account of Marquette— in whom the apostolic ardor of the early Jesuits still glowed, and whose "Maryolatry" evokes one of his most sympathetic passages— Parkman writes:

We turn from the humble Marquette, thanking God with his last breath that he died for his Order and his Faith; and by our side stands the masculine form of Cavelier de la Salle. Prodigious was the contrast between the two discoverers: the one, with clasped hands and upturned eyes, seems a figure evoked from some dim legend of medieval saintship; the other, with feet firm planted on the hard earth, breathes the self-relying energies of modern practical enterprise.

Likewise, minor incidents serve to add touches that round out the conception—as, for instance, regarding the "Great Comet of 1680," what Parkman makes of the strain of latter-day rationalism in La Salle:

As night came on, the travellers saw a prodigious comet blazing above this scene of desolation. On that night it was chilling with a superstitious awe the hamlets of New England and the gilded chambers of Versailles; but it is characteristic of La Salle, that, beset as he was with perils, and surrounded with ghastly images of death, he coolly notes down the phenomenon, not as a portentous messenger of war and woe, but rather as an object of scientific curiosity.

And, finally, the whole is summed up in the magnificent valedictory sketch of La Salle that follows the account of his death:

The enthusiasm of the disinterested and chivalrous Champlain was not the enthusiasm of La Salle; nor had he any part in the self-devoted zeal of the early Jesuit explorers. He belonged not to the age of the knight-errant and the saint, but to the modern world of practical study and practical action. He was the hero, not of a principle nor of a faith, but simply of a fixed idea and a determined purpose.

Thus, to repeat, La Salle, as a type of character, embodies for us above all else the complex of Western drives—of Western will, activism, and "self-relying" energy in their most extreme form— that seemed to reach a cultural climax in the individualist ethos of Parkman's own day. And, to come back to what we started with, it is, above all else, as such that La Salle is the focus for us of tragic feeling in the book—the projection on the one hand of Parkman's sense of creative *élan* in his own commitment to the drives that rule his hero, but as unmistakably the projection likewise of his sense of the nemesis latent in that commitment, of the *misères* as well as the *grandeurs* that gather round the archetypal figure for Western culture of the explorer or pioneer.

But if all this, like the rest, is to some extent made explicit in the book, it is most evident in the tone and atmosphere Parkman creates by his handling of the natural setting; and for the central strain of tragic emphasis in *La Salle,* we shall need to examine in some detail the patterning of the book achieved by this means. Here we may look first at the crucial scene or passage that articulates the whole—the scene, significantly, not of La Salle's failure and death, but of his greatest triumph, the completion of the Mississippi voyage.

This scene occurs roughly in the middle of the book, and consists of a paragraph on the arrival of the explorers at the Gulf, an account of the ceremonies of taking possession, and a closing paragraph evoking with ambiguous irony the continental immensities which thus "on parchment" pass under the sway of the "Sultan of Versailles"; all "by virtue of a feeble human voice, inaudible at half a mile." As with passages of a similar tenor in *Pioneers* I have spoken of, only now with augmented effect because of its recurrence in the climactic scene, this sudden dwarfing of the human scale seems, even as it underlines the hollowness of the French claims to domination, to cast a shadow of dubiety on the signal "conquest" of Nature by "Anglo-Saxons" that will shortly follow. This is again that spatial vision by which in one mode or another, Parkman links the present of his histories with the present of his own time, and projects the ends of things from their beginnings. But if these enigmatic ironies add their note to the scene, it is the opening paragraph on the arrival of the expedition at the Gulf that strikes its ground-tone. Here the whole movement of the book reaches its counterclimax of abstraction; and the great cycle of exploration ends in a spatial vision more primordial than that of any terrestrial vastnesses and immensities, and one that not so much dwarfs the human scale as annihilates it altogether.

And now they neared their journey's end. On the sixth of April, the river divided itself into three broad channels. La Salle followed that of the west, and D'Autray that of the east; while Tonty took the middle passage. As he drifted down the turbid current, between the low and marshy shores, the brackish water changed to brine, and the breeze grew fresh with the salt breath of the sea. Then the broad bosom of the great Gulf opened on his sight, tossing its restless billows, limitless, voiceless, lonely as when born of chaos, without a sail, without a sign of life.

Thus, in a sense, the cycle ends as it began, and we come back again to the "wilderness of waves" from the "wilderness of woods" —the "waste of verdure which rolled in shadowy undulation far to the unknown West" of Ribaut's landfall; or, reaching to the "bounds of Mexico," the "leafy desert . . . sunk in savage torpor" of Cartier's Pisgah sight from the Mountain of Montreal. But these land visions are vibrant with anticipations of the forces of spirit that will disrupt the "savage torpor" and, for good or evil, begin the process of its conquest. As we have seen, the record of the incursion of these forces moves to its culminating point in *Pioneers* through more and more highly charged and richly realized sequences of sensory evocation, instinct with a feeling of the most creative accord of human drives and the task in hand. In *La Salle*, on the other hand, the vision that concludes the cycle is the climax of a movement of deprivation and denudation, which, as it expresses itself in images of external nature, reaches a nadir of blankness in the most primordial of all such images. The prodigious dynamism of will and act that from the beginning implements the venture now exerts itself in a vacuum of blighting solitariness and inhuman isolation; overmastering every capacity of spirit that does not serve its imperatives, it takes on a character of ultrapersonal fatality; and the atmosphere of bleakness and blankness that gradually envelopes its workings to reach the ultimate *nada* of the central scene is above all a correlative of the inner blankness of obsession and monomania, of resources of spirit strained beyond the human limit, of psychic death-in-life.

Or at least some such meaning attaches itself to the spectral quality we feel in this scene, if we follow the interlinked sequences of which it is the focal point and which create for the descent of the great central river, the cardinal historical fact of the narrative, the same atmosphere and tonality as the culminating scene creates for the arrival at the sea—a sense of mere undifferentiated, unremitting flow that finds us embarked on a Mississippi as spectral as the Gulf, in which this blind, denuded energy of flow reaches its stasis: the "dark and inexorable river . . . rolling, like a destiny, through its realms of solitude and shade."

This tonality is achieved by a double process of modulation in Parkman's treatment of the natural setting, simply in its physical aspects. On the one hand, we have a gradually decreasing incidence of sensory detail of the kind on which *Pioneers* builds to its climax; and, conversely, a constantly heightening negative charge, so to speak, that brings to pervasive predominance the single motion of water flow. The atmosphere of bareness, desolation, and at last of utter blankness, that is thus created has for its elements the baldest actualities of what is given Parkman by the primary data of his narrative: the literal fact that the main direction of exploration is now downstream, away from the interior, instead of upstream, toward the interior, as in *Pioneers;* the literal convergence, geographically speaking, of all the rivers on the master-stream—to say nothing of the geographical platitude that rivers finally reach the sea; the actual times and seasons of most of La Salle's exploits; and the actual impressions of landscape conveyed by his own notations on this score in the *Relations.* The process of modulation that brings these elements to predominance in *La Salle* may be traced through a series of key passages, graduated in their incidence of effect, not by the actual order of their occurrence, but by the relation of their geographical locus and the events they deal with to the culminating traverse of the lower Mississippi. These events are Frontenac's ascent of the St. Lawrence to establish a base for Western expansion on Lake Ontario; Joliet's and Marquette's discovery and exploration of the Wisconsin and middle Mississippi; Hennepin's exploration of the upper Mississippi as a prisoner of the Sioux; and La Salle's appearance, in preparation for the culminating voyage, at the headwaters of the master-stream by way of the St. Joseph portage.

The account of the first of these events—Frontenac's progress of state up the St. Lawrence to establish the post at Cataraqui—

is the only passage of the book wholly informed by the same heightening intensities of perception as *Pioneers* and quickened by the same ardors of the upstream voyage. Thus the fleet of a hundred and twenty canoes and two flatboats, "painted in red and blue, with strange devices," intended to dazzle the Iroquois, fights its way up the Lachine Rapids—the men "shouldering canoes through the forest, dragging the flat-boats along the shore, working like beavers, sometimes in water to the knees, sometimes to the armpits," while Frontenac, drenched to the skin, directs their "amphibious toil"—until they reach the Thousand Islands, and the flotilla glides in long file

by rocky islets, where some lonely pine towered like a mast against the sky; by sun-scorched crags, where the brown lichens crisped in the parching glare; by deep dells, shady and cool, rich in rank ferns, and spongy, dark green mosses; by still coves, where water-lilies lay like snow-flakes on their broad, flat leaves; till at length they neared their goal, and the glistening bosom of Lake Ontario opened on their sight.

The episode demands the kind of emphasis this coloring gives it for several reasons. Thus Frontenac, the chief sponsor and backer of the policy of which La Salle is the agent, here makes his first direct appearance in the narrative to the full diapason of the explorer's theme, and in the full deployment of the qualities of will and energy he shares with Champlain and La Salle, energies which, thanks to the reverberations of this passage, make themselves felt "off-stage" through the rest of the book. Likewise, these reverberations have not ceased to sound when two volumes later the workings of Frontenac's energies are unfolded in detail, and the question of the retention or abandonment of the Western base he founds in this scene becomes the key to his quarrel with Versailles over the whole course of policy he has concerted with La Salle for New France. Indeed this stroke of Parkmanian vivification is one of the most archetectonic of the series. But here we are most concerned with this one full recurrence in *La Salle* to the note of *Pioneers* for its crucial part in shaping the pattern of evocation of the book

in relation to La Salle himself. Linked as it is, verbally, as well as
in context, to the climactic passages of both books—to the Ottawa
voyage on the one hand ("amphibious toil"; "with toil and trouble,
made their amphibious way") and to the final arrival at the sea
on the other ("till at length they neared their goal, and the glistening bosom of Lake Ontario opened on their sight"; "and now they
neared their journey's end . . . then the broad bosom of the Gulf
opened on his sight")—the passage at once associates La Salle with
the mode of *Pioneers* and serves as the base point, the immediate
ground of reference, for the process of transmutation through the
book that converts the material of the cycle from this mode to
its polar opposite in the emergence on the Gulf: the reduction or
abstraction of all this rich specificness of scene to the "turbid current" and "low and marshy shores" of the culminating passage;
the progressive muting of these heightened tensions of perception
to whatever faint response of the kind the breeze "fresh with the
salt breath of the sea" momentarily evokes, until the final vision
of the sea extinguishes every such response.

Thus we begin to be aware of this transforming process even
in the two epiphanies of the unknown already mentioned—the
voyages of Marquette and Joliet, and of Hennepin—the first of
which, indeed, as a voyage of prime discovery, outranks in importance La Salle's descent of the lower river. So the missionary and
the trader, embarked "they knew not whither,—perhaps to the
Gulf of Mexico, perhaps to the South Sea or the Gulf of California,"
float down the Wisconsin past "broad bare sand-bars" and wooded
islands, "matted with entangling grape-vines," as prairie and grove
or the "brow of some woody bluff" reveal themselves in parklike
vistas through the screen of trees on the bank. After the day's run
they camp on shore:

At night the bivouac,—the canoes inverted on the bank, the flickering fire,
the meal of bison-flesh or venison, the evening pipes, and slumber beneath
the stars; and when in the morning they embarked again, the mist hung
on the river like a bridal veil; then melted before the sun, till the glassy
water and the languid woods basked breathless in the sultry glare.

So they make their discovery of the master-stream, and continue down its course to the mouth of the Arkansas, while the shores, now "buried in a dense growth of the cane, with its tall straight stems and feathery light-green foliage," assume their southern aspect; and the sun glows "through the hazy air with a languid stifling heat." All this is striking enough as a realization of the midland river scene, and its trancelike quality is true enough to the physical actualities of season and circumstance. Nevertheless, in a way beyond the physical, the hypnotic effect of flowing water already begins to dominate our perception of details and particulars.

Again, as we descend with Hennepin "the young Mississippi, fresh from its northern springs," the panorama of a new world forms and re-forms vividly enough before our eyes, as we watch from the canoe

a wilderness, clothed with velvet grass; forest-shadowed valleys; lofty heights, whose smooth slopes seemed levelled with the scythe; domes and pinnacles, ramparts and ruined towers, the work of no human hand. The canoe of the voyagers, borne on the tranquil current, glided in the shade of gray crags, festooned with honeysuckles; by trees mantled with wild grape-vines, dells bright with flowers of the white euphorbia, the blue gentian, and the purple balm; and matted forests, where the red squirrels leaped and chattered.

But here too, in spite of the brilliant coloring, what dominates our impressions is the sense of the lapse and drift of water, and the passage moves to its close with the quiet flow of the river itself, as, after crossing Lake Pepin, we encamp again in the stillness of the summer night:

And when at evening they made their bivouac fire, and drew up their canoe, while dim, sultry clouds veiled the west, and the flashes of the silent heat-lightning gleamed on the leaden water, they could listen, as they smoked their pipes, to the mournful cry of the whippoorwills and the quavering scream of the owls.

Again, taken by itself, this passage, like the other, seems on the face of it simply a realization of a particular scene and action in

terms of sensory immediacy; and the movement of downward
flow that pervades both passages creates most apparently an atmosphere of relaxation, of release from the strenuous ardors of *Pioneers*. Nevertheless even here, as we come to the passages in their
context, the impression of flow imperceptibly takes on a different
coloration; a note of insistence begins to be felt in this pervasive
movement, even as it relaxes the tensions of every other kind of
perceptual response; and the "and" sentence of arrival and departure, the parataxis of the river voyage, that figures so prominently
in both—"At night the bivouac . . . and when in the morning
they embarked again," "and when at evening they made their
bivouac fire, and drew up their canoe"—begins to project itself
from the immediate detail it conveys, and articulate itself with the
movement of flow to become the essence of the narrative.[1]

[1] Indeed this "and" or "and when" sentence is the chief syntactical
means by which Parkman establishes the ultimate tonality of *La Salle;* and
it constitutes in fact the rhetorical framework of the whole cycle. From
the beginning, if at first only to incidental effect, we find the varied material of Parkman's sources fitted to its repeated pattern of phrase.

Thus we meet it at the opening of *Pioneers,* in the account already cited
of Ottigny's ascent of the St. John's, where, incorporating matter from
Bartram's *Travels,* it closes a richly evocative catalogue of the flora and
fauna:

". . . and when at sunset the voyagers drew their boat upon the strand
and built their camp-fire under the arches of the woods, the owls whooped
around them all night long, and when morning came the sultry mists that
wrapped the river were vocal with the clamor of wild turkeys."

Again—to pass over minor instances—it recurs as we follow Champlain's climactic progress up the Ottawa, unobtrusively threading itself
through the extraordinary sunrise piece we have examined, fashioned from
Parkman's own memories of the Magalloway:

"All day they plied their paddles, and when night came they made their
camp-fire in the forest. . . . Day dawned. . . . The canoes were
launched again, and the voyagers held their course."

But if this repeated phrasal pattern links voyage to voyage to give unity
to Parkman's treatment of the whole cycle, and establishes itself sufficiently in *Pioneers* for what he later makes of it, its effect in the earlier
book is of course subordinated to the ardors and intensities of the upstream *Drang* and the crescendo of perceptual richness with which the
discovery theme is there set forth. In *La Salle,* on the other hand, as the
trend of exploration turns downstream and the movement of the voyage
merges with the movement of the rivers, it becomes predominant.

Meanwhile, with the appearance of La Salle himself on the Mississippi scene—his traverse in December, 1679, of the St. Joseph portage to the Kankakee marshes and the headwaters of the Illinois —we reach a further stage in the process of modulation we have been following. The passage shapes itself to the same general pattern as the foregoing ones, vivifying with specific detail the day's run of the canoe and closing with the "and" sentence of the bivouac. Here, however, there is a radical change of tone; and the recurring parataxis now associates the pervasive movement of flow with an atmosphere of utter bareness and bleakness (but if to however "subjective" an effect, nevertheless in authentic accord with Parkman's sources, as may be seen from the material inserted below, mainly from La Salle's *Relations*).

Thus, after crossing the St. Joseph portage, the voyagers

soon reached a spot where the oozy, saturated soil quaked beneath their tread [*terres tremblantes, sur lesquelles on peut à peine marcher*]. All around were clumps of alder-bushes, tufts of rank grass [*des joncs et des aulnes*], and pools of glistening water [*une espèce de mare qui communique avec plusieurs autres de differentes grandeurs*, Charlevoix]. In the midst, a dark and lazy current, which a tall man might bestride, crept twisting like a snake among the weeds and rushes [*elle coule à travers des vastes marais, où, elle fait tant de destours . . . qu'après avoir vogué une journée entière, on trouva quelquesfois qu'on n'avoit pas avancé de deux lieues en droite ligne*, Relations; *la rivière . . . est si étroite, et il a faut continuellement tourner si court, qu'à chaque instant on est en danger de briser son canot*, Charlevoix]. Here were the sources of the Kankakee, one of the heads of the Illinois. They set their canoes on this thread of water, embarked their baggage and themselves, and pushed on down the sluggish streamlet, looking, at a little distance, like men who sail on land. Fed by an increasing tribute of the spongy soil, it quickly widened to a river [*elle s'augmente de telle sorte en peu de temps qu'elle est presque aussi large et aussi profonde que la Marne*]; and they floated on their way through a voiceless, lifeless solitude of dreary oak barrens, or boundless marshes overgrown with reeds [*on ne voyait aussi loin que la veue pouvoit s'estendre, que des marais, des joncs et des aulnes*]. At night they built their fire on ground made firm by frost, and bivouacked among the rushes [*l'on n'auroit pu trouver à s'y cabaner . . . sans quelques mottes de terres glacées, sur lesquelles on couchoit et faisoit du feu*].

So the voyagers reach the prairie country below, to find it too a dreary waste, burnt over by the Indians, and abandoned by the game in which it ordinarily abounded.[2]

For the content of this passage, as I have indicated, Parkman drew almost wholly on his sources, or on what, tested by personal observation, struck him as most salient in them for giving this entry of the chief actor of his drama on the scene of his chief exploits the kind of emphasis the episode called for. Likewise, for that matter, his most telling addition to what he takes from his sources—"solitude of dreary oak barrens" and its modifiers, which are crucial for the effect of the passage—are enough of a piece with La Salle's "*marais, aussi loin que la veue pouvoit s'estendre,*" "*vastes marais,*" and so on, not to obtrude themselves as more than vivification in a literal, physical sense. Nevertheless, of course, nothing could make more for thematic coloration than what the passage achieves under cover, so to speak, of this impeccable literalness and material authenticity— the suggestion of some vital inner correspondence of scene, action, and character it sets in train by way of connotative phrase, incantatory rhythm, and the repetitive patterns of syntax and paragraph structure that link it on the one hand with the river voyage passages we have discussed, just as its radically different tonality establishes the atmosphere that envelopes the account of the master-voyage and the preparatory exploits, more arduous than the voyage

[2] Parkman's descriptions of the Wisconsin and Mississippi in his accounts of Marquette and Hennepin were drawn from his own impressions on a trip he made in the summer of 1867, in preparation for *La Salle*. If he kept a journal of this trip, it has apparently not survived, but his itinerary can be reconstructed from the text and notes of the book and from letters. It does not explicitly appear from these sources that he visited the region of the Kankakee and the St. Joseph. George A. Baker, however, in a publication of the Northern Indiana Historical Society (1, 1899) states that "Francis Parkman, the historian, who went over the trail in the year 1848, graphically describes the portage and the Kankakee River." The date is hardly possible, but is more likely to have been mistaken than the fact of the visit itself. In this case, of course, unlike the other two, the season of Parkman's visit did not coincide with the season of the historical event, as La Salle made his traverse in December.

itself, which follows. Still detailed and graphic as the passage is in its way, even the particularities of bleakness it sets forth seem to lose their identity in the abstract and general bleakness created by the group of phrases—"boundless," "voiceless," "lifeless," "dreary," "solitude"—that now interweave themselves with the insistent movement of flow; landscape, river, and voyage, for all their faithfulness to external reality, take on to a further degree the trancelike reality of the projective and the oneiric; and, with this appearance of the *dux facti* on the remote headwaters of the master-stream he is to "conquer," the note of the journey's end already begins to sound, and, even verbally, the substance of the concluding sea vision begins to shape itself: "limitless, voiceless, lonely, without a sign of life."

The tonality which this passage establishes is reinforced throughout the train of episodes it introduces—the setbacks, fresh starts, disasters almost incredibly retrieved, obstacles, natural and manmade, faced down with an iron tenacity of purpose, which La Salle's preparations for the Mississippi voyage involved and which constitute indeed the main matter of the venture. So we have the river, "gliding dark and cold between its banks of rushes," "the vast white meadows," "the empty lodges, covered with crusted snow," at the deserted town of the Illinois Indians, as he makes his way up the ice-choked current from Fort Crèvecœur on his extraordinary relief journey of 1680; or the prairie in the interseason of freeze and thaw, "one vast tract of mud, water, and discolored, half-liquid snow," over which he struggled in the later stages of this journey. So, again, the heavy-laden canoes crawl on, "day after day, and week after week," past the "monotonous ranks of bristling moss-bearded firs," as he returns acoss Lake Huron from his relief journey of the following year; and the smoke from the wigwams of his Indian allies creeps "upward in the sullen November air," as he makes his final preparations at Fort Miami.

And so, meanwhile, for the passage which brings us to the most crucial of these episodes, when La Salle arrives at the Illinois town for the rendezvous with Tonty, essential to his plans, to find it a scene of ruin and massacre:

They embarked again, and soon approached the great town of the Illinois. The buffalo were far behind; and once more the canoes glided on their way through a voiceless solitude. No hunters were seen; no saluting whoop greeted their ears. They passed the cliff afterwards called the Rock of St. Louis, where La Salle had ordered Tonty to build his stronghold; but, as he scanned its lofty top, he saw no palisades, no cabins, no sign of human hand, and still its primeval crest of forests overhung the gliding river. Now the meadow opened before them where the great town had stood. They gazed astonished and confounded: all was desolation. The town had vanished, and the meadow was black with fire. They plied their paddles, hastened to the spot, landed; and, as they looked around, their cheeks grew white, and the blood was frozen in their veins.

In what follows—La Salle's grim search for the bodies of Frenchmen in the wake of the Iroquois raid that has caused this devastation; his persistence in exhausting this negative evidence before coming to conclusions as to Tonty's fate; his refusal, until he could complete the search, to go on with the Mississippi voyage, though for once his men had caught his own enthusiasm and urged him to it; his discovery at last of indications that Tonty's party had escaped destruction—in all this we see La Salle at the height of his powers, at his heroically and humanly most "magnanimous"; and the paragraph that introduces the episode builds with typically Parkmanian strokes to a complete immediacy of involvement in the situation as it presents itself to the *dramatis personae*, on the spot, at the moment, so that the reader shares in the quick the challenge that confronts La Salle and participates under the same pressure of uncertainties in the weighing of evidence, the surmises, decisions, and actions that follow. Nevertheless, for all it contributes to dramatize the immediate action, the paragraph also casts over it the implications of the sequence with which it is articulated. Again, we have the hypnosis of flow, evoked by the incantatory echoing of "glided" and "gliding" and the recurrent "and" sentences of the river voyage; again, we have the telltale phrase group woven through them—

"voiceless," "solitude," "no sign of human hand," "desolation"; and La Salle's actions, even at the height of heroic *arete* at which we see them in the episode the passage leads to, are tinged with the atmosphere of spectrality that has begun to envelope them from the beginnings of the venture on the Kankakee.

And so for the conclusion of the venture. Though the season of the culminating voyage is spring—the luxurious southern spring of "hazy sunlight" and "warm and drowsy air"—these hints of sensory richness are left undeveloped. Nothing could be barer or more low-keyed as to details of scene and setting, than Parkman's presentation. Instead, the flowing monotone of the river voyage sentence, its freight of particulars reduced to a minimum, wholly takes possession of the narrative; while, sounding for the last time as La Salle passes Marquette's and Joliet's farthest mark and completes this signal conquest of the unknown, even the discovery theme itself comes to us muted and deadened through the atmosphere of blankness the writing creates:

Towards evening, they saw on their right the mouth of a great river; and the clear current was invaded by the headlong torrent of the Missouri, opaque with mud. They built their camp-fires in the neighboring forest; and at daylight, embarking anew on the dark and mighty stream, drifted swiftly down towards unknown destinies. They passed a deserted town of the Tamaroas; saw, three days after, the mouth of the Ohio; and, gliding by the wastes of bordering swamp, landed on the twenty-fourth of February near the Third Chickasaw Bluffs. They encamped, and the hunters went out for game. . . . Again they embarked; and, with every stage of their adventurous progress, the mystery of this vast New World was more and more unveiled.

Then with their arrival at the Gulf, the process of modulation we have been following reaches its term. The pervasive sentence of the river voyage, now stripped of all syntactical overlay, and abstracted to its barest elements, at once brings to a stasis the long, lapsing movement of downward flow, and, as I have said, seems to comprehend in one vast parataxis the whole interlinked series of voyages that coalesce to form the cycle: "A lonely ship sailed up the St. Lawrence. . . . And now they neared their journey's end." In turn, the talismanic phrase group, of which this opening "lonely" in *Pioneers* is the germ, now brings to complete dominance the sense of denudation and deprivation its incremental echoing through the book has created; and, as we have seen, the cycle ends is a vision of utterly primordial blankness:

the broad bosom of the great Gulf . . . limitless, voiceless, lonely as when born of chaos, without a sail, without a sign of life.

Likewise this nuclear passage sets the tone for the rest of the book—the account of the grandiose attempt at empire building, to which, in La Salle's eyes, the Mississippi voyage was merely a preliminary; his failure to regain the mouth of the river on his colonizing expedition from France; the debacle of his forced landing in Texas; and his assassination by mutineers on his desperate sortie to bring relief to the "dying germ of civilization" he had planted. The narrative here, dramatic as it is, is almost wholly bare of the kind of vivification which, as we have seen, connotes in Parkman a creative accord of psychic drives and the task in hand. Instead, it unfolds throughout in the somnambulistic atmosphere of the sea-vision. So, when Tonty redescends the Mississippi, seeking in vain for his lost leader, already at the extremity of his fortunes on the plains of Texas, the key phrases sound in a last ghostly echo: "All was solitude, a voiceless desolation of river, marsh, and sea." Likewise, when, after La Salle's assassination, the survivors—innocent and guilty—of his forlorn hope make their way overland to the mouth of the Arkansas and reach at last the stream of his obsession, the Mississippi they reach is the "dark and inexorable river . . . rolling, like a destiny, through its realms of solitude and shade." [3] This note, informing the image of the river with the same ultimate resonance as the image of the sea, has been struck

___

[3] Even here, however, Parkman does not go beyond the range of his sources. As he notes elsewhere, Joutel habitually refers to the Mississippi as the "fatal river."

earlier in the book. For all the midsummer glow of Parkman's account of Marquette and Joliet, it is, nevertheless, the current of the "dark and gloomy stream" its discoverers turn back to stem. Again, though the actual time of La Salle's voyage which completes their discovery is spring, the phrases of the sequence recur with accumulated suggestions of a Mississippi beyond the changes of the seasons: "at daylight, embarking anew on the dark and mighty stream, the [voyagers] drifted swiftly down towards unknown destinies." So, finally, the Miltonic, abstracting simile in which the sequence culminates—"dark and gloomy stream," "dark and mighty stream," "dark and inexorable river . . . rolling like a destiny"—wholly charges its cadenced repetitions with intimations of an inner fatality, and we emerge at last on a Mississippi altogether out of time and space, a river as oneiric as the sea into which it flows.

Thus, blending sensorily to a single impression of unremitting, undifferentiated water flow through vast, denuded landscapes to a vaster, more elemental blankness, the controlling images of river and sea establish themselves as the correlative of La Salle's monomania and project for us, to an effect beyond the reach of explicit statement, the nemesis of creativity which is the underlying theme of the book—the rigidifying of the fixed idea, the divorce of the inner world from the world of external reality that, step by step, brings about the grandiose debacle of La Salle's last phase; the blank inhuman grayness of the compulsive and the obsessive; the blind automatism of imperatives of will and action become ends in themselves, as overmastering as an external fate.

And, equally with the climactic passages of *Pioneers,* Parkman is drawing on the deepest personal sources for what the tone and atmosphere of the book achieve by way of setting forth La Salle's monomania. Nothing could project more effectively than his handling of its master-images what he himself had known of possession by a fixed idea: the obsessive turning of the mind, "despite of judgment," to "remote objects of pursuit" (to cite again his letter to Ellis); the straining, beyond human limits, of every faculty to attain them; the compulsions that made "labor . . . a pas-

sion and rest intolerable"; the condition like that of a "locomotive . . . rushing on to the inevitable smash." Likewise, as the
book draws on inner depths of experience, so this nexus of personal
experience articulates itself with the subject matter on broader
and broader levels of meaning. Parkman's La Salle is an "isolato"
from real life comparable only to Melville's Ahab as an embodiment
of atomic Western individualism; and in the commitment to the
central complex of Western drives of which he is an archexemplar
we have a sense of possible shipwreck latent in a whole culture
and ethos.

Yet the subtle modulations that transmute the coloring of *Pioneers* to the coloring of *La Salle* likewise link both books together
to make a single entity of the great cycle of voyages that is their
subject and a unitary complex of the volitions of spirit that implement it. *La Salle* subsumes the creative and positive aspects of these
drives, of which *Pioneers* is the apotheosis; *Pioneers* hints at the
nemesis of this creativity set forth in *La Salle*. Parkman's tragic
version of the Western quest has little in common with Henry
Adams's hysterical catastrophism—or our own. Instead it is tragic
in the classic sense of springing from a double but integral vision
of life beyond optimism or pessimism, which finds its account where
commitment is most exacting and dualities sharpest—that vision
of interdependent good and evil, symbiotic creativeness and destructiveness, complementary qualities and excesses or defects of
qualities, which is Parkman's reading, at once, of nature, man, and
man's second nature of culture and civilization.

Or so at least Parkman's handling of character, incident, and
setting impress us in its wider ramifications of suggestion. Yet the
aura of symbol and evocation that gathers for us around La Salle
never obscures the objective historical figure, and shapes itself
impalpably from the most solid and realistic portrayal of character.
One cannot leave the book without quoting further from the closing sketch of La Salle from which I have already quoted in part,
and in which Parkman's art of tragic portraiture reaches its culmination:

Serious in all things, incapable of the lighter pleasures; incapable of repose, finding no joy but in the pursuit of great designs, too shy for society and too reserved for popularity, often unsympathetic and always seeming so, smothering emotions which he could not utter, schooled to universal distrust, stern to his followers and pitiless to himself, bearing the brunt of every hardship and every danger, demanding of others an equal constancy joined to an implicit deference, heeding no counsel but his own, attempting the impossible and grasping at what was too vast to hold,—he contained in his own complex and painful nature the chief springs of his triumphs, his failures, and his death.

It is easy to reckon up his defects, but it is not easy to hide from sight the Roman virtues that redeemed them. Beset by a throng of enemies, he stands, like the King of Israel, head and shoulders above them all. He was a tower of adamant, against whose impregnable front hardship and danger, the rage of man and of the elements, the southern sun, the northern blast, fatigue, famine, and disease, delay, disappointment, and deferred hope emptied their quivers in vain. That very pride which, Coriolanus-like, declared itself most sternly in the thickest press of foes, has in it something to challenge admiration. Never, under the impenetrable mail of paladin or crusader, beat a heart of more intrepid mettle than within the stoic panoply that armed the breast of La Salle. To estimate aright the marvels of his patient fortitude, one must follow on his track through the vast scene of his interminable journeyings, those thousands of weary miles of forest, marsh, and river, where, again and again, in the bitterness of baffled striving, the untiring pilgrim pushed onward towards the goal which he was never to attain. America owes him an enduring memory; for, in this masculine figure, she sees the pioneer who guided her to the possession of her richest heritage.

For the full effect of these valedictory paragraphs, one needs of course to take them in the context of the rest of the sketch, as one needs to take the sketch in the context of the whole book. But the mingling of psychological realism and tragic amplitude, of objectiveness of manner and inwardness of feeling, of depth of penetration and breadth of reference, is evident enough; and, likewise, one needs no more to recognize stylistically a crowning example of that nervous, masculine, expressive, and many-leveled prose, which, without the slightest trace of surface peculiarities, nevertheless strikes as idiosyncratic a note as any in our literature.

CHAPTER XII

LATER LIFE

⚜ ⚜ ⚜

The twenty years of Parkman's middle life which saw the production of the bulk of his work were also his most expansive, relatively speaking, in other directions: in the pursuit of his hobby of horticulture; in scholarly and social relations; in public service and public utterance.

For the domestic arrangements, and the domestic tranquility and companionship, which were the setting of these activities— and indeed of all Parkman's later life—he was indebted to the whole-souled devotion of his sister Lizzie. On his return from Paris after the death of his wife, he lived during the winters with his mother and sisters—Lizzie and Mary—first at 8 Walnut Street, then, from 1865, at 50 Chestnut Street. Meanwhile, as we have seen, he carried on his horticultural activities at the summer place on Jamaica Pond he had acquired shortly after his marriage. In 1852, his oldest, and, in early days, his favorite sister, Caroline, had married the Reverend John Cordner, a Unitarian minister in Montreal; his second sister Mary, latterly an invalid, died in 1866; and after the death of his mother in 1871, he and Lizzie shared the Chestnut Street house until his own death in 1893. (His daughters, Grace and Katherine— who, during the dark year of his absence in Paris, had been cared for by his sister-in-law, Mary Bigelow—both married in 1879.) But well before the death of his mother, the responsibilities of the household and the care of his daughters had devolved upon Lizzie, and she seemed to find the fulfillment of her life in dedicating herself to her brother's interests.

Indeed, from the start, Parkman had been more or less idolized by all his sisters—more so, it would seem, than is commonly the case with a gifted elder brother, and perhaps because, besides his gifts, he brought into the family atmosphere a dash of assertive masculinity, which the ministerial blandness of the father—though he was anything but a weak man—failed to supply. At any rate, as the chances of life opened to Lizzie an opportunity for its practical exercise, this family brother-worship concentrated itself in her to become the mainspring of her existence. We have seen her reading law books aloud to Parkman in bed, during the distresses of an earlier time; and her diary, or the few printed extracts which appear to be all that is extant of it, show with what solicitude she had already, during the first years of his widowhood, come to regard "F" 's welfare.

1862, June 11. F. has seemed in very good spirits for a day or two.
Sept. 9. F. is suffering from the most severe attack in his eyes he has had for years. He cannot attend to his gardening at all. Mother feels very anxious.
Sept. 10. F., if anything worse. He seems in very low spirits.
Sept. 15. F. seems better.

1863, Jan 24. F. is highly entertained by "Pickwick," as much as if he had never read it before.
Feb. 11. F. is beginning to work upon his French History, though, as he says, at a snail's pace. His eyes are very troublesome now.
Sept. 20. F. has not slept for some nights, and his head is in a bad state.
Oct. 1. F. still has very poor nights and seems miserably.

1864, June 25. This is the day of the Rose Show. Grace and I went in to help Frank. We worked steadily for two hours, and barely had time to prepare the great quantity of roses. F. took four 1st prizes and a large "gratuity."

1865, July 18. Frank and I have been to a reception at the Lyman's to meet Gen. Meade and Staff.
Nov. 7. Frank came down to breakfast very lame; thinks the old trouble is all coming back.
Nov. 22. The anxiety about Frank's knee is passing away.

1867, July 10. Frank is going to the Mississippi River; he is now writing history connected with its discovery, and he goes on that account. What a good summer he has had so far; his book [*Jesuits*] out this spring and well received, and his flowers so successful, and he seems so well.

Aug. 15. Frank arrived none the worse for the 5 weeks journey, though he has used head and eyes much. He has brought many photos of Sioux Indians and of Mississippi scenery.

1868, Sept. 25. Mother is 75 today. F. brought in white roses.

Oct. 29. Frank's head is in a bad state, the first time for a long time.

Nov. 1. F's head is very bad, worse than for some time; he says, years.

Nov. 27. Frank has determined to go to Paris for the winter. His head seems a little better, but he cannot do much with it, and he would rather be idle there than here. He seems disposed to go, and in good spirits, so we are very glad to have him, but it leaves a great gap.

So this record of the minutiae of Frank's condition and doings continues as far as the extracts take us, until the death of their mother left the brother wholly the focus of the sister's gifts of tacit care and affection.

1869, March 27. F. arrived this ev'g. He seems in very good spirits and health.

April 12. Frank's head is almost as bad as before he went away.

1870, March 24. F. is having sleepless nights, and suffering very much.

Sept. 16. F's birthday. He got no sleep last night, and I never saw him more affected by it in health or spirits. It is a year since he has been sleepless, more or less.

Sept. 23. F. did not sleep at all last night. It is wonderful that he can do anything by day, and he does not do much.

Sept. 24. F. slept between 5 and 6 hours. It is such a relief. Yesterday it was mournful enough at breakfast, though he plays with the cats and the children and says nothing.

Sept. 25. Mother is 76 [77] today. As I came down to breakfast, I saw F. coming in with a bunch of roses already tied, and another of ribbons and daisies. He looked so well I knew he had slept, and found he had had a very good night. That alone made mother happy.

1871, March 12. Mother feels very happy that F. has just been chosen professor of Horticulture in the new Bussey Institute of H[arvard] C[ollege]. Frank himself likes the appointment, as he thinks he can do the work without giving more time than he can give, and the fact that he can take such a responsibility is a delight as a proof of how much better he is.[1] June 8. Mother moved out of town with great difficulty [she died that summer] but at last was safe in her room, rhododendrons and roses of Frank's gathering all about her.

Obviously, up to a point, the relationship indicated by these diary entries was a one-sided one. Family tradition has it that Lizzie, from her regard to "F," refused an admirable suitor, who remained single for the rest of his life on that account; and her friends are said to have felt that she was sacrificing herself to her brother with a devotion that the object of it did not fully appreciate. And, habituated as Parkman had been from boyhood to the hero-worship of the home circle of mother and sisters, it is probable enough that in the dark years after his wife's death he more or less took for granted their affection and services. Nevertheless, it is equally obvious that, with time, the bond to Lizzie on his part became one of far deeper reciprocity than familial use and wont; and if her dedication of herself to his interests passed for a sacrifice in the eyes of the world, it was sufficiently grounded on mutualities of feeling, temperament, and understanding to make it a genuine partnership and a genuine fulfillment of her nature. At any rate, inheriting with her brother the same blend of inner warmth and outer reticence that made them temperamentally kindred spirits, sharing with him the same tastes, literary and personal, she not only managed with quiet efficiency the difficult housekeeping the necessities of his condition entailed, but, perhaps alone of the family, entered deeply into the spirit of his work and a comprehension of his larger purposes. Likewise, his independent and self-sufficing nature came to realize even here the degree of its dependence on her. It is eloquent of this aspect of their relationship that

---

[1] Parkman held this post for a year. The duties, according to Farnham, were not exacting, "no preparation being needed to go twice a week to the greenhouses and talk to a class of young women about the cultivation of flowers."

Parkman proposed to memorialize it by dedicating a volume of
the series to her—and it is equally characteristic that, after discussing the matter, the pair should have decided against his doing
so, as making, even in this guarded way, too public a revelation
of their intimacy. (The volume in question was no doubt the last
written, *A Half Century of Conflict*, for which, after some infelici-
tous attempts of his own, Lizzie had devised the title and which,
unlike the others of the series, lacks a dedicatory page.) It is also
characteristic that the one recorded occasion when the feeling which
informed their intimacy came to something like overt expression
between them should have been, likewise, through the medium of
his work, and her recognition of the personal depths from which
it was drawn. She herself set down the incident, after his death,
in some notes she furnished his biographer, C. H. Farnham, which,
in this instance, he left unused. She had been reading back Parkman's dictation to her of the last part of *Montcalm and Wolfe*,
full of a sense of his own resemblance to his invalid-hero. When
she came to the chapter telling of Wolfe's victory and death, she
goes on, "in spite of having braced myself to coolness in order
to read it properly, I fairly broke down and could not finish that
m'g. I do not think he was sorry and I like to think of that morning."

But for the most part, with their common reserve, their common
dislike of "scenes" and the emotionally overaccented, it was in an
atmosphere of tacit understanding that Parkman's life now followed its quiet/tenor under Lizzie's auspices—given always the
background of pain and suffering, the weeks and months of occultation, the never wholly stilled threat of the "enemy." Chestnut
Street, running down Beacon Hill, a block away from, and parallel
with, Beacon Street and the Common, is still, in its physical air and
aspect, the quintessence of late Federalist Boston; and Number 50
is still extant, with its dark-painted front striking a rather somber
note among its more ornately façaded, red-brick neighbors. Indeed, without and within, it was a "twilight house, of subdued
colors," according to Farnham, who, as Parkman's secretary, had
been familiar with it in the eighties. So, or to the same effect,

Lizzie herself had earlier described it in a letter of invitation to Mary Dwight Parkman and her daughter: "Frank and I both want you both. . . . Since you are not fond of sunshine, I can accommodate you beautifully." Yet this opacity, necessitated, in any case, by the hypersensitiveness of Frank's eyes to bright light, seems to have produced no impression of gloom. On the contrary, house and household, with their comely quietness and order, struck observers most of all by their complete suitability to the common tastes, needs, and temperamental traits of the inhabitants.

Here Parkman passed his days mostly in the study on the third floor; a north-lighted room, with a large, double-fronted writing desk, a soft-coal fire in an open stove, some of Barye's animal statuettes on the mantelpiece, the relics of the Oregon Trail trip fixed to the wall above, and bookshelves and engravings of historic personages filling the other walls. As a rule, except for meals, he only descended from these quarters to pass the evenings in the quietest sort of domesticity. Farnham has sketched for us the usual evening scene in the Chestnut Street sitting room: the soft colors and simple furnishings of family heirlooms further subdued in tone by the mild light of a low-shaded lamp; Lizzie, or Lizzie and her nieces, at the table, talking or reading; and Parkman himself at a distance from the light, by the side of the fireplace, in a solid, straight-backed chair. "In the shadows of his corner he was hardly visible. He often rested his elbows on the chair-arms, and meditatively adjusted the finger nails of one hand to those of the other, from time to time separating his hands to see if he could bring them together accurately again with a sharp little blow. Meanwhile the reading or the talking of the others went on. He occasionally looked up at a speaker with a direct and decided way to ask a question or pass a remark; but generally he saved his eyes by keeping them lowered on his finger-tips or on the floor. . . . He often passed the evening without joining much in the conversation. At other times he would be full of quiet talk."

For the rest, with out-of-doors additions, the same ordered tenor of things ruled the seasonal sojourn, from spring to late fall, at the Jamaica Pond cottage, where Lizzie was her brother's guest, so to speak, as he was hers at the Chestnut Street House, which came to her at their mother's death. The cottage stood on the southwestern shore of the pond, the grounds falling off at the rear to a dock, from which Parkman embarked for a daily row of one hour, never omitted or shortened; a form of exercise, indeed, which was his only recourse during particularly acute spells of lameness. But besides the steadily maintained routine of historical work, the chief activity of his summers was of course the famous gardening, of which I have already spoken, with its concomitants of Horticultural Society exhibits and offices; the professorship at Bussey; and, during these years of his main historical production, the output also of a little literature on gardening: *The Book of Roses*, already mentioned, in 1866; a score or so of contributions to Tilton's *American Journal of Horticulture* from 1867 through 1872; and in 1878, for the *Bulletin of the Bussey Institute*, a paper on the "Hybridization of Lilies," regarded by experts as a model of its kind. In the early eighties, because of increasing lameness, he gave up the more exacting of his horticultural activities; and thereafter maintained his garden simply for his own pleasure. Its physical scene was the slope of land above-mentioned, from the rear of the cottage to the pond, where the beds flanked the walk to the dock, against a diversified background of trees and shrubs, familiar or rare. It is said to have been planted more with an eye to the flourishing of individual species in the perfection of their kind than to niceties of color juxtaposition or "landscaping"; but the effect seems nevertheless to have been sufficiently harmonious as well as striking. In any case, for many persons who came to some degree within the orbit of Parkman's privacy, this atmosphere of floral amenities was the characteristic setting of his later years. So Henry James writes of "that delightful back verandah of yours at Jamaica Plain, from which the world seems all festooned with wisterias" (and at least one strain of which—*Wisteria floribunda violacea plena*—Parkman himself first brought to flowering). So, likewise, John Fiske, going out one morning for what he supposed to be a short session of Harvard College business, recalls an "enchanted day in the season of apple blossoms," prolonged until late evening, as host and guest "ransacked the world of thought" amid perambulations of garden, pond, and greenhouse.

And indeed beyond what could be ascribed to material conditions, this sense of amenity in Parkman's way of life was equally expressive for observers of an inner amenity, a serenity and tranquility of spirit, which stand in marked enough contrast to the *Sturm und Drang* of his earlier years. Such impressions, to be sure, emphasize equally, as we should expect, a sense of latent force and fire, of animation and incisiveness, behind the quiet unobtrusiveness of manner; as they do the unaffected simplicity and frankness of personal address which, from the beginning, had opened Parkman's way for him at all levels of life; and the lack, even physically, of any appearance of invalidism: the firm chin, square-set frame, upright bearing, and good color—or, even when he had to resort to crutches, his briskness in managing them. Nor, decidedly, are we to suppose an atrophying of the old instinct of command, or a lack of consciousness of power. "His modesty was not the modesty of naiveté or humility," Farnham notes. "On the contrary, he was always, in a quiet way, a masterful rather than a humble spirit. He held his virtues by a firmer grasp than unconscious possession." Nevertheless, it is the grasp of certain rather unexpected virtues that is persistently emphasized in impressions of Parkman's later years: the presence of an unsentimental but deeply genuine strain of kindliness and sympathy; the manifestation of an essential humaneness of spirit, of which, to be sure, we are always aware enough in his writing, but which hitherto had asserted itself somewhat intermittently in his personal life, and in a way painfully at odds with elements of character that might easily have congealed to a rather hard sort of egoism. "What most impressed one, in talking with him," Fiske writes, "was the combination of power and alertness with extreme gentleness." This testimony of honey from the lion is forthcoming on the part of almost all who knew Parkman in later life; and for closer intimates, who knew, as Fiske did not, the extremity of temperamental discordances that he had had to bring into balance, the force of the innate propensities to violent assertion and action he had had to curb, the pressure of pain and suffering that might have excused any degree of them, the result seemed a triumph of character of no small order.

And, likewise, for all Parkman's self-discipline and the limitations imposed on him by the demands of health and work, his nature was not that of a solitary or recluse. He had sufficiently strong propensities for both "the freedom of intimate friendship and the decorum of ceremonious intercourse," as Farnham puts it; and was a sufficiently familiar figure in the various worlds, social, scholarly, and literary, of Boston and Cambridge, to which his birth and circumstances or his tastes and pursuits variously allied him. So, we find him a member of the Union Club, started during the Civil War as a protest against the Copperhead tendencies of the fashionable Somerset; a member of the famous Saturday Club; and, later, an active organizer of the St. Botolph Club, of which he was chosen the first president, both his social gifts and his emphatic antiprohibition sentiments being warrantably deemed a safeguard against the chilling proposal of another of the founders—Edward Everett Hale, who soon resigned—that "the use of wines and liquors be interdicted in the clubhouse." [2] He had a particular predilection for the Saturday Club, which Emerson had been instrumental in founding, a few years before the Civil War, as a common meeting ground for men of the world and the lights of Concord transcendentalism, of Cambridge scholarship, and of New England letters generally—or as a "mutual admiration society" of the local literati, as it sometimes seemed to visiting outsiders, not wholly overawed by august names and the conversational pyrotechnics of a Holmes or Lowell. If its palmiest days had perhaps closed by 1873 when

[2] In an undated pamphlet, *An Open Letter to a Temperance Friend*, Parkman stigmatized the "corrupting force of a prohibition which does not prohibit, which in large communities does not prevent or even diminish drunkenness, but which is the fruitful parent of meanness, fraud, lying, and contempt of law."

Parkman was elected to it—of the early group Agassiz died that year, and Emerson himself had entered his long decline—it still provided a vantage point for observations of the great and near great of an elder generation, whose traits he later occasionally sketched for Farnham in a "kindly and impartial" but sharply realistic strain; and in its roster of closer contemporaries, provided the opportunities for intimate discourse he particularly relished: foregatherings with such various spirits as Martin Brimmer, fellow Brahmin and fellow original; the painter William Morris Hunt, boon companion of his college years and his Italian journey; or non-Bostonians like Howells, or Godkin, of the *Nation*, resident for a time in Cambridge.

As a social figure Parkman is not recalled for witticisms or anecdotes, and seldom took the lead in general conversation. Barrett Wendell speaks of the "normal impersonality, the animated objectivity of his talk," its "frank, idiomatic raciness of phrase," and a quality of unpretentiousness and friendliness that made one forget he was a celebrity and forget "even that he was not exactly of an age with you. Like his own literary style . . . the man himself was steadily contemporary." On particularly favorable occasions, or in a particularly congenial group, his powers of conversation could be fired to highly memorable effect, as we have seen from John Fiske's recollections, or as is witnessed by a much younger contemporary than Wendell, and one much less disposed to take the Bostonian scheme of things at its own value. During the early seventies, John Jay Chapman, then an undergraduate at Harvard, became an intimate of Martin Brimmer's household, and thus records his impressions of the symposia—composed mostly of Saturday Club members—to which this intimacy admitted him: "At Beverly [where the Brimmers summered] as in Boston, rare spirits would often gather—Tom Appleton, Frank Parkman, William Hunt, Frank Parker, and others; and *le causeur des Lundis*, Sainte-Beuve himself, might sometimes have envied those long, inspiring talks, with the pine-trees whispering overhead and the surge of the summer sea not far away."

Not all observers, to be sure, strike this note; and Howells, enthusiastic admirer as he was of Parkman's histories, in which he found no alloy of parochialism, sets down with a certain asperity some occasions in personal intercourse of what he felt to be characteristically Bostonian circumscriptions: "those limitations I nearly always found in the Boston men."

I remember his talking to me of *The Rise of Silas Lapham*, in a somewhat troubled and uncertain strain, and interpreting his rise as the achievement of social recognition, without much or at all liking it or me for it. I did not think it my part to point out that I had supposed the rise to be a moral one; and later I fell under his condemnation for certain high crimes and misdemeanors I had been guilty of against a well-known ideal in fiction. These in fact constituted lese-majesty of romanticism, which seemed to me disproportionately dear to a man who was in his way trying to tell the truth of human nature as I was in mine.

Nevertheless, Howells continues, these displeasures passed,

and my last meeting with our greatest historian, as I think him, was of unalloyed friendliness. He came to me during my final year in Boston for nothing apparently but to tell me of his liking for a book of mine describing boy-life in Southern Ohio a half century ago [*A Boy's Town*]. He wished to talk about many points of this, which he found the same as his own boy-life in the neighborhood of Boston; and we could agree that the life of the Anglo-Saxon boy was pretty much the same everywhere.

And, indeed, whatever conversational points of discord may have arisen, Parkman's own letters to Howells give the impression of considerably less formidable barriers to communication than the latter's reminiscences suggest—and not least in regard to *Silas Lapham*, though no doubt Parkman's conception of the "moral" of that book takes a sufficiently Brahminesque turn. Likewise, with whatever vehemence of manner we may suppose Parkman to have rallied to the defense of romantic fiction, it was certainly, as can be seen, from no defect of response to the fictional realism of Howells's own practice.

I have just finished your *Chance Acquaintance*, and cannot help telling you the pleasure and the admiration I have felt in reading it. The truth, subtle penetration of character, kindly satire, and wholesome genuine feeling that fill it throughout, make it charming. . . . If you are like me, you do not object to the expression of an honest liking for your book. I wish you would find time to dine over here before the end of the month, with Mrs. Howells.

I cannot help telling you of a pleasure I have enjoyed lately in common. My siste.: read to me *The Lady of the Aroostook*, and we were both delighted. It seems to me as near perfection in its kind as anything terrestrial can be. . . . Ladies appear to be of one mind as to the truth and delicacy of its feminine analysis; and, on the other side, it paints a gentleman realistically, a thing so rare in American fiction as to be a conspicuous distinction in itself. I know you have had this said over and over again, but I like the book so much that I am impelled to add my voice to the rest.

My sister has just been reading *Silas Lapham* to me and I cannot help writing to tell you how much I have been interested and delighted. It is admirable portraiture, realistic in the best sense of the word. It must touch the consciousness of a great many people, and—as we descendants of the Puritans are said to be always on the lookout for a moral—it will teach the much needed lesson that money cannot do everything. . . . I think I never admired your genius more than in this capital book.

As we have seen, Parkman was also on friendly terms with Henry James, an acquaintance begun no doubt like that with Howells, early in James's Cambridge years. During this time, in fact, James wrote reviews of *Jesuits* and *The Old Régime* for the *Nation*. The chief personal memorials of their friendship, however, belong to a later period, being an exchange of letters occasioned by James's reading of *Montcalm and Wolfe* and Parkman's of *The Bostonians*. James writes from Dover in 1885:

This is only three lines, because I cannot hold my hand from telling you . . . with what high appreciation and genuine gratitude I have been reading your *Wolfe and Montcalm*. (You see I am still so overturned by my emotion that I can't even write the name straight.) I found the right time to read it only during the last fortnight, and it has fascinated me from the first page to the last. You know, of course, much better than any one else how good it is, but it may not be absolutely intolerable to you to learn how good still another reader thinks it. The manner in which you have treated the prodigious theme is worthy of the theme itself, and that says everything. It is truly a noble book, my dear Parkman, and you must let me congratulate you, with the heartiest friendliness, for having given it to the world. So be as proud as possible of being the author of it, and let your friends be almost as proud of possessing his acquaintance.

Perusing the book, James goes on, "here by the summer smooth channel," with the French coast in view, and above him, on the downs, "the guns of old England pointed seaward, from the rambling, historic castle," he has been stirred under these influences to "all sorts of feelings—none of them, however, incompatible with a great satisfaction that the American land should have the credit of a production so solid and so artistic." He then makes the allusion I have quoted to the wisteria-festooned verandah at Jamaica Plain and launches into a discussion of the current state of English politics, characteristically expanding the "three lines" of his opening to an epistle of more than as many pages.

Parkman answers with characteristic brevity, if no less warmly, thanking James and expressing his own pleasure in *The Bostonians*, the instalments of which his sister was reading aloud to him—a pleasure, to be sure, which perhaps a little misconstrues the novel into an *exposé* of a "vile and rotten stratum of our society." For the rest, he hopes that Varena "is to return to nature and common sense," finds Miss Birdseye "a masterpiece," and congratulates James on his knowledge of the "types of progress and reform" that figure on the Boston scene. But, as we shall see presently, there are grounds for surmising that Parkman himself, or at least certain public activities in which he had been engaged not many years before, may well have played their own part in the inception and germination of James's book.

Meanwhile, as a complement to Parkman's Boston life, we have to note the resumption, also fertile in friendships, of his travels of historical investigation, so much intermitted during the time of his worst troubles. As has been seen, we have only two such to record for the seventeen years between the Oregon Trail trip and the publication of *Pioneers* in 1865—the Quebec-Montreal-Ottawa visit of 1856 and the winter in Paris after his wife's death, undertaken primarily for his health. Following *Pioneers*, on the contrary, these journeys, until the early eighties, became an almost biennial occurrence.

The first of them, to be sure, was made in a scholarly interest altogether off Parkman's own beat. This was a journey to Richmond at the close of the Civil War, undertaken at the instance of William F. Poole, the librarian of the Boston Athenaeum—of which Parkman was a trustee—to collect, while the opportunity was fresh, files of newspapers and similar matter, unavailable outside the Confederacy. So we find him in June of 1865 at work on this errand in the ruins of the recently burned city, to an effect, as might be supposed, that materially helped Poole lay the foundations of a Confederate collection "second to none," according to James Ford Rhodes. Unfortunately, nothing appears to survive as to Parkman's impressions of this eventful time and scene.

For the staple of his own investigations, we have to begin with eight or nine Canadian journeys, from 1866 through 1879, comprising almost always a stop at Quebec, and often at Montreal and Ottawa, but including also forays through New Brunswick, Nova Scotia, and Cape Breton Island, and revisitings of his old haunts at Lake George. In 1873 he spent several weeks at the Abbé Casgrain's family estate, Manoir Airevault, at Rivière-Ouelle, on the south bank of the St. Lawrence below Quebec—a visit which contributed notably to the impressions in his work, especially in *The Old Régime*, of preconquest Canadian life. Of his four European trips during these decades, the first was the 1868–1869 winter in Paris which Lizzie notes left such a "great gap" in the family circle. It was at this time that he struck up a friendship with Pierre Margry, the curator of the Archives de la Marine et des Colonies, with whose own scholarly fortunes, as we shall see, Parkman's work, especially on *La Salle*, was to be peculiarly bound up. We find him again in Europe in 1872, crossing on the *Siberia*, with Lowell and the Henry Adamses for fellow passengers, and joining Lizzie in Paris. (Adams writes to Charles Milnes Gaskell from Beverly Farms, June 23, 1872: "We are to have a pleasant party on the *Siberia* . . . James Russell Lowell and his wife, and Professor [of horticulture, that is] Francis Parkman, our best American historian and a very agreeable man.") Further European trips, to Paris and London followed, in 1880 and 1881, on which he appears as something of a celebrity, Henry James proffering him a guest membership at the Reform Club, and the Earl of Carnarvon at the Athenaeum. Meanwhile, to go back, he had also been supplementing the American forays of his earlier years with fresh travels, particularly the important Western trip of 1867, in preparation for *La Salle.* This took him to the country of the upper Mississippi, the Wisconsin, the Illinois, and the Kankakee; and at St. Louis was the occasion for a reunion with Henry Chatillon. In 1870 he explored Mt. Desert on a visit to his classmate, Judge Gray; and, in 1885, made the Florida journey which he turned to such effective account in the revised version of *Pioneers.*

Parkman kept brief notebooks of many of these trips, and, in some part, for the purpose, as with his earlier journals, of recording on the spot impressions of landscape and setting. This is particularly true of the 1871, 1873, and 1879 Acadian notebooks, when he was viewing for the first time many of the historic sites—Louisbourg, the "Evangeline country," and so on—that figure in *Montcalm and Wolfe* and *A Half Century of Conflict.* Likewise the little 1870 Mt. Desert notebook is wholly composed of such impressions; though, in comparison with what he makes of one or two of them in the revised *Pioneers,* to a rather heavy-handed and overadjectival effect—a curious reversal of the relationship that sometimes holds, for his earlier books at least, between the journals and the passages based on them. But for the most part—except, again, for the Florida journal—the contents of these later notebooks are, like the trips themselves, of a purely scholarly nature: archival, bibliographical, or cartographical references, notes as to projects in hand or in prospect of fellow tillers of his field, and the like. As such they have a high degree of professional and technical interest; but we touch on them here only as they round out the impressions his correspondence and other sources give us of the personal relationships which his scholarly activity involved.

These relationships, indeed, had begun to develop from the time of Parkman's return from Europe in 1845, first, mainly with American antiquarians and archivists—particularly a group engaged during the eighteen forties in establishing state archives of early history—but coming with the years to comprise almost every historical worker in the United States, Canada, and Europe, whose labors touched at all on his own field of activity. Two of these scholarly friendships—with Pierre Margry in Paris and the Abbé Casgrain in Quebec—were particularly intimate and cordial, though both also involved elements of discord. Margry, as I have said, was the director of the French colonial archives, and had earlier been the agent in the selection and copying of documents from them for a collection relating to the old Northwest made by General Cass, and a similar collection relating to the early history of New York, made for the state by John Romeyn Brodhead. Finally, when Parkman first knew him, he had gathered on his own account a vast collection dealing with French exploration in America, and including, among much else relevant to Parkman's purposes, the private letters of La Salle on which the official *Relations* of his voyages were based. Margry, with the common desire of scholars for priority of publication, had gone about ensuring it in this case by the somewhat questionable method of withdrawing the documents he needed from the public archives of which he was in charge and refusing other scholars access to them until he could print them himself, a matter for which no financial arrangements had been made. This procedure has been sharply criticized as an abuse of his official position. Parkman, however, with a genuine personal liking for Margry, and realizing that on this point he was intractable to either indignation or blandishments, set himself to gain his own end by seeing to it that Margry gained his, meanwhile publishing the first version of *La Salle*, subject to what revision might be necessary in the light of the withheld material. To get this material into print proved a sufficiently formidable undertaking, and involved in the end the arduous business of lobbying through Congress an appropriation for the purpose. An earlier attempt of the kind on the part of the Americanist, Henri Harrisse, in concert with the U.S. Minister to France, had come to nothing. Nevertheless, Parkman assiduously marshaled his forces—the officers of state historical societies, General Garfield in the House of Representatives, Senator Hoar of Massachusetts, Howells, then editor of the *Atlantic,* and others—and this time, after the usual delays, an appropriation of ten thousand dollars was voted. He still had the task of keeping the peace between Margry in Paris and the Librarian of Congress in Washington while the printing was in process, but finally the relevant volumes of the monumental compilation—*Découvertes et Etablissements des Français dans l'Ouest et dans le Sud de l'Amérique Septentrionale (1614–1754), Mémoires et Documents Originaux*—were off the press, and Parkman could begin his revision of *La Salle.* Except for his estimate of Beaujeu, the naval commander on La Salle's last expedition, he did not, as it happened, have to alter materially the main lines of his book. Nevertheless, the chief treasure for Parkman of Margry's hoard—La Salle's private letters, mentioned above—furnished the basis for an added chapter, "La Salle Painted by Himself," which remarkably confirms from La Salle's own words Parkman's view of his character and gives the finishing touches to an almost unrivaled achievement in historical portraiture. It is doubtful whether the documentary material for any other fifteen pages of historical writing ever cost their author quite such protracted and far-reaching effort to come by, or so much justified the effort.

But if Parkman questioned at all the validity of Margry's position in this matter, he did not let any such feeling appear, and, in spite of the trouble he was put to, remained on the most cordial terms with him. Margry, for his part, except as touching his collection, spared no pains in forwarding Parkman's investigations, and warmly reciprocated his friendship, where his Gallic vivacity and volubility seem to have found a highly congenial complement in Parkman's capacity for listening and drawing people out. Besides a long correspondence, pleasant memorials of their intimacy are forthcoming in Margry's nickname for Parkman of *"le cerf agile"*— from the rapidity of his gait—and some *vers d'occasion* he composed for a dinner with Parkman and Lizzie to celebrate the historian's forty-ninth birthday, on his Paris visit of 1872. For the rest, Margry's views were of a pronounced anticlerical and anti-Jesuit cast—"[he] is of the modern French school continually yelping at the Jesuits," to quote a letter to Parkman from John Gilmary Shea, the translator of Charlevoix—and the question has been raised of Margry's influence on Parkman's work in this sense. Two pieces of evidence bearing on the point are to be found in his 1869 Paris notebook. The first has to do with a long letter from Margry to Sainte-Beuve, in response to a request for Margry's opinion of *The Jesuits in North America,* of which Parkman had sent Sainte-Beuve a copy. In his answer to Sainte-Beuve, Margry expresses himself to the effect that Parkman had been misled by his clerical sources and that the miscarriage of the Jesuits in Canada was brought about, not by Iroquois intractability, but by the arbitrariness of their rule at Quebec. Margry read this letter to Parkman, who was sufficiently impressed to set down a summary of its contents. "He insists that I have not exposed their political character—that . . . they held the colony in a subjection so irksome that it could not long be tolerated. . . . He says that he has a document . . . 'very damaging for them.' " Parkman then concludes:

It might be added to the text that the "Northern Paraguay" could not long have endured, as the growth of political and commercial interests must sooner or later have subverted the Jesuit empire.

Whether or not he would have made some such addition to *Jesuits* cannot be known, as he died before he could revise the book.

On the other hand, Parkman did not hesitate, in spite of Margry's opinion, to discard an anti-Jesuit interpretation of events when he felt fresh evidence contradicted it. Thus he also set down in his 1869 notebook Margry's views as to the conduct of the naval commandant Beaujeu, referred to above. "He says that he has positive proof of the treachery of Beaujeu and that he was in league with the Jesuits . . . Margry says that Beaujeu had an understanding with the Jesuits to defeat La Salle's plans, as, he thinks, may be inferred from the following," and so on. In the first version of *La Salle*, Parkman accordingly adduced Jesuit influence as at least a possible explanation of the difficulties between La Salle and Beaujeu, which he interprets throughout in a sense unfavorable to Beaujeu. But in the revised version of the book, based on a firsthand examination of the hitherto unavailable documents of Margry's collection, he came to a different conclusion; discarded entirely in this connection the hypothesis of Jesuit intrigue; and ascribed Beaujeu's difficulties mainly to La Salle's own vagaries and unfitness for a divided command. As regards particular cases, Margry's influence on Parkman would seem to be confined to circumstances where Parkman was without means of forming an independent judgment.

Likewise, for anticlericalism in general, as point of view or mode of feeling, Parkman would seem to owe little to Margry and the "modern French school." *Jesuits* itself, written and published before Parkman knew Margry, is sufficient evidence on that score. In fact, leaving aside the issues of historical causation raised by Margry, it is precisely the matter of Jesuit rule at Quebec that called forth on Parkman's part perhaps the most emphatic and sweeping assertion of anticlerical sentiment to be found in his work:

The instinct of domination is a weed that grows rank in the shadow of the temple, climbs over it, possesses it, covers its ruin, and feeds on its decay. The unchecked sway of priests has always been the most mischievous of human tyrannies; and even were they all well-meaning and sincere, it would be so still.

In sum, Parkman's anticlericalism was a perfectly autonomous and autochthonous growth, for the origins of which we need hardly look beyond his native eighteenth century heritage—the strain of libertarianism and rationalism that was part of the environment in which he was born and that blends so curiously, in his histories, but to

such an integral effect, with the counterimpulses of romanticism.
But it was, of course, hardly a deficiency of anticlerical emphasis
that gave rise to his differences with the Abbé Casgrain; just as,
besides the personal affinities and joint historical interests that over-
rode these differences, their common responsiveness to the impulses
of romanticism was a bond of mutuality in this liveliest, warmest,
and most intimate of Parkman's scholarly friendships. The Abbé
Henri-Raymond Casgrain, eight years younger than Parkman, was
on the faculty of Laval University, and perhaps the leading figure
in a circle of Catholic scholars and writers, lay and clerical, bent
on reviving the forgotten glories of the French Canadian past and
creating a distinctively French Canadian literary culture. This
movement represented the awakening to cultural self-consciousness
of an ethnic group in some danger of submersion by a predominantly
"Anglo-Saxon" world, and, like other movements of the sort elsewhere through the nineteenth century, was highly charged with
currents of nationalist and religious feeling. The Abbé's contributions to the movement were manifold. As an historical scholar, he
and a colleague, Abbé Laverdière, had brought out in 1858 the
first modern reprint in full of the Jesuit *Relations* (which Parkman had reveiwed in the *North American*, making his review the
occasion for part of the monograph on Indian life that forms the
introductory chapter to his own *Jesuits*). This was followed by
the *Histoire de la Mère Marie de l'Incarnation* and *Histoire de
l'Hôtel-Dieu de Québec*. Then, in the eighties, came *Un Pèlerinage
au Pays d'Evangéline*, in which the Abbé gathered up every shred
of evidence an impassioned industry had been able to unearth telling against the English side of the Acadian question. This work of
revindication was intended to refute Parkman's treatment of the
question in *Montcalm and Wolfe*, and brought about their most
acute difference of opinion. Finally, the Abbé returned to his editorial labors with *Montcalm et Lévis*, a huge compilation of documentary sources in eleven volumes, for one of which, their breach
of friendship now healed, Parkman wrote the introduction.
Likewise, besides the production of these works of erudition—to

go back to an earlier period—the Abbé busied himself with a variety of other activities, literary and personal, in furtherance of the movement he had at heart—particularly the founding and editing, in the eighteen-sixties, of its chief organs, *Les Soirées Canadiennes* and *Le Foyer Canadien*. One fruit of these miscellaneous activities was a series of sketches and critiques, later collected in book form as *Biographies Canadiennes*, of the principal literary figures of the French revival. Among them, on the ground that *"c'était servir la cause nationale,"* he included a sketch of Parkman, in recognition, with due reservations, of what his books had done to make French Canada known to the world at large.

Parkman, as we have seen, was familiar with Casgrain's earlier scholarly work, but otherwise their paths did not cross until 1866, when the Abbé happened to come on a copy of *Pontiac* in the Parliamentary Library at Quebec. Struck by its scholarship, *"aussi rare que sûr,"* and by its evocatory power, which at once stirred his literary sensibilities and appealed to the cultural interests he cherished, he wrote the author, expressing his sense of this, and putting himself at Parkman's service in matters of scholarly investigation. His advance was reciprocated, an exchange of photographs followed, and the pair were soon launched on the full tide of a correspondence which, with minor intermissions, continued until Parkman's death twenty-seven years later. Through a series of mischances, they did not meet in person until 1871, when the Abbé made a trip to Boston to gather material for the above-mentioned sketch of Parkman. He has recorded there his impressions of his visit—his meeting with Parkman on the steps of the Revere House, the drive to the Jamaica Pond cottage in the season of rhododendrons, and calls in Cambridge on Longfellow and Agassiz. The author of *Evangeline*, white-bearded and majestic, struck the Abbé as the embodiment of an elder-day bard or seer—*"c'est ainsi qu'on représente Ossian, Baruch, ou le Camoëns"*—and Mrs. Agassiz particularly moved him by taking him aside and speaking with "tears in her voice" of the revelation of old Canada and the heroism of its missionaries and martyrs that Parkman's books had been to her and her husband. His host himself, with his engaging simplicity of manner "*toute américaine*," he felt had a face that Leonardo would have loved to paint, an "harmonious combination of intelligence, *finesse*, and energy," expressive of the thinker rather than of the poet, but with something nevertheless in the eyes, half-shut against the sunlight, that suggested the flame within. This visit was repaid, as we have seen, by Parkman's stay in the summer of 1873 at Manoir Airevault—a sojourn that might be called the Oregon Trail in little of his investigations of preconquest Canadian life. At least, he seems to have ingested every surviving trait of that life the region had to show, down to the details of the St. Lawrence porpoise fishery—the "white whales floundering in the bay of Tadoussac" of *Pioneers*—on which the Abbé had written a monograph.

Meanwhile, with the bonds of amity thus knit closer by personal intercourse, they were also being put to some strain by the mission Casgrain had undertaken of familiarizing Canada with Parkman's histories, where they were almost unknown, or becoming known only through the garbled translations of the Comtesse de Clermont-Tonnerre.[3] Casgrain's enthusiasm for them was of course

[3] The Comtesse de Clermont-Tonnerre, a descendant of the Vaudreuil family of Canadian fame, had given free rein to her ultraclerical sensibilities in making these translations, for which Parkman had accorded her permission together with whatever financial profits might accrue from them. Her tamperings with *Pioneers* he let pass, but he could not ignore her flagrantly garbled version of *Jesuits* and indignantly repudiated it:

"You express a wish I may have been satisfied with the translation of the *Jesuits*. I am unable to regard it as in any proper sense a translation at all. Large and essential parts of the book are omitted. The arrangement of the rest is in some parts entirely changed, sentences are in some places interpolated and sometimes suppressed, often in such a way as to make me appear to express views contrary to those of the original. My name is put on the title-page of a book which is not mine, either in form or substance, and not an indication is anywhere given that any alterations have been made."

Parkman's histories met no such instant response from the general public as those of Bancroft, Prescott, and Motley; and even among English-speaking readers, it was only during the eighteen-seventies that they began

subject to serious reservations, which, in turn, as he voiced them privately or in reviews and articles, called forth some vigorous countersallies from Boston. It would take too much space to follow these exchanges in detail; and interesting as they are, it must be confessed that they have a somewhat marginal bearing on our sense of Parkman's work as a whole. Parkman's approach to the history of French Canada certainly involved some debatable prepossessions; but whatever fundamental points Casgrain might have raised in respect to them became obscured, as the debate developed, by the emotionalism of his attachment to the *"cause nationale"* and the compulsion he was under, beyond the necessities of his case, to preserve intact the idealized and sentimentalized image of old Canada the interests of the cause seemed to postulate. Consequently, the debate is hardly a contest between equals, and misses a kind of centrality it might have had. Nevertheless, we must glance

---

really to make their way outside historical circles. Casgrain's work of vulgarization was thus very much of a pioneer undertaking. In spite of the differences of point of view on which he felt increasingly bound to insist, he can be credited as much as anyone with the first recognition of Parkman's real stature as an historian and as a writer.

In the United States, Howells was perhaps most instrumental in making Parkman known to a wider public, with his review of *The Old Régime* in the 1874 *Atlantic*, and other reviews. John Fiske was also an early enthusiast, doing much, particularly, to establish Parkman's reputation in England.

In 1879, repeating in Boston a series of lectures he had given the year before at University College, London, Fiske had occasion to mention Pontiac's conspiracy. Among other things, he said it was memorable as "the theme of one of the most brilliant and fascinating books that have ever been written by any historian since the days of Herodotus." Then followed perhaps as rewarding a moment as could come to a lecturer, making an allusion of the kind:

"The words were scarcely out of my mouth when I happened to catch sight of Mr. Parkman in my audience. I had not observed him before, though he was seated quite near me. I shall never forget the sudden start which he gave, and the heightened colour of his noble face, with its curious look of surprise and pleasure,—an expression as honest and simple as one might witness in a rather shy schoolboy suddenly singled out for praise. I am so glad I said what I did without thinking of his hearing me."

at it, if only for the plane on which it was conducted, and the scrupulous balance the participants were at pains to strike between the claims of conviction and the claims of friendship. Some excerpts from Casgrain's letter to Parkman on *Jesuits* and from Parkman's answer to Casgrain's review of *The Old Régime* will perhaps give a sufficient idea of its tone and temper.

Parkman had sent Casgrain a copy of *Jesuits* with a cautionary note: "Remembering that I am a heretic, you will expect a good deal with which you will be very far from agreeing . . . I meant to give a candid view of my subject in the best light in which I could see it." To this Casgrain replied:

You speak of the impression that the reading of a book by one whom you call a heretic, and to whom I give the kinder name of *separated brother* (belonging to that chosen class who trample prejudices under foot to look the truth squarely in the face), must have made on me, a Catholic priest. Your book, in my opinion, is a *masterpiece*, and I dare not tell you so, for fear of passing for a flatterer, without adding that it is *masterpiece* of contradictions. Pardon my frankness. It is useless for me to attempt to reconcile the conclusions with the premises; it would be a waste of time. We live at two opposite poles; you at the pole of naturalism; I at that of supernaturalism; but there is one point on which we meet: that is the love of humanity.

Like me you cannot withhold your admiration of these men who sacrificed themselves with so much constancy and heroism for the love of mankind. The only reproach you make them is that of an inoffensive credulity. What is this speck of dust, if it is one, before the grandeur of their deeds? What colossuses, you say, and justly. But are you indeed sure that they would have been such great men without their blind obedience, without their enthusiastic faith? . . . However that may be, your book is the work of a thinker and of a great painter; and Canada owes you an eternal debt for having made its history so much admired.

Agreeing that they were, indeed, at opposite poles of faith (though adding that "my faith—such as it is—is strong and earnest") Parkman made no particular demur to this, nor to an elaboration of essentially the same points—enlarging the place of praise to give

criticism elbowroom, as Casgrain put it—in the essay on Parkman
I have referred to, first printed as a series of magazine articles in
1872.

With the publication of *The Old Régime*, however, Casgrain
found himself on less certain footing in respect to what, besides
their literary merits, he had made the chief ground of his champion-
ship of Parkman's books—their service to the *"cause nationale,"*
that is, in making "our history" generally known and admired. *The
Old Régime* necessarily dealt more conspicuously than Parkman's
earlier books with some less admirable aspects of old Canada; and
instituted some unflattering comparisons of a topical nature, particularly in the last chapter, which ends with the statement: "A
happier calamity never befell a people than the conquest of Canada
by the British arms." Casgrain's objections accordingly took on a
sharper edge; and his review of the book likewise evoked from
Parkman a more positive response to his friend's criticisms than
he had hitherto felt called on to make:

Mon cher ami:
   I am an *abonné* of the *Revue Canadienne* and have just read your article
on *The Old Régime*. It is very much what I had expected, knowing your
views and the ardor with which you embrace them, as well as the warmth
and kindliness of your feelings. I could take issue squarely on the principal
points you make, but it would make this letter too long, and I do not care
to enter into a discussion with a personal friend on matters which he has
so much at heart. Moreover, I wish to preserve an entirely judicial, and
not a controversial, frame of mind on all that relates to Canadian matters.
   Let me set you right, however, on one or two points personal to myself.
My acquaintance here would smile to hear me declared an advocate of
democracy and a lover of the Puritans. I have always declared openly my
detestation of the unchecked rule of the masses . . . and the corruption
which is sure to follow in any large and heterogeneous community. I have
also always declared a very cordial dislike of Puritanism . . . and I should
not spare criticism if I had to write about [it]. Nor am I an enthusiast for
the nineteenth century, many of the tendencies of which I deplore, while
admiring much that it has accomplished. . . .
   If you have mistaken my views, I could also point out a good many
other mistakes in your article. You say I see Canadian defects through a

microscope and merits through a diminishing glass. The truth is, I have suppressed a considerable number of statements and observations because I thought that while they would give pain, they were not absolutely necessary to the illustration of the subject; but I have invariably given every favorable testimony I could find in any authentic quarter; and after I had finished the volume, I made careful search in Ferland and Garneau to see if they had discovered anything which had escaped me. . . . The end of the paper stops me. I have space only to tell you how much I value your testimony to my conscientiousness as a writer and your remarks, too partial, I fear, on the literary qualities of the book.

[New sheet]. P.S. I am well aware that the conduct of the British government towards the Canadians was for a long time unjust, and in some respects grossly so; but it is not the less true that it was the conquest to which Canada owes the introduction of the institutions by which she has so greatly prospered.

In exhibiting the different workings of the two political systems, it was necessary to make comparisons which seem invidious, but these comparisons are not, as you say, *continual;* for they are confined to three or four pages at the end of the book. . . . As for the *cri de haine* which you impute to me, I assure you that my patriotism is not of the sort to be disturbed at this late date by any vision of Puritan scalps.

But, if these clashes of opinion had begun to sharpen, they did not yet strain the bonds of amity, or diminish the fund of mutual esteem the years had built up. Three years later, in 1878, the warmth and solidity of Parkman's relations at Quebec, across the lines of difference, were further demonstrated by the proposal of Laval University to grant him an honorary degree. And, likewise, these relations were proof against the storm raised by a certain section of Catholic opinion when the intention of the university was inadvertently divulged. This outbreak was largely the work of Jules-Paul Tardivel, a journalist of pronounced ultramontane views, with a violent dislike of the United States. He was no respecter of persons, and having disposed of the alien heretic as a matter of course, turned with equal vigor on the Abbé and the university for their traffickings with this "traducer of our race and our religion." The controversy spread; the Protestant and anticlerical press joined in; and by March of 1879 the atmosphere had become so heated that

Monsignor Hamel, the rector of Laval, reluctantly wrote Parkman that, for the good of the university, it seemed better to defer the question of the degree. Shortly after, with the Catholics at odds among themselves, McGill University improved the occasion by offering Parkman its own degree, which he accepted. Nevertheless, he had been genuinely moved by the kind of recognition that Laval intended. The previous December, he had expressed to the Abbé his sense of this and in view of the Tardivel affair, had taken pains to smooth the university's path if it should have to withdraw from its position.

It was to me extremely gratifying that men like these, while differing profoundly from me and disapproving much that I have written, should recognize the sincerity of my work by expressing their intention to honor me with a degree of *docteur-ès-lettres*. It was this generous recognition which gave me particular pleasure; and greatly as I should feel honored by a degree from Laval University, I prize still more the proofs of esteem which its directors have already given me. I trust that they will not feel themselves committed to any course which circumstances may have rendered inexpedient, and that they will be guided simply by the interests of the university.[4]

The one controversy which, eight years later, brought the relations of the two historians to a temporary breaking point was, as I have said, over Parkman's treatment of the Acadian question in *Montcalm and Wolfe*. Though Casgrain did not come off without honor in this historical duel, his highly emotional manner, and his refusal to face unpleasant facts where his emotions were involved, touched off in Parkman a charge of exasperation which

[4] Actually, this incident of Parkman's Laval degree was only a minor skirmish in the long and bitter contest between opposing Catholic factions known in the annals of Quebec as The Holy War. Bishops Bourget and La Flêche were the clerical leaders of the ultramontane party, and Tardivel its chief lay spokesman; Archbishop Taschereau and the university headed their opponents. For the most part, the questions at issue were decided by the Vatican in favor of the anti-ultramontanists. On the occasion of one such decision the irrepressible Tardivel pronounced the pope himself (Leo XIII) in error as to the facts of the matter.

one sees accumulating through occasions of disagreement I have omitted—particularly over Rameau de St. Pierre's *Une Colonie Féodale* and over *Frontenac*. Whatever Parkman's own bias, he had to a preeminent degree that feeling for the evidence in the round and in its relative bearings that marks off the genuine historian from the special pleader; and on this score, partisanship for partisanship, there was a disparity between the two which was bound sooner or later to trouble the waters of friendship. At any rate, when, in 1887, Casgrain set him a copy of *Un Pèlerinage au Pays d'Evangéline*, he allowed himself at last to speak directly on issues close to the Abbé's heart, with a bluntness that put a stop for a time to their correspondence:

You say that the charges against the priests are "laughable." . . . In reality, however, you are far from thinking these charges laughable, and you call them so only because you cannot answer them.

The quotation in your note to me—"*Amicus Plato, sed magis amica veritas*"—would have fitted the case better if you had written, "*Amica veritas, sed magis amicae patria et ecclesia.*"

The book would inspire more confidence but for the passionate animosity it shows against the actors on our side, and the equally vehement determination to justify those on the other at any cost.

Let me correct . . . a remark in one of your former volumes to the effect that I was attracted to the history of Canada by its nobleness and purity. The truth is that I had a taste for the woods and the Indians, and it was this that turned my attention to forest themes. . . . The splendid self-devotion of the early Jesuits and some other members of religious communities is worthy of all praise, but the history of the colony itself is throughout anything but pure.

Writing to Farnham the next year, he summed up his sense of the matter in plainer English: "The Abbé is no more fit than a chicken to deal with questions of history."

Nevertheless the Abbé's counterattack was by no means wholly without effect. If he failed to clear the French side of the case of its uglier aspects, which *Montcalm and Wolfe* had brought to light, he unearthed new material further blackening the English record, and was able to show that one of Parkman's sources, a compilation of documents from the Nova Scotia archives, had been bowdlerized in the English interest. The influence of his findings is evident in *A Half Century of Conflict*, where Parkman deals with the earlier phases of the Acadian episode, and noticeably shifts his emphasis as to the causes of the final catastrophe.

Who were answerable for the anomalous state of affairs in the province . . . ? It was not mainly the Crown of France nor its agents, secular or clerical. Their action under the circumstances, though sometimes inexcusable, was natural, and might have been foreseen. Nor was it the Council at Annapolis, who had little power either for good or evil. It was mainly the neglect and apathy of the British ministers, who seemed careless as to whether they kept Acadia or lost it, apparently thinking it not worth their notice.

Meanwhile, Parkman had spoken his last word of direct controversy with the Abbé by way of a review of a new edition of *Un Pèlerinage* in the March, 1889, *Nation*. This, like his letters, is unsparing of Casgrain's historical shortcomings. Due credit is given, however, for the fresh evidence he had gathered; and the review closes with the words: "The truth is, that the treatment of the Acadians was a scandal on both sides." By this time passion was spent and the air had cleared. Shortly after, the two resumed their correspondence on the old friendly basis; and it continued, without further jars, until Parkman's death in 1893.

And, indeed, throughout, though the differences that strained their amity figure larger in the telling, geniality of personal feeling is the dominant note of the relationship. For Parkman, working in isolation, Casgrain played an indispensable rôle of scholarly confidant, of a colleague with whom he could talk shop. Dissimilar performers as they were on the historical stage, they were perfectly at home behind the scenes of each other's projects; and this exchange of professional shoptalk and of scholarly services is in fact the main matter of their letters. At the same time, Casgrain's warmth and *gentilesse* melted Parkman's shell of reserve and quickened the inner warmth of his own nature to an expressive responsiveness, of a kind rare enough in his life. Conversely, Casgrain, for his part, found in the response he thus awakened the requital of a touching hero worship, kindled by the attraction of the stronger and more forceful personality, whose suffering he divined, and whose genius, for all in its workings that wounded his sensibilities, had cast its magistral spell on him from the beginning. At any rate, it is through some such affinity of contrasted temperaments that their friendship had started, had weathered its storms, and now came to its tranquil end, its flavor lingering in the fine French closes of their letters: "*Croyez toujours à ma sincère amitié: la votre m'honore infiniment*, Casgrain." "*Que Dieu vous aide, tout-à-vous*, Parkman."

But the amenities of Parkman's friendship with the Abbé made themselves felt in their degree through all his scholarly relationships, particularly in Canada, where, naturally, such relations were most numerous and most intimate. His correspondence came with time to comprise almost every worker in the field of early Canadian history; and, during his active years of scholarly travel in the eighteen-sixties and seventies, he himself became a familar and remarked figure at Montreal—where, as we have seen, his brother-in-law was a Unitarian minister—at Ottawa, at Quebec, and elsewhere. But it is of course at Quebec above all that we think of him at this time: the center alike of his studies and of the matter of his histories, and the city of his own predilection. Here he had nearly as wide a circle of acquaintances as at Boston, and was regarded almost as an adopted son—"*le Touriste aimé, qui, chaque printemps, nous revient avec les hirondelles; le brillant et sympathique historien, qui a su entourer d'une auréole notre vieux Québec*," as James LeMoine put it in the dedication to Parkman of his *L'Album du Touriste*. He stayed usually at Russell's Hotel in St. Louis Street; or sometimes with Judge George O'Kill Stuart among his Protestant friends; or with Dr. Hubert La Rue, of the

Abbé Casgrain's circle, who figures with him in the Abbé's *Biographies Canadiennes.* *"Rendez-vous tout droit à la maison,"* La Rue writes him, *"où votre petite chambre du fonds vous attends avec impatience."* Another close friend was Sir James Macpherson LeMoine, mentioned above, an antiquarian of note and president of the Quebec Literary and Historical Society, who was often the companion of Parkman's explorations of the battlefields around the city. And, finally, relations with less eminent figures also testify to the harvest of good will and amity he reaped at Quebec. Thus, in forceful if not native English, M. N.-E. Dionne—later head of the Parliamentary Library—recalls his admiration for the man and the craftsman, when he was Parkman's copyist on his 1871 visit:

Being poor, I was glad to gain some dollars, but I was chiefly proud to accompany this well-known Bostonian through his peregrinations from the Seminary to the Episcopal Palace, from the Registrar office to the Terrier's office, compulsing together every document which he intended to use. . . . So I must say, and everybody can say so, that if I am something today, I owe this to Mr. Parkman.

These scholarly travels, running their non-Bostonian thread through the ways and days of Chestnut Street and Jamaica Plain, complete the main sum of Parkman's activities during the twenty years from 1865 to 1885 that saw the production of the bulk of his work. Nevertheless, they do not exhaust that sum, and despite the slim margin left by the claims of "the enemy," we also find him playing a part in movements and causes of the day, sometimes publicly, sometimes privately, and if seldom to any great degree quantitatively speaking, almost always at some decisive juncture of action or to some decisive effect of utterance. But an account of these activities demands a chapter to itself.

CHAPTER XIII

PUBLICIST
AND CONTROVERSIALIST

⚜ ⚜ ⚜

To begin with, we find Parkman, though he worked independently, making his contribution to the task of organizing and professionalizing the higher scholarship that was a phenomenon of the years after the Civil War. Here, indeed, he seems to have had little direct connection with developments in his own field; developments which, for the rest, had little to offer him—he had nothing to learn from the "methodology" of historical research that was establishing itself at Johns Hopkins and elsewhere, and less than nothing from such historical theories as that of Teutonic Origins which presided for a time over the new dispensation.[1] On the other hand, he had, for obvious reasons, a lively interest in the field of American ethnology and archaeology, in which his friend Squier had broken new ground and where Henry Lewis Morgan was now a leading figure. Thus he signalizes in *Jesuits* the importance of Morgan's *League of the Iroquois* (though he disagreed with much of it) and corresponded at length with its author. This interest also had practical results. "I wish we had you in Cambridge," he writes Morgan in 1877. "There are the beginnings of an archaeological museum here and I hope something will come of it." Parkman was much concerned with this, and particularly with the founding, in the following year, of the Archaeological Institute of America, of which he was offered the presidency. This he declined because

[1] Except for Sparks, who died in 1866, the American historians with whom Parkman had the closest relations were Bancroft and Henry Adams. See Appendix C.

of his health, but successfully contended from the floor at the organizing meeting for the inclusion of American as well as European projects in the society's program of activities, which at first had been shaped to fit the tastes of the embattled classicists. Likewise, as a member of the executive committee and the council, he vigorously promoted this line of work, and also did much, privately and individually, to further the careers of promising Americanists, such as Captain John Bourke, the Indian ethnologist; and Adolphe Bandelier, a pioneer investigator of Mexican and New Mexican antiquities.

At the same time, as may be supposed, he had his eye on the Indian question as a current issue as well as a matter of ethnological study. Thus in 1875, during the Comanche troubles, he took occasion, in a review for the *North American* of H. H. Bancroft's *Native Races of the Pacific States*, to sketch out an Indian policy, which, could it have been followed, would have had the merit of preserving tribal life and culture from the attempt at root-and-branch eradication that later actually occurred at the hands of a misguided humanitarianism. Its essential flaw was the flaw of any Indian policy that demanded the same degree of firmness in dealing with whites as in dealing with Indians. Another cause that naturally engaged him, and to more viable effect, was that of conservation, to which George Perkins Marsh's pioneer work *Man and Nature*—which we find Parkman borrowing from the Athenaeum in 1872—had given the initial impetus. Thus, reviewing Sargent's *The Forests and the Census* for the *Atlantic* in 1885, and later in a plea for the preservation of the White Mountain forests, he outlines a national policy of forest conservation, such as began to take actual shape in the Weeks Act a quarter of a century later.

But it was a more comprehensive movement of the time, subsuming these sporadic if related activities, that called forth Parkman's chief efforts in the arena of public, or quasi-public, service. This was the movement for the general reform of American higher education, of which of course his own bailiwick of Harvard was for a time the center, and in which he played a part of some importance, both as publicist and as a member of the governing boards of the college. We have seen his dissatisfaction as an undergraduate with what the college had to offer him; and this dissatisfaction could hardly have been allayed by his service, at a time of low institutional vitality, on the committee for examining in history to which he had been appointed in 1852 at the instance of Jared Sparks. Nor, himself a pioneer of latter-day scholarship, could he fail to have been struck by the incongruously marginal position at Harvard of its own most seminal thinkers and scholars, particularly its brilliant group of scientists, with most of whom—Asa Gray, Agassiz, Jeffries Wyman (together with F. J. Child and Ephraim Gurney in other branches of learning)—he was on more or less close personal terms. Finally, as a lay alumnus of socially conservative but pragmatic views—of a type to which the divorce in 1865 of the college from the control of the Massachusetts legislature had now given a direct voice in its affairs—he was acutely aware of the new demands the whole development of the country after the Civil War was making on its institutions of intellectual culture and of their inadequacy to meet these demands in a formative way.

Thus on several counts Parkman was predisposed to figure as a backer of innovation and change when the movement of reform locally came to its head with the portentous election of Charles W. Eliot as President of Harvard in 1869. A few months after that event he made his sentiments publicly evident by way of a notable manifesto in the New York *Nation*, to which we shall return; and he was able to give practical effect to these sentiments from behind the scenes, through his official position at the college. Thus, elected an Overseer in 1868, under the recent dispensation which vested in the alumni the right of electing to the Board, he had at first favored Ephraim Gurney for the vacancy in the office of president that occurred the next year; but is credited by Eliot himself with having taken a leading part in breaking the deadlock between Overseers and Corporation when the former body had balked at ratifying the Corporation's unprecedented choice.

Likewise, through the crucial years of the new administration—as Overseer from 1868 to 1871, and 1874 to 1875, and as Fellow of the Corporation from 1875 to 1888—he was a stanch and influential supporter of Eliot's momentous program of reforms, which, if long since itself subject to revision, was decisive for the reestablishment of American higher education on the solid footing which made it an integral part of the complex new world that the years after the Civil War saw come into being. "Charles Eliot is more a live man than any incumbent of his presidential chair since I knew anything about it," he wrote Norton in 1870.

The only specific measure of moment for which Parkman is known to have been responsible was the setting up of a course in public speaking, "English 6." Started in 1879, under Albert Bushnell Hart, it became a celebrated undergraduate forum for the discussion of controversial issues.[2] But the details of policy were not his official function; and the general ground of his support of Eliot is sufficiently clear from the 1869 *Nation* article I have referred to: "The Tale of the 'Ripe Scholar.'" Rejecting, on the one hand, the "effete and futile scholasticism which the popular mind justly holds in slight account," and, on the other, the popular demand which "would 'improve' our colleges into schools of technology," Parkman aims in this article to rally to the idea of a reinvigorated liberal education the body of responsible, public-spirited lay opinion he represented and to set forth, from this point of view, some of the functions such an education might be expected to perform in the light of current conditions and needs. The arguments he rehearses

---

[2] Parkman's part in the storm aroused by Eliot's interim appointment of John Fiske to a chair of history is noted in Appendix A. A later anecdote shows him in a less liberal light; or at least in the position of injecting a personal foible into college affairs—if not perhaps with altogether serious intent. But, according to John Knowles Payne, whenever questions of economy were before the Corporation, he habitually singled out the Music Department for the ax of retrenchment, winding up his remarks with the phrase "*Musica delenda est.*" As we have seen, music was a closed world to him. In his later years, Farnham tells us, he did have one favorite song—the "Ballad of Sam Hall," "whose dramatic force, grim humor, virility, and anticlerical sentiments delighted him."

were to become familiar enough, but at the time they were still by no means commonplaces, and in any case have seldom been so cogently put.

His exordium is a scathing indictment for its marginality and thinness of what—except for "some notable results in the matter of theology"—had hitherto, or until recently, passed for scholarship on his native heath. In the main, he envisages the New England man of letters, "when he happened not to be a minister," as usually "some person whom constitutional defects, bodily or mental, had unsuited for politics or business . . . a recluse, ignorant of the world, bleached by a close room and an iron stove . . . sometimes reputed a scholar merely because he was nothing else," the products of whose mind were "as pallid as the hue of his face, and, like their parent, void of blood, bone, sinew, muscle, and marrow." Edward Everett he finds "the most finished and altogether favorable example of this devitalized scholarship," which, with the decline of clerical influence, understandably failed to make head against the dominant set of national life to practical pursuits and material achievement. The article then rises to one of its most eloquent passages, as Parkman indicates the need of a genuine intellectual culture to fill the vacuum thus created, and sketches some of its functions:

In times of agitation, alive with engrossing questions of pressing moment, when all is astir with pursuit and controversy, when some are mad for gold, and some are earnest and some rabid for this cause or for that, the scholarship of the past is naturally pronounced not up with the times. . . . Only a slight reason is wanted for depreciating the scholar, and a strong one is offered. Because the culture which our colleges supplied, and which too many of them still supply, was weak, thin, and unsuitable, it was easy to depreciate all culture.

[Yet true] culture is with us a supreme necessity, not for the profit of a few but of all. The presence of minds highly and vigorously developed is the most powerful aid to popular education, and the necessary condition of its best success. In a country where the ruling power is public opinion, it is above all things necessary that the best and maturest thought should have a fair share in forming it. Such thought cannot exist in any force in the community without propagating its own image, and a class of strong thinkers is the palladium of democracy. They are the natural enemies of ignorant, ostentatious, and aggressive wealth, and the natural friends of all that is best in the popular heart. They are sure of the hatred of charlatans, demagogues, and political sharpers. They are the only hope of our civilization; without them it is a failure, a mere platitude of mediocrity, stagnant or turbid, as the case may be. The vastest aggregate of average intelligences can do nothing to supply their place, and even material growth is impeded by an ignorance of its conditions and laws.

Taking this central ground as to the uses of culture, Parkman then traces in detail the conditions adverse to the achievement of it, as they disclosed themselves at the onset of the Gilded Age; the "ascendancy of material interests among us," in which "art, literature, philosophy, and science—so far as science has no direct bearing on material interests—are regarded as decorations, agreeable and creditable, but not essential"; the growing taste for the sensational and the mediocre, resulting from the spread of popular education in a democracy where material interests were paramount; the exacerbation of these developments by the excitements of the Civil War and the new surge of material growth, "the morbid stimulus applied to all departments of business," that accompanied it; and the consequent debasing of intellectual currency in a market where "the public which demands a second-rate article is so enormously large in comparison with the public which demands a first-rate article" and where "educated tastes are completely outridden by uneducated or half-educated tastes."

As I have said, Parkman here touches on phenomena that were to become and remain familiar enough subjects of remark, but with the freshness and force of primary recognition, at a time when such phenomena, at least in their latter-day shape, had first defined themselves prominently on the social landscape. Likewise he presents with the same primary force, and with the special force of his own proclivity toward a life of action, the effect on the individual of the pressures of the time, as they told against high intellectual or artistic endeavor—the urge to participation on the age's own terms and the temptations of the compromises it offered:

The drift towards material activity is so powerful among us that it is very difficult for a young man to resist it; and the difficulty increases in proportion as his nature is active and energetic. Patient and devoted study is rarely long continued in the vortex of American life. The dusty arena of competition and strife has fascinations almost irresistible to one conscious of his own vigor.

Intellectual tastes may, however, make a compromise. Journalism and the lecture-room offer them a field midway between the solitude of the study and the bustle of the world of business; but the journal and the lecture-room have influences powerfully adverse to solid, mature, and independent thinking. . . . That which pleases . . . pays so much better in money and notoriety, and is so much cheaper of production, than the better article that does not please . . . that the temptation to accept light work and high wages in place of hard work and low wages is difficult to resist. Nothing but a deep love of truth or of art can stand unmoved against it.

Yet, as can be seen, it is not from any attitude of genteel aloofness or merely negative distaste for the energies at work in the age that all this is presented. On the contrary, it is precisely as a channeling of this dynamism to other ends that Parkman calls for a "powerful re-enforcement of the higher education" as a corrective, in part, to the conditions he has sketched—and calls for this redirecting of central forces with the authority of one who, at the highest level, and not only by grace of independent means, had himself achieved in "the solitude of the study" such a canalizing of the age's energies to nonmaterial ends. Thus, invoking for the task in hand the full impetus of these central drives, Parkman then puts the matter in terms of the same *Anschauung* by which the age itself justified them and closes with a highly pragmatic plea, the substance of which was to become very familiar indeed:

He who gives or bequeaths money to a well-established and wisely-conducted university confers a blessing which radiates through all the ranks of society. He does a service eminently practical, and constitutes himself the patron of the best and highest utilitarianism.

In sum, appearing when it did, and under the circumstances it did, and written as it was, from Parkman's double vantage point of scholar and lay participant, this article was a notable manifesto of the movement that called it forth. Making explicit the background of social conditions and needs implied or glanced at in other discussions, it is perhaps as cogent an appeal as could be found to the particular body of lay opinion it aimed to reach, whose support would be necessary, on more than one level, to implement the work being taken in hand by Eliot, Gilman, White, and others.

Likewise as it brings Parkman's social conceptions to focus on a special issue for a special purpose and applies them to it with the immediacy of direct participation, "The Tale of the 'Ripe Scholar' " is perhaps the most effective of his occasional writings. It was not, however, his first or last production of its kind; and, just as a few years before, in the Civil War letters to the Boston *Advertiser* I have spoken of, he had begun to expound the complex of social ideas "The Tale of the 'Ripe Scholar' " makes evident, so, a decade later, he was to develop them further and more comprehensively in two articles for the *North American Review* on the question of popular suffrage: "The Failure of Universal Suffrage" and "The Woman Question" (together with an answer to critics of this last, "The Woman Question Again"). This group of papers as a whole articulates the development of Parkman's social views from the grudge-ridden caste feeling of his early years to the more broadly based, more realistic and pragmatic conservatism of his maturity.

The response of the Northern democracy to the challenge of the Civil War quickened to fresh life for Parkman the perceptions of his early travels. "Here, indeed, democracy revealed itself in its grandest aspect," he later wrote of the war; and this revelation of a fund of ideality, latent beneath the politics of mediocrity and the "pursuit of material success," is a recurring theme of the *Advertiser* letters. "Material interests and base political rivalries ruled us. . . . The national mind and heart were fast subsiding into one vast platitude. . . . All that was best and ablest dwindled in obscurity, and an ill-instructed zeal, often assumed to cover mean designs, was left to battle after its own fashion with unscrupulous self-interest and the passions of demagogues and adventurers." [3] Nevertheless, "though buried deep in ashes," the old fire was not dead; on the day of Sumter, "the forked flame leaped up," and the North became "a people disenthralled . . . roused from deathly torpor." Under the impact of these recognitions Parkman turns fiercely on the fraction of his own class, who, as the war prolonged itself, would bargain for peace at the price of restoring the *status quo:*

Well is it said that extremes meet. The Conservatism that anchors on rottenness and grapples to forms without life,—that struggles with infatuated dullness to dam back the flowing current instead of guiding it to safe and beneficent issues, is destruction in disguise. Conservatists and destroyers, timid respectability on the one hand, and Woods, Vallandighams, and Copperheads on the other, circle on their convergent paths till they seem on the point of joining hands. . . . Must we again be . . . entangled in the same wretched meshwork of compromises and compliances? Shall all that is noble in our national life again be borne down and smothered . . . ? To buy a transient and hollow peace . . . shall all that makes the soul of a nation be choked and starved into annihilation, and shall this ruin be wrought in the name of Conservatism?

But for the most part the war had of course the same electrifying effect on our "best character and culture" as on the democratic generality; and—which is the particular reason for Parkman's scoring of a conservatism that would stem the flow of the currents the war had set in motion—it had created a situation which seemed to him ripe with promise. The military exigencies of the emergency, especially as touching officer material for the vast citizen armies it had called into being, put a premium on qualities that had hitherto been at a discount in public life, and demanded a kind of leadership that hitherto the "fallacies of ultra democracy" had driven from the public arena. In sum, an opportunity now seemed to be opening for the return of the "educated minority" to the field of public affairs from which to its own and the nation's loss it had been so

[3] For other expressions of Parkman's views of abolitionism see Appendix D.

long divorced. "Democracy has played her low cards long enough. She must play her trumps now or lose the game." In this need, looking beyond the war, one could discern the beginnings of a great *rapprochement* of minority and majority and the dawning of a day of national regeneration.

Such at least, beyond their more immediately topical concerns, is the main tenor and drift of these perfervid letters. As may be gathered, their manner is overwrought and declamatory to a degree; and their apocalyptic reading of the signs of the times illusory enough. Whatever portents the response of the North to the war held forth, they hardly heralded the immediate regeneration of public life that Parkman envisaged; and the hopes and expectations he voices, like other war-engendered hopes, then and later, were doomed to a speedy enough disappointment, of which, in a sense, "The Failure of Popular Suffrage" is a reflex. If the stock of the "educated minority" was at a discount in the public market under Jacksonism, it had never fallen to a lower figure, as Henry Adams was painfully discovering, than under the régime of Demos and Plutus ushered in by the presidency of General Grant.

Nevertheless, the feeling of solidarity, the revelation of the "popular heart," that Parkman gained from the Civil War also left its residue and made its enduring mark. Though the postwar years were to sharpen sufficiently his criticisms of democracy, the tone of resentment, the accents of personal frustration that we hear in his early diaries give place to a sense of possibilities of response, however latent for the moment, within the democratic scheme of things; his ideas as to the sources and means of conservative reform widen to a broader conception than the integral restoration of his own class to its old place on the old terms around which the Civil War letters uncertainly hover; and in general, with the fading of illusions of this sort, Parkman's whole approach to the questions with which he deals takes on, as I have said, a more realistic character. Indeed, in spite of the line of thought its title indicates, what perhaps most strikes one today about "The Failure of Popular Suffrage" is this positive quality in relation to actualities—also evident in "The Tale of the 'Ripe Scholar' "—which sharply sets it off from the kind of high-toned, high-minded "viewing with alarm" it superficially resembles.

What most struck Parkman's contemporaries, however, and gave the article the notoriety it gained—it was widely and heatedly commented on, both at home and abroad—was the vigor, boldness, and forthrightness of its attack on democracy, or at least on the false equalitarianism, which, as Parkman conceived it, democratic theory and practice embodied: the tyranny of "organized ignorance, led by unscrupulous craft, and marching, amid the applause of fools, under the flag of equal rights." As to the practical workings of "equal rights," developments during the decade since "The Tale of the 'Ripe Scholar' " were hardly of a sort to leave untroubled the most sanguine democrat; and Parkman's indictment of conditions at the onset of the Gilded Age is duly broadened to comprehend the phenomena that marked its high tide—the scandals of the spoils system, the sinister alliance of politician and plutocrat, the spread of municipal corruption, and so on. Again, he touches on matters that have become commonplaces of the history books, but again with the freshness of primary observation and the instinct for essentials of the 1869 piece. Indeed, he was now in a position to envisage as a whole the transition from the republican simplicities of an earlier day to the industrialized, urbanized world that presented itself so startlingly to the postwar view; and, however different one's context of interpretation, it would be hard to equal his summing up of the process for sweep, scope, and relevance:

A generation or more ago, a cry of "Eureka!" rose over all the land, or rather over all the northern part of it. . . . The enthusiasm had its focus in New England, at that time perhaps the most successful democracy on earth—a fact which, however, was mainly to be ascribed to wholesome traditions, which had become part of the popular life. These the jubilants overlooked, and saw the fountain of all political and social blessings in the beneficent sway of an absolute Demos. . . . A little cloud, no bigger than a man's hand, rose presently above the sea, the herald of an invasion of peasants. With this in-pouring of labor came railroads, factories, and a thousand prolific industries, which heads without hands could not have awakened or sustained. Population increased, wealth grew apace; men became rabid in making money, and women frivolous in spending it. The same influences were at work through all the Northern States. A vast industrial development, an immense prosperity, rested safely for a while on the old national traditions, love of country, respect for law, and the habit of self-government. Then began the inevitable strain. Crowded cities, where the irresponsible and ignorant were numerically equal, or more than equal, to the rest, and where the weakest and most worthless was a match, by his vote, for the wisest and the best; bloated wealth and envious poverty; a tinseled civilization above, and a discontented proletariat beneath— all these have broken rudely on the dreams of equal brotherhood once cherished by those who made their wish the father of their thought, and fancied that this favored land formed an exception to the universal laws of human nature. They cried out for elevating the masses, but the masses have sunk lower. They called for the diffusion of wealth, but wealth has gathered into more numerous and portentous accumulations. Two enemies, unknown before, have risen like spirits of darkness on our social and political horizon—an ignorant proletariat and a half-taught plutocracy. Between lie the classes, happily still numerous and strong, in whom rests our salvation.

These are, perhaps, unmistakably the views of a Boston Brahmin, but they strangely resemble, at least in the sense they give of perils "unknown before," beyond the range of older categories and formulations, the misgivings which an observer of very different social origins, surveying the same scene from a very different social orientation, had already voiced in *Democratic Vistas*. Indeed, as to "equal rights," simply on the political level, Whitman, it will be recalled, had there spoken of "the appalling dangers of universal suffrage in the United States," which he would not "gloss over"; and had expressed himself to the effect that, as things then stood, American democracy, even "in its social aspects," was "an almost complete failure."

Needless to say, this is hardly Whitman's final word on the subject; nor is it Parkman's, as witness the closing sentence of the above passage, and the matter of other passages to which we shall come. Nevertheless, from any point of view, the time was one for the soberest stock-taking in regard to the progress and meaning of democracy; and as, in the light of ugly actualities, Whitman reassesses and reaffirms the democratic "dream of equal brotherhood," so Parkman reformulates the counter—or, rather, one should say, the complementary—theme of "intrinsic inequality," which from the start had been the chief ground of his quarrel with democracy, or with the leveling of human diversity to a "platitude of mediocrity" which he conceived to be of its essence. But, as can be seen from the following truncated version of his argument, his conception of diversity, for all the extremity of his emphasis on human differences rather than human likenesses, is now no longer involved with any particular scheme of class or caste; and the ideal of commonalty that emerges is something not far removed from Jefferson's open society of the "natural aristocracy."

Liberty was the watchword of our fathers, and so it is of ourselves. But in their hearts, the masses of the nation cherish desires not only different from it, but inconsistent with it. They want equality more than they want liberty. Now, there is a factitious inequality and a real and intrinsic one. Rank, titles, privileges, and wealth make up the first; and character, ability, and culture, the second. Excepting only the distinctions of wealth, we have abolished the artificial inequality, and now we are doing what we can to abolish the real one. . . . A jockey may be a democrat in the street, but he is sure to be an aristocrat in the stable. And yet the essential difference between man and man is incomparably greater than that between horse and horse, or dog and dog; though, being chiefly below the surface, the general eye can hardly see it. . . . Through the long course of history, a few men, to be counted by scores or by tens, have planted in the world the germs of a growth whose beneficent vitality has extended itself through all succeeding ages; and any one of these men outweighs in value to mankind myriads of nobles, citizens, and peasants, who have fought or toiled in their generation, and then rotted into oblivion. . . . The highest man may comprehend the lowest, but the lowest can no more comprehend the highest than if he belonged to another order of beings, as for some purposes he practically does. . . .

We have said that intrinsic equality is inconsistent with liberty. It is so because, in order to produce it, very unequal opportunities of development must be granted to different kinds of mind and character, and an even distributive justice refused to human nature. The highest must be repressed and the lowest stimulated in order to produce a level average. In such an attempt no political or social system can completely succeed; but in so far as it tends this way it is false and pernicious. . . . A society where liberty was complete, and where all men had equal opportunities of development, according to their several qualities, would show immense diversities of all kinds; like the vegetable world, where the tallest trees and the humblest shrubs, plants climbing and crawling, poisonous and wholesome, all grow out of the same soil and are formed of the same essential elements. . . . Shall we look for an ideal society in that which tends to a barren average and a weary uniformity . . . ; or in that which recognizes the inherent differences between man and man, gives the preponderance of power to character and intelligence, yet removes artificial barriers, keeps circulation free through all its parts, and rewards merit wherever it appears with added influence? This, of course, is a mere idea, never to be fully realized; but it makes a vast difference at what a republic aims, and whether it builds on numbers or on worth.

A partisan of democracy would, of course, have something to say to this dilemma which propounds for its antidemocratic horn the idea of a "society . . . where all men had equal opportunities of development, according to their several qualities"—as he would have something to say to much else. It is, for instance, precisely the demand for "1st, a large variety of character—and 2nd, full play for human nature to expand itself in numberless and even conflicting directions" that Whitman takes from John Stuart Mill for the opening text of *Democratic Vistas;* and in the perennial debate to which both essays are contributions the question of democracy is thus perennially and paradoxically apt to entangle itself with the question of individualism or "personalism." Here, however, we need only note that if Parkman, as always, advances what, in the context of his own thought, he conceives to be an antidemocratic or aristocratic principle, it is conceived in such a way as to bring it into complementary relationship with its opposite; and his quarrel with democracy now rages over common ground.

Thus, if after his castigation of the sins of equalitarianism, we looked for any interestingly drastic assertion of alternatives we should be disappointed. So he dismisses with contempt whatever notions of the sort were currently in the wind. An "oligarchy" would be one made up of "the 'boss,' the 'railroad king,' and the bonanza Croesus—a tyranny detestable and degrading as that of the rankest democracy, with which it would be in league"; and "imperialism"—or, as we should say, a dictatorship—would only produce "a demagogue on a throne, forced to conciliate the masses by giving efficacy to their worst desires." Likewise, for all the saliency with which he brings into view the darker shadows on the democratic scene, if we looked for any interestingly thorough-going vein of pessimism we should be equally disappointed. So, with a parting salvo at the "weary twaddle of the optimists," he nevertheless underscores the presence of forces already available to counteract the dangers of a "debased suffrage," and addresses himself pragmatically in the last part of the paper to what can be done for the better within the equalitarian scheme of things.

But why descant on evils past cure? Indiscriminate suffrage is an accomplished fact, and cannot be undone. Then why not accept it, look on the bright side, and hope that, "somehow or other," all will be well in the end? Because the recognition of an evil must go before its cure, and because there is too much already of the futile optimism that turns wishes into beliefs, and discourses in every tone of sickly commonplace about popular rights and universal brotherhood. Beneath it all lies an anxious sense of present and approaching evil. Still the case is not yet desperate. The country is full of recuperative force, latent just now, and kept so by the easy and apathetic good nature which so strangely marks our people. . . . But complete disruption and anarchy are, we may hope, still far off, thanks to an immense vitality and an inherited conservative strength.[4]

[4] Complacency was a national trait that never failed to stir Parkman's ire—"the senseless optimism" (as he put it later in *Our Common Schools*) "which leads so many Americans to imagine that all will go well in the end, whatever they may do or fail to do; and that our Ship of State cannot be wrecked, whether the crew do their duty or not." So he enlarges on the theme in "The Woman Question Again":
"This last remark will pass, no doubt, as an effect of that 'distrustful solicitude' which one of our critics contrasts with the 'more manly hopefulness' that 'trusts all the virtue of the community to take care of all the vice of the community.' But has the virtue of communities always taken

For specific means of neutralizing the effects of a "debased suffrage" Parkman looks to the movement for civil service reform which was already making itself a political force; and particularly to the movement for municipal reform which was to gather strength in the coming decades. ("It is in the cities that the diseases of the body politic are gathered to a head, and it is here that the need of attacking them is most urgent. . . . The reform of the cities would be a long and hopeful step toward the reform of the states and the nation.") At the same time, he urges, as before, the strengthening of higher education and the increased participation, despite obstacles, of the "educated minority" in public affairs. In sum, he outlines with a fund of prescience and acuteness the features of the whole "good-government" movement which the future was to see establish itself firmly enough on the American scene, and which, in the main, was to be successful in driving at least the grosser forms of corruption from American public life. And, finally, he is particularly prescient, perhaps under the impulse of his own activities, as to one aspect of this and of later more broadly based movements, that is to say, the prominence they gave to the rôle of the "intellectual" in the public arena. "Ain't he one of those damned literary fellers?"—so Senator Cameron is alleged to have explained the then recent rejection by the Foreign Affairs Committee of Richard Henry Dana's appointment as Minister to England; and the remark called forth one of Parkman's liveliest and not least prophetic sallies:

The low politician is not a noble foe, but he is strong and dangerous enough to make it manly to fight him; and the cause of his adversary is the

---

care of their vice? Has not the world been filled with triumphant wrong; and have republics and democracies never fallen under anarchy and despotism? What makes and saves nations is not the blind and fatuous security which our friend calls 'manly hopefulness.' . . . That faith is manly which can see as well as dare, not that which dares because it can not see. It is by such manhood that liberties are won—by watching, forecast, and conflict, through year after year and age after age; and by watching, forecast, and striving, they must be preserved. There is no more dangerous weakness in American nature than that sickly notion that we have only to believe, and let things take their course."

cause of the people, did they but know it; or at least of that part of the people that is worthy the name. . . . The "literary feller" may yet make himself a practical force, and, in the presence of the public opinion which he has evoked, the scurvy crew who delight to give at him may be compelled to disguise themselves in garments of unwonted decency.

The whole article, indeed, is a striking manifesto of the *Nation*-mugwump school of reform, which, for all its outspoken distrust of "ultra democracy" and its rigid adherence to the tenets of laissez faire, was nevertheless a lineal ancestor of the more popularly oriented progressivism that, two or three decades later, was to dominate the American political scene. At least the voice that speaks in the article is hardly the voice of the unreconstructed Federalist, the mere *laudator temporis acti*, for which its author too often passes.

But however that may be, the piece, as I have said, created a sufficient noise in the world; and Parkman, having tasted battle, followed it up with the aforementioned article on female suffrage—"The Woman Question"—which also raised the same or a greater stir of controversy. In fact, it struck home so far as to evoke from suffrage quarters a joint effort at rebuttal on the part of five leading lights of the cause—Julia Ward Howe, T. W. Higginson, Lucy Stone, Elizabeth Cady Stanton, and Wendell Phillips—and this critique, in turn, was answered by Parkman in a second article.

Prescience is hardly a quality one could postulate of these antisuffrage articles, at least, as regards Parkman's forecasting of the probable political results of female suffrage. Here, in the light of the actual event, his prophecies wear a ludicrous enough air; and the whole conclusion of the main article is a classic "parade of imaginary horribles" of the most lurid variety. Thus we have the mistress "outvoted in her own kitchen"; Delilah "spreading her snares for the Congressional Samson"; posses of viragoes outshouting him on the legislative floor; and for a climax, a female majority voting reluctant males into a war which they would refuse to fight. Even the rhetorical effect of this culminating *argumentum ad terrorem* is undone by Parkman's own perception of its chimerical quality. "The above contingency is not likely to occur," he lamely concludes; "but that it is simply possible shows the false position of a government subject to female suffrage."

But if, as specific political prophecy, the article for the most part makes us smile, the case is otherwise with what it has to say of "feminism" in general—with its insistence in this connection on the primary facts of sexual differentiation and sexual reciprocty; or rather, simply, to begin with, its insistence on sex itself as of the essence of the question, an approach which, perhaps more than its political illiberalism, was responsible for the storm of controversy it stirred up. Here Parkman sounds a realistic enough note—or as nearly so as he felt to be possible in the current climate of discussion —and, however different our own climate, a note with vibrations of meaning that have not lost their pertinence in a world where the triumph of feminism has long since become an accomplished fact. But a few quotations from the article, or its sequel, will perhaps best give an idea of their direction, emphasis, and incidental insights:

Nothing is more certain than that women will have the suffrage if they ever want it; for when they want it, the men will give it to them regardless of consequences. A more than readiness to conform to the wishes of the other sex is a national trait in America, though whether it would survive the advent of the female politician is matter for reflection.

A disposition to ignore differences of sex is so common that few persons can fail to observe it. Sometimes it takes curious forms. A few days ago, a . . . gentleman told us the following: Being on the examining board of a school in a country town, he asked the pupils what was meant by gender in nouns and pronouns. As they could not answer, he looked to the teacher for explanation, whereupon she said, with flushed cheeks and some sharpness, "Nothing is taught about gender in *this* school!"

It has been said that the question of the rights and employment of women should be treated without regard to sex. Mr. Wendell Phillips tells us that all those who so treat it are "high-minded," and all the others "lowminded." It should rather be said that those who consider it regardless of sex do not consider it at all. . . . If it could be treated like other subjects, and discussed fully and freely, the cause of the self-styled reformers would have been hopeless from the first. Hence their extreme sensitiveness whenever the subject is approached on its most essential side.

A remedy [for the disadvantages under which women are placed] is looked for in a change of public opinion which shall visit the breach of chastity with equal condemnation in men and women. This remedy has long been urged, and probably at this moment there is in the world at large as little disposition to accept it as ever. . . . In [conforming to an unequal standard, women] are generally aided by more delicate sensibilities, by passivity of temperament, and by being protected from the countless temptations that beset every man who mingles much with the world. Nor to him is the temptation from within less than those from without. To impose the same penalties on him that are imposed on a woman . . . would be a far greater hardship.[5]

Notwithstanding limitations on one side and comparative freedom on the other, it would not be safe to say that the allotment of happiness to the two sexes is unequal. . . . It is among women who have no part in the occupations and duties of the rest of their sex that one is most apt to find that morbid introversion, those restless cravings, that vague but torturing sense of destinies unfulfilled, and activities without an object, which rarely receive much pity, but perhaps deserve it as much of any of the more positive woes. There is no misery like the misery of a vacuum.

A certain benign influence, indefinite and almost mystical in character, has been ascribed to "woman," which, it is proclaimed, will purify our politics. That, in some relations of life, the instincts of women are preeminently delicate and true . . . is, happily, not to be denied; but they are no whit less human than men. Like them, they have "the defects of their qualities." . . . There are circumstances under which they rarely appear to advantage, or avail much for good.

But it was of course hardly as a depreciator of the feminine that Parkman conceived himself to be entering the lists against woman suffrage, but as the defender of reciprocities based on intrinsic differences between the sexes, which, as he saw it, the triumph of feminism would minimize to the impoverishment of both. Difference

[5] It will be recalled that Parkman's perception here of an intrinsic difference between the sexes as regards "the temptation from within" (the psycho-biological basis of the famous Victorian "double standard") has recently been confirmed statistically for us by the late Dr. Kinsey, somewhat to that investigator's surprise at his own findings. It was of course given neither to Parkman nor his opponents to pierce the veil of a future where "the breach of chastity" would impose no very drastic social penalites, relatively speaking, on either sex.

is his leading theme; and the symbiosis of opposites of which the cultivation of difference is a precondition. He is nowhere more eloquent than in his articulation of the meaning for civilizaton of those "reciprocal principles" of sex which his friend Squier had traced through the world of primitive cultures in *The Serpent Symbol:*

The natures of the two sexes are like the two electricities of the magnet. Each needs the other, and is drawn to the other; and as each is emphatically masculine or emphatically feminine, so is the strength of this mutual need. . . . The reciprocity between the two separate halves of human nature extends over a wide field, not only in passions and emotions, but in the regions of moral and intellectual life. Most intelligent men have felt the stimulus and refreshment of the faculties that spring from the companionship of an intelligent and congenial woman, and which is unlike anything resulting from the contact of a male mind. It is a fructifying power, with which neither the world of thought nor the world of action could well dispense. . . . This principle of sexual reciprocity . . . is the most pervading among the forces of human life . . . and none is so prolific in results of all kinds, for evil and for good. It is the spring of the chief pleasures and the chief pains of life, and, misplaced or abused, becomes the source of unspeakable degradation. . . . Yet what we are to observe is, that this imperial and all-essential power is founded not on resemblances but on differences of nature and function. The differences are so great that it may be doubted if men and women can ever quite understand each other. Women have a nice perception of male psychology in certain phases of life and character; but there are regions of masculine nature in which their perception is exceedingly faint and dim, because there is nothing that answers to them in their own consciousness; and no doubt the same holds good of men in their comprehension of women.

Again we note the extremity of Parkman's emphasis on differences; nor is our own shift of emphasis without its claims to an equally "intrinsic" basis in the range of human possibilities. But neither is it, to say the least, without its problems; and if the social arrangements as to the position of women which Parkman championed suppressed too much else in their cultivation of the "emphatically masculine" and the "emphatically feminine," the balance of gains and losses is hardly unequivocal in a condition of things which has tended to the opposite extreme of disregard of sexual differences—or rather, if one wishes, has tended, in derogation of the masculine principle, to feminize altogether an already overfeminized *ambiente*. At any rate, it is not, again, merely the voice of the pleader of a lost cause that makes itself heard in these antisuffrage articles. Perhaps our best guide to their scope and impact is the affiliation, already noted, they suggest with James's *Bostonians*. At least Basil Ransom's "reactionary" magazine article in the novel is very much, as James describes it, such a one as Parkman had actually contributed to the *North American Review* on "The Failure of Universal Suffrage"; the views of feminism ascribed to Basil by James are more or less identical with those Parkman sets forth in "The Woman Question" and "The Woman Question Again"; and if such views are scarcely original with Parkman (as he expressly disclaims their being) the deployment of them in both the articles and the novel is informed by a feeling for sex itself, for the higher values of emphatic sexual differentiation, and the "imperial and all-essential power" of sexual reciprocity, that hardly appears elsewhere and is expressed with a frankness that, in the atmosphere of the time, largely accounts for the aversion which both articles and book aroused. Considering these affiliations of content and approach, and considering James's friendship with Parkman, their common social milieu, and the stir of discussion Parkman's articles caused, it is hard not to reckon them as one of the more important nuggets of suggestion around which James's creative instinct shaped the substance of a novel on the "woman question." [6]

Meanwhile, at the time these "reactionary" forays on the subject of popular suffrage—male or female—were stirring up the hornet's nests of reform at home, Parkman, as we have seen, was under attack

[6] James of course was living abroad when Parkman's articles were published; but he almost certainly would have seen them—in fact, his own essay on Sainte-Beuve's letters appeared in the same number of the *North American* as "The Woman Question Again." For the articles as a subject of discussion among Bostonians in Europe belonging to his circle of friends, one notes Mrs. Henry Adams's tart comment in a letter to her father from Seville, November 30, 1879: "Mr. Parkman had better go to Morocco—his ideal woman is found in perfection there. If I talked much with him, I should take the stump for female suffrage in a short time."

at Quebec for opposite reasons, as an exponent of democracy, progress, and other monstrous progeny of the godless, Anglo-Saxon "nineteenth century." "*C'est assez curieux*," he writes Margry, "*que de servir à la fois de cible vivante aux democrates et aux ultramontanes*" adding that it was also "*assez amusant*" and didn't keep him from eating or sleeping. Nor were Parkman's *North American* articles his last appearance in the public forum. He entered the antisuffrage lists again with a paper, read by proxy, at a hearing in Boston in 1884 on municipal suffrage for women (at which, in a curious juxtaposition, the future Justice Brandeis also figured among the antisuffragists); and later with a pamphlet, *Some of the Reasons against Woman Suffrage*, "printed at the request of an Association of Women." In 1890 the controversy over parochial schools also evoked a brief pamphlet in defense of public education (*Our Common Schools*), deprecating equally an attitude of indifference or an attitude of fanaticism on the part of Protestants in regard to the question. But, tempting to his combative instincts as public controversy may have been, he had, in the main, said his say on issues of the time in the *North American* pieces of the late seventies. Thereafter, with his revision of *La Salle* in 1879, he turned to work on *Montcalm and Wolfe*, and the last phase of his project engrossed him. Meanwhile, the publication of *The Old Régime* in 1874 and *Frontenac* in 1877 had brought him measurably in sight of his goal.

CHAPTER XIV

THE OLD RÉGIME, FRONTENAC

⚜ ⚜ ⚜

With *La Salle* Parkman reached what to the present writer seems
the consummate point of his historical artistry. This is not because
of any slackening of his powers in the later volumes of the series,
but because to a greater degree than the novelist, the historian is at
the mercy of his material for the deployment of his powers. The subject matter of *La Salle*, that is to say, and the personality of its chief
actor engaged Parkman more deeply at more points than the matter
of any other of his volumes, and evoked the widest range of reference
of which his subject as a whole was capable. Likewise, in spite of
the advantage of a single, dominating central character, *La Salle*
presented to its author perhaps his most exacting and most signally performed task of organization; and even *Montcalm and Wolfe*, which
Parkman himself regarded as his masterpiece, owes its effect more
largely than *La Salle* merely to what is "given"—the concentration
of its events to the span of six years, their climactic importance independently of what a writer makes of them.

Nevertheless, the thematic coloring which Parkman gives to the
opening epos of exploration is so firmly established as to pervade the
whole. The narrower question now predominant of which form of
Western civilization, the more archaic or the more "advanced,"
shall prevail in the New World, is comprehended throughout in the
question of civilization itself evoked by the image of the wilderness
and the Indian, and the question of Western civilization in particular,
as its central drives have unfolded themselves through the figures of
Champlain and La Salle. If New France, in its attempt to consolidate
the gains these exemplars of the Western spirit have won for her,

perishes from the defects of the qualities it embodies as an anachronistic social organism, its victorious adversary is potentially vulnerable to counterdefects of counterqualities, and the shadow of tragedy falls likewise on the triumph of Western "progress," as it clears its way to hegemony of the continent. Throughout, the organizing principle is Parkman's sense of the permutations of culture and civilization— the perennial tragedy of selection and suppression under a perennial law of imbalance, to the effect that, as William James put it, human nature cannot seem to have enough of anything without having too much. Thus it is not in a spirit of merely romantic nostalgia, but at once of critical realism and of Scott-like piety that Parkman reconstructs for us the world of New France in its more archaic aspects— its singular adaptation of a complex of clericalism, absolutism, and neofeudalism to the conditions of the wilderness—and traces the conflict of past and future that its struggle with its rival signified.

The Old Régime is mainly a depiction of Canadian social and economic institutions as they were established during the 1660's by the reorganization of the colony at the hands of Colbert and Louis XIV which brought to an end the missionary period. The first part of the book, in its original form, covers the closing phase of clerical rule— the near extinction of the colony by the Iroquois after the ruin of the Huron mission in 1649—and the opening phase of the civil régime, both of which Parkman had passed over in order to treat as a unit the matter of French exploration. Finally, just before his death, he added a new opening section, on Acadian affairs, so that, as a whole, the book has a somewhat heterogeneous effect.

The most strikingly handled episode of what was originally its opening part is the famous exploit of Daulac des Ormeaux and his companions at the Long Saut, which, at the cost of their own lives, preserved the life of the colony at one of its most critical moments. Here matter and manner recall Parkman's account in *Jesuits* of the founding of Montreal—"Is this true history, or a romance of Christian chivalry? It is both." So the motive forces of Daulac's feat are "the enthusiasm of honor, the enthusiasm of adventure, and the enthusiasm of faith" and Daulac himself "a knight of the early crusades among the forests and savages of the New World." Parkman's emphasis on this example of lay martyrdom, so to speak, complements his accounts in *Jesuits* of clerical martyrdom, and, as his narrative turns to more mundane considerations, leaves on us a final impress of the quintessential spirit of the missionary period.

The less edifying matter that brings us to the main part of the book comprises the internal dissensions that shook the minuscule and beleagured colony even during its times of direst external peril—the quarrels between Jesuit and Sulpician; between Jesuit and fur trader; and above all, with the appearance on the scene of François Xavier de Laval-Montmorency, Vicar Apostolic and titular Bishop of Petrea, the contest between church and state that raged as this archultramontane and champion of the Jesuits imperiously made and unmade a series of royal governors until the reforms of Colbert, if by no means effacing the effect on the church of Laval's genius for organization, put an end to the period of direct ecclesiastical ascendancy. With Laval's establishment of the Canadian church on a permanent footing, and with the setting up of the state machinery of royal absolutism, the initiation of a quasi-feudal social order, and the paternalistic encouragement of emigration and economic activity that took place under the governorships of Tracy and Courcelle and the intendantship of Talon, the life of the colony began to assume the form it kept until the English conquest. The rest of the book examines in detail the workings of its institutions as they adapted themselves to the New World environment of wilderness and frontier.

As the presentation of a culture, at once in terms of its material, social, political, and spiritual components and as a living and distinctive whole, *The Old Régime*, as I have said, was something of a pioneer achievement in American historical writing. John Fiske is an eloquent witness to the freshness and novelty of effect of the book for Parkman's contemporaries:

The author never preaches like Carlyle, nor does he hurl huge generalizations at our heads like Buckle; he simply describes a state of society that has been. . . . It is a picture painted with consummate art; and in this instance the art consists in so handling the relations of cause and effect as to make them speak for themselves. . . .

It is the whole national life of New France that is displayed before us. Historians of ordinary calibre exhibit their subject in fragments, or they show us some phases of life and neglect others. Some have no eyes save for events that are startling, such as battles and sieges; or decorative, such as coronations and court balls. Others give abundant details of manners and customs; others have their attention absorbed by economics; others again feel such interest in the history of ideas as to lose sight of mere material incidents. Parkman on the other hand conceives and presents his subject as a whole. He forgets nothing, overlooks nothing; but whether it is a bloody battle, or a theological pamphlet, or an exploring journey through the forest, or a code for the discipline of nunneries, each event grows out of its context as a feature of the total development that is going on before our eyes.

In considering this estimate, to be sure, one must allow for the relatively small-scale and uncomplex nature of the society Parkman is describing—the just sufficiently limited compass that permitted him to treat it as a cultural whole without benefit of specialized monographs, and, here as elsewhere, with the particular first-handedness of effect imparted by his synthesizing of the finished product directly from the raw material. But to grasp as vitally as Parkman does the lineaments of any society in its "total development" is a rare enough historical feat; and the book retains, as an example of its kind, the freshness and authority with which it impressed his contemporaries.

Its conclusions, of course, have not gone unchallenged: those "invidious comparisons" of the last chapter—between absolutism and self-government, between paternalism and laissez faire, and so on— where Parkman joins issue squarely on the fundamental questions involved. The closing paragraph, particularly, drew fire from French Canadian critics. A culture struggling to preserve its identity and ensure its future in the face of "Anglo-Saxon" dominance could hardly relish Parkman's insistence there on its debt to the conqueror —to the "boon of rational and ordered liberty," as he puts it, "imposed by the sword on reluctant Canada."

With England came Protestantism, and the Canadian Church grew purer and better in the presence of an adverse faith. Material growth; an increased mental activity; an education, real though fenced and guarded; a warm and genuine patriotism—all date from the peace of 1763. . . . Through centuries of striving [England] had advanced from stage to stage of progress, deliberate and calm,—never breaking with her past, but making each fresh gain the basis of a new success,—enlarging popular liberties, while bating nothing of that height and force of individual development which is the brain and heart of civilization; and now, through a hard-earned victory, she taught the conquered colony to share the blessings she had won. A happier calamity never befell a people than the conquest of Canada by the British arms.

But if this, however true, seems to turn the knife in the wound of the vanquished, Parkman had not spoken his last word on the subject of the conquest. When he came to do so, at the end of *Montcalm and Wolfe*, addressing himself, this time, to the legatees of the victor—that is to say, his own compatriots—it was equally little in terms calculated to inspire on their part any undue afflatus of complacence at the result.

Likewise, Parkman's portrait of Laval, the chief character of the book, has been a bone of contention, the more so for the very life-likeness with which he recasts in a human mold a figure who had been the object of an almost hagiological veneration. Laval was another hero of the will, but in a mode from which Parkman's sympathies recoiled. Of this he was well enough aware, and lays his cards on the table with his usual frankness in such matters. "We are touching on delicate ground. . . . Laval is one of those concerning whom Protestants and Catholics, at least ultramotane Catholics, will never agree in judgment. The task of eulogizing him may be safely left to those of his own way of thinking. It is for us to regard him from the standpoint of secular history." The character sketch that follows is conceived in Parkman's most trenchant vein, with flickerings of Gibbonesque irony and a highly idiosyncratic feeling for the human drive to mastery that fed the zeal of the ecclesiastic for his cause.

And, first, let us credit him with sincerity. . . . Of the faults which he owed to nature, the principal seems to have been an arbitrary and domineering temper. . . . He fought lustily, in his way, against the natural man; and humility was the virtue to the culture of which he gave his chief attention; but soil and climate were not favorable. His life was one long assertion of the authority of the Church, and this authority was lodged in himself. . . . His principles and his instinct of domination were acting in perfect unison, and his conscience was the handmaid of his fault. . . . Austerities and mortifications, playing at beggar, sleeping in beds full of fleas, or performing prodigies of gratuitous dirtiness in hospitals, however fatal to self-respect, could avail little against influences working so powerfully and insidiously to stimulate the most subtle of human vices. The history of the Roman Church is full of Lavals. The Jesuits, adepts in human nature, had made a sagacious choice when they put forward this conscientious, zealous, dogged, and pugnacious priest to fight their battles.

It is as the protagonist of the complex quarrels, springing from the theocratic conceptions he shared with the Jesuits, and embittered by his own aggressive temper, that Parkman's Laval figures most immediately for the reader—a type par excellence of intransigent clericalism. Resting on evidential detail that formidably "speaks for itself," and developed with all Parkman's psychological skill, the portrait is a masterpiece in its undisguisedly hostile vein.

Yet the book also makes manifest other aspects of Laval's character—the creative strain evident in his organization of the Canadian church, with its novel system of removable curés dependant on the seminary at Quebec, which, "old and worn . . . and driven almost to despair," he defended to the end against his successor Saint-Vallier and the misgivings of Louis XIV. As Parkman notes, the contest of "the crozier and the sword" provoked by Laval's attempt to keep Canada an absolute theocracy was not a fundamental one; and division of absolute authority with the civil powers left ample enough margin for a work which, by its masterly adaptation of old forms to new conditions, made the church the one genuinely cohesive social force of the old régime, and of all its institutions the one to leave the most enduring mark on Canadian life. Doubtful as Parkman considered the results for Canada of this commitment to ecclesiastical tutelage—tempered only by the wild and demoralizing freedom of the forest —he is sufficiently emphatic as to the viability of Laval's handiwork.

One great fact stands out conspicuous in Canadian history,—the Church of Rome. More even than the royal power she shaped the character and the destinies of the colony. She was its nurse and almost its mother; and, wayward and headstrong as it was, it never broke the ties of faith that held it to her. It was these ties which, in the absence of political franchises, formed under the old régime the only vital coherence in the population. . . . The English conquest shattered the whole apparatus of civil administration at a blow. . . . Governors, intendants, councils, and commandants, all were gone; the principal seigniors fled the colony. . . . Confusion if not anarchy, would have followed but for the parish priests, who, in a character of double paternity, half spiritual and half temporal, became more than ever the guardians of order throughout Canada.

And likewise, more specifically, Laval's genius speaks through Parkman's emphasis on the viability of the particular system devised by him that thus, to use the clerical phrase, set Canada on "the good path." Indeed, Laval's itinerant curé, the rank-and-file worker in his vineyard, is almost the hero of the book. It is his labors which the incidence of Parkman's arts of vivification through the book brings into most immediate focus for the reader, and which evoke from his New England chariness of direct praise his most explicit words of admiration: "The splendid self-devotion of the early Jesuit missions has its record; so, too, have the unseemly bickerings of bishops and governors. But the patient toils of the missionary curé rest in the obscurity where the best of human virtues are buried from age to age." In sum, if Parkman leaves to others the task of eulogizing Laval, the materials for eulogy are at hand in what he makes, on this side of the ledger, of the fruits of his work; and if we are certainly not spared the unprepossessing aspects of his character, Laval emerges from the book with qualities that witness his kinship to La Salle or Frontenac, the capacity, at least within the limits of his sphere of action, for significant and creative response to the challenge of new conditions and the indomitable will to implement his response.

And so, throughout, the little world of New France "speaks for itself," in a double sense: convincingly enough for what we may make of it in the frame of interpretation by which Parkman judges it; and also convincingly enough for what else we may make of it, in the living reality of light and shade by which he re-creates it. Again, this objectiveness of effect is a matter mainly of dramatic presentation. Here, as a particular adaptation of Parkman's dramatic gifts to the particular mode of the book, one might mention the generalized, if highly concrete, sketches of representative types, by which he sums up the processes of institutional development he is tracing and exhibits their meaning on the plane of their results for social character. A notable example is the portrait of the native seignor that closes his discussion of Canadian feudalism—a passage in which a whole process of social evolution suddenly seems to unfold itself physically before our eyes; and yet, for all its deceptively novelistic brilliance, almost every phrase of which is the condensation of paragraphs of analytical discourse.

Others learned the same lesson at a later date, adapted themselves to soil and situation, took root, grew, and became more Canadian than French. As population increased, their seigniories began to yield appreciable returns, and their reserved domains became worth cultivating. A future dawned upon them. . . . The beggared noble of the early time became a sturdy country gentleman,—poor, but not wretched; ignorant of books, except possibly a few scraps of rusty Latin picked up in a Jesuit school; hardy as the hardiest woodsman, yet never forgetting his quality of *gentilhomme;* scrupulously wearing its badge, the sword, and copying as well as he could the fashions of the court. . . . He was at home among his tenants, at home among the Indians, and never more at home than when, a gun in his hand and a crucifix on his breast, he took the war-path with a crew of painted savages and Frenchmen almost as wild, and pounced like a lynx from the forest on some lonely farm or outlying hamlet of New England.

But, mainly, as elsewhere, meanings are underscored by the immediacy of effect Parkman imparts to specific scenes and actions. The setting of these passages for the most part is of course the St. Lawrence, now the river of settlement as it was the river of exploration, from which, and its tributary the Richelieu, almost every house in old Canada, as Parkman notes, was literally visible. Thus, early in the main part of the book, this fact is utilized, on the whole factually and literally, to give a physical description of the colony, comprising the settlements of the north bank on an up-river voyage and of the south bank on the return. Then at the end of the book the voyage is resumed, as it were, as we embark from Quebec on the last ship of the year, and the low-keyed suggestions of setting and atmosphere of the opening voyage are heightened to make predominant the immediate sensory effect of the scene: a patch of snow on Cape Tourmente catching the chill gleam of an autumnal sunset; "the sharp spires of fir-trees on the heights of Sillery" standing "stiff and black against the pure cold amber of the fading west." In its context this passage revives retrospectively a suite of heightened passages through the book, fusing to a whole in our minds the elements of a culture and an ethos thus underscored, and, once more, steeping our imagination in the tincture of their own colors, before, on this farewell voyage, we "ponder what we have seen on the banks of the St. Lawrence" and turn to the wider considerations of the last chapter.

But of this St. Lawrence sequence, the scene which leaves on us the most vivid single impression is, as I have said, that of the itinerant curé at his labors. It occurs in the chapter on "Priests and People"; and is compounded of factual material from the *Plan Général de l'estat présent des missions du Canada*, made for Laval in 1683; of Parkman's own impressions gathered on his 1873 visit to the Abbé Casgrain; and of his youthful memories of the Magalloway and Mackinaw frontier. We pass abruptly but congruously from expository discourse—"Nature as well as Bishop Laval" threw difficulties in the way of settling the curés in fixed parishes as in France—and find ourselves on a ship from France, the "last of the season," entering the lower St. Lawrence through "wilderness and solitude" to the "far verge of the ocean-like river." This is the "watery solitude, twenty miles from shore to shore" of Champlain's founding voyage in *Pioneers;* but now "you are not so solitary as you think." As we veer toward the south bank, the autumnal setting is developed with details that link it to the closing passage we have looked at—the slap of waves against the ledges in the north wind, the sweep of its

gusts through "the quivering spires of stiff and stunted fir-trees."
Then Father Morel and his canoe-man appear around a point,
paddling hard to keep their craft off the shingle and the breakers.
They land by "a shattered eel-pot high and dry on the pebbles";
make their way through the belt of firs; and reach the desolate aftermath of a clearing, studded with dead trees, "branchless, barkless,
pierced by the woodpeckers, in part black with fire, in part bleached
by sun and frost." Picking their path through the debris of charred
limbs and trunks, "the cat-bird mewing, and the blue-jay screaming
as they pass," they emerge on an open space, fringed with the yellow
and purple of goldenrod and aster, where the settler's scanty crops
are growing among the stumps. Then, with this increasing incidence
and heightened immediacy of detail, the little episode comes to its
climax as the *habitants* appear on the scene to meet the pair—"wild-
looking women, with sunburnt faces and neglected hair," running
from their work; a man or two, following "with soberer steps and
less exuberant zeal"; and a troop of "half-savage children, the *coureurs
de bois* of the future, bareheaded, barefooted, and half-clad," gathering to wonder and stare. For the rest, the portable altar is set up;
and at this point, with great artistic tact, Parkman quietly resumes the
expository mode. The functions of the curé, which constitute the
nodal process of interaction between church and people the passage
is intended to set forth—"to say mass, hear confessions," and so on—
are simply enumerated; further factual details are adduced bearing
on the conditions of the curé's work in the early days; and the passage leads to the words I have quoted on the obscurity in which the
"best of human virtues are buried from age to age," and from
which, for a moment, Father Morel emerges. But, meanwhile, with
nothing but bare statement as to the main point, the filaments of
the institution that was chiefly to mold the life of the colony seem to
root themselves for us along its attenuated length with the physical
actuality of a plant's growth; again, a process of social formation is
realized to the life and in the quick; and, again, whatever our ultimate judgments, we are forced, before arriving at them, to apprehend, to the limits of our imaginative capability, the meaning of the
process in its own terms.

Or at least so much may be said of passages of the sort that bear on the internal life of the colony. Nevertheless, our attention is also claimed by one or two other moments of heightened writing, not comprehended in the St. Lawrence framework. Such, for example, are the winter description of Lake Champlain and the autumn description of Lake George which set forth the expeditions of Courcelle and Tracy against the Iroquois. These begin a sequence which runs through the rest of the series to reach its climax in *Montcalm and Wolfe*, when this highway of Indian warfare becomes for a time a key also to "white" hegemony of the continent. But most of all we have to note the strange Lucretian vision of the inner forest, already alluded to, which meets us, incongruously enough, in Parkman's chapter on "Trade and Industry," where it is intended, somewhat unnecessarily, to vivify for us the activities of the *coureurs de bois*. Indeed, so far as concerns its immediate context, the passage has the effect of a detached and gratuitous piece of "fine writing." Instead of passing swiftly and surely to the dramatic mode, as in passages like the one discussed above, Parkman thus laboriously introduces it: "Though not a very valuable member of society . . . the *coureur de bois* had his uses, at least from an artistic point of view. . . . At least, he is picturesque, and with his redskin companion serves to animate forest scenery. Perhaps he could sometimes feel, without knowing that he felt them, the charms of the savage nature that had adopted him." As if this were not chilling enough, Parkman practically disavows the passage when he has written it, so far as it has any immediate bearing on what he is saying: "Yet it would be false coloring to paint the half-savage *coureur de bois* as a romantic lover of Nature. He liked the woods because they emancipated him from restraint. . . . His life has a dark and ugly side, which is nowhere more strongly drawn than in a letter written by the Jesuit Carheil [who] describes the state of things around him [at Michilimackinac] like one whom long familiarity with them had stripped of every illusion."

Yet, farfetched as the passage seems in relation to its ostensible context, it holds us and compels us by its articulative force in relation to the series as a whole. The matter of it is a generalized forest scene, based on Parkman's memories of the little bushwhacking expedition to the Pool and the Flume in Franconia Notch of his freshman vacation trip: first, we have the forest stream at its sources, "stealing . . . through breathless caves of verdure," or glancing to the sun in crag-walled clefts; then the foisoning tangle of the inner forest itself, which forms the main element of the piece; and finally at the close, an emergence to a spatial vision of lake and mountain and the "transparent azure" of the summer sky. As I have indicated, the passage does for the northern forest what related passages we have examined do for the midland scene in *Pontiac*, the exotic Florida wilderness in *Pioneers*, and the great wilderness river routes of the explorers in *Pioneers* and *La Salle*. Indeed, in its literal sense, it sets the stage for the whole last part of the series, where we turn from the river arteries, the lines of least resistance along which exploration penetrates, to the heart of the forest itself, which, except for the siege of Quebec, is the terrain of the coming struggle for hegemony, and the doom of which is implicit in the English victory. This is the forest of innumerable French and Indian border raids; of Rogers's exploits; of Braddock's defeat; of Forbes's road; of Lord Howe's death; of rout and retrieval at Ticonderoga; and above all, beyond the immediate action, the forest of man's encroachment—that "grand world of woods which the nineteenth century is fast civilizing out of existence."

And, likewise, the passage brings to a climax the train of quasi-symbolic intimations that gather around the other wilderness pieces to which it is related and that make themselves felt in its incantatory rhythms and in the cumulative force of its complex syntactical scheme, which articulates the whole in a single enormous sentence, running to over a page.[1] As to the close, with its evocation of in-

---

[1] "Perhaps he could sometimes feel, without knowing that he felt them, the charms of the savage nature that had adopted him. Rude as he was, her voice may not always have been meaningless for one who knew her haunts so well,—deep recesses where, veiled in foliage, some wild shy rivulet steals with timid music through breathless caves of verdure; gulfs

finite space, enough perhaps has already been said of the implications beyond mere physical description that invest such passages in Parkman's writing. So, too, figures or epithets that elsewhere Parkman uses conventionally enough now take on imaginative life. One notes, for instance, in the first part, the image of cave and river—"stealing through caves of verdure" (reinforced later by "depths of immemorial forests . . . silent as a cavern")—which recalls the fascinated dwelling in Parkman's early journals on underground or hidden streams. Or, again, perhaps imbued in this context with subconscious memories of his friend Squier's book *The Serpent Symbol*, the rendering of an elsewhere commonplace comparison of gnarled roots to snakes—"roots intertwined beneath like serpents in an agony of contorted strife"—here charges itself with the phallic force of the vision of the generative cycle that follows and constitutes the heart of the piece: "fallen trunks . . . bent in the impotence of rottenness . . . while around, and on and through

---

where feathered crags rise like castle walls, where the noonday sun pierces with keen rays athwart the torrent, and the mossed arms of fallen pines cast wavering shadows on the illumined foam; pools of liquid crystal turned emerald in the reflected green of impending woods; rocks on whose rugged front the gleam of sunlit waters dances in quivering light, ancient trees hurled headlong by the storm, to dam the raging stream with their forlorn and savage ruin; or the stern depths of immemorial forests, dim and silent as a cavern, columned with innumerable trunks, each like an Atlas upholding its world of leaves, and sweating perpetual moisture down its dark and channelled rind,—some strong in youth, some grisly with decrepit age, nightmares of strange distortion, gnarled and knotted with wens and goitres; roots intertwined beneath like serpents petrified in an agony of contorted strife; green and glistening mosses carpeting the rough ground, mantling the rocks, turning pulpy stumps to mounds of verdure, and swathing fallen trunks as, bent in the impotence of rottenness, they lie outstretched over knoll and hollow, like mouldering reptiles of the primeval world, while around, and on and through them, springs the young growth that battens on their decay,—the forest devouring its own dead; or, to turn from its funereal shade to the light and life of the open woodland, the sheen of sparkling lakes, and mountains basking in the glory of the summer noon, flecked by the shadows of passing clouds that sail on snowy wings across the transparent azure." *The Old Régime in Canada,* Chapter XX.

them springs the young growth that battens on their decay—the forest devouring its own dead." [2]

But most of all it is this central vision itself that haunts us as the ultimate rendering of something we have seen beginning to shape itself from these wilderness pieces in Parkman's earliest writing— that recurrent vision of the interdependent strife of opposites, the symbiotic interplay of beauty and horror, good and evil, or here, most primordially of all, of birth and death that, in the symbolic vocabulary of natural objects, is the expression of his sense of the human, a metaphor of the psyche, and its projection of itself in man's second nature of culture and civilization. Without abating in the slightest our response to the imperatives of choice and commitment, will and act, that present themselves on the human plane in the perennial parturition of the new from the old, the future from the past—or, historically speaking, the perennial supersessions of culture and civilization—this controlling image of nature and human

---

[2] The serpent as a symbol of reproduction is a leading theme of Squier's book. E.g., pp. 157–158: "Perhaps there is no circumstance in the natural history of the serpent [more striking] than . . . the annual sloughing of its skin, or supposed rejuvenation. . . . It was probably this which connected it with the idea of an eternal succession of forms, constant reproduction and dissolution. . . . In all [of various mystery rites] the serpent was more or less conspicuously introduced, and always as symbolical of the invigorating or active energy of nature. . . . The doctrine of the unending succession of forms was, not remotely, connected with that of regeneration . . . which was part of the phallic system." As we have seen, Parkman was sent a copy of *The Serpent Symbol* by Squier at the time of its publication in 1851, and notes in his acknowledgment its "captivating pictures of snakes, and unseemly phallic emblems."

Parkman's passage perhaps also owes something to Bartram's version of the generative cycle (*Travels*, Part 2, Chap. III): "The plant, or tree [of the palm], when grown old, sometimes divides into two or three stems . . . but generally, when they arrive to this age and magnitude, their own weight brings them to the ground, where they soon decay, the heart or pith first, leaving a hollow, fibrous, reticulated trunk or sleeve, which likewise soon after decays, and in fine, all is again reduced to its original earth, and replaces the vegetative mould. But the deceased are soon replaced by others, as there are younger ones of all ages and stature, ready to succeed their predecessors, and flourish for a time with the same regal pomp and splendor."

nature invests the process with the fullest recognition of its costs, pains, and exactions, and involves the waxing as well as the waning ethos in the symbiotic interplay of gain and loss, of psychic deprivation in one quarter to release novel energies in another—in fine, gives to Parkman's tragic conception of the drama of Western man its ultimate depth and resonance.

This passage of *The Old Régime* is the last of quite the same sort we find in Parkman's history. The thematic overtones established in the sequence of which it is the culmination are sufficiently powerful to be set vibrating through the rest of the series by a passing phrase; and the clash of cultures whose remoter meanings such passages set forth now "speaks for itself" in the direct form of overt physical conflict. As a result, though Parkman deploys his skills of vivification no less effectively than in the earlier volumes, he can do so more sparingly with the stage thus prepared; and, likewise, the bare, terse, kinetic, functional prose that throughout is the staple of his writing becomes more markedly the predominant stylistic element of the last three volumes.

The Old Régime traces the internal development of the colony during its formative years. *Frontenac* deals with its external policy, the implementation of which in the field, as it involved the control of the West, *La Salle* has already illustrated. Now we are shown the evolution of this western policy as a matter of statecraft—despite bitter opposition in France and Canada—at the hands of La Salle's chief supporter and fellow spirit in energy, will, and vision. Frontenac came to New France as royal governor at the age of fifty-two, a professional soldier with a European reputation, and an impecunious courtier, bent on retrieving his private fortunes. Recalled in something like disgrace after a term of ten years, he returned at seventy to consummate during the last eight years of his old age the achievements on which his fame chiefly rests. In this respect he is perhaps the most remarkable of Parkman's heroes. Champlain and La Salle accomplished their chief feats as comparatively young men: La Salle, indeed, had explored the Ohio before he was thirty and died at forty-three. Champlain's name, furthermore, is almost wholly identified with his American career, and La Salle's wholly so. Both were schooled to American conditions from the start. For Frontenac, on the contrary, America was a completely new beginning; and, if his military abilities were sufficiently evident, this flowering in later life of latent capacities of statecraft and this fresh release of energies as prodigious as those of his young coadjutor make him in certain ways Parkman's most signal example of European response to the challenges of the New World.

Nevertheless, though Frontenac shares with La Salle the continental vision that impelled the explorer to his achievements and his death, it is in a wholly different mode. La Salle, "attempting the impossible and grasping at what was too vast to hold," is the focus of a configuration of drives and purposes that seems to postulate a transcendence of the whole French scheme of things for their realization. Frontenac, on the other hand, is a consummate practitioner of the art of the possible, playing his cards, such as they were, with the same coolness, address, and skill that won him, as a professional soldier, the admiration of Europe for his protracted defense of Candia against the Turks, in the face of overwhelming odds.

Frontenac's instinctive grasp of the imperial strategy of New France—of the lines of development, within the limits of the colony's impeded conditions of settlement, best calculated to equalize it with its rival—was evident almost from the moment of his landing. This was particularly signalized by the alliance he at once made with La Salle, and the establishment on Lake Ontario of the post at Cataraqui (Fort Frontenac) which was vital to his and La Salle's plans for control of the West, the abandonment of which by his successors marked the nadir of the policy of retreat and retrenchment that again brought the colony to the verge of ruin, and the reestablishment of which during his second governorship—in the teeth of express and repeated prohibitions from Versailles—sealed the triumph of his own policy of Western expansion as the most effective countermove to English occupation of the seaboard.

As we have seen, the founding of Fort Frontenac was the subject in *La Salle* of one of Parkman's most highly wrought and richly evocative passages, and one matched by few others of his histories for articulative and architectonic effect. Thus in *La Salle*, this brief but prestigious appearance of the hero of the later book, at once establishes Frontenac as a kindred type to the great explorers in will and vision; and creates for us a sense of energies at work behind the scenes, an apprehension of which, if their workings are not then spelled out in detail, is necessary for our understanding of La Salle's activities. So now, when his senior partner takes the center of the stage and what was background in the earlier book constitutes the foreground of the action, the passage continues to pay dividends, so to speak, as the subsequent fortunes of the post become the index to the fortunes of the grand scheme of policy initiated by its founding.

Finally, near the end of the book, when Frontenac's reestablishment of the post brings to a climax the conflict of views of which it has been the focal point, the carrying power of the initial passage charges with equal dramatic force the bare, terse counterchange of sentences, already quoted, which narrate the action that precipitates this crisis of policy:

The representations of the intendant and his faction had such effect, that Pontchartrain wrote to the governor that the plan of reestablishing Fort Frontenac "must absolutely be abandoned." Frontenac, bent on accomplishing his purpose, and doubly so because his enemies opposed it, had anticipated the orders of the minister and sent seven hundred men to Lake Ontario to repair the fort. The day after they left Montreal, the letter of Pontchartrain arrived. The intendant demanded their recall. Frontenac refused. The fort was repaired, garrisoned, and victualed for a year.

But, most of all, the hints of significance that have gathered round Parkman's evocative narration of the founding of the post now find their account in an equally striking series of expository passages, setting forth the repercussions of the act in terms of its remoter historical causes and consequences, and defining the limits and possibilities open to Frontenac as an architect of policy. With their trenchancy of statement and their effect of simply

underlining with a minimum of comment what is already self-evi-
dent from the presentation of facts and events, these passages are
particularly characteristic of Parkman's manner in expository analysis. The series begins with a review of the proximate causes of
the growing disparity between the rival colonies in population
and wealth. As elsewhere, Parkman finds the Achilles's heel of the
French venture in the zeal for religious unity which led Louis XIV
to exclude the Huguenots from his American domain and attempt
to people it "not [with] those who wished to go, but [with] those
who wished to stay at home."

From the hour when the edict of Nantes was revoked, hundreds of thousands of Frenchmen would have hailed the permission to transport themselves, their families, and their property to the New World. The permission was fiercely refused. . . . Had it been granted . . . the valleys of the
west would have swarmed with a laborious and virtuous population,
trained in adversity, and possessing the essential qualities of self-government. Another France would have grown beyond the Alleghanies, strong
with the same kind of strength that made the future greatness of the
British colonies. British America was an asylum for the oppressed and
suffering of all creeds and nations, and population poured into her by the
force of a natural tendency. France, like England, might have been great
in two hemispheres, if she had placed herself in accord with this tendency,
instead of opposing it; but despotism was consistent with itself, and a
mighty opportunity was for ever lost.

As in *The Old Régime*, Parkman's immediate ground of approach
is the contrast of institutions indicated by "laborious and virtuous
population," "self-government," "asylum for the oppressed and the
suffering of all creeds and nations" on the one hand, and "despotism"
on the other (or, in the rest of the passage, "priest-ridden king" or
"fatal policy of exclusion"). Yet, as before, it is not only the superiority of libertarian institutions in the abstract on which the emphasis falls, but on their empirical adaptability to the particular
demands of a particular situation. Here the key phrase is "by force
of a natural tendency," and the conceptions Parkman attaches to
the phrase become evident as he develops the reverse side of the

picture: the possibilities of creative response within the rigidities of the Bourbon system itself; the degree of accordance with "natural tendency" imposed by the American *ambiente* even on the "vigorous mediocrity" of Louis XIV, at the hands of a Frontenac (or, for that matter, as we have seen, at the hands of a Laval).

These northern conflicts were but episodes. In Hudson's Bay, Newfoundland, and Acadia, the issues of the war were unimportant, compared with the momentous question whether France or England should be mistress of the west; that is to say, of the whole interior of the continent. There was a strange contrast in the attitude of the rival colonies towards this supreme prize; the one was inert, and seemingly indifferent; and the other, intensely active. The reason is obvious enough. The English colonies were separate, jealous of the crown and of each other, and incapable as yet of acting in concert. Living by agriculture and trade, they could prosper within limited areas, and had no present need of spreading beyond the Alleghanies. . . . In Canada, all was different. Living by the fur trade, she needed free range and indefinite space. Her geographical position determined the nature of her pursuits; and her pursuits developed the roving and adventurous character of her people, who, living under a military rule, could be directed at will to such ends as their ruler saw fit. The grand French scheme of territorial extension was not born at court, but sprang from Canadian soil, and was developed by the chiefs of the colony, who, being on the ground, saw the possibilities and requirements of the situation, and generally had a personal interest in realizing them.

With its emphasis on economic and geographical factors in general, on the influence of the West in particular, and on the native and autochthonous elements of American development, this passage, like much else in Parkman, strikingly anticipates—if to a very different effect—a ground of approach, which, in the form of the "frontier hypothesis" and otherwise, was to dominate the writing of American history after his death. This strain of interpretation is developed, as, having thus indicated the general background of Frontenac's Western policy, Parkman sets forth its catalytic effect on the internal affairs of the colony. First, however, he interrupts the train of analysis to narrate the immediate events that brought this domestic crisis to a head. These are the refounding of Fort

Frontenac itself and the campaign against the Iroquois Frontenac immediately launched to vindicate by a military victory his flouting of Versailles in regard to the crucial post (where, as usual, if by a more flagrantly narrow margin, he had taken advantage of the slowness of communications with his superiors to make a *fait accompli* of proposals he had with reason expected them to reject).

Parkman then resumes his exposition and sets forth in detail the conflict of issues that has reached its climax of action in the intendant's demand and Frontenac's refusal at Montreal and that now finds its resolution in the tacit disengagement of Versailles from this strange overseas duel with the American wilderness. These three paragraphs pull together the threads of the book, demonstrating the relationship to the central Western question of a whole series of diverse and wide-ranging subsidiary questions, the bearings of which have hitherto been indicated partially and incidentally; and making good the central point of the preliminary discussion: "the grand French scheme of territorial extension was not born at court, but sprang from Canadian soil."

Most of these quarrels, however trivial in themselves, had a solid foundation, and were closely connected with the great question of the control of the west. As to the measures to be taken, two parties divided the colony; one consisting of the governor and his friends, and the other of the intendant, the Jesuits, and such of the merchants as were not in favor with Frontenac. His policy was to protect the Indian allies at all risks, to repel by force, if necessary, every attempt of the English to encroach on the territory in dispute, and to occupy it by forts which should be at once posts of war and commerce and places of rendezvous for traders and *voyageurs*. Champigny and his party denounced this system; urged that the forest posts should be abandoned, that both garrisons and traders should be recalled, that the French should not go to the Indians, but that the Indians should come to the French, that the fur trade of the interior should be carried on at Montreal, and that no Frenchmen should be allowed to leave the settled limits of the colony, except the Jesuits and persons in their service. . . .

Strong personal interests were active on both sides, and gave bitterness to the strife. Frontenac, who always stood by his friends, had placed Tonty, La Forêt, La Motte-Cadillac, and others of their number, in charge of the forest posts, where they made good profit by trade. Moreover, the licenses for trading expeditions into the interior were now, as formerly, used largely for the benefit of his favorites. The Jesuits also declared, and with some truth, that the forest posts were centers of debauchery, and that the licenses for the western trade were the ruin of innumerable young men. All these reasons were laid before the king. In vain Frontenac represented that to abandon the forest posts would be to resign to the English the trade of the interior country, and at last the country itself. The royal ear was open to his opponents, and the royal instincts reinforced their arguments. The king, enamoured of subordination and order, wished to govern Canada as he governed a province of France; and this could be done only by keeping the population within prescribed bounds. Therefore, he commanded that licenses for the forest trade should cease, that the forest posts should be abandoned and destroyed, that all Frenchmen should be ordered back to the settlements, and that none should return under pain of the galleys. . . . Frontenac was also directed to make peace with the Iroquois, even, if necessary, without including the western allies of France; that is, he was authorized by Louis XIV to pursue the course which had discredited and imperilled the colony under the rule of Denonville.

The intentions of the king did not take effect. The policy of Frontenac was the true one, whatever motives may have entered into his advocacy of it. In view of the geographical, social, political, and commercial conditions of Canada, the policy of his opponents was impracticable, and nothing less than a perpetual cordon of troops could have prevented the Canadians from escaping to the backwoods. In spite of all the evils that attended the forest posts, it would have been a blunder to abandon them. This quickly became apparent. Champigny himself saw the necessity of compromise. The instructions of the king were scarcely given before they were partially withdrawn, and they soon became a dead letter. Even Fort Frontenac was retained after repeated directions to abandon it. The policy of the governor prevailed; the colony returned to its normal methods of growth, and so continued to the end.

This is a sufficiently anticlimactic upshot to the long drama of challenge and response we have been following, but the "off-stage" reference at the end—"even Fort Frontenac"—once more revives our sense of the ardors and endurances, the imaginative vision, the political boldness, sagacity, and adroitness required to establish even this limited degree of accordance between the Bourbon system and "natural tendency," between European preconceptions and American conditions. Finally, the concluding paragraph of the book, summarizing its main themes, projects the future results of this struggle and shows us Frontenac's work firmly woven into the fabric of Canadian statecraft—always against the background of failure in the larger adaptations that was to doom the colony at the end.

The chief objects of the late governor were gained. The power of the Iroquois was so far broken that they were never again very formidable to the French. Canada had confirmed her Indian alliances, and rebutted the English claim to sovereignty over the five tribes, with all the consequences that hung upon it. By the treaty of Ryswick, the great questions at issue in America were left to the arbitrament of future wars; and meanwhile, as time went on, the policy of Frontenac developed and ripened. Detroit was occupied by the French, the passes of the west were guarded by forts, another New France grew up at the mouth of the Mississippi, and lines of military communication joined the Gulf of Mexico with the Gulf of St. Lawrence; while the colonies of England lay passive between the Alleghanies and the sea till roused by the trumpet that sounded with wavering notes on many a bloody field to peal at last in triumph from the Heights of Abraham.

As I have said, this sequence of passages is characteristic of Parkman's handling of the framework of "conditions" which determine the form and direction of events and policies and the scope of individual action. Because he sums up in them a vast deal which has been conveyed to the reader by incidental comment in the course of the narrative and because he has shaped narrative itself so that events become their own comment on the conditions which are their matrix, such passages of overt expository analysis are relatively rare in Parkman and yet extremely trenchant in effect. As interpretation they anticipate the emphasis on economic factors and the influence of the frontier which for a later generation of historians became the all-sufficient key to American developments, yet in a fashion wholly free from the naïve "scientism" and reductiveness of his successors. Instead they form one element in the kind of synthesis possible only to "narrative" history, at least at the hands of a master: a multifaceted presentation which by various means—vivification, portraiture, analysis—discriminates the interplay of causal factors and sets them in dynamic relationship to their issue in action. And if, as we have noted, the actions of individuals bulk large in the particular complex of historic cause and consequence Parkman sets forth, it is for empirical reasons, and within a framework of incisive exposition of the broader, impersonal factors that determine the limits and possibilities of individual action.

But however remarkable Frontenac's design for French imperial policy in America as a display of creative adaptability under unfavorable circumstances, the question was one of tactics rather than of strategy; and as to the general French scheme of things his quarrel with Versailles was no more fundamental than Laval's.[3] And however remarkable the flowering of his latent capacities for statecraft under the impact of American conditions—of all that receives its stamp of vivification in the controlling passage in *La Salle* on the founding of Fort Frontenac—it was his military abilities, which from the necessities of the colony's case, both as regarded the Iroquois and the English, were most immediately in demand. Thus, within the limits of the book itself, the episode on which the incidence of vivification most tellingly falls is that of

[3] Nevertheless, shortly after his first arrival in Canada, Frontenac also attempted in domestic policy a series of sufficiently audacious innovations —revivals of "faded liberties"—designed to give the colony a modicum of self-government. These took the form of an assembly modeled on the ancient Estates of France, elective aldermen for Quebec, and a semiannual town meeting for the discussion of public business. As Parkman puts it: "The boldness of these measures will scarcely be appreciated at the present day. . . . Frontenac, filled with the traditions of the past, and sincerely desirous of the good of the colony, [had] rashly set himself against the prevailing current [of absolutist centralization]. His municipal government, and his meetings of citizens, were, like his three estates, abolished by a word from the court, which, bold and obstinate as he was, he dared not disobey. Had they been allowed to subsist, there can be little doubt that great good would have resulted to Canada."

the repulse of Sir William Phips's expedition against Quebec, to outfit which Massachusetts, still exhausted from King Philip's War, had strained her last resources; and to repulse which, ineptly as it was conducted, required the full strength of her chronically impoverished rival and the full deployment of its chief's formidable energies. As Parkman handles the episode, we see Frontenac in all the outward hierarchical circumstance of his position as governor and commander, and through the personal mana with which he makes good these outward attributes, the vital focus, at this moment of crisis, of all the forces of this quasi-military, hierarchical, yet frontier-formed society which, in *The Old Régime*, we have watched come into being.

Thus, in the opening scene we follow the blindfolded emissary bearing Phips's preposterous demand for surrender up the steep streets to the Château, "amid a prodigious hubbub intended to bewilder him and impress him with a sense of immense warlike preparation." When his blindfold is removed, he—and the reader with him—are suddenly confronted by the old soldier-courtier in the midst of his officers, French and Canadian—"Maricourt, Sainte-Hélène, Longueuil, Villebon, Valrenne, Bienville, and many more" —in full panoply of "gold lace and silver lace, perukes and powder, plumes and ribbons, and all the martial foppery in which they took delight," "regarding the envoy with keen, defiant eyes," while Frontenac rejects the pompous ultimatum out of hand, and refuses to honor it with a written answer. Thus for the currents of morale emanating from the Château; and the currents meeting and mingling with them from below are made as tellingly evident in the scene of the arrival by night of the reinforcements from Montreal: Callières with seven or eight hundred men, part regular troops, part "bands of *coureurs de bois* and other young Canadians, all full of fight, singing and whooping with martial glee as they passed the western gate and trooped down St. Louis street." Likewise, the conjunction of the man and the hour compels the recognition of even his clerical enemies and brings into full play the offices of the colony's predominant institution. So we have the bishop, St.

Vallier, absent on a pastoral tour, returning "at night, by torch-light, to the great joy" of the inhabitants, to invoke the blessings of heaven on the governor's endeavors, and Laval—at odds with both—fervently seconding his successor's efforts. And, throughout, as I have said, the episode is so managed as to constitute our impression par excellence of the Frontenac of the Château, so to speak, of the actualities of the Canadian world in being, such as the interplay of institutions and conditions have made it, bringing to bear its forces at the maximum of capacity, to achieve its moment of power and glory. And thus in turn the episode complements and completes the effect of the initial episode in *La Salle*, where we see Frontenac in no less characteristic a posture, directing the flotilla up the Long Saut, "without his cloak, and drenched to the skin"; and which, through Parkman's arts of evocation, constitutes our impression par excellence of the Frontenac of the frontier, of the continental vision and the continental future. Again, by the incidence of vivification, the nature and style of the French venture, as the range of Frontenac's activities sums them up, speak for themselves in a double sense, forcefully enough on their own terms and in their own colors, and forcefully enough in the light of the libertarian and pragmatic criteria—the fundamental material and social prerequisites of peopling the new continent and developing its resources—which constitute Parkman's own frame of judgment and the various bearings of which, for all the éclat of his re-creation, we are never for a moment unaware: the shakiness of the foundations, social and economic, on which New France of the Château rested; the inadequacy of the means at its command—"a musket, a rosary, and a pack of beaver skins"—for realizing the possibilities that opened before it on the frontier; the "fatal policy of exclusion" and the rest that impeded and choked the flow of central Western drives which its initial confrontation of the challenge of the New World had evoked.

For the rest, without projecting the figure of the man beyond the framework of historical agency, Parkman rounds out his portrait of Frontenac to match as a character piece, if in a different vein, his tragic portrait of La Salle. Many traits of his subject, indeed, lend themselves patently to comedy: Frontenac's unabashed relish for ceremonious pomp and circumstance, "above all when he himself was the central figure in it"; or the disputes over points of protocol—though they also had deeper causes—to which he intermittently devoted his redoubtable energies, in a mood of explosive irascibility when his opponents were strong enough to thwart him, or of ironically suave urbanity when he himself had the upper hand.

Yet the comic force of Parkman's rendering of these episodes is also quickened by a recognition from very inward sources of the irritability of temperament and the will to mastery that animated Frontenac in such forays. Likewise the same inner response makes itself felt through his comments on other traits of the govennor: his taste for the wilderness, for instance, and his remarkable affinity with Indians. So we have the scene at a council of the Western tribes when "the punctilious old courtier . . . himself half Indian at heart," and "as much at home in a wigwam as in the halls of princes," seizes a hatchet, and, stamping and whooping, leads the war dance in person.

His predecessor would have perished rather than play such a part in such company. . . . Another man would have lost respect in Indian eyes by such a performance. In Frontenac, it roused his audience to enthusiasm. They snatched the proffered hatchet and promised war to the death.

And there is also a very idiosyncratic turn in Parkman's remarks on the genuine rapport which almost alone of the royal governors, the old aristocrat established, not only with the Indians and the *coureurs de bois*, but with the native Canadian populace at large.

Indeed, as regards the Canadians generally, he refrained from the strictures with which succeeding governors and intendants freely interlarded their despatches. It was not his instinct to clash with the humbler classes, and he generally reserved his anger for those who could retort it.

And throughout, infusing his sources with his own penetration of character, Parkman achieves, stroke by stroke, a piece of portraiture with very much the savor of the great French memoir writers of Frontenac's own time—Cardinal de Retz or Parkman's favorite, the Duc de St. Simon—and with the same first-handedness of effect.

Then Frontenac, with the ease of a man of the world and the loftiness of a *grand seigneur*, delivered himself of the harangue he had prepared [for the meeting of the Estates]. He wrote exceedingly well; he is said to have excelled as an orator; certainly he was never averse to the tones of his own eloquence.

Frontenac has been called a mere soldier. He was an excellent soldier and more besides. He was a man of vigorous and cultivated mind, penetrating observation, and ample travel and experience. . . . He had the air of distinction natural to a man familiar all his life with the society of courts, and he was as gracious and winning on some occasions as he was unbearable on others. When in good humor, his ready wit and a certain sympathetic vivacity made him very agreeable. At times he was all sunshine, and his outrageous temper slumbered peacefully till some new offense wakened it again. . . . He was full of contradictions; and, intolerant and implacable as he often was, there were intervals, even in his bitterest quarrels, in which he displayed a surprising moderation and patience. By fits he could be magnanimous.

Not every voice in the colony sounded the governor's praise [during his second term]. Now, as always, he had enemies in state and Church. It is true that the quarrels and the bursts of passion that marked his first term of government now rarely occurred, but this was not so much due to a change in Frontenac himself as to a change in the conditions around him. The war made him indispensable. He had gained what he wanted, the consciousness of mastery; and under its soothing influence he was less irritable and exacting.

His own acts and words best paint his character, and it is needless to enlarge upon it. What perhaps may be least forgiven him is the barbarity of the warfare that he waged, and the cruelties that he permitted. He had seen too many towns sacked to be much subject to the scruples of modern humanitarianism; yet he was no whit more ruthless than his times and his surroundings, and some of his contemporaries find fault with him for not allowing more Indian captives to be tortured. Many surpassed him in cruelty, none equalled him in capacity and vigor. When civilized enemies were once within his power, he treated them, according to their degree, with a chivalrous courtesy, or a generous kindness. If he was a hot and pertinacious foe, he was also a fast friend; and he excited love and hatred in about equal measure. His attitude towards public enemies was always proud and peremptory, yet his courage was guided by so clear a sagacity that he never was forced to recede from the position he had taken. Towards Indians, he was an admirable compound of sternness and conciliation. Of the immensity of his services to the colony there can be no doubt. He found it, under Denonville, in humiliation and terror; and he left it in honor, and almost in triumph.

In spite of Father Goyer, greatness must be denied him; but a more remarkable figure, in its bold and salient individuality and sharply marked light and shadow, is nowhere seen in American history.

Together with *Jesuits* and *The Old Régime*, *Frontenac* completes in the main Parkman's depiction of French Canada and the versions, sacred or secular, of continental conquest that were the losing alternatives to the forces maturing along the English seaboard. Already the disparity between the rival colonies in growth of population and economic productiveness was the determinant of French policy; and Phips's attack on Quebec heralds the closing phase of direct military conflict which Parkman traces in the last volumes of the series.

CHAPTER XV

A HALF CENTURY, MONTCALM AND WOLFE, LAST YEARS

⚜ ⚜ ⚜

A Half Century of Conflict traces the development of Frontenac's policy in the West, almost unopposed at first by the English; the sporadic border war of raids and massacres in the East, motivated largely by the exigencies of French relations with the Indians; and the response of the rival colony, from Phips's unsuccessful attempt on Quebec, through the occupation of Acadia, to the taking of Louisbourg, provoked by the threat to New England commerce and fisheries which that "Dunkirk of America" added to French harassment of the land frontier. This phase of the struggle was mainly provincial on the English side: Phips's expedition had been entirely a native product; and the lucky stroke at Louisbourg, though assisted by the Royal Navy, was also a colonial undertaking (the fruits of which were lost by the restoration of the fortress to France by the Treaty of Aix-la-Chapelle).

In *Montcalm and Wolfe* the conflict broadens, deepens, and reaches its climax. Hostile contact spreads along the whole frontier, as the westward push of trade and settlement meets the chain of French posts intended to contain it, and the key areas of conflict become the Lake George-Lake Champlain gap, Oswego and Niagara on the Great Lakes, and the approaches to trans-Appalachia and the Ohio Valley. At the same time the struggle assumes on the English side the imperial character it had always had on the French side; the main battles are engagements of professional European armies, in which local forces, colonial or Indian, play a subsidiary part; and the decisive stroke of this war for the forest is delivered from the sea as part of a world-wide conflict, whose "Agent of Destiny" is William Pitt. Yet the fall of New France which imperial and colonial interests converge to effect—and its postlude as regards the Indian, set forth in *Pontiac*—likewise strengthens the forces preparing to harvest the results in their own autonomous fashion and paves the way for a conquest of the wilderness, independent of the mother country.

A Half Century of Conflict, written at a considerable interval after *Montcalm and Wolfe,* shows the effect of this displacement in the order of composition. Except for the explorations of the Vèrendryes, the working out of Frontenac's policy for New France in the West is rather perfunctorily treated, at least for Parkman; and the internal affairs of the colony are hardly touched on. Thus, though the state of the colony on the eve of the conquest is depicted vividly enough in *Montcalm and Wolfe, A Half Century* does not maintain the continuity and cohesion of the series evident in the rest through *Frontenac.* On the other hand, Parkman's extremely detailed treatment of the sporadic war of raids and massacres on the New England border and of the Louisbourg expedition makes the book seem disproportionately long in relation to the series as a whole. Besides *Montcalm and Wolfe* (and the earlier written *Pontiac*) it is the only unit that runs to two volumes.

Yet Parkman relates these New England events to their social context, and, for a society whose forces are so largely local and autonomous, harnessed to workaday ends and dispersed through its whole fabric rather than concentrated in the activities of a few individuals at the head of a hierarchical structure, some such minuteness of treatment was necessary to paint it in its characteristic colors and, so far as the scope of his subject allowed, to authenticate concretely the contrast of institutions and cultures he had first sketched at the beginning of *Pontiac.* At any rate the incidents of border war—the raids on Wells and York (narrated in *Frontenac*); on Deerfield, Haverhill, and Keene; the captivities of the survivors; the scotching of the Abnakis and Father Rale at Norridgewock; Lovewell's fight, the defense of Number Four, the loss of Fort Massachusetts, and so on—are the occasion for a development on the scale of a town history, with the same closeness of view, yet with a presentation in depth that re-creates the whole life-style of frontier and rural New England. Likewise Parkman's handling of the collective efforts at reprisal the provocations on the frontier set in train— Phips's attack on Quebec, in *Frontenac*, and the Louisbourg expedition—completes the picture in respect to merchant and maritime New England, the workings of the colony's quasi-autonomous political institutions, its relations with the royal governors, its economy and finances. In their dispersed way, and though martial events, guerrilla or otherwise, are their foreground matter, the New England parts of *A Half Century* form something of the same kind of cultural and institutional view of the colony that Parkman had attempted for its rival in *The Old Régime*. Nor, though he does not conceal his main allegiances, is this conspectus of his own ancestral background notably less objective in tone.

For the rest, the book shows Parkman's prose at its most characteristic in pace, economy, finely shaded incisiveness, and balance between rhetorical pointing and a natural, almost colloquial, manner. The following sketch of the younger Dudley is an example— to give as a last specimen in this kind a shorter biographical piece that can be quoted as a whole:

Joseph Dudley, governor of Massachusetts and New Hampshire, was the son of a former Governor of Massachusetts, that upright, sturdy, narrow, bigoted old Puritan, Thomas Dudley, in whose pocket was found after his death the notable couplet:

> "Let men of God in courts and churches watch
> O'er such as do a toleration hatch."

Such a son of such a father was the marvel of New England. Those who clung to the old traditions and mourned for the old theocracy under the old charter, hated Joseph Dudley as a renegade; and the worshippers of the Puritans have not forgiven him to this day. He had been president of the council under the detested Andros, and when that representative of the Stuarts was overthrown by a popular revolution, both he and Dudley were sent prisoners to England. Here they found a reception different from the expectations and wishes of those who sent them. Dudley became a member of Parliament and lieutenant-governor of the Isle of Wight, and was at length, in the beginning of the reign of Queen Anne, sent back to govern those who had cast him out. Any governor imposed on them by England would have been an offence; but Joseph Dudley was more than they could bear.

He found bitter opposition from the old Puritan party. The two Mathers, father and son, who through policy had at first favored him, soon denounced him with insolent malignity, and the honest and conscientious Samuel Sewall regarded him with as much asperity as his kindly nature would permit. To the party of religious and political independency he was an abomination, and great efforts were made to get him recalled. Two pamphlets of the time, one printed in 1707 and the other in the next year, reflect the bitter animosity he excited. Both seem to be the work of several persons, one of whom, there can be little doubt, was Cotton Mather; for it is not easy to mistake the mingled flippancy and pedantry of his style. He bore the Governor a grudge, for Dudley had chafed him in his inordinate vanity and love of power.

If Dudley loved himself first, he loved his native New England next, and was glad to serve her if he could do so in his own way and without too much sacrifice of his own interests. He was possessed by a restless ambition, apparently of the cheap kind that prefers the first place in a small community to the second in a large one. He was skilled in the arts of the politician, and knew how, by attentions, dinners, or commissions in the militia, to influence his Council and Assembly to do his will. His abilities were beyond question, and his manners easy and graceful; but his instincts were arbitrary. He stood fast for prerogative, and even his hereditary Calvinism had strong Episcopal leanings. He was a man of the world in the better as well as the worse sense of the term; was loved and admired by some as much as he was hated by others; and in the words of one of his successors, "had as many virtues as can consist with so great a thirst for honor and power."

This little masterpiece, finally, is as characteristic in matter as in manner for its ironical detachment from "filiopietistic" attitudes in regard to both the royal governors and their opponents. That

Shirley, Dinwiddie, or even Dudley figured on the American scene as more than mere instruments of tyranny was a novel view at the time and again anticipates a later strain of interpretation. As Parkman had already put it in *Montcalm and Wolfe*:

Mind and heart [of the colonists] were engrossed in strife with their governors: the universal struggle for virtual self-rule. But the war was often waged with passionate stupidity. . . . In the interest of that practical independence which they had so much at heart, two conditions were essential to the colonists. The one was a field for expansion, and the other was mutual help. Their first necessity was to rid themselves of the French, who by shutting them between the Alleghanies and the sea, would cramp them into perpetual littleness. . . . But in the middle of the last century the vision of the ordinary colonist rarely reached so far. . . . The governors, representing the central power, saw the situation from the national point of view. . . . [Dinwiddie's] instincts were on the side of authority; but it is hardly to be imputed to him as a very deep offense against human liberty that he advised the compelling of the colonists to raise men and money for their own defense. . . . As [he and Shirley] both defended the royal prerogative and were strong advocates of taxation by Parliament, they have found scant justice from American writers. Yet the British colonies owed them a debt of gratitude, and the American States owe it still.

By and large, however, *A Half Century* is the least compelling of Parkman's histories—partly, no doubt, for reasons intrinsic to its subject matter; but also partly because, in defect of a central predominant figure, he failed to find some less loosely strung, dispersed way than is the case of organizing its diverse material. Certain more personal passages of the book will demand our attention elsewhere.

With *Montcalm and Wolfe* we emerge on a world stage; the concentration of decisive events within a brief frame of time makes for a natural coherence of effect, which Parkman's instinct for pace and proportion reinforces to the fullest; and this climactic series of events is so managed as to bring to a focus all the lines of thematic suggestiveness of the previous volumes.

Montcalm and Wolfe is of course first of all the history of a war. The battle pieces, of which the account of Frontenac's repulse of Phips or the account of the first Louisbourg expedition in a *A Half Century* are types, now hold the center of the stage throughout— Washington's backwoods brush with Jumonville at Great Meadows which opened this conflict that "set the world on fire"; Braddock's disaster on the Monongahela; Johnson's unexploited defeat of Dieskau at Lake George; Montcalm's brilliant victories at Oswego and Fort William Henry; the second siege and capture of Louisbourg; the death of Lord Howe and Abercrombie's fiasco at Ticonderoga; Forbes's retrieval of Braddock's defeat; and above all Wolfe's culminating stroke from the sea at Quebec, with its aftermath in the battle of Sainte-Foy and the capitulation of Montreal. Coming now to that part of his undertaking which had first aroused his interest and turned him to the vocation of history when he was little more than a boy; dealing on the grand scale with a type of event that, besides the challenges of exploration, most appealed to his instinct for action; Parkman makes these battle pieces the occasion for the deployment of his most brilliant gifts of narrative. So the figures of the opposing military leaders command his finest arts of portraiture; and the issues at stake having come to the stage of naked physical conflict, the moments of conflict on which the settlement of issues now hangs are the immediate focus of the drama.

This fact, however—though the background is as solidly filled in as the foreground is brilliantly lighted—did much to obscure Parkman's reputation in the period after his death. To a school of historians for whom brilliance of narrative was almost per se evidence of lack of depth, and whose preconceptions almost automatically ruled out war and battle as elements of historical actuality worth a serious historian's attention, *Montcalm and Wolfe* could pass for mere romantic pageantry, a specimen of outmoded "drum and trumpet" history. Time, however—or rather history itself—quickly and signally corrected this astigmatism of view; and the living experience of two world wars casts a very different light on Parkman's account of their eighteenth century forerunner. What perhaps most strikes us about the book today is precisely its realism and relevance, both as to the more dramatic and less dramatic aspects of its subject. Again and again, in spite of changed conditions, Parkman awakens an astonishing sense of closeness through a whole range of connections: the Churchillian coloring, for example, with which he presents the familiar series of English fiascos at the start and the energies of the master spirit who sustained and retrieved them; his emphasis on problems of logistics (though the word had not yet come into use), of adaptation to new conditions of warfare, and of Anglo-colonial cooperation; his discussion of the differing strategic conceptions of the contestants, as it determines the apportionment of forces to the European and American theaters of war; his discrimination of the conflict of parochial and national views that was to project itself after the Revolution from the struggle for self-government between the colonial legislatures and the royal governors; or, in general, his adumbrations of the difficulties of a democratic, locally autonomous society face to face with an authoritarian régime. And as for the larger lines and deeper issues, so for the details. Take, for example, the following, with its glimpse of children at play among the ruins, which Parkman fashions from his sources for his account of the English occupation of Quebec:

The troops, driven by cold from their encampment on the Plains, were all gathered within the walls. Their own artillery had so battered the town that it was not easy to find shelter. The Lower Town was a wilderness of scorched and crumbling walls. As you ascended Mountain Street, the Bishop's Palace, on the right, was a skeleton of tottering masonry, and the buildings on the left were a mass of ruin, where ragged boys were playing at seesaw among the fallen planks and timbers.

For a generation to whom the sight was to become a hundredfold familiar, such touches, as Mr. Otis Pease points out, have a living pertinence of actuality that makes short work of a "drum and trumpet" view of the book.

The book, of course, is not a general history of the Seven Years'

War. Parkman deals with its European background and developments only so far as is necessary to place the American phase of it in the perspective of the whole. These European chapters involve a highlighting and foreshortening of their material to which historians have not altogether unjustifiably demurred. Still, they sufficiently serve their main purpose of demonstrating the Old World connections of this New World conflict, and their bearing on its remoter results: the relationship of American independence, for instance, to such a phenomenon of historical contingency as the emergence on the European scene of Frederic II. At any rate, breaking new ground in the American field as the book does, this sense of wider ramifications it nevertheless conveys strikes a particularly fresh and contemporary note in contrast to the parochialism that was to mark so largely the work of Parkman's successors. Indeed, fifty years later, we can still perhaps subscribe to John Fiske's judgment that, of all American historians, Parkman "is the most deeply and peculiarly American, yet . . . at the same time the broadest and most cosmopolitan."

His main story, as I have said, has a double aspect: an emphasis at once on the convergence and divergence of imperial and colonial interests in the prosecution and outcome of the war. Naturally, because the colonies could not mobilize their full strength, Great Britain's desire for imperial gain comes to the fore, as a defensive conception of the war changes to a conception of total victory— "*Canada delenda est*"—under the impetus of Pitt's energies, and this train of events reaches its climax in the amphibious operation utilizing control of the sea for a direct thrust to the heart of New France. Yet the decisiveness of this stroke depends also on mastery of the Lake Champlain and Lake Ontario-St. Lawrence invasion routes that give interior access to New France through its wilderness bulwarks. Likewise the third main area of conflict is the wilderness frontier of the middle colonies, where the westward push of English settlement across the Alleghanies—or at least its fur-trading forerunners—comes up against the French chain of posts intended to contain it. Thus, except for the action at Quebec in the final phase, the war is a forest war; or rather, on the English side, a war against the forest, both in its immediate problems and its remoter consequences—the conquest, literally and symbolically, of that "world of woods the nineteenth century is fast civilizing out of existence."

So the French style of fighting is based on a long-practiced adaptation of regulars and militia to the conditions of the forest as it is; the English style, if shaped in part by a similar and dearly learned lesson is, nevertheless, based more on altering the conditions of the forest itself. Braddock's rout at the hands of the forest and the Indian is retrieved by the laborious and prosaic process of hewing a road across the densely wooded ridges of the Alleghanies; thereby winning Fort Duquesne, the "Key to the West," without a battle—or in spite of a subsidiary skirmish which is also a temporary victory for the forest and the French. Likewise the characteristic response to the brilliant series of French victories in the "operations at Lake George" is Amherst's careful solidification of each step of his counteradvance: the destruction of broad belts of woods along his line of communication to the Hudson; the opening of a road across the Vermont wilderness to the New England frontier at "Number Four." "Never was the problem of moving troops encumbered with baggage and artillery, a more difficult one," Parkman writes of the war as a whole. "The question was less how to fight the enemy than to get at him." But there are also broader questions of "logistics": the bringing to bear of the disparity produced by the economic and cultural differences between the rival systems; the mobilization on the English side of native resources which was as indispensable to the war as an imperial venture as professional armies were to its prosecution as a colonial venture. The éclat of Parkman's account of Braddock's defeat does not obscure the significance of Franklin's procurement of the hundred and fifty wagons without which the expedition could not have started at all. So in the wake of the disaster, colonial apathy gives way in widening ramifications to a realization of the native interests at stake and the nature of the war as an assault on the wilderness.

The struggle on the Alleghany frontier is naturally the part of the book where Parkman's handling most emphasizes these remoter and more specifically American consequences of the war. The setting is largely that of his first book; and theme, action, and characters strike a familiar note. We have the counterattack of the wilderness and the devastation of the frontier that repeat themselves in *Pontiac;* the same civil jars between the borderer and Quaker over what is to be done; and, among the *dramatis personae,* Lieutenant-Colonel Bouquet, preparing himself in Forbes's advance on Fort Duquesne for his rôle in the postlude that completed the work of this forest war that first "opened the Great West to English enterprise." Descriptive touches likewise echo earlier passages, and reawaken the dualities of Parkman's first broaching in *Pontiac* of the theme of wilderness conquest: "forests crashing to the axe, dark spires of smoke ascending from autumnal fires." So now, even for military purposes, the ax is as potent a weapon as the gun, and behind the military incursion into this "realm of forests ancient as the world" Parkman evokes the encroaching tide of settlement that is to consolidate the conquest and turn it to its own purposes: the long, thin fringe of log cabin and clearing, where

the victims of the settler's axe lay strewn about . . . in a chaos of prostrate trunks, tangled boughs, and withered leaves, waiting for the fire that was to be the next agent in the process of improvement, while around . . . stood the living forest . . . biding its own day of doom.

These touches keep alive our sense of the complex of ambiguities and affirmations from which in *Pontiac* Parkman had projected his version of the advance of civilization and the "doom of the forest and the Indian"; while now on an earlier but already crucial stage of this advance civilization likewise composes its dissensions, rallies willy-nilly to the support of its vanguard, and in the persons of Braddock, Forbes, Bouquet, or the young Washington schools itself ill or well to the conditions of the wilderness in order to subdue it.

Yet for immediate strategic purposes the Allegheny front was a minor one; and the forest rout of Braddock mainly an Indian affair. It is in the Lake Champlain-Lake George area that a "compact military absolutism" exploits most strikingly its advantages of forest mastery and interior lines of maneuver against the superior numbers and resources of a "heterogeneous group of industrial democracies" hampered by "diffusion and incoherence," and against the efforts of the professional armies unused to forest war that have come to their aid. Or, correspondingly, it is here that the military challenge of the forest is most complex for the English; and its demands of adaptation hardly less disastrously enforced than by Braddock's rout. Montcalm, at least in the purely military sphere to which his activities are confined, plays the cards dealt him with the vigor and skill of Frontenac before him; and, indeed, in a strictly military sense, the English finally carry the day at Lake George more by default, as Wolfe strikes at the vitals of the French from the sea, than by fighting. Nevertheless, the lessons of adaptation are mastered, if late and painfully; and, in the person of Lord Howe, only untimely death deprives the English of a practitioner of forest war worthy of his opponent.

The chief actions of this phase of the war are Montcalm's capture of Fort William Henry, the English wilderness outpost at the head of Lake George, and his repulse of Abercrombie's counterattack on Ticonderoga, guarding the Champlain gap for the French. The first episode, with the near massacre of the defenders by the French Indians after the surrender, is a forest sortie that spread a wildfire of fear and panic through the English settlements. The second is a magnificent last stand of the forest against odds, as Lord Howe meets his death in the tract of "mountain and valley . . . wrapped in primeval woods" at the foot of Lake George, and Abercrombie, blindly attempting to carry Ticonderoga by a *coup de main*, hurls the flower of the army his nominal subordinate has organized and trained to its destruction on the freshly felled abattis of trunks and branches Montcalm has prepared in front of the fort.

The ground sloped away like a natural glacis. . . . To a distance of a musketshot from the works, the forest was cut down, and the trees left

lying where they fell among the stumps, with tops turned outwards, forming one vast abattis. . . . But the most formidable obstruction was immediately along the front of the breastwork, where the ground was covered with heavy boughs, overlapping and interlaced, with sharpened
points bristling into the face of the assailant like the quills of a porcu-
pine. . . . Montcalm had done what he could; but the danger of his position was extreme and inevitable. His hope lay in Abercrombie; and it was
a hope well founded. The action of the English general answered the
utmost wishes of his enemy. . . . The regulars, who had formed in
columns of attack under cover of the forest, advanced their solid red
masses into the sunlight, and . . . pushed forward to the assault. . . .
They had been ordered to carry the works with the bayonet; but their
ranks were broken by the obstructions through which they struggled in
vain to force their way, and they soon began to fire. The storm raged in
full fury for an hour. The assailants pushed close to the breastwork; but
they were stopped by the bristling mass of sharpened branches, which they
could not pass under the murderous cross-fires that swept them from front
and flank. At length they fell back. . . . Abercrombie, who was a mile
and a half in the rear, sent orders to attack again, and again they came on
as before.

The scene was frightful: masses of infuriated men who could not go forward and who would not go back; straining for an enemy they could not
reach, and firing on an enemy they could not see; caught in the entanglement of fallen trees; tripped by briers, stumbling over logs, tearing
through boughs; shouting, yelling, cursing, and pelted all the while with
bullets that killed them by scores, stretched them on the ground, or hung
them on jagged branches in strange attitudes of death. . . . Montcalm,
with his coat off, for the day was hot, directed the defence of the center,
and repaired to any part of the line where the danger for the time seemed
greatest. He is warm in praise of his enemy, and declares that between one
and seven o'clock they attacked him six successive times. . . . Till half-
past seven a lingering fight was kept up by the rangers and other provin-
cials . . . to protect the retreat of the regulars, who fell back in disorder
to the Falls. As twilight came on, the last combatant withdrew and none
were left but the dead. Abercrombie had lost in killed, wounded, and
missing, nineteen hundred and forty-four officers and men [out of a total
of 15,000 against a French force "not one fourth so numerous"].

Here English ineptitude in the forest dialectic of challenge and
response reaches its nadir; and, in the framework of evocation built

up through the rest of the series, only the literal facts are needed to make Montcalm's *chevaux-de-frise* at Ticonderoga an emblem of the whole great belt of wilderness that guards New France, with whose fate that of the wilderness and the Indian is identified. But if, so far as actual fighting is concerned, the battle, as Parkman recounts it, is the climactic scene in the ebb and flow of forest war through this "route of mutual invasion," it is nevertheless a last stand of the forest and the wilderness. Abercrombie's blundering is only a temporary setback. Lord Howe's innovations in training and equipment to fit the English regulars for forest war bear their fruit; his cooperative attitude toward the colonials has reconciled divergences sufficiently for the purpose in hand; and the latent strength of the "industrial democracies" is mobilized, in part at least, for the joint assault on the forest.

Again, the enterprise moves forward to a retouching of familiar themes. So the main chapters on this phase of the war open with a bird's-eye view, as the wild fowl stream "in long files northward to their summer home," of the whole "seat of war . . . spread beneath them like a map" from the Hudson to Montreal: Fort William Henry "amid charred ruins and a desolation of prostrate forests"; Lake George "like some broad river, trenched between mountain ranges still leafless and gray"; Ticonderoga with the Bourbon flag "a flickering white speck" on its ramparts; Crown Point and its stone tower; the widening reaches of Lake Champlain; the Adirondacks on the left; on the right, "the long procession of the Green Mountains," and "far beyond, on the dim verge of the eastern sky, the White Mountains throned in savage solitude"; Fort St. John and Fort Chambly guarding the Richelieu; and "the broad belt of the St. Lawrence, with Montreal seated on its bank." This, of course, is a last appearance of that recurrent spatial vision evoked for Parkman by decisive turns in the conquest of the wilderness, the germs of which we have seen in his first sketch of his subject at the beginning of *Pontiac*. Complementing it, the axwork of Amherst's uncontested advance with which the campaign anticlimactically ends needs only literal statement to revive the intimations that gather in the earlier passage around the "ploughs and axes of Virginian woodsmen" enforcing a surer title to the wilderness than Céleron de Bienville's armorial plates. Thus the war declares itself as a "strife of the past against the future, the old against the new"; the prosaic energies of exploitation take over the wilderness world to which the French energies of exploration have staked their vast claims; and behind the imposing façade of the military absolutism that supports these claims the failure of response of the "Bourbon system" to the larger challenges of the wilderness finds its account in the economic chaos that overtakes the colony, the orgy of peculation among its officials, and the growing war-weariness of its scanty population with no vital stake of its own in the retention of continental hegemony.

For all this forest phase of the war, as I have said, accent and emphasis—or so much so as serves to awaken the evocatory intensities of earlier passages—make for an underlining of meanings in their more remote and peculiarly American terms. Here we come back full circle to Parkman's first book, where the postlude to the war in this sense is played out and the doom of the forest and the Indian, implicit in the fall of New France, is finally sealed. But with the decisive episode at Quebec we are out of the forest altogether. The Indian allies hardly figure; the colonials on the English side play only a subsidiary part, and, on the French side, an unreliable part; victory hangs on a clash of regular troops, encountering European fashion on an open field of battle; and naval power, both remotely and immediately, is the predominant factor in Wolfe's success.

And, in a near view at least, the outcome was far from inevitable. Montcalm, if hampered by division of authority with a jealous governor, had the advantage of an almost impregnable position, and, like Frontenac, could concentrate his scanty manpower to present his assailant with superiority of numbers. The odds were not vastly greater against Phips than against Wolfe. Heavily repulsed at Montmorency, his situation was becoming desperate; and but for the lucky combination of circumstances that made good his audacious gamble for the Plains of Abraham, "New France might have lived a little longer, and the fruitless heroism of Wolfe would have passed, with countless other heroisms into oblivion." The Quebec–St. Lawrence scene is of course a familiar one, and Parkman's descriptions of it are now confined to functional, map-like surveys setting forth the military situation, or to a few evocatory strokes to mark critical junctures of the action. The approach of the English fleet, for example, is thus signalized from the point of view of a forest observer:

The ships that had gone before lay to till the whole fleet was reunited, and then all steered together for the St. Lawrence. From the headland of Cape Egmont, the Micmac hunter, gazing far out over the shimmering sea, saw the horizon flecked with their canvas wings, as they bore north-ward on their errand of havoc.

So we have a moment of heightened description of the natural setting as Wolfe makes his first, abortive attempt at a land approach to Quebec by way of the Montmorency:

The position of the hostile forces was a remarkable one. They were sepa-rated by the vast gorge that opens upon the St. Lawrence; an amphitheatre of lofty precipes, their brows crowned with forests, and their steep brown sides scantily feathered with stunted birch and fir. Into this abyss leaps the Montmorency with one headlong plunge of nearly two hundred and fifty feet, a living column of snowy white, with its spray, its foam, its mists, and its rainbows. . . . It was but a gunshot across the gulf, and the senti-nels on each side watched each other over the roar and turmoil of the cataract.

Finally, in the culminating episode of the Anse du Foulon, a descriptive touch or two remarkably intensifies the climactic effect. Parkman first recounts very briefly and factually the climb to the plateau of the advance party and their successful surprise of the French outpost. Then, with a sudden heightening of immediacy, the focus of the narrative is shifted; the course of the action is re-peated in terms of the auditory impressions that come through the darkness to Wolfe and the army waiting in the boats below; and the whole complex of issues at stake hangs for a moment in the suspense of a silence only deepened by the noise of a brook and the suck of the tide.

The main body of troops waited in their boats by the edge of the strand. The heights nearby were cleft by a great ravine choked with forest trees; and in its depths ran a little brook, called Ruisseau St-Denis, which, swollen by the late rains, fell plashing in the stillness over a rock. Other than this no sound could reach the strained ear of Wolfe but the gurgle of the tide and the cautious climbing of his advance-parties as they mounted the steeps at some little distance from where he sat listening. At length from the top came a sound of musket-shots, followed by loud huzzas, and he knew that his men were masters of the position. The word was given; the troops leaped from the boats and scaled the heights, some here, some there, clutching at trees and bushes, their muskets slung at their backs.

With this quickening of pace the final action unfolds itself and the fate of the continent is determined by the brief shock of arms on the Plains of Abraham to which the moment of silent waiting at the Anse du Foulon is the crucial prelude.

Thus the decisive blow of this war for the wilderness is a field battle of professional armies, fought *dans les règles;* and the decisive factor that makes Quebec the Achilles's heel of French wilderness empire is naval power. The point is brought home on the foreground scene with characteristic immediacy in Parkman's account of Lévis's all but successful attempt to retake the city the next spring:

In the autumn Lévis, with a view to his intended enterprise, had sent a request to Versailles that a ship laden with munitions and heavy siege-guns should be sent to France in time to meet him at Quebec in April; while he looked also for another ship, which had wintered at Gaspé, and which therefore might reach him as soon as navigating opened. The arrival of these vessels would have made the position of the English doubly critical; and, on the other hand, should an English squadron appear first, Lévis would be forced to raise the siege. Thus each side watched the river with an anxiety that grew constantly more intense. . . . Bad and scanty fare, excessive toil, and broken sleep were telling ominously on the strength of the garrison when, on the ninth of May, Murray, as he sat pondering over the fire in his quarters in St. Louis Street, was interrupted by an officer who came to tell him that there was a ship-of-war in the basin beating up towards the town. Murray started from his revery, and directed that British colors should be raised immediately on Cape Diamond. . . . The news had spread; men and officers, divided between hope and fear crowded to the rampart by the Château . . . and every eye was strained on the approaching ship. . . . Slowly her colors rose to the masthead and unfurled to the wind the red cross of St. George. It was the British frigate "Lowestoffe." She anchored before the Lower Town, and saluted the garrison with twenty-one guns. . . . The "Lowestoffe" brought news that a British squadron was at the mouth of the St. Lawrence, and would reach Quebec in a few days.

Finally, after the destruction of the French river fleet, Wolfe's amphibious operation is completed by Murray's junction at Montreal with the forest forces of Haviland and Amherst and the ensuing capitulation of the "Bourbon system" in America. And, as we return to the world scene in Parkman's discussion of the Treaty of Paris, it is again the establishment of English "maritime supremacy" which, among the larger consequences of the war, complements the beginnings of the history of the United States implicit in Wolfe's victory on the Heights of Abraham—and which was to be such an important, if tardily acknowledged factor in guaranteeing the continental developments that resulted from those beginnings. At any rate, Parkman's whole handling of the war in relation to American destiny underlines both its national and world connections, its elements of independence and interdependence, with an effect that gives the book a centrality of view hardly to be appreciated at the time when it was written.

Nor, for the rest, have Parkman's own conclusions, in the light of his time, altogether lost their pertinence. As might be expected, they are hardly conceived in a mood of complacence, firmly committed in general as he was to what he felt was signified by the outcome of this "strife of the past against the future; of the old against the new; of moral and intellectual torpor against moral and intellectual life; of barren absolutism against a liberty, crude, incoherent, and chaotic, yet full of a prolific vitality." After a harshly astringent paragraph in the same vein on contemporary French Canada, which if it "would fulfil its aspirations . . . must cease to be one of the most priest-ridden communities of the modern world," he thus projects the present from the past as regards his own fellow countrymen:

Those who in the weakness of their dissensions needed help from England against the savage on their borders have become a nation that may defy every foe but that most dangerous of all foes, herself, destined to a majestic future if she will shun the excess and perversion of the principles that made her great . . . resist the mob and the demagogue as she resisted Parliament and King, rally her powers from the race for gold and the delirium of prosperity to make firm the foundations on which that prosperity rests, and turn some fair proportion of her vast mental forces to other objects than material progress and the game of party politics. She has tamed the savage continent, peopled the solitude, gathered wealth untold, waxed potent, imposing, redoubtable; and it now remains for her to prove, if she can, that the rule of the masses is consistent with the highest growth of the individual; that democracy can give the world a civilization as mature and pregnant, ideas as energetic and vitalizing, and types of manhood as lofty and strong, as any of the systems which it boasts to supplant.

That these resonant adjurations, like Parkman's last words on French Canada, have their shortcomings of apprehension is a point hardly worth disputing. As to types of character which democracy had already given to the world, one need only indicate his estimate of Lincoln: the "feeble and ungainly mouthpiece of the North," as he wrote Mary Parkman in 1862, whose displacement of Washington as the hero of schoolboys Barrett Wendell found him deploring thirty years later. This valedictory passage can pass, and has passed, for a tissue of commonplaces of the *Nation*-mugwump school, the expression of disgruntlement of a patrician class relegated to political impotence. Yet, in the context of Parkman's whole work, the familiar items of the arraignment take on a different ring; and the key phrase —"A nation that may defy every foe but that most dangerous of all foes, herself"—strikes a note that transcends any bias of the kind: the pervasive note of genuine tragic feeling, beyond optimism or pessimism, springing as much from engagement, involvement, and commitment as from alienation, comprehending the writer's own deepest sense of life, and voicing a challenge the right to which had been "earned" in the most inward and exacting way.

After the publication of *Montcalm and Wolfe* in 1884, the main productive years of Parkman's life were over. The connecting volume that completed the series did not appear until 1892, the year before his death. This and the chapters on the early history of Acadia he prepared for a revised edition of *The Old Régime*, published the year he died, were the only new works of his last period. In general, this time of life, which normally sees a taking in of sail, was also marked for Parkman by a sharp aggravation of the disorders that had always afflicted him.

Still, even with the completion of *Montcalm and Wolfe*, he undertook soon after the very thorough revision of *Pioneers* which appeared in 1885, and in preparation for which he made the trip to Florida we have noted to acquaint himself at first hand with the setting of the opening episode of the book—a matter he had had to leave in abeyance when he wrote it, because of the Civil War. The little notebook of the trip sets down his impressions with all the freshness of vision of his youthful wilderness travels, sharpened by the horticulturalist's response to the novelty of a half-tropical flora. So too, as we have seen, he put to use these impressions in refashioning the opening wilderness piece of his histories with an undimmed imaginative energy that makes it one of his most magistral efforts of the sort. These years likewise saw a curious flickering up of his old appetite for wilderness living, which, not a person to do things by halves, he had made no attempt at after his breakdown had denied him the freedom of full physical activity. Nevertheless, in 1875, we find him on a visit to Moosehead Lake with Judge Gray, climbing mountains with something of the impetuosity that disconcerted the companions of his youthful expeditions—or at least at a pace not relished by the judge, a colossus of six feet four, weighing two hundred and fifty pounds, Parkman wrote Margry (in French), "whom you can imagine scrambling up the rocks with his rifle—for he is a good shot—and stopping now and then to wipe his forehead while he cursed me for getting him into such execrable country." Again, in October, 1883, he had made a horseback trip around his cherished White Mountains, where he was caught coming through Crawford Notch by a drenching rainstorm that turned to snow—an adventure, however, that left him none the worse, "though a grandfather of sixty."

So, in 1886, the enthusiasm for the backwoods of C. H. Farnham, his secretary at the time, led to a month's encampment on the Batiscan River, a tributary of the St. Lawrence, which it enters near Trois Rivières. Here, in spite of his lame knee, he insisted on helping as he could with building the camp and doing the camp work. For the rest, though he was too lame to attempt more with a rifle than target practice, he took to canoeing again for the first time in forty years, and was initiated by Farnham into the art of fly fishing. He found this sojourn so beneficial that he went later in the summer to a sporting camp at the Rangeley Lakes, where he had a cabin built with the idea that he and his sister might vacation there from time to time. The proprietor of the camp was a Maine guide, F. C. Barker, in whose adventures his guest had reason to take a particularly lively and personal interest. Ten years earlier Barker and a companion, J. S. Danforth, had spent a winter trapping in the region of Parkman's wilderness forays of the 1840's, and had written an attractive account of the experience—*Hunting and Trapping on the Upper Magalloway River and Parmachenee Lake*—where we find they used for their supply base Parkman's campsite of thirty years before at the junction of the Magalloway and Little Magalloway. The flow of mutualities thus called forth is attested by a copy of the book, now in the Harvard Library, inscribed to "Mr. F. Parkman with kind regards of F. C. Barker, Bemis Camp, Sept. 11, 1886." Parkman, in turn, was stirred to a further range of wilderness reminiscence, and reciprocated the gift as Barker records in his autobiography:

In the season of [1886] Mr. Francis Parkman was a guest at Camp Bemis for six or eight weeks, and many were the pleasant walks I had with him on the piazza of Cleft Rock Hall, after supper, he telling me of his early experiences in the West, and the early French History of Canada, and Arnold's famous trip through Maine to Quebec; but I did not know he was an author until I received through the mail his book, *The Oregon Trail.* He was a man whose acquaintance was much sought after by the guests, and he was pleasant and genial to all. The following winter I built him a camp at Bemis, but ill health before the next season caused him to give up his trip here.

Nor was he ever to come back. Even at the best, after sixty—and above all on the American scene—the Magalloways or Oregon Trails of one's youth are hardly to be recaptured from the diminished actuality except in memory; and this wilderness episode fittingly closed with these evocations of the *temps perdu* to which the Rangeleys and Barker prompted him.

And Parkman's case, after sixty, was far from the best. From 1886 on his infirmities increased markedly, if not to a diminution in quality of what he did, at least to a rather drastic curtailment of the range of his activities. As we have seen, he gave up his gardening, except for ordinary maintenance, in the early eighties. So, in 1888, he felt compelled to resign from the Harvard Corporation because of his condition. The year before he had made his last trip to Europe, which was cut short at Madrid, soon after his landing, by a particularly severe onslaught of "the enemy." Its chief manifestations were, as before, besides the "whirl in the brain," the arthritis and insomnia which now afflicted him with renewed force. Lameness of the knee indeed so crippled him during the last years of his life that he seems hardly to have been able to walk at all without a cane or crutches, and had to have an elevator installed in the Chestnut Street house to reach his study on the third floor. The worsening of his insomnia levied a more serious toll. As he wrote the Abbé Casgrain in 1889: "For the past five years I have done very little historical work. . . . Two or three hours of sleep in the 24—which have been until lately my average allowance for long periods together—are not enough to wind up the human machine, especially when exercise is abridged by . . . rheumatism. . . . Perhaps, however, the rheumatism is a stroke of retributive justice for writing *Montcalm and Wolfe*. Though I have slept better in the past year, it is still an open question whether I shall ever manage to supply the missing link between that objectionable work and its predecessor, *Count Frontenac*." Some alleviation was afforded him by the famous Philadelphia physician, S. Weir Mitchell, who, Parkman felt, had done more for him than anyone else. We find in his last notebook a careful record of the few extra hours of sleep gained by the use of various sedatives; and he seems to have benefited from his physician's advice not to watch his diet, and allow himself to grow stout. Howells, in the account already cited of his last conversation with Parkman, speaks of this change in his appearance. "I had noticed . . . that he had put on weight; his fine face was full; whereas when I first knew him, he was almost delicately thin of figure and feature. He was always of a distinguished presence, and his face had a great distinction."

But, whatever his condition, he avoided, as always, any attitude of invalidism, in private life or at large. If he had to resort to crutches, he manipulated them in a characteristically Parkmanian fashion. On the street he would proceed with all his old vigor of gait, then rest a little, and start off again at the same quick pace. Or, as his grandchildren recall, he would negotiate the descent of a staircase by sending his crutches clattering in front of him, while he himself slid down the bannister. Nor did the more inward ravages of "the enemy" reveal themselves even in his domestic life, which now comprehended a widening circle of nieces and grandchildren, for whose entertainment he deployed resources of humor and fantasy to an effect that, except for the patent fact of his lameness, left them largely unaware of his illness and suffering. Likewise, on his part, this traffic provided exactly the means of relief he needed between mere silence and the overstimulation of too serious or provocative conversation. Farnham sketches for us some of the rituals of comic fantasy with which, schooled to make the most of little things, he freshened the daily round of his life:

At breakfast, after replying briefly to inquiries as to health, he would begin a tale and carry it on throughout the meal, and even continue it from day to day. The chief characteristic of these stories was a jocose exaggeration. Any subject would serve; now he would reconstruct a character from some novel; or would take a name on a sign as the starting point, and carry the imaginary owner through various experiences more or less impossible. He married off his daughters to persons they detested, and then teased them with making such unwise selections. Frequently he chose subjects more or less theological; he invented a minister in Florida who was so ill supported by his congregation that he had to eat crocodile eggs, which turned him into an amphibious divine; and a Miss Simpkins, who conducted a Sunday School for young demons; as her pupils were rather restless, she passed their tails through holes in the bench, and tied knots underneath. Or he would now and then take up one of the Prophets, and give him a character and history hardly in accord with Biblical traditions. Another string to his bow was humorous verse. During sleepless hours he often composed parodies; one was on the "Psalm of Life"— cats being the heroes. At breakfast he would often make additions to these compositions, and thus enrich and expand a topic to its utmost.

So he drew for entertainment on the stores of verse he had by heart, reciting extracts from Byron's "Vision of Judgment"; or from "The Baby's Debut," Horace Smith's parody of Wordsworth in *Rejected Addresses;* or from *Bombastes Furioso,* that raucous little farce we have spoken of earlier in which he himself had acted as a boy. Or again, he enlivened what otherwise might have been the insufferable monotony of his row on Jamaica Pond by the invention of a comic mythology for the geographical, floral, and faunal features of that minuscule body of water, peopling its depths with a sea-serpent and an icthyosaurus, or endowing the cats along its shore—seen or unseen—with names, characters, and the most astonishing experiences. Indeed, he had a great fondness for cats; and was almost always to be seen in the evenings at Chestnut Street or on the verandah at Jamaica with a cat in his lap or curled up on the floor beside him. Naturally they figured large in his intercourse with the young; his letters to his grandchildren taking the form of imaginary epistles from "Flora" or "Creem." So, for many years, on arriving for a visit to his daughter's family, a flannel cutout of a cat, which one of his granddaughters had made for him for Christmas, was produced from under his coat, with intimations, by no means skeptically received, that it has spent the winter there, followed by an equally convincing recital of its adventures since its last appearance.[1]

Meanwhile, the visits of which this little comedy were the occasion, marked a change during his last years from the previous course of his life at Chestnut Street and Jamaica Pond. In 1879 his daughter Katherine became the wife of the architect J. T. Coolidge, who later acquired and restored for their summer home the mansion built in colonial days by Governor Benning Wentworth at Little Harbor, near Portsmouth, N.H., on the point of land where the Piscataqua reaches the sea. Here Parkman now habitually spent a large part of his summers in the congenial company of his daughter and architect son-in-law—for whom he had a particular liking—

---

[1] Parkman's gifts of impromptu fantasy, and his rapport with the young, are attested for a very much earlier period of his life by the son of Dr. Elliott at Staten Island, where he had gone to be treated for his eye trouble and where a branch of his Shaw cousins had moved from Boston:

"Frank Parkman, or 'Cousin Frank,' as he was called by the Shaw family, was a great favorite with the boys; with whom he played and to whom he told wondrous tales of adventure by field and flood—he having recently returned from one of his frontier expeditions. Later his stories began to vary from the strictly historical, and to take on the guise of fictions. And at last one evening when we were out rowing on the river in front of our house 'Cousin Frank' told of a frightful struggle which he and his companions had with sharks, in the Bay of California, which lasted over two hours and during which he and his two companions—Mexican pearl divers—were in 90 feet of water, so that when the party reached the surface, they were all nearly out of breath. We boys looked at each other silently for a while, until Bob Shaw, who being a relation was less shy of speech—did ejaculate 'g'long!' so forcibly that the passage from the credible to the incredible was recognized. On another occasion—also in the boat—he told us about a row among the animals at an Eastern menagerie, during which he had tied the trunk to the tail of the biggest and most savage elephant, under his belly, till he surrendered by holding up his paw and purring. We were never quite sure after that whether the tales of adventure so freely narrated were meant to be taken literally or not, as 'Cousin Frank's' face gave no outward or visible sign for grave or gay. . . . He was an excellent talker among his peers, the adults, and we boys liked him even better than James Russell Lowell, who had taken more notice of our adolescence, but who somehow appeared condescending and Bostony to our untutored fancy."

and their four children; and in the congenial setting of seacoast, harbor, and tidal creek, where he could bait-fish and maneuver a rowboat more adventurously than on his home pond. His rowing was no less brisk for having to hobble to the boat on crutches or having to blow a whistle for help in getting out of it when he docked. The Wentworth mansion was perhaps so called from its one state chamber for meetings of the governor's council. Otherwise it was a rambling farmhouse of angles and gables, little rooms, odd corners, and crooked passages. To landward of it stood the remnant of an apple orchard; and old lilac bushes softened its weathered frame. On one side an outlet of the river, on the other a creek, brimmed with water at high tide, or laid bare at the ebb their complex of channels, sandbanks, mussel beds, seaweed, rocks, and glistening mud flats. The farther prospect comprised the spires and masts of Portsmouth; at the harbor mouth, the large island of Newmarket, with its attendant train of islets and island rocks, "battered with the rack of ages, studded with dwarf savins, or half clad with patches of whortleberry bushes, sumac, and the shining wax-myrtle"; and beyond, the open Atlantic, where "in the dim distance the Isles of Shoals seemed floating on the pale gray sea." So, writing "at a window of this curious old house," Parkman took occasion to describe the scene, in his account, in *A Half Century of Conflict*, of William Pepperell, whose own house stood across the channel from the Wentworth mansion. Much of the book, in fact, was composed on these summer visits to Portsmouth.

And the material of *A Half Century*, indeed, called forth this personal note in several connections—particularly as it quickened in old age the memories of boyhood and youth Parkman so tenaciously retained. Thus he traces the fortunes of the "Outagamies" or Fox Indians, after their defeat by the French in 1713, through Blackhawk's rising to an occasion of which, at the age of fourteen, he was himself a witness:

Three or four years after [Blackhawk's rising] a party of their chiefs and warriors was conducted through the country by order of the Washington government. . . . At Boston they danced a war-dance on the

Common in full costume, to the delight of the boy spectators, of whom I was one.[2]

Likewise an incident of New Hampshire border war stirred him to memorialize the attractions of Keene and the time of his college visits, when he was courting Pamela Prentiss:

In the valley of the little river Ashuelot . . . was a rude border settlement which later years transformed into a town noted in rural New England for kindly hospitality, culture without pretence, and goodbreeding without conventionality.

But the chief crossing point of history and personal experience in the book is his account of the French in the trans-Mississippi West— the last great thrust into the unknown of French exploring energy which culminated with the 1742 expedition of the brothers La Vérendrye, in the company of a band of Sioux, to the foot of the Big Horn Mountains (or so at least Parkman interpreted the meager and confusing data, though later historians incline to make the Black Hills the Vérendryes' farthest west).

Here he found the correlative in objective historical fact for the most unforgettable experience of his life; and an experience which had now become historically retrievable, on the external scene as well as inwardly, in memory alone. Once before in his histories, as we gaze with La Salle at the swarming buffalo herds of the Illinois prairie, images of the Oregon Trail had charged his writing with the immediacy of participation, while at the same time an elegiac note had begun to sound.

The boundless waste was thronged with life. He beheld that wondrous spectacle, still to be seen at times on the plains of the remotest West, and the memory of which can quicken the pulse and stir the blood after

[2] The occasion also made a considerable impression on a spectator of maturer years. Longfellow wrote of it to his father:

"There is a grand display of Indians in Boston,—Black-Hawk and some dozen other bold fellows, all grease and red paint; war-clubs, bears-teeth, and buffalo scalps in profusion; hair cut close, like a brush, and powdered with vermillion; one cheek red, one black; forehead striped with bright yellow, with a sprinkling of flour between the eyes,—this will fit almost any of them. They are to have a *pow-wow* on the Common tomorrow."

the lapse of years. Far and near, the prairie was alive with buffalo; now like black specks dotting the distant swells; now trampling by in ponderous columns, or filing in long lines, morning, noon, and night, to drink at the river,—wading, plunging, and snorting in the water; climbing the muddy shores, and staring with wild eyes at the passing canoes.

When he came to write of the Vérendryes, the buffalo had vanished even "on the plains of the remotest West"; the Indian had followed; and as, with the same quickening of the pulse, he re-creates, through the eyes of the explorers, the scenes that had stamped themselves so indelibly on his mind during his own sojourn with the Sioux, the valedictory note swells to full diapason:

At length the camp broke up. The squaws took down the lodges, and the march began. . . . The spectacle was such as men still young have seen in these Western lands, but which no man will see again.

Thus the circle completes itself from the account in the opening volume of Parkman's histories of Champlain on the Ottawa, crepitant with memories of his own first wilderness forays; again, the personal and the historic, the inward and the outward, merge to open up wider and wider planes of meaning; and this most authentic of farewells to that lost world of the West whose image has become a stereotype of our culture also writes finis to more besides than even now perhaps it is possible to reckon.[3]

[3] So Melville, at about the same time, and in the same spirit, spoke the valedictory of that other lost world of the South Seas, the stereotyped image of which has also fixed itself in our culture:

Where is the world we roved, Ned Bunn?
Hollows thereof lay rich in shade
By voyagers old inviolate thrown
Ere Paul Pry cruised with Pelf and Trade.
To us old lads some thoughts come home
Who roamed a world young lads no more shall roam.

. . . .

Marquesas and glenned isles that be
Authentic Edens in a Pagan sea.

Parkman, meanwhile, had already marked the passing of the old West in the preface to the 1872 edition of *The Oregon Trail* and was to do so

Yet, in the sum of Parkman's work, the word "spectacle" is the key word of the passage, and all it comprehends with him beyond the elegiac or nostalgic, the remote or the exotic—that Shakespearean sense it expresses of the whole human show of things, in its worth and interest *sub specie temporis*, which is at once the deepest ground note of his writing and the most quintessentially historical note of history itself.

Parkman spent the last summer of his life quietly at his daughter's in Little Harbor. Though the great series was completed, he had plans for recasting it as a continuous whole and emending the unrevised volumes—the last entry in his notebooks, fittingly enough, is a minute detail of the sort: "*Jesuits*, 257, correct '*evening* mass.' " In the fall he celebrated his seventieth birthday at Jamaica Pond. A few weeks after, he was struck with appendicitis on coming back from a row. Peritonitis set in before he could be operated on, and he died November 8, 1893. He was buried at Mt. Auburn, in the fullness of fame and honors, and to an accompaniment of official eulogy which has perhaps done more to eclipse his stature than the almost total obscurity that attended the burial two years before of Herman Melville, his greater contemporary, the major experience of whose life, nevertheless, that of his own so strikingly paralleled.

---

again in the preface to the 1892 edition, illustrated by Frederic Remington —one of those "men still young" who had seen "in these Western lands" what Parkman himself had seen, or, as the preface has it, who "knew the prairies and the mountains before irresistible commonplace had subdued them." In his correspondence with Remington, Parkman introduced him to the work of his ablest predecessor as a pictorial recorder of the wild West. "I immediately went to the library," Remington writes January 2, 1892, "and got Maximilian's book [Prince Maximilian of Wied's *Journey Through North America*] and Bodmer's drawings. Before that I had never heard of the book and I was delighted. Bodmer drew much better than Catlin."

Religious Beliefs

According to Farnham, Parkman began "with the early Unitarian opinions found in Channing; then embraced the more manly and natural religion of Parker; and ended in the agnosticism that makes it impossible to subscribe to any definite statement regarding the Unknown. His attitude is shown by this bit of intimate conversation with his sister Eliza. One day when they were rowing on Jamaica Pond she said, 'If I should be asked about your religious beliefs, it seems to me I might say that you were a reverent agnostic.' 'Yes, that's about it.'"

In another connection, Parkman recorded himself as feeling that, whether or not we believe in the supernatural origin of Christianity, it is to be accepted "on its ethical side . . . with reverent gratitude as a vast boon to mankind." In a letter of 1870 to Charles Eliot Norton, concerning the storm raised among the Harvard Overseers by President Eliot's appointment of John Fiske to a temporary professorship of history, he writes: "Some call Fiske 'Positivist,' and some 'Atheist' . . . I shall go for Fiske on one condition—that I become satisfied that, heretic or not, he will deal with serious questions in a spirit of candor and reverence, and will practically admit the accountability of man to a higher power." But whatever such statements indicate, the agnosticism of his sister's phrase—in which mingled a strong strain of rationalism and anticlericalism—was the attitude which Parkman consistently held to in his histories, as touching the supernatural claims both of Catholicism and Puritanism.

Yet Farnham's conclusion that Parkman "was a stranger to religious emotion, so far as we can judge," is perhaps stronger than the biographical data warrant. In his discussion of the question,

Farnham passes over altogether the Catholic episode of Parkman's youth; and evidence that has recently come to light shows him responsive at least to religious considerations at one other juncture of his life. This is a letter of 1852, written at a time of great personal distress, to his cousin-in-law Mary Dwight Parkman, who took a deeply Christian view of the *ultimata* of life with which the letter is concerned. Even here the note is more Stoic than Christian, but the letter is stamped with Parkman's fundamental seriousness of thought and feeling; and whatever may be deduced from it as to his beliefs, it is perhaps the most intimate revelation he has left of the spirit with which he faced obstacles that seemed to him insuperable.

In your kind note of last Sunday, you wish you might return me a helpful answer. Your answer was doubly helpful. Your sympathy is a balm and a cordial . . . I have pondered, also, the graver consolations which you offer. You express fully and clearly views toward which I have long been tending. I believe profoundly in the truth of what you say. It is the only key which can explain the mystery of life: and even if this key does not in every instance suffice, I am content to rest in the assurance of a clear light hereafter. It was, many years ago, my prayer that my lot in life might be such as might tend to the advancement of my highest interests, irrespective of happiness or suffering. It may be that the prayer is granted. I accept whatever destiny is assigned to me and shall seek to draw from it whatever germs of good it may conceal. Yet I hold that, where action is possible, passive resignation is no virtue, but a weakness. At present I am fast bound—hand and foot—and there is little possibility of my ever regaining even a moderate share of liberty. Yet, if by God's mercy, a single finger is unloosed, its feeble strength will not lie idle. In *achievement* I expect to fail, but I shall never recoil from endeavour, and I shall go through life, hoping little from this world, yet despairing of nothing.

You have done me a great service. Truth from the lips of a friend brings with it a double conviction. Your views are not hard and gloomy, for they embody a glorious hope.—You and I have certain vital aims and feelings in common, and I feel that a friendship founded on such sympathies must be enduring—not wholly dependent on the accidents of intercourse or separation.

Revision of Descriptive Passages in the Florida Episode of *Pioneers*

In writing the first version of *Pioneers* Parkman was unable to examine the Florida scene at first hand because of the Civil War, and drew for descriptive detail mainly on William Bartram's *Travels*, which had earlier kindled the romantic imagination and had been put to use by Chateaubriand in *Atala*—on the grand scale—and by Coleridge and Wordsworth. Nor did he by any means eliminate all reminiscences of the *Travels* from his revision. The account of Ottigny's encampment on the St. John's, for instance, echoes two of Bartram's most imaginative passages:

. . . and when at sunset the voyagers drew their boat upon the strand and built their camp-fire under the arches of the woods, the owls whooped around them all night long, and when morning came the sultry mists that wrapped the river were vocal with the clamor of wild turkeys.

Bartram writes of the owls:

I was awakened and greatly surprised by the terrifying screams of Owls in the deep swamps around me, and what increased my extreme misery was the difficulty of getting quite awake, and yet hearing at the same time such screaming and shouting, which increased and spread every way for miles around, in dreadful peals vibrating through the dark extensive forests.

And of the wild turkeys:

I was awakened in the morning early, by the cheering converse of the wild turkey-cocks (Meleagris occidentalis) saluting each other from the sun-brightened tops of the lofty Cupressus disticha and Magnolia Grandiflora. . . . The high forests ring with the noise . . . the watchword being caught and repeated, from one to another, for hundreds of miles around. . . . A little after sun-rise, their crowing gradually ceases, they quit their high lodging places, and alight on the earth, where, expanding their silver bordered train, they strut and dance about the coy female, while the deep forests seem to tremble with their shrill noise.

Nevertheless, the sequence was drastically revised in the 1885 version to achieve a more realistic effect, a greater economy of presentation, and a closer thematic relationship with the narrative as a whole. A striking example is the culminating passage, with its overelaboration of detail in the first version, and its incongruously idyllic close:

The wilderness through which they passed holds its distinctive features to this day,—the shady desert of the pine-barrens, where many a wanderer has miserably died, with haggard eye seeking in vain for clue or guidance in the pitiless, inexorable monotony. Yet the waste has its oases, the "hummocks,"—where the air is sweet with woodland odors, and vocal with the song of birds.

Then the deep cypress-swamp, where trunks rise like the columns of some vast sepulchre; above, the impervious canopy of leaves; beneath, a black and root-entangled slough. Perpetual moisture trickles down the clammy bark, while trunk and limb, distorted with strange shapes of vegetable disease, wear in the gloom a semblance grotesque and startling. Lifeless forms lean propped in wild disorder against the living, and from every rugged stem and lank, outstretched limb hangs the dark drapery of the Spanish moss. The swamp is veiled in mourning; no breath, no voice; a deathly stillness, till the plunge of the alligator, lashing the waters of the black lagoons, resounds with hollow echo through the tomb-like solitude.

Next came the broad sunlight and the wide savanna. Wading breast-deep in grass, they view the wavy sea of verdure; headland and cape and far-reaching promontory; distant coasts, hazy and dim; havens and shadowed coves; islands of the magnolia and the palm; high, impending shores of the mulberry and elm, ash, hickory, and maple. Here the rich gordonia, never out of bloom, sends down its thirsty roots to drink at the stealing brook. Here the halesia hangs out its silvery bells, the purple clusters of the wistaria droop from the supporting bough, and the coral blossoms of the erythrina glow in the shade beneath. From tufted masses of sword-like leaves shoot up the tall spires of the yucca, heavy with pendent flowers of pallid hue, like the moon, and from the grass gleams the blue eye of the starry ixia.

In the 1885 version the passage is cut to half its original length; and the closing evocation of the savanna—charmingly as it interfuses recollections of Bartram and Chateaubriand with Parkman's horticultural interests—is omitted altogether. A new opening dispenses with the melodrama of the lost traveler to incorporate material from Parkman's own impressions of the pine barrens. Most importantly, the elements of the description are rearranged and the emphasis shifted to bring to predominance in this finale the note that has sounded through the rest of the sequence.

The wilderness through which they passed has not yet quite lost its characteristic features—the bewildering monotony of the pine barrens, with their myriads of bare gray trunks and their canopy of perpetual green, through which a scorching sun throws spots and streaks of yellow light, here on an undergrowth of dwarf palmetto, and there on dry sands half hidden by tufted wire-grass, and dotted with the little mounds that mark the burrows of the gopher,[1] or those oases in the desert, the "hummocks," with their wild, redundant vegetation, their entanglement of trees, bushes, and vines, their scent of flowers and song of birds; or the broad sunshine of the savanna, where they waded to the neck in grass; or the deep swamp, where, out of the black and root-encumbered slough, rise the huge buttressed trunks of the Southern cypress, the gray Spanish moss drooping from every bough and twig, wrapping its victims like a drapery of tattered cobwebs, and slowly draining away their life, for even plants devour each other, and play their silent parts in the universal tragedy of nature.

[1] Cf. *Journal*, March 13, 1885: "Woods opposite Jacksonville. Tall, lank, bare-stemmed pines. Wire grass, etc., below. Sun easily penetrates, Palmetto thickets."

Relations with Bancroft and Henry Adams

Bancroft afforded Parkman scholarly assistance in several connections, and wrote him a warmly appreciative letter on the publication of *Montcalm and Wolfe:*

I take delight in your honors as much or more than I should my own. You have just everything, which goes to make an historian: persistency in collecting materials, indefatigable industry in using them, swift discernment of the truth, integrity and intrepidity in giving utterance to truth, a kindly humanity which is essential to the true historian and which gives the key to all hearts, and a clear and graceful and glowing manner of narration.

Parkman had likewise marked the completion of Bancroft's history, with a warm sense, at least, of the magnitude of the task, carried on, unlike his own, through the press of other affairs. "It must be a prodigious satisfaction," he writes,

to contemplate as one of the results of your crowded life the grand monument which you have built on such a vast and solid basis of research. It is a work the boldest man would hardly hope to finish or dare at the outset to contemplate in all its extent. It is a marvellous triumph to see it nobly achieved.

Yet heartfelt as this is, so far as it goes, it does not convey the feeling of any great depth of response to the work itself; a point on which Parkman seems to have shared the sentiments of posterity. At any rate, he is reported (in Herman Ausubel's *Historians and Their Craft*) to have confessed to Edward Eggleston that he found Bancroft unreadable. Nevertheless he owed much to the parts of Bancroft's history which treated his own field.

Evidence is not at hand as to Parkman's views of Henry Adams as an historian. Their personal relations seem to have been highly congenial. Adams's attitude toward his elder's work is colored by ambiguities which there is not space to set forth here. They were resolved, so far as they could be resolved, in a letter written the year before Parkman's death, on the receipt of a copy of *A Half Century of Conflict:*

My dear Cousin:

Your two volumes have lain on my table only long enough for me to read them before sending my acknowledgment. You have had the singular good fortune to complete successfully a great work which puts you at the head of our living historians; and I leave the dead ones out of account only because we cold-blooded Yanks detest the appearance of exaggeration so much more than we love what the French call *mesure.* Let the dead rest in peace, but pray accept my warm congratulations on your arrival.

Certainly it is an event in our literary history, and I wish you had been here to celebrate it with me, who am probably about the only man who has in this country grown sufficiently weary in the same service to join in the celebration in a thoroughly religious and penitent spirit. To be sure, I have none of your courage, for I have not even preserved enough self-respect to express so much as an opinion about our society or its tendencies. With abject selfishness, I recognize that our society has been much more civil to me than I deserve, and I feel grateful to it for leaving me alone. You hold a higher ideal, and have worked in a more generous spirit. Peace be with you,

Ever yrs

---⊰ APPENDIX D ⊱---

Views of Slavery and Abolition

Oregon Trail Journal, Oct. 1, 1846. "Stuck on a sandbar in the river. There is a gang of slaves below. Two of them are chained together. Another fellow, with an immense mouth, is beating the banjo, and a dance is going on with the utmost merriment. None are more gay and active than the two fellows chained together. They seem never to have known a care. Nothing is on their faces but careless, thoughtless enjoyment. Is it not safe to conclude them to be an inferior race?

> " 'The mind is its own place and of itself
> Can make a Heaven of Hell, a Hell of Heaven!' "

Letter to Charles Eliot Norton, Nov. 10, 1850. "Just now we are on the edge of an election—a great row about the Fugitive Slave Law, and an infinity of nonsense talked and acted upon the subject. A great union party is forming in opposition to the abolitionists and the Southern fanatics. For my part, I would see every slave knocked on the head before I would see the Union go to pieces, and would include in the sacrifice as many abolitionists as could be conveniently brought together."

Letter to Mary Dwight Parkman, Sept. 27, 1862 (referring to the presidential order of Sept. 22, 1862, later reissued as the Emancipation Proclamation). "Among all the doubts, one thing seems sure—slavery has its death blow, and the North, through Abe Lincoln, her feeble and ungainly mouthpiece, has vindicated herself at last."

Letter to Boston Daily Advertiser, *Oct. 17, 1862.* "An ill-instructed zeal, often assumed to cover mean designs, was left to battle after its own fashion with unscrupulous self-interest and the passions of demagogues and adventurers."

"*The Failure of the Universal Suffrage*," North American Review, *July-August, 1878*. "Some half a century ago, a few devoted men began what seemed a desperate crusade against a tremendous national evil. American slavery has now passed into history. It died a death of violence, to our shame be it said; for the nation had not virtue, temperance, and wisdom enough, to abolish it peacefully and harmlessly; but it is dead. We would not compare the agitation against it to the far more complex and less animating movement by which alone our present evils can be met and checked. Conviction and enthusiasm, with very little besides, served the purpose of the abolition agitators. Their appeal was to sentiment and conscience, not to reason; and their work demanded a kind of men very different from those demanded by the work of political regeneration. The champion of the new reform will need no whit less enthusiasm, but it must be tempered with judgment and armed with knowledge. One idea will not serve him. He must have many, all tending to one end; an integrity that can neither be tempted nor ensnared, and a courage that nothing can shake."

"*The Woman Question*," North American Review, *October, 1879*. "This impetuous property of feminine nature, no doubt, may have its uses at times. When a people is afflicted by some overwhelming evil, to be thrown off at any risk or sacrifice, then a one-idea vehemence of attack is not out of place. Such modes of attack are not confined to women. Ardent philanthropic reformers have commonly shown feminine characteristics, and assumed corresponding attitudes toward the objects of their zeal. But, useful as men of this stamp are in exceptional emergencies of a certain kind, the habitual reformer is generally a nuisance when he tries to deal with the broad and many-sided questions involved in the government of nations. These demand qualities very different from his; and, as the foundation of them all, the essentially masculine one of justice."

The main sources for Parkman's life, besides his letters and journals, are the memoirs by O. B. Frothingham (*Proceedings of the Massachusetts Historical Society*, 2nd series, VIII, 1894) and Edward Wheelwright (*Publications of the Colonial Society of Massachusetts*, I, 1894); and Charles H. Farnham's *Life of Francis Parkman*, 1900. Henry Dwight Sedgwick's *Francis Parkman*, 1904, adds fresh material, as does Mason Wade's *Francis Parkman: Heroic Historian*, 1942, especially from Parkman's journals. Mr. Wade's recovery of the complete text of these, and his editing and annotating of them in *The Journals of Francis Parkman*, 2 vols., 1947, has put all students of Parkman permanently in his debt.

Previous partial collections of letters by Don C. Seitz (letters to Squier), John Spencer Bassett (letters to Margry), Arthur Merlieux (letters to the Abbé Casgrain), and Howard Doughty (letters to Mary Dwight Parkman) are now superseded by Wilbur R. Jacobs's definitive and admirably edited *Letters of Francis Parkman*, 2 vols., 1960, published after I had finished my book.

Though Farnham made a strangely limited use of the material at his disposal relating to Parkman's early years, and occasionally gives a coloring of false pathos to his later life, I found his biography on the whole the most critically interesting, particularly for its tracing of the traits of its subject's personality in his work. The fullest critical studies are John Fiske's "Francis Parkman," *A Century of Science and Other Essays*, 1899; and Otis Pease's penetrating and excellently written *Parkman's History: The Historian as Literary Artist*, Yale Historical Series, 1953. Shorter pieces which I found interpretatively suggestive are: Melville's unsigned review of *The Oregon Trail*, *Literary World*, March 31, 1849; Lowell's posthumous fragment, *Century*, November, 1892; Bliss Perry, "Some Personal Qualities of Francis Parkman," *Yale Review*, April, 1924; Melvin Lasky's review of Wade's *Parkman*, *Partisan Review*, July–August, 1943; Bernard De Voto, "The Editor's Easy Chair" (on Parkman and narrative history), *Harper's Magazine*, April, 1949; and the introduction to Samuel Eliot Morison's volume of selections, *The Parkman Reader*, 1955. I regret that Wilbur Jacobs's "Some of Parkman's Literary Devices," *New England Quarterly*, June, 1958, and David Levin's *History as Romantic Art: Bancroft, Motley, Prescott, and Parkman*, 1959, appeared too late for me to take advantage of their insights.

I should also mention the following for the light they throw on one aspect or another of Parkman's life or background: Samuel Eliot Morison, *Maritime History of Massachusetts* and *History of Harvard College*, Vol. 3; O. B. Frothingham, *Boston Unitarianism, 1820–1850;* Wayne Andrews, *Architecture, Ambition, and Americans* (for George Parkman's and Jacob Bigelow's relations with Alexander Jackson Davis); Bernard De Voto, *Year of Decision;* Ruth Benedict, *Patterns of Culture;* Edward Waldo Emerson, *The Early Days of the Saturday Club;* and Mason Wade, *The French Canadian People* (for the background of political and ecclesiastical controversy during the years of Parkman's visits to Quebec).

Wilbur Schramm's volume of selections, *Parkman,* American Writers Series, 1938, contains an exhaustive bibliography of material up to that date.